Borders of Chinese Civilization

ASIA-PACIFIC: CULTURE, POLITICS, AND SOCIETY

A Series Edited by Rey Chow, H. D. Harootunian,
and Masao Miyoshi

Borders of Chinese Civilization

Geography and History at Empire's End

D. R. Howland

Duke University Press   Durham & London   1996

© 1996 Duke University Press
All rights reserved
Printed in the United States of America on acid-free paper ∞
Designed by Cherie H. Westmoreland and typeset in Adobe Caslon
by Keystone Typesetting, Inc.
Library of Congress Cataloging-in-Publication Data appear on the last
printed page of this book.

Contents

Acknowledgments

This book originated with the doctoral dissertation I completed at the University of Chicago in 1989. To the official readers of that dissertation—Guy Alitto, Leo Lee, and Harry Harootunian—I remain grateful for the intellectual freedom they allowed me as I developed my ideas on this diffuse topic. Chicago in the 1980s was a stormy but creative environment for interdisciplinary explorations. My grounding in Chinese texts and traditions was cultivated by Edward Ch'ien, Ping-ti Ho, David Roy, and Anthony Yu. My appreciation for historiography as a theoretical practice was stimulated by the seminars of Michael Dalby and Ron Inden, Harry Harootunian, and Tetsuo Najita; and my interest in linking history to anthropology and language was expanded by Marshall Sahlins, Michael Silverstein, and William Hanks. Crucial in fostering the endurance to finish were my friends, seniors, and peers, who provided invaluable answers to periodic questions and graciously commented on various drafts; I am especially thankful to Professors Norma Field, Paul Friedrich, Michael Geyer, and Bill Sibley, and to Wah-kwan Cheng, Kevin Doak, Linn Freiwald, David Gitomer, Susan Griswold, Jim Hevia, Howard Kaplan, Jim Ketelaar, Matt Levey, Kai-shyh Lin, Stanley Murashige, Leslie Pincus, Lisa Raphals, Naoki Sakai, Natalie Silberman-Wainwright, Julia Thomas, and Tom Wilson. During a year at the University of Iowa, Geeta Patel, David Tucker, and Stephen Vlastos offered new friendship and feedback as my revisions commenced. Stefan Tanaka did me the great favor of reading through the penultimate draft and offering last-minute advice.

The research and writing of this work were made possible through the generous support of several organizations. A research fellowship from the Japanese Ministry of Education allowed me to work on the first phase of my research between 1984 and 1986; dissertation writing was subsidized by a Charlotte W. Newcombe Dissertation Fellowship from the Woodrow Wilson National Fellowship Foundation. Revisions were undertaken with a grant from the National Endowment for the Humanities and a fellowship from the American Council of Learned Societies. I deeply appreciate the encouragement of my dean, Richard Meister, in permitting my leaves of absence to finish my writing.

My research in Japan was facilitated by Professors Maeda Ai and Tai Kuo-hui at Rikkyō University. The "brushtalking" through which Professor Maeda and I communicated when I first arrived in Japan confirmed the hunch that motivates this study, and I regret that he did not live to see the results of his encouragement. Professor Igarashi Akio introduced me to the National Diet Library, and Christian Daniels and Gregory Pflugfelter came to the rescue by borrowing materials from Tokyo University Library and Waseda University Library respectively. The generosity of the late Sanetō Keishū, who donated his vast collection of materials to the Tokyo Public Libraries, allowed me to see many rare works; the staff of the Sanetō Archives at the Chūō Library were always accomodating and willing to share their knowledge. During the stage of revisions, my several trips to the Harvard-Yenching Library were facilitated by Timothy Connor; I would particularly like to thank him and the staff there for their expert and eager assistance.

Finally, I am grateful to Reynolds Smith of Duke University Press for his confidence and reliability. Maura High edited the manuscript with perspicacity, and Pam Morrison expertly guided my work through production.

This book is dedicated to the memory of T. F. Mayer-Oakes, my undergraduate mentor, who taught me to juxtapose the detail and the larger historical context, encouraged me to treat ideas with imagination, and first inspired me with the possibility of an academic career.

Note

I use the *pinyin* romanization herein, in sympathy with its aspirations to international scholarship. However, I take the liberty of making two adjustments. I refer to the Chinese dynasty of Soong (rather than Song), to distinguish it from the English noun "song"; and I refer to the surname of one of my subjects as Hê (rather than He), to distinguish him from the English pronoun "he."

Because of my occasional double references to Chinese and Japanese pronunciations of Chinese-character words, I distinguish the two with the following notation: (C: Liuqiu / J: Ryūkyū).

In citing works published prior to the adoption of the Gregorian calendar in China and Japan, I follow the convention of bracketing Gregorian calendar years transposed from Chinese or Japanese reign years. I have eliminated *juan* ("volume") from my citations, with the exception of some sets or large series, where multiple "volume" notations require *juan* or related terms for clarity.

My citations of the Chinese Classics are parenthetical and, after the manner of the Bible, direct the reader to book and chapter of the text in question.

Unless otherwise noted, translations from the Chinese and Japanese are my own.

Introduction

In antiquity, the Yellow Emperor undertook a journey that would bring relief to all the disunited. He traveled Under-Heaven in all directions, established coordinates of a myriad leagues, delineated the wild, demarcated the administrative districts, and produced the domains of a hundred leagues and the myriad precincts. The *Classic of Changes* germanely relates, "The ancient kings enfeoffed the myriad domains and treated the various lords as relations"; and the *Classic of Documents*, "[He] pacified and harmonized the myriad domains."
"Treatise on Earth's Patterns," *History of the Han*

If Jan defines the border for himself as the line of the greatest admissible repetition, I must correct him. The border is not a product of repetition. Repetition is only a means of making the border visible. The line of the border is covered with dust, and repetition is like the whisk of a hand removing the dust.
Milan Kundera, *The Book of Laughter and Forgetting*

This study concerns, most centrally, borders—those cultural, social, and political borders that work to define and delimit human relationships in our world. These borders, according to Kundera, are always present: from the most idiosyncratic preference for the shape of an eye, to the most tenuous boundary between ill-defined nations, to the arguably most constitutive feature that distinguishes human societies: language. Although creatures of habit, we may, if thoughtful, perceive the borders of our worlds in the space between the familiar and the possible—in the arena of repetition. The present study specifically concerns the borders between Chinese and Japanese in the changing world of the 1870s and eighties, and the activities of a certain group of these men as they worked to maintain and reproduce a distinctly Chinese understanding of the human world. It was in these acts of repetition—the activities of conversing and writing— that these men disclosed the borders separating themselves not only from one another, but also from their own histories—as well as from the third party that increasingly figured in cultural, social, and political matters, whom both Chinese and Japanese named the "West."

This study explores these borders of cultural identities. It is not a book about Japan, nor is it primarily concerned with the content of what Chinese thought about Japan; rather, it explores the ways in which Chinese categorized Japan as an object of knowledge. Historians have well documented the intricacies of Chinese and Japanese diplomacy and the intense debate that ensued in both the Chinese court and the Japanese government over Westernization policies. Here I will be only marginally concerned with official policy, or with the success or failure of Westernization. The primary issue is not politics or diplomacy; it is the cultural epistemology that informs certain forms of cultural interaction. I am interested in disclosing those cultural practices that enabled Chinese observers in Japan not only to identify Japan with Chinese Civilization but also to differentiate Japan from China. In time, some Chinese would identify Japan with the West.

Accordingly, I examine Chinese perceptions and representations of Japan in the nineteenth century. At the beginning of the century, Japan remained an inaccessible and insignificant island kingdom at the eastern edge of Chinese Civilization, much as it had been since the 1640s; at century's end, Chinese were debating the meaning of their deplorable 1895 defeat at the hands of the presumptuous and aggressive empire of Japan. Chinese perceptions of Japan underwent marked vicissitudes in the course of the century, and it is the main purpose of this study to elucidate the Chinese understanding of Japan during the critical decades of the 1870s and 1880s, when Chinese perceived an alarming shift taking place in Japan. Japan was leaving behind the universal order known as Civilization, and establishing itself within another, alien order based on a new "international" principle forced upon the world of East Asia by the West. Among Chinese observers, this corresponded to a shift in worldviews: from a Chinese worldview based on hierarchy and unification to a Euro-American world view based on equality and differentiation. My argument is simply that Japan, which had periodically caused some awkwardness to Chinese Civilization, proved to be instrinsically destabilizing to Chinese sensibilities in the late nineteenth century. Once Japan was removed from the Chinese worldview, that worldview was irreparably changed. The encounter with Japan, in other words, presented Chinese scholars and officials in Japan with concrete evidence of the practical limits to the world-view of their Civilization; it is these limits that I identify as "borders of Chinese Civilization."

From the perspective of Chinese knowledge and representations of the world, this categorization of Japan as an object of knowledge was above all geographical. To the educated mind of the 1800s, Chinese represented foreign peoples and kingdoms—be they tax-paying subjects of the Chinese emperor, tribute-bearing participants to the Chinese Empire, or barbarians beyond the borders of Chinese Civilization—under the rubric of either "Lands of the Earth" (*yudi*) or, most often, "Earth's Patterns" (*dili*). While this understanding of the lay of the land corresponds to our conception of geography (and in fact "*dili*" is the standard contemporary Chinese translation for "geography"), there are ways in which our geography differs significantly from *yudi* and *dili*.

As scholars of European and American history have observed, our study of geography is closely related to the expanding capitalism of the nineteenth century. Raymond Schwab, Edward Said, and others have noted that the European heritage of exploration and plunder, of conquest and colonization, was reconstructed after Napoleon's invasion of Egypt to form the new science of geography in western Europe. In France, for example, university geography was institutionalized as an academic discipline in the 1870s, in reaction to France's defeat in the Franco-Prussian War (a consequence, some claimed, of inadequate maps) and as France expanded its colonial empire into Southeast Asia. There are, in short, formal relations between our economics and politics, our social sciences, and our practice of geography; whatever these may be, it is worthwhile to remember, in the words of one scholar, that "space, as a social fact, as a social factor and as an instance of society, is always political and strategic."[1] It is with an eye to the consequences of this observation, then, and another to the difference between geography and *dili,* that one purpose here will be to elucidate Chinese geographical representations as primarily historical knowledge and, specifically, to elucidate Chinese representations of Japan as geographical and historical knowledge.

In China, this matter of *dili,* or geography, was traditionally subordinate to the historical claims of imperial rule. The first in the series of official dynastic histories, *History of the Han* (*Han shu*), was completed in the first century A.D. and inaugurated the tradition of including a "Treatise on

Earth's Patterns" (*Dili zhi*) within the official dynastic history.[2] It was the purpose of this treatise to record changes in place-names and local administrative districts comprising the empire, as well as descriptions of mountain ranges, river systems, taxable products, and so on. Over the centuries, as the Chinese Empire expanded southward and westward, descriptions of more distant regions and foreign peoples were included in, respectively, the "Treatise on Earth's Patterns" and the sections entitled "Arrayed Biographies" (*Liezhuan*) in the official dynastic history. Although independent works on geography, modeled after the official "Treatise on Earth's Patterns," were written from the fifth century on and evolved into geographical encyclopedias by the thirteenth century, the production of such books inexplicably declined thereafter, their place taken by travel diaries, treatises on localities, collections of poetry on foreign themes, and other minor and more personal or immediate genres. Meanwhile, official Chinese geography remained intimately involved with the claims of imperial rule, and was primarily historicist and textual (rather than iconic—relying on diagrams and maps) for much of the imperial age.[3]

As I demonstrate in my examination of Chinese representations of Japan, there were two fundamental modes of geographical representations available to scholars in the late nineteenth century. One of these I call the poetic, or performative, by which I mean that a geographic representation provides the *experience* of an encounter abroad. As I show, this was the primary claim made on behalf of travelogues and travel poetry. The other I call the expository, by which I mean that a third-person and abstracted representation of reality makes a certain claim to truthfulness as objective *knowledge*. This latter was in fact the dominant mode of geographical representation officialized in the dynastic history "Treatise on Earth's Patterns." Although the expository corresponds to what we might think of as quintessentially "historical," these representations are nonetheless historical in ways that may seem unusual to the Euro-American reader.

Moreover, it is not the case that these are two strictly distinct and incompatible modes of representation. Although loosely associated with two traditional explanations of textuality, one concerning the natural capacity of poetry to give voice to human intention (*shi yan zhi*) and the other concerning the capacity of truthful writing to serve as a vehicle for the Way of the Ancient Sages (*wen yi zai dao*), these two modes of representation can be traced to a duality as old as the self-consciousness of

Chinese Civilization: poetry and historical document, collected respectively in the ancient *Classic of Poetry* (*Shi jing*) and *Classic of Documents* (*Shu jing*). One consequence of intellectual movements during the eighteenth century was a deliberate historicism among certain scholars, one of whom, Zhang Xuecheng (1738–1801), attempted to eradicate the difference between poetry and history—he asserted that *all* texts, even the *Classics,* should be considered equally the objects of history. These are, in other words, fundamental epistemological strategies of Chinese geographical representations, and my extensive interest in the scholar, poet, and diplomat Huang Zunxian (1848–1905), for example, lies precisely in his unusual attempt to integrate the two.

In effect, this study examines the epistemology underlying Chinese perceptions of Japan and Japan's Westernization. Rather than discuss these problems only in terms of diplomatic relations, I treat them as problems of knowledge and representations. This approach seems preferable, because, in the first place, it is important to begin by validating a Chinese worldview so different from our own. Too often Chinese historians have seen the nineteenth century in terms of "tradition versus modernity," a dichotomy that has had the effect of characterizing nineteenth-century Chinese leaders as misguided or ill prepared for modernizing China. The fact remains that most Chinese scholars saw the world differently from us, and, as I hope to demonstrate, it is worthwhile to begin by taking seriously what they took to be valid representations of their world.

So, in addition to elucidating these strategies for geographical knowledge and the literary forms in which they are represented, I examine the grounding of geography in this Chinese worldview. Geographical representation in China is not simply an inert body of texts, but a participant in the intellectual activity of informing and interpreting the world; geographical texts attest both to ways in which Chinese scholars and officials understood the outside world and to ways in which that perceived outside world began to change in the late nineteenth century. To the degree that Chinese perceptions of Japan reflect China's position in the world, Chinese perceptions of change in Japan reflect the movement of China's changing position in the world.

The Chinese had of course known of Japan for some fifteen hundred years, and Japan had appropriated a great deal of Chinese culture beginning in the seventh century A.D. Chinese dynastic histories systematically document that through the centuries, the Chinese court had received Japanese embassies, tribute missions, students, and merchants, in a manner enacting for both peoples distinctive roles befitting, on the one hand, the suppliant Japanese, and on the other, the imperial lords of the "Central Kingdom," benevolent dispensers of Civilization. If this Chinese version of such interaction impresses us with the overall agreeability of both parties, we are perhaps reassured by the occasional testaments of Chinese ire toward the Japanese—for example, in reaction to Japanese ill treatment of Kubilai Khan's Chinese messenger in the late 1200s, or the Japanese invasion of Korea in the 1590s. Nevertheless, the intense and mutually satisfying exchange that took place between the seventh and tenth centuries lingered long after the fact, immortalized in poetry attesting to the friendship of the two peoples, and this available store of textual evidence habitually reappeared as proof of and justification for Japan's inclusion within Chinese Civilization.

Accordingly, the historical actors who both orient and actuate this essay—mainly Chinese and Japanese scholars and officials—joined together out of their common interest in Chinese Civilization. Since most of these men could not speak the language of the other group, they "conversed" with each other in writing—in the literary Chinese language—a practice called "brushtalking." As I describe, these brushtalks took place in Tokyo in the late 1870s and early 1880s. The Chinese were scholars and diplomats connected to the first Chinese embassy in Japan, as well as distinguished Chinese travelers to Japan; the Japanese were mainly conservative educators and officials, not hostile to the Meiji Restoration, but somewhat suspicious of both its "chaotic" offshoots (the Freedom and People's Rights Movement of 1874–1889) and the Meiji government's authoritarian reaction to that series of events. These men instead hoped to supplement Meiji ideology with a moral training based in the models provided by Chinese texts.

As members of the educated and ruling classes in the nineteenth century, these Chinese and Japanese men understood that the authority legitimizing their worldview was based in a literary tradition claiming a history two thousand years old; they understood that they participated in administration *because* they were learned, and that the goal of all learning was, after self-cultivation, the proper administration of one's family, one's state, the universe. If in China by the 1870s, learning and the testing of learning for purposes of entry into the ruling bureaucracy had grown formulistic, pedantic, and stagnant, the two were nonetheless based upon the two most established branches of writing, history and poetry. Ideally, the best official was a scholar learned in history and the Confucian classics, who could not only formulate policy based on sound historical precedent and express his opinion in well-composed memorials that included both eloquent turns of phrase and allusions that gave evidence of his learning, but also compose poetry suitable for a variety of official functions and public occasions, poetry that in its choice of word again gave evidence of a solid grounding in antecedent allusions, and in its form attested to the balance and regularity of the author's character.

That this literary Chinese language, this set of classical texts, and this understanding of the human world persisted for so many centuries surely testifies to the hegemonic persuasiveness of the Chinese worldview. To be sure, Chinese rulers were exceedingly successful at institutionalizing this worldview through academies and the examination system, but such success does not account for the persistence of the language, the texts, and the worldview *outside* of China—in Japan, Korea, Vietnam, and others of China's neighbors. Indeed, this "international" aspect of the Chinese understanding of the human world offers a measure of truth to Chinese claims of the universality of their worldview, which, in the words of my subjects in the 1870s, was essentialized and referred to as *wenming*, or "Civilization." (So in this study I treat "Civilization" as a proper noun and indicate it with a capital.)

In fact, I have chosen Japan to examine as an object of Chinese geographical understanding largely because the position of Japan vis-à-vis China was so contestable in the nineteenth century. Chinese travelers to Japan at the time quite comfortably declared Japan a *tongwen zhi guo*, a "country sharing language," or as I argue, by virtue of the synecdochal relationship between the literary Chinese language and Civilization in the Chinese worldview, a "country sharing Civilization." However, these claims of Japanese cultural affiliation to China were not matched in political relations. Of particular ire to Chinese officials in the late nineteenth century was Japan's perverse disregard for Chinese diplomatic principles and its insistence on following the Western pattern. The changing world order in the nineteenth century presented Chinese with a critical choice: was China to deal with Japan as kin, in terms of *tong wen* (shared language/Civilization), or as an alien of the Western sort? Ultimately, this was a question of rival claims to universality: the Chinese model of Civilization described relations with foreign domains in terms of proximity, and proposed to order the various domains according to principles of hierarchy and unification; the Westerners, by contrast, described foreign relations in terms of an international legality that promised equality and differentiation. In the end, this study suggests, growing contradictions undermined the Chinese model of Civilization as a viable possibility.

There is a gifted dancer and choreographer in Taiwan, Lin Huaimin. In one of his solo pieces, the stage lights up to reveal a man, front-stage corner, left, dressed in a white court robe (white: read "funeral/mourning"). He proceeds to move diagonally across the stage, seeming to gather momentum, but the further he gets, the more we see that his progress is hindered by the train of the robe, which finally extends thirty feet across the stage. The dance then consists of the man's attempts to overcome this restraint, his twisting and turning, and grabbing at the train of his robe, until finally he has gathered it all up in his arms, only to realize that the sheer weight of the entirety makes him immobile, and then tottering, unable to stand still, and so the innumerable folds of the train begin to slip through his arms, sliding along the stage again. The stage blackens. No curtains are drawn.

In the program notes that particular night, Lin Huaimin added an explanation for those in the audience who preferred their dances less abstract, to the effect that this was a portrayal of a man burdened with five thousand years of Chinese history.

This, then, is the image I am confronting here—that time in the nineteenth century when, like that Chinese dancer on the stage, the immense historical totality of Chinese Civilization began slipping through its grasp.

I Encountering Japan

1 Civilization from the Center

The Geomoral Context of Tributary Expectations

Our Illustrious Ancestor taught us
To bring the people near, and cast them not aside;
For the people are the root of the kingdom:
With the root firm, the kingdom is tranquil.
Classic of Documents

And, as it is with this, so too with all things.
The pages of our lives are blurred palimpsest:
New lines are wreathed on old lines half-erased,
And those on older still; and so forever.
The old shines through the new, and colors it.
Conrad Aiken, "Palimpsest"

During most of the long and expansive rule of the Qing dynasty (1644–1912), Japan remained a largely inaccessible island kingdom on the eastern reaches of the Chinese world—the land of *Riben,* where the sun took root. Within the extensive array of tributary domains offering obeisance to the celestial Qing emperors, Japan was silent—physically absent from the imperial court, yet persistingly present within All-under-Heaven. This ongoing abstention from official communication with the Qing court was one major consequence of Shogun Tokugawa Iemitsu's policy of "locking up" Japan in the 1630s, and putting Riben—what the Japanese themselves called "Nihon"—out of reach of Qing military might and administrative influence. To most Chinese, Japan endured as an inaccessible silence for over two hundred years.

Accordingly, in the most comprehensive and most widely read geographic anthology of the nineteenth century, Wei Yuan's *Illustrated Treatise on the Sea Kingdoms,* Japan was simply appended to the section on the Nan Yang, or "Southern Sea"—that is, the island kingdoms of maritime Asia, which included the Philippines, Borneo, Java, and Sumatra. Japan was appended—and not featured in the formal enumeration—because it was not among the official tributary kingdoms. Nevertheless, Japan retained its place on Chinese maps, because it still lay there, as it had for centuries, just off the coast of Civilization. In the nineteenth century, it took on added significance to Wei and other Chinese who saw Japan as a potential target of Western encroachment.[1]

Incidents of Western aggression and the violent events sparked in their wake ensued with alarming speed by the middle of the nineteenth century. In 1839 Great Britain provoked the first of the Opium Wars in south China. In 1851 the Taiping rebels began their fourteen-year rampage that devastated much of China south of the Yangzi River. In 1853 Commodore Perry and his "Black Ships" demanded forcibly that Japan open its ports to American traders. By 1858 the second series of Opium Wars were under way in China, and calls for administrative reform and study of Western science and armaments were thereafter officially supported by the "Foreign Affairs Clique" at court; so began the Tongzhi Restoration. In 1868 the Meiji Restoration was proclaimed in Japan—a curious "revival of ancient ways" that overthrew the ruling Tokugawa shogunate, restored the emperor, and quickly turned into a wide-ranging program of "civilization and enlightenment" according to Western models. With the world of East Asia thus forced into the "international community," China and Japan were brought closer to reestablishing official contact. The conduct of this relationship, however, was to be hotly contested from the start.

Because Chinese policies had begun to change by 1870, when Japan requested a treaty of trade and friendship, consensus was lacking among Chinese officials advising the court on its dealings with Japan. A number of officials—certainly the most irate—continued to consider Japan in the terms of the long-standing diplomacy of tributary relations, "Civilization" and "proximity." But others were willing to consider Japan in light of the newer practice of international treaties, to which the Chinese court had committed itself in its relations with the Westerners. The problem faced by both positions, I will demonstrate in this chapter, is that they were informed by the legacy of Chinese writings on Japan, which remained quite inadequate during the first two centuries of Qing rule. The question thus arises: What was the state of Chinese knowledge of Japan by 1870, and how did it inform Chinese diplomacy both in that year, when Japan requested a treaty, and in 1874, when a conflict over Taiwan delayed the projected exchange of ambassadors between China and Japan?

Civilization and Proximity

Civilization, or *wenming* to the educated Chinese class in the nineteenth century, ultimately signified the expansive process of Chinese imperial lordship. In part, "*wenming*" meant "clarifying-" or "enlightening-through-patterning." One patterned the world and thus ruled it, with the assistance of a largely civil bureaucracy staffed by literati ideally entrusted to spread enlightened virtue throughout the realm. In explicit contrast to the rule of military subjugation (*wugong*), this active administering, termed "*wenhua*" ("transforming by patterning" or "civilizing"), was accomplished in the name of the emperor, or "Son of Heaven," whose direct access to the clarity of the heavenly bodies made him the exemplar of illustrious virtue and guaranteed that the regularity of Heaven might be manifested in an analogous regularity of human life on earth. Because the basis for such virtuous example was provided by the set of histories and classics—the latter the putative writings of the ancient sages—writing was thus understood to be the quintessential patterning of Civilization, and we may further understand *wenming* as "enlightening through writing." In other words, *wenming* described quite literally a superior state of human society made luminous (*ming*) through writing or civilization (*wen*); when all was at peace in the world, the world was *wenming*. A man's knowledge of the received texts and their language, which was demonstrated as virtuous behavior in accordance with the very recommendations of the texts, meant that he too was *wenming*, or "civilizing."[2]

Implicit in the bookishness of this Chinese conception of Civilization was an encouragement of historical analogy as a primary method of reasoning about man in the world. To the degree that one understood how the world was to be patterned after the writing of the classics, one could proceed to regulate human agency in the world. Analogical knowledge of the human world concentrated on human behavior, which was marked in terms of "lordship" (*jun*) and specified analogically as the reciprocal positions of the Confucian "Three Bonds": the ruler-servant, father-son, and husband-wife relations. To pattern one's behavior after the models provided by the classics, specifically indicated by properly submitting to one's rightful lord, was to be among the "civilizing." Those who did not display such behavior comprised the various ranks of the uncivilized; if the "black-haired masses" of Chinese subjects at least benefited from the example of local officials and scholars, the outsiders, the rudest of whom made no ritual attempt to acknowledge the universal sovereignty of the Chinese emperor, lived in a wilderness beyond the border of recognition.[3]

Civilization was, accordingly, a spatially expansive and ideologically infinite project. From the point of view of the emperor at the center, the realm was instantiated by the establishment of regional and local bureaucratic offices, by the voyages of imperial envoys to and from the emperor's capital, and by the foreign envoys who came to call. In time, and assuming that imperial virtue shone forth, distant outsiders too would understand the Chinese classics and take a place within the civilizing realm. When outsiders did participate in Civilization, as when they sent tribute missions to the imperial court, they wrote in the literary Chinese language, expressing the decorous and submissive sentiments proper to their station. Literati in Korea, Vietnam, Japan, and other kingdoms became fluent in literary Chinese, and Chinese officials thus included those peoples within Civilization.[4]

In this context of diplomacy, and in reference to these nearby east Asian nations, Chinese officials had recourse to the ancient concept of "proximity" (*jin*). More a correlative than a causal concept, proximity proposed a connection between space and morality: humankind would approximate moral behavior in proportion to their proximity to the moral rule of the Chinese emperor. This understanding of the world was fostered by the texts of Confucianism, and it assumed the expressly hierarchical world noted above. In the ancient *Classic of Documents,* the legendary founder of Chinese Civilization, the Great Yu (or Illustrious Ancestor), is lauded first for his paternal manner of rule: bringing the people close, or cherishing them (3.3). Other early formulations underline this conflation between nearness in space and appropriateness in moral behavior; most explicit perhaps is the statement attributed to Confucius in the *Analects* (6.28): "To be able to take one's example from what is close at hand can be called the direction of reciprocity." That is, if one treats others as one treats "oneself" (what is close at hand), one "follows the form" of reciprocity.

Diplomacy, in terms of traditional tributary relations, pursued the same ideal.[5] The emperor brought close the outside peoples, who, insofar as they appeared in the Chinese court and thereby participated in the moral action of reciprocity, acknowledged a minimal acceptance of Chinese Civilization—the nominal lordship of the Son of Heaven and his calendar. In return, the foreign lord was confirmed as ruler of his domain. Neverthe-less, this was but one area within an all-encompassing system of rites, or propriety (*li*), which extended to dress, language, food, and so on, and constituted the cultural substance of Civilization. To the degree a foreign people participated in the totality of Civilization—above and beyond their participation in tributary protocol—they could be considered "Chinese." The kingdom of Korea, for example, was so closely integrated into Chinese Civilization that its nominal status during much of the Ming (1368–1644) and Qing periods was more akin to "adopted son" than outsider.[6] Japan, by contrast, had not been a consistent participant since the eighth century, and accordingly, when Japan requested a formal treaty with China in 1870, an intense debate arose among Chinese advisors as to the position of Japan within the order of Civilization.[7]

But this view of an expanding realm embracing other peoples did not guarantee that outsiders would in fact participate in Civilization; Chinese texts promised an ideal scenario to which actual practice did not neces-sarily conform. The issue at hand, however, is *not* whether or not the ideological bookishness of the model discredits it as an adequate descrip-tion of historical reality; rather, the present issue is how this textual model operated in the worldviews of historical agents in the 1870s and 1880s.[8]

The Bounds of Diplomatic Protocol

Models, after all, are but guides to reality; and the assumption is patently false that an ideal scenario (or ideology) will fully comprehend social interactions, whether they are as elemental as two individuals sharing a language and culture or as complex as ruling classes of two distinct so-cieties. Although Chinese Civilization provided an explanation for actual relations diverging from the text (in its worst form, conflict)—namely, that one or both of the parties was morally lacking in adherence to reciprocity—there was always the possibility that peoples at the borders of social config-urations—be they subcultural groups, rural and urban communities, prov-inces, regions, or states—would be in a position to interact, simply because they strayed into contact with one another. In other words, when Chinese chose to describe relations with foreign peoples in terms of proximity, they were intending to *ritualize,* and thereby regularize before the act of encounter, the random contacts among people(s) who moved into the vicinity of each other. As Pierre Bourdieu has observed, ritual practice "always aims to facilitate *passages* and/or to authorize encounters between opposed orders."[9] In the interests of regulating contact, Chinese interpreted the commonplace "nearness" between peoples in terms of proximity, an act that formally designated and officially sanctioned a relationship between those peoples.

This comprehensive (if compulsive) concern for ritual is one well-documented aspect of Chinese Civilization. On the ancient precedent of the three classics of ritual (the *Li ji, Yi li,* and *Zhou li*), it was the business of Chinese authorities—both heads of clans and emperors—to issue ritual precedents and regulations for members of the group subject to their respective authority. Although weddings, funerals, and ancestral sacrifices were of greatest general importance, ritual manuals presumed to cover the gamut of human behavior. Emperors, moreover, had rituals appropriate to their universal sphere—the Great Sacrifices to Heaven and Earth and the reception of foreign envoys. Yet as Angela Zito reminds us, ritual was not simply its textual representation, but a *performance* that enacted or represented the knowledge of past organizations described in texts, coupled with those objects or people needed to demonstrate power in present reality.[10]

Given this dual orientation of ritual as written precedent and enacted performance, the interest among Chinese rulers to ritualize diplomacy, and thereby manage the power of foreign states, could be easily and injuriously frustrated, precisely because such encounters were most difficult to prescribe. Chinese demonstration of universal lordship in diplomatic ritual was a precarious undertaking, because a ritual performance, in spite of its express intention to contain the power of a foreign state, did not necessarily do so. Chinese were dependent upon foreigners to come to the imperial court, yet Chinese claims could appear quite preposterous to the foreign party (as with the British in the eighteenth and nineteenth centuries). During the "medieval" age in Japan (roughly 1200–1600), warlord leaders dismissed Chinese claims of universal lordship (especially after Mongolian attempts to invade Japan in 1275 and 1281), and as Japanese political order disintegrated in the sixteenth century, would-be Japanese rulers cynically took advantage of Chinese ritual protocol in attempts to garner their respective claims to lordship in Japan. This development was recorded with repugnance in the *Ming History*, especially because these Japanese supplicants were unable (or unwilling) to control the allegedly Japanese "Dwarf pirates" ravaging the Chinese coast, and later advisors to the Qing emperors inferred the lesson that Japan might best be left alone. The imperial "decision" to ignore a foreign power was, after all, a legitimate choice.

Unofficial Contacts in the Early Qing

This willingness of the early Qing emperors and their advisors to forgo official relations with Japan presents a striking contrast to Qing diplomacy with the southeastern kingdoms of Vietnam, Thailand, Java, Sumatra, and especially the Liuqiu (Ryūkyū) Islands. Relations between the Qing court and the king of the Liuqiu Islands were maintained regularly; as the Qing emperors welcomed ambassadors and tribute missions from the Liuqius, Chinese coastal trade with the Liuqiu Islands flourished.[11] But in the case of Japan, the early Manchu emperors were satisfied with occasional, unofficial diplomacy when mutual interests coincided—typically over trade issues. Evidence has been found in the Yongzheng emperor's *Imperial Comments in Vermilion* (*Zhupi yuzhi*) to demonstrate that both the Kangxi and the Yongzheng emperors carried on secret diplomacy with Japan. Hoping to forestall all potential problems with piracy, the Kangxi emperor banned sea travel in 1684; nonetheless, trade with Japan quickly increased eightfold. Consequently, when the offical Li Xu memorialized the throne in 1700 to express concern for the safety of the seacoast, the Kangxi emperor ordered that Li arrange for the envoy Mai Ersen to visit Nagasaki in order to observe the Chinese trade with Japan. In 1715, the Japanese shogunate instituted a system of "official passes" (C: *xinpai*; J: *shinpai*) in an effort to reduce the quantity of unauthorized trade; this action caused problems in south China when disgruntled merchants complained that those merchants receiving the passes were guilty of sedition. In response, the Kangxi emperor confiscated all passes, effectively prohibiting all trade until he relented two years later. Problems with illicit trade and smuggling grew during the 1720s, until the governor of Zhejiang province, Li Wei, with the personal approval of the Yongzheng emperor, sent emissaries to explore the possibility of a more mutual supervision of ships. In 1729, Japanese officials returned a letter outlining their policies, which was forwarded to the emperor and received his approval. Apparently, the problems were thereby solved.[12]

On the rare occasion, then, when Chinese traders or Japanese policies were a source of dissention in the empire, Chinese officials close to the court sought imperial intervention with Japanese officials in charge of Nagasaki trade. Nevertheless, these contacts between the Chinese court and Japanese officials—conducted in secret and outside of imperial ritual protocol, and never the result of Japanese tributary missions to China— neither developed into more sustained relations nor induced Chinese to take a greater interest in Japan. Indeed, they may have had the opposite effect. Alarmed by stories that Chinese subjects traveled surreptitiously to Japan for the purposes of teaching archery, military formations, Chinese rituals, and other sensitive matters, Governor Li Wei sought to enforce the Kangxi emperor's standing ban on sea travel by more strictly controlling the activities of merchants and all other Chinese in Japan. In 1728, he ruled that no Chinese when in Japan was allowed to leave the Chinese merchants' compound in Nagasaki for free travel or for any reason other than trading.[13]

By 1870, then, the year in which the newly "restored" Japanese state surprised Chinese officials with a request for a treaty of friendship and trade, the problem facing Chinese considerations of Japan was the glaring lack of Qing ritual precedents for Japan: in over two centuries, there had been no official contact.[14] Accordingly, the Chinese debate would dwell on locating a precedent; should Japan be treated in accordance with the principle of proximity and after the example of tributary states like Korea and Vietnam, or should Japan be treated as a distant outsider and granted a treaty, like the Western domains? The outcome of that debate, to which we turn shortly, was guided by the legacy of geographical knowledge informing Chinese scholars and officials about Japan in 1870.

Japan in the Qing Record

Imagine, if you will, what a Chinese scholar might have known about Japan in the years just before China resumed official relations with the Japanese. As a consequence of the first Opium War, Chinese-language works on geography had multiplied quickly in the decade of the 1840s.[15]

Although they were primarily intended to provide information on the Westerners, all of these geographies included sections on Japan, with the prominent exception of the first—Lin Zexu's *Treatise on the Four Continents* (*Si zhou zhi*), published in 1841. This work was followed quickly by Karl Gützlaff's *Complete Illustrated Geography of the Myriad Nations* (*Wanguo dili quantuji*) in 1843; the first and second editions of Wei Yuan's *Illustrated Treatise on the Sea Kingdoms*, in 1844 and 1847 respectively; Robert Morrison's *Concise History of the Foreign Nations* (*Waiguo shi lue*) in 1847; a *Geographical Reference* (*Dili bei kao*) by a Portuguese "Ma Jishi" ("Marques"?) also in 1847; and R. Q. Way's *Survey of Geography* (*Dili shuo lue*) in 1848.[16] The geography second in importance to that of Wei Yuan appeared in 1849; this was Xu Jiyu's *Short Treatise on the Ocean Circuits* (*Ying huan zhi lue*), parts of which Wei Yuan incorporated in his third edition of 1852.[17]

In this third edition of the *Illustrated Treatise on the Sea Kingdoms*, Wei collected the corresponding excerpts on Japan from most of the above works, as well as other well-known Chinese works, and a small number of still uncollated, rare titles. The following texts provide the sources for Wei's section on Japan:[18]

1. The "Japan Biography" (*Riben zhuan*) in the *Ming History* (*Ming shi*) [1739]

2. *A Treatise on Military Preparations* (*Wu bei zhi*), by Mao Yuanyi, a military strategist and poet of the late Ming [1621]

3. *Classified Manuscripts of the Year "Guisi"* (*Guisi lei gao*), by Yu Zhengxie, a leading evidential research scholar of the early nineteenth century [1833]

4. *Recorded News of the Sea Kingdoms* (*Hai guo wenjian lu*), by Chen Lunjiong, a sea traveler [1730]

5. The *Illustrated World Geography* (*Kunyu tu shuo*), by Ferdinand Verbiest, a Jesuit employed by the Kangxi emperor in the Imperial Office of Astronomy [1672]

6. The *Qing Imperial Compendium* (*Huang Qing tong kao*) [1772][19]

7. *A Brief Record of Macao* (*Aomen ji lue*), by Yin Guangren and Zhang Rulin, a pair of customs officials in Macao in the mid-eighteenth century [1751?][20]

8. The *Complete Illustrated Geography of the Myriad Nations* (*Wanguo dili quantuji*), by Karl Gützlaff, a German missionary working in Hong Kong after the Opium War [1843]

9. *Additional Notes from Chun District* (*Chunxiang zhui bi*) by Dong Han, a seventeenth-century traveler and poet [1738?][21]

10. *Geographical Reference* (*Dili bei kao*), by the Portuguese "Ma Jishi" [1847]

11. *Concise History of the Foreign Nations* (*Waiguo shi lue*), by Robert Morrison, the most prominent British Protestant missionary in Macao and Malacca prior to the Opium War [1847]

12. *A Short Treatise on the Ocean Circuits* (*Ying huan zhi lue*), by Xu Jiyu, a leading government official, scholar, and geographer of the mid-nineteenth century [1849]

I should add that Wei reproduced excerpts from at least three additional works, which are integrated among the last two items above (Morrison and Xu Jiyu). Wei himself may have been working from fragments, since his excerpts differ from other versions of the three works. One of these is the celebrated early Qing scholar Huang Zongxi's history of the Ming "pretenders," *Records of the Itinerant Court* (*Xing chao lu*), which was banned as subversive in the eighteenth century; from it, Wei extracted fragments of a chapter on "rebel" efforts to secure military help from Japan.[22] The other two sources are an obscure text by a Yuan dynasty official, Wang Yun, entitled *A Brief Record of a Sea Voyage* (*Fan hai xiao lu*), and the preeminent early Qing scholar Gu Yanwu's massive seventeenth-century compendium on military geography, *On the Gains and Ills of the Administrative Domains under Heaven* (*Tianxia junguo libing shu*).[23] Gu Yanwu's work was printed for general circulation only in 1811 (and again in 1823), but in fact, it was this work that provided a model for the above geographic anthologies of the mid-nineteenth century. In a turn of events reminiscent of the "Dwarf pirate" scare of the sixteenth century, piracy along the south China coast resurged in the late Qianlong and Jiaqing reigns (1796–1820), a situation which renewed interest in military history and frontier and coastal defense. Following Gu, who collected geographic materials in the interest of informing his Chinese compatriots of the defense of China's frontiers against invaders like the Manchus, Wei Yuan collected his materials for the *Illustrated Treatise on the Sea Kingdoms* in the interests of coastal defense against the Westerners.[24]

Narratives: Dwarf Pirates and Treacherous Japanese

The observant reader of Wei's materials on Japan would notice three characteristic types of writing concerning Japan. Two are historical narratives, the third an ethnographic description. Of the two narratives, one chronicles the proliferation, intensification, and ultimate suppression of the Japanese "Dwarf pirates" of the sixteenth century; the other recounts the beginnings, expansion, and ultimate demise of Christian proselytizing among the Japanese at the turn of the seventeenth century. The former narratives painstakingly outline the numerous pirate alliances and invasions flourishing after 1547, and often end with the death of Toyotomi Hideyoshi and the Dwarf abandonment of their invasion of Korea in 1598.[25] The latter narratives much more briefly describe the efforts of Portuguese Catholics or Dutch Protestants in Japan and Taiwan respectively, and end with the anti-Christian massacres in Nagasaki and the establishment of exclusionary laws against Westerners in the early 1600s.[26] Where the former are Chinese historical narratives, based on the many Ming and early Qing accounts of the Dwarf pirates, the latter likely represent the reports of European proselytizers and traders, and Chinese merchants. In other words, the genres of the two sets differ in that the Dwarf pirate narratives are segments from longer Chinese histories, while the anti-Christian narratives are excerpted from collections of much shorter pieces called "notes" (*biji*), a style of writing popular among evidential research scholars in the Qing period (see chapter 5).

Not surprisingly, both narratives attribute utterly negative characteristics to the Japanese. They are rapacious, cruel, cunning, and treacherous; in broader terms, they are a warlike, unlettered people. The compilers of the *Ming History* emphasize the duplicity in the behavior of the Dwarf pirates:

The Dwarf character is exceedingly cunning. They invariably carried on board their ships both local products from their native land and their weapons. They would put to sail and wait along the coast for an opportunity. If it came, they would brandish their weapons and attack, invading inland; if none came, they would display their local products, styling them "tribute to the Court." . . . In short, they were sometimes "tribute bearers," and sometimes "pirates," as it suited them.[27]

The set of narratives concerning anti-Christian activity also highlights expressly devious devices of the Japanese. One repeated incident indicts Japanese authorities in Nagasaki, who inlaid a bronze cross into the threshold of the gates to the city so as to entrap and execute those believers who would deliberately avoid stepping on the cross. (Some versions add an image of the Christ on the cross.)[28]

A critical difference between the two sets of narratives, however, is the name by which the Japanese are known. The pejorative "Dwarfs" (*Wo*) or "Dwarf pirates" (*Wokou*) is consistently used in the narratives concerning the sixteenth-century pirates. There is of course a historical precedent for this name; until the tenth century, Japan was known as the "Wo Kingdom" (*Wo guo* or *Wonu guo*). While the name was probably not a deliberate pejorative prior to the Ming dynasty, it could be literally interpreted as "slave" or "peon." Certainly, in the sixteenth century, *Wo* was recirculated for its pejorative effect—no doubt to indicate Chinese contempt for the illicit behavior of pirates, especially the Japanese variety.[29] By contrast, "Japan" (Riben)—or its derivative, "Japanese"—is typically used in the set of anti-Christian narratives.[30]

I propose two reasons for these distinctive practices. In the first place, "Dwarf" carries over from Ming Chinese usage, while "Japan" is the more established geographical usage of the Qing period. As I indicated earlier, the histories of the Dwarf pirates are based on Ming sources, while the "notes" on anti-Christian activity are strictly Qing writings.[31] In the second place, the geographic content of the semantics of the two names is different. The "Dwarfs" are Japanese when they are outside of Japan and trespass into Chinese territory, while "Japan" is the Chinese geographical name for the land so signified and is the location of the anti-Christian activity perpetrated by Japanese against their own people.

Chen Lunjiong even questions whether the "Dwarf pirates" were truly "Dwarfs" from Japan:

The Dwarf pirates of the Jiajing period [1523–1567] were from Satsuma. When Japanese trading ships first sailed to Yongjia [in Zhejiang Province], eighteen Dwarf fishermen were driven by the winds to China, and certain dissolute characters induced them to participate in rebellious acts. [These Chinese] trimmed their beards and shaved their heads [like the Dwarfs], and bastardized their speech with dialect from some distant place, and thereupon [they all] collaborated in robbery and plunder. This gang was called the "Dwarf pirates," but at the time they were apprehended, there were only eighteen [such Dwarfs].[32]

Indeed, evidence in the accounts of Ming dynasty piracy would seem to support such a position, because the pirate leaders and prominent figures in the narratives are primarily Chinese.[33] In order to strategically compensate for this straying from "Japan," the narratives typically close with identifiably Japanese subjects. One frequent ending is Hideyoshi and his invasion of Korea; another (which appears in examples of both narratives) is the story of Zheng Chenggong (or Koxinga), son of a Chinese pirate and Japanese mother, who abandoned the Chinese mainland and established a Ming refuge in Taiwan, which was ultimately wiped out by the Qing armies in 1683. As Ralph Croizier has pointed out for the case of Koxinga, these endings serve to underline the consistency of historical events—from an imperial Qing perspective.[34]

Descriptions: Civil Japan

The third format for writing about Japan is the more typical ethnographic description, which generally covers such points as the location of Japan, its type of administration, laws, customs, teachings, local products, and so on. If this approach is more prevalent, its details exhibit the most variation. There is no systematic ordering of information, and little is consistent aside from the often repeated introductory assertion that "Japan was known as the Dwarf [Wo] Kingdom in ancient times."[35]

Nevertheless, it is clear that above all, Chinese writers of these descriptions understood "Japan" as an administrative unit. In addition to whatever assortment of details, all texts make a point of this topic in one form or another. Several texts begin with the analysis that Japan "consists of five principalities, seven circuits, and three islands, which are altogether 115 departments encompassing 587 districts."[36] Another analysis mentions either thirty-six or seventy-two islands, each being an independent domain.[37] In both cases, all mention that the Japanese are ruled by some combination of king, lord, or general (shōgun), and generally have the idea that there are two important administrative offices. Most state that there is a "domainal king" (guowang), who has either an empty or a ceremonial position, and a general, who is the focus of privilege and power.[38] Others mention two kings who share the same functional division of ceremony and power: a "true" or "spirit" king, and a "secondary king."[39] Finally, some writers mention a group of lords who rule the various islands in the name of the king—akin to the ancient Zhou king's "noble ranks."[40]

In these descriptions of Japan, the Dwarf people are presented much more congenially than in the historical narratives. They live amid mountains, rivers, and lakes; they produce gold, silver, hemp, wood, and silk, and manufacture lacquerware, bronze vessels, beautiful cloth, and exquisite swords. Their laws may be strict, but they are a well-mannered people; they honor the graves of their ancestors, keep their streets clean, believe in the teachings of the Buddha, and delight in poetry and the Chinese dynastic histories. They use the Chinese writing system; their dress resembles that of the ancient Tang style. Like the Chinese, they eat rice.[41]

These generally favorable assessments are possible, I believe, because of two kindred premises. In the first place, the Japanese are often said to be "similar" to the Chinese in these accounts. This characterization renders them much more sympathetic, because every point of resemblance to "the Chinese" is a moment at which the writer leaves the details of such resemblance to the imagination of his Chinese reader. To the reader aware of regional variations in China, Japan becomes a similar, albeit more distant, variation. In the second place, there is an *order* in these representations, one that would have been familiar and therefore reassuring to Chinese readers: Japan is subdivided into units that are in turn administered by a hierarchy of rulers. This class division patterns the Japanese after Chinese Civilization, especially in contrast to the disharmony represented in the narratives about the Dwarf pirates. These two favorable premises often combine in direct comparisons between Japan and China. For example, some texts complete the above analysis of Japan's administration with a Chinese point of reference: "Japan consists of . . . 587 districts, all of which are bound by water and smaller islands; the largest does not exceed the size of a Chinese village."[42] Or again, Japanese government officials are said to "hold offices and stipends generation upon generation, honoring the Han dynasty system, the standard for which was one thousand stones of grain for the rank of district magistrate."[43] One text observes a truly favorable set of similarities with Chinese behavior: "In Izumi Province, the people ring a bell when meals are laid out, as in Chinese customs. The people of Oka hamlet in Satsuma understand propriety and righteousness, and regard law-breaking with gravity."[44]

Whether or not Japanese are like Chinese, or even share Chinese ways, was an issue hotly contested when contact was renewed between the two peoples—as we shall see shortly. Only rarely do voices in the Qing record dissent from these positive assessments of the Japanese and recognize ways in which they unfavorably differ from China. Consistently, it is the European missionaries' texts that devalue Japan, and do so on the basis of an awareness of the different social classes in Japanese society. Morrison, for example, comments on the shogun's practice of keeping hostages in the capital and connects this to the general "haughtiness" of the lordly class.[45] Gützlaff notes the rigid divisions of privileges among classes, one result of which is that the common people fear their rulers; this is an unfortunate departure from the Chinese ideal of reverence or affection for one's rulers. He also observes that the Japanese too often drink to excess and are sexually dissolute, with the entire land full of courtesans.[46] Gützlaff is as well the only one to declare: "The Japanese people are not similar to the Chinese people [the Han race]. Their facial appearance, bearing, and the sound of their speech are different [from Chinese]. Although they borrowed Chinese written characters and the ritual practices of Tang Chinese, their intentions and views are vastly different."[47]

Apart from these descriptions and narratives, Qing writings on Japan also include a few series of directions for Chinese wishing to sail to Japan. Chen Lunjiong locates Japan in units of *geng*, the two-hour watch, recording that such-and-such a place in Japan lies the distance traveled in so many *geng* from a given place in China. He is apparently the originator of this information, which is reproduced in the *Qing Imperial Compendium* and elsewhere. Chen adds further directions of questionably practical help, stating simply that a ship sailing from Amoy in south China, heading toward Jilong in Taiwan with a southerly wind, will continue to pass certain landmarks en route, depending on certain winds, and arrive in Nagasaki.[48] Much more detailed directions are reproduced in Gu Yanwu's *On the Gains and Ills of the Administrative Domains under Heaven*; most interesting is a quite technical set of directions in terms of "compass" points, evidence that Chinese knowledge of seafaring had early on situated Japan in an abstracted system of references.[49] By comparison, Chinese were confused by the first European geographies in Chinese that introduced the latitude and longitude system, because they typically gave contradictory values for Japan. Wei Yuan's *Illustrated Treatise on the Sea Kingdoms* includes two versions, one in the *Dili bei kao* and one by Morrison; Wei notes at the end of his section on Japan that the English outsiders in Hong Kong offer misinformation as knowledge—since they have never personally gone to Japan, their mapping system is not to be trusted.[50]

Given this preponderance of received knowledge, based not on current, first-hand accounts of Japan but on conventional narratives and descriptions of Japan one or more centuries old, it is not surprising that by the time of China's awkward entry into the "international order," anyone dealing with Japan inevitably relied on "facts" and incidents only distantly bearing upon the contemporary era. Since scholars had for so long been unable to verify what they had heard and read, this general ignorance of Japan created two related difficulties. On the one hand, scholars or officials interested in Japan were confronted by a host of received "facts" that often conflicted with each other; one couldn't tell if the Japanese were treacherous Dwarf pirates or a people patterned after Chinese Civilization. On the other hand, when officials had occasion to formulate political recommendations on the basis of these received "facts," their opponents exploited the dissonance between textual representations from the past and the contemporary world of action. It is the effects of this received knowledge in the activity of diplomacy to which we shortly turn.

An Aside: The Aborted Legacy of the Ming

The scarcity between 1640 and 1840 of information concerning contemporary Japan is remarkable, when compared to the number of writings completed by the end of the Ming dynasty (1368–1644). Scholars commonly interpret this output of the late Ming in terms of need and practicality; these writings on Japan were directly prompted by the widespread problem of Japanese Dwarf pirates. The appearance of works like the *Japan Investigations* (*Riben kao*) by Li Xingong, printed in 1575, is explained as evidence of the effort to better understand Japanese character and conditions in order to more effectively suppress the Dwarf pirate raids of the time.[51]

The most significant fact about these writings is that Ming scholars created an unprecedented set of monographs on Japan. Quite unlike the standard narrative "Japan Biography" in the official dynastic histories, these works treat Japan as the individual object of an independent history. The works constituting this history were produced largely between the 1520s and the 1620s; the first among them was Xue Jun's *Concise Investigations of Japan* (*Riben kao lue*), published in 1523. Xue initially reiterates the widespread Ming perception that the Dwarfs are cunning and devious barbarians against whom China must defend herself, but he then offers a quite detailed analysis of Japan. His analysis proceeds according to what became a standard geographical representation during the Qing period (see chapters 3 and 5 on local treatises) and is divided into the following categorizations: successive administrative changes (*yan'ge*), borders, provinces and prefectures, tributary domains, mountains and rivers, local products, dynastic records, population, regulations, customs, history of tribute to the Chinese court, tribute items, pirates, and writing. These "concise investigations" are followed by a series of poems on memorable Japanese sites, events, and persons; and the work ends with a lengthy and fascinating list of Japanese "transmitted vocabulary" (*jiyu*) items, each of which is the reputed sound of a Japanese word or phrase, phonically transliterated into Chinese characters, and accompanied by a Chinese (character) translation. (There is no written Japanese.)[52]

None of these Ming works received any sustained attention during the Qing dynasty. Quite apart from the issue of the need to understand Japan and the fact that these texts were not widely reprinted, this nascent Ming discourse on Japan was "aborted" primarily as a result of a significant shift in scholarly sensibilities. When the Qianlong emperor commissioned the massive encyclopedic collection of texts that came to be known as *The Complete Books of the Four Treasuries* (*Siku quanshu*), his eighteenth-century editors considered only three of these texts on Japan for inclusion among geographic works: the two works by Li Xingong and Xue Jun mentioned above, and one other, the *Illustrated Compendium on Japan* (*Riben tu zuan*), attributed to Zheng Ruoceng. All three received less than satisfactory evaluations. The editors reported that Li had gathered his information in the process of combating pirates and had simply written down what he had heard. Zheng, they reported, had interviewed merchants who had traded in Nagasaki and recorded errors and truths indiscriminately. Xue, by contrast, had interviewed Japanese officials bearing tribute to the Chinese court and had had the opportunity to differentiate the true from the false; nevertheless, errors remained in his account.[53] None of the works were included in the final edition of the *Four Treasuries,* and all fell into obscurity. If Zheng's work alone had an audience, it was known through the larger work from which it was excerpted, the *Illustrated Collection on Coastal Defense* (*Chou hai tu bian*), attributed to Hu Zongxian.[54]

Although the "investigation" remained a significant genre of critical history and geography during the Qing period, no further monographs devoted to Japan were produced until the 1870s. In spite of this hiatus of three centuries or more, there is a remarkable parallel between the production of works on Japan between 1520 and 1620 and the resurgence of works on Japan in the 1870s and 1880s (the subject of chapters 3, 4, and 5): conflict with Japan inspired some Chinese to develop a better understanding of their neighbor across the sea.

The Matter of International Treaties

By 1870, the Chinese ruling class had encountered an exceptional series of foreign challenges that questioned the veracity of the model of Civilization. The Westerners waged war upon the realm over the right to import opium; they understood nothing of virtuous conduct. Worse, they were simply not interested in Civilization; and the alternative world they proposed, an international order in which sovereign powers were differentiated and equal, threatened to subvert the very essence of Civilization—the literary Chinese language, the Confucian classics, and the Chinese emperor. The Westerners would not go away; neither could they be ignored, dismissed, or left to their recalcitrant immorality. By 1870, many among the ruling class were struggling to reach some ideological mediation of the two opposed, if not antagonistic, positions.

Although Wei Yuan's readers in 1852 had indications from Morrison that English and Americans had begun contacting the Japanese as early as 1837, news of current affairs in Japan was not widely available for a few decades. As reports of Japanese success at copying Western technology were brought to China by Western travelers and diplomats, Chinese literati made increasingly substantive mentions of Japan in their writings—with particular reference to China's own efforts at Westernization. Both those officials who would strengthen China with Western armaments (so-called self-strengtheners), and those who would modify Chinese administrative institutions so as to effect some integration of Chinese and Western learning (so-called reformers), used Japan as a point of comparison in their efforts to impress upon the Qing court the urgency of building "strong ships and effective guns." Chinese attention was caught—and jarringly so—by the Meiji Restoration of 1868, and several scholars and officials made much of the fact that Japan had quickly managed to build its own iron foundries and steamships so as to return diplomatic visits to the

United States and Europe. In feeling such dissonance between the activities of the "small domain" of Japan and the hesitation of "great" China, some even suggested that China follow the example of Japan.

The issue at the heart of these evaluations and comparisons of Westernizing change in China and Japan was whether or not Civilization could accommodate Westernization—both the technology of weapons and industry as well as the diplomatic practice of creating treaties. A minority insisted that all elements of Westernization were heretical and threatened to destroy the very fabric of China's relations with its nearby neighbors, if not Chinese society altogether. As we will see, this group of officials rejected Japan's request for a treaty in 1870. Other officials, however, inclined toward a more positive assessment; many had grown to accept the treaty system as a part of Civilization, but remained ambivalent about Western industry and social forms. Zuo Zongtang, for example, declared that Japan was foreign and thus beyond the borders of Civilization; like the other Westerners, Zuo maintained, Japan's interest in Western technology was based on the same immoral act of mistaking superfluous mechanical details for fundamental principles of virtue. But in the same way that Chinese protocol could accommodate a new treaty system—making it effectively a component of Civilization—Zuo believed that China could accommodate practical matters like the industrial production of ships and guns. Because both outsiders and Chinese were human beings, Chinese were inherently capable of placing increased emphasis on mechanical details and thereby producing competitive ships. In other words, Zuo displaced the quality of sameness to the more universal category of human being, which was securely grounded within Civilization. Implicitly, however, Zuo deferred the day that Chinese Civilization reasserted its preeminence over the West and Japan, and accordingly, his understanding acknowledged a weakness of Civilization—China was neither practical nor strong enough, and would have to become so if Chinese Civilization were to survive.[55]

A third group of scholars, by comparison, were similarly accepting of Westernization and also believed that Japan was still within the Chinese domain of Civilization. Scholars like Feng Guifen, Wang Tao, and Li Hongzhang acknowledged with Zuo Zongtang that the new diplomatic protocol was properly part of Civilization, but these men went further than Zuo when they imagined China incorporating much more Westernization. In urging the court not only to follow the example of Japan, but also to sign a treaty with Japan, such scholars imagined more porous boundaries to Civilization, and their view, I will argue, included the possibility of actively renegotiating the relationship between Civilization and Westernization.

What is suggestive about these attitudes is that acceptance of Westernization began with treaties—legal documents grounded in an alternative ritual of diplomacy. Although much has been made of China's "unequal treaties" after the Opium War, the making of international treaties was not new to China in the nineteenth century. As Joseph Fletcher has shown, the Qing emperors signed several treaties with the czar of Russia as well as with Moslem kingdoms in central Asia.[56] Chinese treaties with Russia, beginning with the Treaty of Nerchinsk in 1689, were in part the work of European Jesuit advisors, and were explicitly agreements between *equals*; the Kangxi emperor reasoned that Russia was so vast and so far away that the czar could be acknowledged to possess an equivalent status. But this magnanimity in the early Qing was no longer available in the nineteenth century. According to Fletcher, who describes the Chinese treaty with the Moslem khan of Kokand in 1835 as the first "unequal" treaty, the Daoguang emperor was willing to relinquish his claim to the revenues from customs and commercial taxation in Altishahr (Xinjiang) in return for a cessation of hostilities in the area. That this treaty was perhaps less than honorable may explain why it was omitted from the otherwise complete "Veritable Court Records" of the activities of the court.[57] In other words, in addition to both the traditional tributary ritual described above and the occasional practice of unofficial contact, the Manchu emperors of the Qing dynasty employed a third alternative in managing foreign relations, the international treaty, but the status of this practice changed greatly between the late seventeenth and early nineteenth centuries. The violence of the Opium Wars in 1839 and 1858 soured many Chinese attitudes toward the Westerners and their practice of international treaties, because, repeatedly, the foreigners forced China to agree to treaties that in practice not only contradicted their pretext of equality but also subverted Chinese superiority.

Nonetheless, it is noteworthy that some Chinese officials were in time encouraged to begin to take this treaty arrangement seriously. This was, I believe, because such an ordering of the world did promise to empower all nations to treat each other as equals according to the strict provisions of these mutual agreements. It was precisely this emergent "universalism" re-flected in the practice of treaties and their promise of mutuality and equal-ity that legitimized such arrangements to Chinese proponents. That is to say, to some Chinese, an implicit universalism bridged the traditional and Western approaches to diplomacy.[58] Both the notion of proximity and the practice of treaties promised universal order, although each vision of uni-versality was structured quite differently. While Civilization imagined a universal unity hierarchized under the person of the Chinese emperor, the universality posed by an international order of sovereign states was that of equality—an equality that not only necessitated differentiation, but made a virtue of it. Accordingly, when Japan's Ambassador Yanagihara began by claiming that "Civilization had changed" and "near and far had ceased to be," he was giving voice to the new Western universalism, which to some promised a new international order, but to others threatened to subvert traditional Chinese diplomacy, and Chinese Civilization altogether.

The Decision to Grant Japan a Treaty (1870)

To express their interest in normalizing Japan's relations with the Chi-nese empire, in the manner of already "normalized" relations with the Western powers, Japanese authorities of the new Meiji state sent Am-bassador Yanagihara Sakimitsu to Tianjin in September 1870 to petition Chinese authorities with an official Japanese request for a joint treaty of friendship and trade. Yanagihara's letter reasoned that "recent changes in Civilization had unfolded in great measure," and that "paths to interna-tional communications were multiplying daily, so that near and far had ceased to be"; since Japan had recently signed trade agreements with the Western nations, she would like to do the same with her closest neighbor, China.[59] Japan's request was regarded favorably by Chenglin, the northern superintendent of trade, who had received Yanagihara in Tianjin. In re-porting the matter up to the court, both Chenglin and his superior at the International Office, Prince Gong, proceeded cautiously in advising the court.[60] Both expressed sympathy with the good intentions of Japan. Prince Gong drew particular attention to the proximity of Japan, evident in Japan's skill with Chinese writing, and noted that because Japan too had borne the mistreatment of the West, China should show solidarity by cooperating with her sole eastern neighbor. But he advised against signing a treaty; he saw no need—Japan could simply petition the court and request permission to trade with China.[61] The Japanese ambassador, however, aware that such a move would encourage Chinese claims to superiority, insisted. In the ensuing debate over whether or not to establish a treaty with Japan, the governor of Anhui, Ying Han, condemned the proposed treaty; Ying's points were refuted by the two most celebrated officials credited with the recent suppression of the Taiping rebels and the "self-strengthening" reforms, Li Hongzhang and Zeng Guofan.[62]

The argument engaged conflicting interpretations of Chinese and Japanese relations in the past. Because the imperial court had always been the Chinese institution managing foreign affairs, and because proper relations were instantiated by proper ritual behavior, a consideration of contact with Japan turned immediately to the question of historical precedents. Specifically at issue was whether Japan should be considered a Chinese dependency (*shuguo*), a tributary domain (*chaogong zhi guo*), or neither.[63] Corollary to this dispute was an argument over the moral nature and intentions of the Japanese. What attitude befitted their status? To Ying Han, the Japanese were like other outside domains—"having the nature of dogs and sheep." That is, they made their plans in terms of profit and threatened others in terms of might. Worse, Japan was none other than the "Dwarf Kingdom" of old, whose "Dwarf pirates" had been responsible for "the two hundred years of calamity" afflicting the Chinese coast during the Ming dynasty. They plotted secretly; their manner was condescending. And unlike England or France, with whom China had granted treaties, the Dwarfs had always been a servant and tributary domain; hence their request was without propriety and should be spurned. Otherwise, a dangerous precedent might result, and China would find its other dependencies requesting treaties.[64] In other words, Ying Han analyzed the situation as a long-standing Japanese transgression against the ancient principle of proximity: Japan's immorality corresponded to her violations of tributary expectations.

In response, Li Hongzhang acknowledged that Japan was the former Dwarf Kingdom, but pointed out that they had stopped sending tribute after the time of the Yuan dynasty founder, Kubilai Khan. Even if they had once been a tributary domain, they had never been a dependency, and therefore, could not be classed with Korea, the Liuqiu Islands, or Vietnam.

Some might say that the Dwarf pirate problem during the Ming had arisen because of the "cunning" nature of the Dwarfs, but Li insisted that the problem was due to the harmful Ming policy of restricting Chinese trade with Japan.[65] As further support for his claim that the Japanese nature was benign, Li pointed out that Japan had never taken advantage of China during either the Taiping problem or the recent wartime troubles of 1860–1861.[66] Zeng Guofan reiterated many of Li's points and, furthermore, denied emphatically that the Japanese had any intention apart from a desire for a trade agreement. Zeng saw no harm in giving Japan the treaty she wanted, but urged the court to specify Japan's privileges under the treaty rather than grant Japan the customary most-favored-nation status. Both Li and Zeng were especially concerned to contain the issue; they sought to avoid the possibility that Japan might turn to the Western nations for help and "introductions" on this matter and thereby create complications. At the same time, they took the opportunity to advocate further self-strengthening measures, urging the court to send ambassadors and observers to Japan, so as to learn from Japan's Westernizing changes.[67] The judgment of Li and Zeng prevailed, and a treaty was ratified in 1871, to take effect in 1873.

These two attitudes toward contacts with Japan persisted at least through the first two decades of resumed official relations. If the precedent established by Li and Zeng carried greater weight, adherents of the opposing view continued to raise similar protests on historical grounds. I would characterize the former attitude as a "legalistic pragmatism," insofar as this group of Chinese officials took Japanese claims and requests at face value and attempted to formulate solutions to misunderstandings and diplomatic problems on the basis of the terms of the friendship treaty. Although one can identify a background of such adherence to law in China, traceable through codes of law to the ancient legalist philosophers, what especially distinguishes these men in the nineteenth century is their capacity to *imagine* a new history for Chinese and Japanese relations. By contrast, the latter attitude might be considered an "idealistic historicism," in that this group of Chinese officials compared the present to past accounts with the understanding that the received imperial history not only provided standards for Civilization that had to be maintained in the present but also assigned to Japan a predetermined rank and moral expectations, both of which the Japanese had spurned in more recent history. The present Japanese were the descendents of the Dwarf pirates and, as such, had treacherously abandoned Civilization. These men are often referred to as reactionaries or xenophobes, but again, I am especially struck by their rigid adherence to an ideal Confucian interpretation of Civilization.

Be that as it may, these designations of "pragmatic" and "historicist" are in the end heuristic devices, because all of these officials were historicists insofar as they were all informed by—but gave different weight to—the received history. The "pragmatic" officials all rejected any present pertinence of the narratives of Dwarfish treachery, and some among them noted the optimistic descriptions of a civilized Japan. By contrast, "historicist" officials could not look beyond the Dwarf pirate narratives, which provided damning evidence of past Japanese failures to maintain civilized standards. In other words, we have here a pair of alternative readings of the received history on Japan, and thus a pair of alternative understandings of Japan's relationship of proximity to Chinese Civilization. Where "historicists" gave precedence to Japan's tributary relation to the Chinese court, the "pragmatists" instead gave priority to Japan's filiation to certain cultural attributes of Civilization. But these two attitudes were not mutually exclusive, and I am not suggesting that Chinese officials can be classified as one type or the other. Individuals evaluated the historical narratives and descriptions differently and inconsistently when they constructed their criteria for the present. Indeed, the fact that certain "historicists" accepted the legitimacy of the treaty with Japan *after* it was signed is a significant indication of the degree to which Chinese perceptions of foreign relations continued to change after the second Opium War.

Ultimately, the debate in 1870 alerts us to a fracture in the notion of proximity, a new disjunction between its spatial and moral attributes. When Zeng Guofan, speaking for the "pragmatists," observed that "the Japanese are familiar with the incidents of the past [i.e., Kubilai Khan's ruined efforts to invade Japan], so rather than fear us, they simply call us their neighbor," he asserted that geographical proximity invited diplomatic relations on the model of a treaty.[68] His observation, however, did not assuage "historicist" concerns, because "historicist" officials took that brazen assertion of neighborliness as proof of their claims that the Japanese Dwarfs were wanting in honesty and propriety. Proximity, to their understanding, demanded moral submission and tributary ritual rather than any treaty arrangement. In other words, Japan's request in 1870 had the consequence of placing Japan squarely in an ambivalent position: neither as distant and different as the Westerners, nor as close and commensurate as China's dependencies. Indeed, much of this study is an investigation of the working out of that ambivalence in the 1870s and eighties.

Japanese Incident/Dwarf Intrusion (1874)

The story of Chinese and Japanese relations in the last three decades of the nineteenth century is most often a story of deliberate Japanese hostility toward China, from acts intended to detach intermediate lands like the Liuqiu Islands and Korea from Chinese tributary relations, to the invasion and annexation of Chinese territories.[69] It is not my purpose here to retell or to contest this story. Rather, I am interested in a certain style of argument, the "historicist" argument, that was repeatedly used in discussions of Japan. As Chinese became more knowledgeable in international law and more accustomed to the ways of international diplomacy, they became better able to defend the empire in those terms. And yet some scholars continued to take the "historicist" position described above, producing policy statements that elaborately shuffled arguments and points of view, and persistently refused to relinquish the Dwarf pirate narrative.

An instructive case is provided by the furor over what came to be known as the Taiwan Incident of 1874. In what Chinese felt was an act of utter contempt for the friendship treaty, a Japanese expedition headed by Saigō Tsugumichi invaded Taiwan in order to punish certain Taiwanese aborigines who had earlier killed some Liuqiu islanders when the latter had inadvertently fished Taiwanese waters. The Japanese claimed that because the Liuqiu Islanders were Japanese citizens and because China had taken no measures to punish the aggressors or compensate the victims, Japan's own army was justified in seeking direct recourse. This developed into a major international incident; European ships patrolled the Taiwan coast to observe developments, and the British ambassador to China, Sir Thomas Wade, volunteered to mediate the dispute. In the end, Japan received an indemnity and strengthened its claim over the Liuqius.[70] As we might expect, the more "pragmatic" position throughout the crisis, exemplified again by Prince Gong and Li Hongzhang, was to turn to the treaty for standards of behavior. Their memorials to the court repeat the need to "act according to the treaty"; their official communiqués to Japanese officials reiterate their ultimately ineffectual protests that Japan has failed to act in accordance with either the treaty or recent official negotiations.[71]

By contrast, and in the spirit of Ying Han's case against establishing a treaty with Japan, "historicist" arguments condemning Japan's conduct in Taiwan make much of historical evidence. They begin by rehearsing the history of Dwarf and Japanese tribute missions to China, which were documented from the Wei through the Soong dynasties—that is, the third through twelfth centuries—but ceased with the Yuan (1279–1368) and were resumed only intermittently during the Ming period. After citing these ritual precedents for Japanese submission to China, "historicist" officials typically recall the Dwarf pirate problem during the Ming dynasty, which culminated in the Dwarf invasion of Korea in 1592. Their most significant source of information was the "Japan Biography" in the *Ming History*; in fact, the *Investigation of the Eastern Dwarfs*, a discussion of the Taiwan incident written by Jin Anqing around 1875, incorporates those sections of the "Japan Biography" concerned with pirate raids after 1552 under the leadership of Wang Zhi.[72] Through this use of historical evidence, Jin and his colleagues establish what turns out to be a circular argument. First, the Dwarfs were a "cunning" and "treacherous" people, and thus unwilling and unable to act according to Civilized moral principles. Second, because Japan had long been China's tributary domain, and then cosigner of a friendship treaty, she had in recent actions violated all established order between herself and the Chinese court. To bring the argument full circle, Japan had violated established order because, as Dwarfs, Japanese did not act according to principle. What is fascinating about this argument is the way in which it entwines not only a history of Dwarfs with a history of Japan, but also a history of tributary ceremony with a history of treaty relations, so as to recommend that China go to war with Japan.

An extended example will illustrate the logical procedures in this argument. The *Notes on the Recent Japanese Incident*, written by Chen Qiyuan around 1875, begins by describing the "haughtiness" of the Dwarfs since the time Kubilai Khan failed to invade Japan, and then turns to the "viciousness" of the Dwarf pirates during the Ming. To emphasize Japan's disregard for the righteous precedents of their own forebears, he reproduces the Wei emperor Ming Di's decree to the "original" Dwarf tribute mission sent allegedly by Jingū Kōgō in 239. The Wei emperor commends the Dwarf queen for her loyalty and filiality, and bestows upon her both the epithet "Friend of Wei" and a sizeable collection of gifts.[73] Chen establishes the connection to the present incident when he concludes:

In truth, it can be seen that our nation-family calls together the distant peoples in kindness and conciliation, and across the expanse of a common Heaven. Yet, in the thirteenth year of Tongzhi [1874], Japan took the Taiwan aborigines' killing of Liuqiu islanders as cause to command a sortie of several thousand troops into Taiwanese territory, set up base camps, construct fortifications, and wage war against the aborigines. Who could have foreseen this covert intention![74]

Implicit in Chen's argument are two corollary beliefs. First, Chen intimates that although something had gone awry in the thirteenth century, earlier arrangements between China and Japan should be recoverable. And second, these arrangements should be recoverable because they had an *origin* in righteous intent. Now, we today would likely credit Japanese leaders with a decision to forgo Japanese tributary missions to China (indeed, Chinese scholars toward the end of the nineteenth century blamed the establishment of a non-Chinese dynasty under Mongol domination in 1279), but scholars like Chen in the 1870s attributed the break in relations between China and Japan to the failure of Kubilai Khan's planned invasion of Japan, which they described as a "legitimate punitive expedition" in retaliation for Japan's assassination of the Chinese envoy in 1276. Chen and Jin noted that the inept leadership of the surrendered Soong general Fan Wenhu had sabotaged the expedition, but critical fault for the break in relations must be placed on Japan, because imperial intent was in accord with Heaven, and Heaven had earlier brought Dwarf tribute missions to the Chinese court.[75] This was the natural order implicit in Civilization, and Chen, Jin, and others could not consider a reversal of this hierarchical model.

By implication, the Japanese must have lost a measure of virtue during the intervening eras, and Chen confirms this when he discloses the "covert intention" of the Japanese in Taiwan. He goes even further when he recounts his dissatisfaction with the solution to the Taiwan Incident, and sarcastically questions the basic humanity of a people that would be appeased by monetary retribution for the deaths of their fellows: "Two Dwarfs were pleased to receive our compensation, thereby 'alleviating their sorry burden'; they considered the situation remedied and returned to

Japan, even though the number of dead among their forces was considerable."[76] This overriding purpose of attributing a base character to the Dwarfs is, I believe, the reason why "historicist" arguments make use of the Dwarf pirate raids of the sixteenth century. As Dwarfs, the Japanese lack virtuous intent. In this respect, Jin Anqing's careful analysis of Japanese foreign trade expansion after the 1840s and the consequent collapse of the shogunate is indicative; Jin details the tremendous *profit* earned by the shogun, and implies that his improper intention led to his downfall in 1868.[77]

The remainder of Chen's essay is the text of a memorial that he and Ying Baoshi, provincial administration commissioner of Jiangsu, wrote to the emperor and sent by way of Zhang Shusheng, provincial governor of Jiangsu. (The memorial, to my knowledge, has never been reported to have reached the emperor.) The text begins with a similar castigation of the base intentions of the Dwarfs, in language evocative of the "Japan Biography" in the *Ming History*:

Japan is alone in the eastern sea, and lies very close to China. Their people are accustomed to deception of a great many sorts, and quite simply lack honesty and righteousness. Recently, they imitate the ways of Westerners in everything; they indulge in wild thoughts of self-strengthening, and secretly design to expand their territory. In sum, their intentions are underhanded—how long have they plotted so willfully?[78]

Chen and Ying expand on this reasoning by bringing in the matter of the treaty, which, we see, has been subverted in a larger web of cunning intentions:

Today, they spurn treaties and start wars, giving excuses as they provoke other states; they force their way into our borders, massacring our aboriginal peoples. China desires to maintain old relations, and to get along with others on the basis of principles. How could we unashamedly use military force—or even permit such use? That we build watchtowers could be said to exemplify extreme generosity and to celebrate propriety and righteousness—they are an expression of how we protect their trading ships. But who could have fathomed their cunning plots? Even as they stall us with empty words, they have already long occupied aboriginal shrines and coerced the aborigines over to their side.[79]

Criticism of Japan is inseparably ethical and cultural, based on the notion of proximity. Japan lies *close* across the eastern sea; Japan may know Chinese ways but it has forsaken them, and consequently its invasion of Taiwan is proof of unprincipled and barbarian behavior. The damnable act here is disclosed in the projection "How could one use military force?" Chinese modes of action are predicated on modeling—one imitates the good example of better others. What Japan lacks, honesty and righteousness, is what China offers. That an established set of behaviors deserves imitation is implicit in China's "desire to maintain old relations." China would not use military force so provocatively, nor sanction such activity—the implication remains, "How could Japan?" In the tautological simplicity of the piece, Japan has ceased to follow the good example of China—because it has perversely declined to do so. Where China's military defenses express paternalistic concern, and give evidence of generosity, propriety, and righteousness, Japanese munitions become a sign of their devious plotting. What makes Japan's betrayal of principles so heinous is that they, unlike the West, once participated in civilized relations. They once followed Chinese models of propriety. Where the West chose instead to rely on the legalistic treaty for standards of behavior, there was no reason for Japan to do so. It has deliberately abandoned Chinese propriety.

In addition to this argument based on Chinese history, Chen and Ying make use of a second point of reference. Given that Japan has chosen to imitate Western ways, it is appalling that it does not respect even that set of standards. Chen and Ying are not so single-mindedly "conservative" as to hold Japan accountable only to Chinese principles; they do acknowledge the new ways of containing power in the world. They advocate obeying treaties, and significantly, make a precedent of international law:

Furthermore, now that all nations are opening up to international trade, they can take advantage of official boundaries without awakening a martial spirit of invasion, *because they have treaties*. These days, Japan does not honor its treaties. . . . As a present plan, we should publicize Japan's crime of treaty-breaking and report it to all nations. Moreover, on the basis of international law, we should strictly round up all Dwarfs and disengage all armies in Taiwan.[80]

To Chen and Ying, treaties safeguard a nation from potential excesses or perversion of trade; they believe that advantageous exploitation of international boundaries by way of trade might very well turn to warfare. To put it another way, where nations once may have brazenly invaded each other for economic advantages, treaties provide a means to regulate such economic advantages. Again, Japan is acting perversely—not following the ideal behavior exemplified by "all nations." Chen and Ying imagine recourse in international law, which represents an adequate and necessary set of principles applicable equally to all nations. Reporting Japan to these nations should have the effect of singling Japan out for her singularly unprincipled actions. Japan's name and reputation will be tarnished.

The careful reader will notice a striking "division of labor" in the language of these anti-Japanese arguments, which I have tried to reproduce in my above examples. "Dwarf" and "Japan" connote different objects. Where "Dwarf" and its variants signify elements of a textual past, the subjects of Dwarf pirate narratives, "Japan" signifies a collective agent (or set of agents) involved in present incidents, and the linking of the two permits a case to be made about the nature of the problem in Taiwan. Chinese officials refer to the "Dwarfs" and "Dwarf pirates" in history texts so as to establish the base character of the present aggressors in Taiwan. At the same time, officials refer to "Japan" in describing the present activities of Japanese agents in Taiwan, and interweave those motives borrowed from received texts that pejoratively attest to the Dwarfish nature of the Japanese agents. The validity of this exchange of "Dwarf" for "Japan" (and vice versa) depends on the reader's acceptance of a certain reading of history; this is why, I believe, historicist arguments begin by asserting the historical "fact" that Japan was formerly known as the Dwarf Kingdom. Such interchange of the terms "Dwarf" and "Japan," like that in Jin Anqing and Chen Qiyuan, serves to identify the incident in Taiwan as a lack of principles specifically symptomatic of the vile behavior of reprehensible Dwarfs. Without such an account of the "Dwarf" character of "Japan," the Taiwan incident would be incomprehensible, and in fact, as one of the more "pragmatic" officials laments: "How can we *reasonably* discuss [the situation] with them?"[81] The point is that the Dwarfish Japanese do not act in accord with civilized principles, or reason.

The peculiar nature of this account is traceable, I believe, to the geomoral conceptualization of proximity. When Chinese considered foreign lands in relation to their Civilization, they privileged space and morality.

The difficulty with figuring Japan into that relationship in the late nineteenth century is that two versions of Japan were available, referring Japan to two different spaces and correspondingly inconsistent moral natures. There were, as I have documented, the Dwarfs outside Japan and the Japanese inside Japan; and the moral history of the former had degenerated from good to bad, while the moral history of the latter was unpredictable: sometimes commendable, sometimes reprehensible. If "historicist" Chinese commentators on diplomatic policy tended to privilege the accounts of reprehensible Dwarfs outside Japan, that is because both diplomacy itself and "historicist" ideals for foreign relations invoke that very space: Civilization from the center scrutinized Japanese within Chinese territory.

That is to say, "Dwarf," in addition to all its deprecating content, also invokes the abandoned ideal of Japanese tributary relations. It is the one element of early Qing narratives of Japan uncomfortably remaining in the historicist version of events, and accordingly, it is the element Li Hongzhang and other pragmatists had so quickly attempted to negate when they denied that "Japan" was a tributary domain. We see here two versions of a rather straightforward discontinuity over time, and an attempt to work out the fact that conditions had changed. Where historicists began with the assumption that the "Dwarf Kingdom" had been a tributary domain, and showed that "Japan" too continued in the practice, pragmatists cut them short by declaring that Japan was no longer a tributary domain. Relations had changed. This, I believe, is the substance of certain Chinese officals' intellectual difficulty with accepting Japan's new status "under Heaven." But this contradiction highlights two attendant problems of the day: On the one hand, it makes an issue of the pertinence of the past as a guide to action in the present and changing world, a matter I return to in later chapters. On the other hand, it exposes a distinctive weakness in late Qing knowledge of outside peoples; the Chinese had faulty understanding of Japan, and the texts to which they turned for information were quite out of date. This deficiency would soon be remedied.

The exchange of ambassadors provided by the friendship treaty of 1871 had been delayed, first by the 1874 incident in Taiwan, and then by the death of the Tongzhi emperor and the accession of the Guangxu emperor in 1875. Not until late 1877 did the Chinese ambassador Hê Ruzhang depart from

Shanghai, arriving at Nagasaki on November 30—that being the twenty-second day of the tenth month in the second year of the reign of His Highest Majesty the Guangxu emperor. Neither an ambassador nor any members of his entourage can readily engage in the sort of polemics that we have seen here. Theirs is a social and representative function; and the encounters between this first Chinese embassy and their Japanese hosts are for the most part a genial and thoughtful exchange, what we might anticipate from the protégés of Li Hongzhang or Zeng Guofan. The next chapter examines the records of these encounters, and thereafter we turn to the Chinese representations of their experiences in Japan.

2 Civilization as Universal Practice

The Context of Writing and Poetry

To write is to produce a mark that will constitute a kind of machine that is in turn productive, that my future disappearance in principle will not prevent from functioning and from yielding, and yielding itself to, reading and rewriting.
Jacques Derrida, "Signature Event Context"

The power of *wen* is great indeed!
Liu Xie, *The Literary Mind and Carving Dragons*

I have argued that the largely Confucian project of Civilization (*wenming*), as a component of the ideology of the imperial state, served nineteenth-century Chinese scholars as a means to locate Japan within a Chinese worldview, both historically and in terms of present relations. But as we have seen, Japan's was a contested position—for some, a former participant in imperial tributary relations; for others, a sinified and still civilized neighbor across the Eastern Sea; for still others, a renegade and treacherous barbarian. It is perhaps because of the acrimony in this very dispute that when some Chinese in the late nineteenth century encountered Japan in a favorable light, they intensified an aspect of the ideology of Civilization that I examine here: they specifically referred to Japan in terms of *tong wen*—"shared language," and by extension, "shared Civilization."[1] For at the personal level of friendly interactions among Chinese and Japanese scholars, this element of the ideology of Civilization even more successfully served as a means to include Japan within Chinese Civilization. Japanese scholars were able to participate not only in "conversations" conducted in the literary Chinese language but also in the ritualized play that most defined civilized sociability: occasional poetry.

Brushtalking

The men who gathered intermittently over a period of years in the company of Ōkōchi Teruna formed a distinctive society. Ōkōchi, the former lord of Takasaki-han, was living at his Tokyo estate since his forced retirement after the Meiji Restoration. As far as can be known from records these men left, these were the eighth through the fourteenth reign years of the Meiji emperor, or 1875 through 1881 in the new Western reckoning. Ōkōchi's guests were for the most part Chinese and Japanese scholars and officials: the Chinese came largely from the retinue, acquaintances, and associates of the first Chinese ambassador to Japan, Hê Ruzhang; the Japanese came from among their friends, and the friends and acquaintances of Ōkōchi. They all drew together out of a common interest in Chinese literature, history, and poetry—proper Chinese learning, that is—and met irregularly over tea or drink, out of the generous hospitality and curiosity of Ōkōchi, for conversation—of a sort.[2]

Ōkōchi and his Japanese friends spoke little Chinese, and Hê Ruzhang and the Chinese spoke little Japanese. Their solution to this difficulty—indeed the original design for these primarily entertaining encounters—was to converse by writing in *hanzi*, or *kanji*, the Chinese characters used by educated men for literary and official communications. This practice has been called "brushtalking," from *bitan* in Chinese or *hitsuwa* in Japanese, and it provided an opportunity to gather with some of the literary figures of the day, to show off one's erudition and poetry composition, and, as guest in a foreign land or host to visitors from abroad, to share one's everyday experiences and impressions of the changing times.

The peculiar fact is that after each session, Ōkōchi, a man convinced of the historical significance of his "society," would collect all the sheets of paper, rescuing some from the trash, press them, and then mount them on a sturdier backing to be bound into book form. These he saved until his death, whereupon they were stored in the family temple at Hirabayashi, and there they lay until scholar Sanetō Keishū rescued them, badly worm-eaten, toward the end of the Great Pacific War. Today they are housed in the Waseda University Library in Tokyo.[3]

Thus we have in these "brushtalks" material documenting a specific sequence of historical events—encounters between identifiable Chinese and Japanese individuals. Because they are such peculiar and unique phenomena, the brushtalks challenge our usual categories of language activity. To begin with, they are a form of writing that works like speech; that is, they lack the self-enclosure and deliberate continuity that is a property of most written texts. They start with a formal greeting to a friend, they stop for a newcomer or for a trip to a certain tea house or drinking establishment across the Sumida River; they break off and begin again according to unwritten social principles, as in spoken interaction. Like statements uttered in the service of some collective activity, they were disposable once the activity was completed.

Unlike conversation, however, the brushtalks were not entirely "spoken away." There is evidence that they were recorded with the full awareness on the part of some participants that Ōkōchi was collecting them. In fact, it seems that Ōkōchi intended all along to turn the brushtalks into something of a more permanent nature—a text. He added comments indicating whether others were present, whether persons arrived or departed, whether an expected someone was absent because of sickness, and so on; likewise, the small notations in red identifying the writer of a "passage" or "utterance" are probably his.[4] The result is a set of papers that reads vaguely like a collection of playbooks, but lacks all sense of overall organization. There is no sustained narration or development; at best, the persevering reader acquires a sense of the character of individual participants in the interaction.

The Written Code : *Hanwen/Kanbun*

As a language phenomenon, then, the brushtalks are neither speech nor text; they defy these primary categories. The brushtalks are rather, I believe, the purest example I have seen of a *written linguistic code*. I emphasize "written code," because as I will explain shortly the language is better defined in terms of its material and usage than in terms of its users. We can provisionally think of this code as "Chinese writing"—similar to what the Chinese would call *hanwen* and the Japanese *kanbun*. Indeed, the code incorporates aspects of both Chinese and Japanese languages.

In the first place, this Chinese writing of the brushtalks includes elements of both the literary Chinese language and the spoken Chinese language of the nineteenth century. The former is what has come to be called in our century *wenyan wen*, the formal language of China's textual tradition. The latter is what was called *guan hua*, or "official speech," and is the northern Chinese spoken language we now know as Mandarin, *guo yu, putong hua,* or *Zhong wen.*[5] So, for example, the Chinese writing of the brushtalks includes (1) final sentence particles typical of literary Chinese: the *ye* of equation (the copula), the restrictive *er* of "and that's all," and the *yi* of completion; as well as (2) colloquial elements typical of spoken Chinese: noun measures like *yi ge,* the connective particle *de,* and so on.[6]

At the same time, this Chinese writing corresponds with what the Japanese call *kanbun,* which means both "Chinese writing" and "Japanese writing in Chinese." From the ninth century, literate Japanese society treated written Chinese as if it were the same language as Japanese, and (from my own informal survey in Japan) Japanese still ambivalently identify *kanbun* as culturally *both* Chinese and Japanese. In the same way that literary Chinese in China incorporated newer colloquial elements over the centuries, *kanbun* in Japan developed in accord with the introduction of the latest books from China. Although the reading of *kanbun* varied by academy and teacher, Japanese in the eighteenth century—especially as a result of the efforts of Ogyū Sorai and expatriate Chinese scholars—were skilled in writing a *kanbun* indistinguishable from literary Chinese.[7] And because "official speech" courses at the shogunal language academies in the mid-nineteenth century were taught by native Chinese, educated Japanese like those who participated in the brushtalks acquired the fluency for the colloquial elements that we find in the brushtalks.

The brushtalks thus confront us with the fact of the interpenetration of the Chinese and Japanese languages. As the linguistic code of the brushtalks, Chinese writing questions the adequacy of formal descriptions of language, which are generally based on a positivist conception of language that (1) fixes the boundaries of a language in order to speak abstractly about its unity, (2) employs criteria habitually extraneous to language, like racial characteristics or national (political and geographical) demarcations, and (3) privileges one form of language use over others in order to designate a standard. To the contrary, the Chinese writing of the brushtalks is a linguistic code that cannot be identified by posited qualities of its users, because the only feature of these individuals that unifies them as a group is their competence with the code. Instead, Chinese writing must be identified in its own terms, precisely because it entangles what usually passes for two distinct "Chinese" and "Japanese" languages. It is neither a pure literary Chinese nor a pure Japanese *kanbun.* Rather, it is a written linguistic code, characterized by its signs—Chinese characters—and by certain practices of composition.[8]

To give an example: There are characters used in the brushtalks for meanings common in *kanbun* but uncommon in literary Chinese, and vice versa, like the character 藩 (C: *fan*; J: *han*). To the "Chinese" reader, *fan* means a fence, boundary, or outlying fiefdom of the Zhou kings (reigned ca. 1100–255 B.C.). But it does not mean that here. The reader must understand the character as *han*, the domain of a Japanese lord (like Ōkōchi Teruna) during the time of Japan's feudal organization. This of course was as obvious to the participants in the brushtalks as it would be to us reading today; both they and we benefit from a knowledge of the context. Because of context, which necessitates a degree of competence with the subject matter, the problem of pronunciation difference diminishes. This is indeed a remarkable property of the Chinese character, which helps to explain how it is that historically, the Chinese character has managed to overcome, if not silence, many and vast differences in (and among) spoken language(s).[9]

It might be argued, however, that because "*han*" is specifically Japanese, and "*fan*" is specifically Chinese, this systematic differentiation has already distinguished the two. But in fact, such delimitations (definitions) of 藩 as either Chinese or Japanese are wholly external to the practice of brushtalking; *fan* and *han* are among the pool of cultural associations that are available to the persons engaged in brushtalking, and these persons can bring these meanings into play as they will. That is to say, reference is a culturally specific attribute of language, and although pronunciations and meanings of Chinese characters are specific to specific languages, such differences can nonetheless be included by and incorporated within the written code of the brushtalks.[10]

The practical consequences of this interpenetration of Chinese and Japanese languages is the subject of this chapter. Through participation in this common code of brushtalking, Chinese and Japanese scholars actualized a conception of Civilization that gave members of both cultural groups positions in an allegedly universal discourse.[11] To be sure, the Chinese and Japanese participants were quite aware of their different (and often antagonistic) political affiliations—the Chinese and Japanese states respectively. But in the interests of amiable *personal* relations, they preferred to stress the commonality of their shared language and all that it implied.[12] As I will explain, the quintessential practice of this common discourse was poetry writing, the purpose of which was to concretize past and present in a self-perpetuating and universal Civilization.

The Play of the Code

Let us look at an extended example, which demonstrates how it is that in becoming both subjects and objects of the code, both Chinese and Japanese participants in the brushtalks create a new group affiliation existing alongside yet overlapping with their particular Chinese or Japanese cultural identities. The passage below has been dated to the afternoon of May 30, 1878; it was inscribed at Ōkōchi's home, shortly after he had returned from a teahouse, the Rijogo, which he frequented with two of his Chinese friends, Wang Zhiben (literary name Qiyuan) and Wang Fanqing (Qinxian) (both of whom were living in Tokyo and working privately as Chinese teachers and editors) because, he tells us, they all liked the women there. Present with Ōkōchi (Guige) at this occasion were Huang Zunxian (Gongdu), counselor to the Chinese ambassador, and Liao Xi'en (Quxian), an attaché at the embassy. (Shen Wenying [Meishi], who is mentioned below, was another frequent participant in the brushtalks and also an embassy attaché.) Ōkōchi has been questioning Huang about the ambassador's plans to find a new location for the embassy; Huang wonders if the reception area at Ōkōchi's former Han office would be suitable for new buildings:

Guige [Ōkōchi]: I'll ask everyone who would be concerned. As for the size of the property, how much would be needed?

Gongdu [Huang]: About three or four thousand *ping* would be best, on solid ground and in fresh air, and one or two *li* from Tokyo.[13]

Guige [Ōkōchi]: Perhaps the ambassadors could ask Mr. Wei Li to look into the matter with our representatives; since he's most accustomed to this sort of thing, it might be as easy as a turn of the hand.

Gongdu [Huang]: I'm aware of that, but I'll take your advice—to the word.

In a poetry game of ours recently, [Shen] Meishi composed the riddle: "Man-made wagtail mating technique; I am Prince Unmixed-Feathers." It uses expressions from your nation's history—do you know the meaning?

Guige [Ōkōchi]: I know not the first line, and blush red as a skirt; I know not the second, and am shamed to the light of my soul. Whenever I ascend the Banner Pavilion, I've no one to accompany me; I guess that you, sir, are a handsome man—would their maidens be safe from your surprise attacks? Should I invite you on another day, I certainly won't accept a refusal; and even if you decline, I'll force your carriage forward.

Gongdu [Huang]: I couldn't dare disagree.

Guige [Ōkōchi]: I often take Wang Qiyuan and Wang Qinxian to the Rijogo for conversation; it's like discussing family affairs with my wife at my own home— their words are respectful and chosen with care; they bow their heads at my command. But when I go to the Gakkaiin with Huang, Liao, and Shen, it's like coming upon famous beauties in the sultry world of smoke and flowers. Words are graceful and show charm and character; listening to the talk, I'm lost in love and unwilling to leave. Do you have such feelings for us Easterners?

Quxian [Liao]: With conversation, each follows its inspiration. When there's romance, it's romantic; when there's talk of economy, it's economics. There's no difference between Chinese and Japanese. You're an intelligent man, surely you understand this point.

Gongdu [Huang]: The *Yanzi* records, "Entering a kingdom of dogs is merely entering a dog kennel"—but this is only a metaphor; don't take it to mean your own nation. Given your words, we could say it fits the case at hand—as a joke.

Guige [Ōkōchi]: In a dog kennel, which one orders the dogs? Could such a one tame your household, or would the barking frustrate your intentions? After all, dogs and people tame each other. History has transmitted Confucius time and again, like a homeless dog—a dog passing for a monkey—or so Eastern scholars have joked.

Gongdu [Huang]: Wagging its tail without entering by the door—of course a dog could joke. These days foreign learning is spreading; the nature of Westerners is to love dogs. I too have been infected by such habits.

Guige [Ōkōchi]: Pig-tailed grandfather shakes his head, dog wags his tail—ha, ha![14]

The witticisms continue for several more rounds.

This rather arcane passage exemplifies two rivalries that recur in the available brushtalks. In the first place, there is the purely personal tension between Ōkōchi and Huang over Ōkōchi's sexual innuendos. From the first of their brushtalks, Ōkōchi repeatedly urges Huang, whose wife remains in China, to take a Japanese mistress; Ōkōchi's suggestion that Huang is a lusty young man in need of amorous outlets (he was thirty-two years old in 1878) repeatedly leaves Huang supercilious and feisty, and in other instances, leads to the same sort of banter.[15] Unlike Huang's subordinates, Liao and Shen, who delight in Ōkōchi's talk of women, Huang's attitude borders on prudish. Here, Ōkōchi's fanciful suggestion that Huang might take advantage of the waitresses at the Banner Pavilion, a restaurant celebrated in Tang history, elicits an ambiguously formal rejoinder—"I couldn't dare disagree." Huang's remark is standoffishly clipped; he is offended by the suggestion but nonetheless compliant, because, as I will describe momentarily, Ōkōchi is flattering Huang. When Ōkōchi goes even further, making first the exoticist comparison of his Chinese companions to beautiful women, and then the erotic metaphor that it is as if he is in love with Huang, Liao, and Shen, Huang responds pugnaciously with a criticism both Ōkōchi and we have seen before—that the Japanese are dogs, uncivil creatures pursuing personal advantage. Should Huang himself indulge his lust, as Ōkōchi proposes, he would be heeding a maxim on the order of "when in the dog kennel, do as the dogs do."[16]

This second rivalry, that between Chinese and Japanese, is potentially more explosive, and this latent tension is surely a consequence of the practice of brushtalking being so weighted in favor of the Chinese participants. Although the fact that Ōkōchi and Huang joke about the difference is indicative of their friendship, we do witness the speed with which they work to contain their banter.[17] Huang is quick to disclaim that "dog" is a true reference—it is "only a metaphor"—and Ōkōchi counters with a joke of his own, that the Chinese tradition of Confucius is a stray dog masquerading as a monkey. (Is this usage in turn a pun, in that *guo* [Vietnamese langur] is homonymic with "nation"?) Huang then attempts to diffuse the rivalry by bringing in a third party, the West, to serve as both a common target and an excuse to admit that he has gone too far; whereupon Ōkōchi patches up the rift with a wittily poetic sentence that parodies the syntax of moral maxims, *"Bianye yao tou, you gou yao wei"*—that is, if Huang, the pig-tailed Chinese grandfather, shakes his head in disapproval, then Ōkōchi, the Japanese dog, wags his tail in glee. (Like all Chinese scholars of the Qing period, Huang wore his hair in a queue.)

The point here, which is such a truism that neither Ōkōchi nor Huang bothers to address it directly, is expressed in Liao Xi'en's lone contribution:

"Conversation" like this has its own inspiration and rules of development, which render secondary the matter of Chinese and Japanese cultural differences. The written code incorporates these differences within a common order of signs, and so, as Liao rightly states, the subject matter governs. Because the sequence of lines is a play of references and linguistic forms—over which no one has a monopoly—all are welcome to play. The critical factor is a participant's degree of competence with the code.

Take, for example, two peculiar word items in the passage. First, Huang refers to an archaic combination of Chinese characters from the ancient Japanese history, the *Kojiki* (*Record of Ancient Matters*). Anyone unfamiliar with this text—whether Japanese or Chinese—would be unable to read the peculiar and difficult name of Ugayafukiaezu-no-mikoto, which means, literally if nonsensically, "Prince Unmixed-Feathers." The name of this (legendary?) prince is an artifact of his birth, which was interrupted when his father improperly observed his mother in the act of giving birth, hence "unmixed"; the "feathers" refers in turn to the miraculous birth of the prince's father, who was born after his own parents witnessed a pair of wagtails mating.[18] Now, Ōkōchi does not know the reference to Japanese history; his friend Shen's riddle has stumped him too. But not to be outdone by the two, Ōkōchi responds with a hyperbolic confession of his embarrassment, from which he generates a new reference that both needles Huang by way of sexual innuendo and acknowledges the success of the riddle. (The Banner Pavilion was the site of a famous anecdotal rivalry between three Tang poets, Wang Changling, Gao Shi, and Wang Zhihuan; incensed that the voluptuously beautiful girls were singing the poems of Changling and Shi, Wang Zhihuan proved that he was the true master by predicting that the loveliest of the group would sing one of his.)[19] In effect, Ōkōchi is admitting Huang's skill as a poet, and issuing a challenge that is played out in the round of witticisms that follow.

Huang's citation of the *Yanzi* (a fifth-century-B.C. history) responds not only to Ōkōchi's sexual innuendos but also to Liao's comment that romance and economy, like Chinese and Japanese, are interchangeable. In fact, Huang protests, romance and economy are not equivalent, because economy, which epitomized one approach to Westernization in Japan in the 1870s, is the very reason that the contemporary world is going "to the dogs." If Japan (which to Huang has been ostensibly within the Chinese world) suffers in the person of Ōkōchi from too much romance, the nation itself is in danger of reverting to some uncivil status because of its policies of economy. Huang is implying that China and Japan should together raise a barrier against the West, because even he himself has been "infected." The infection to which he refers takes place before his very eyes—and ours, with the introduction of new vocabulary into the written code. An expression like "economy" is a reification of the very process of Westernization that Huang views with suspicion, and which, he feels, deserves some containment.

Like "Ugayafukiaezu-no-mikoto," this second term, "economy," juxtaposes Chinese characters in such a way that what determines one's ability to understand is familiarity and competence. Unlike "Ugayafukiaezu-no-mikoto," however, "economy" is not simply a Japanese peculiarity; it is, rather, what I would describe as a rehabilitated archaism. As the Chinese *jingji* or Japanese *keizai*, "economy" is a collapsed form of an older expression, *jingshijimin* or *keiseisaimin*, which indicated the goal of proper administration: "ordering the world and providing for the people." Although discussion of *jingji/keizai* continued throughout the Chinese dynasties and had a certain hearing in Tokugawa Japan, it came to mean "economy" in the 1870s largely as a result of the popular works of the Meiji "enlightener," Fukuzawa Yukichi. Fukuzawa used *keizai* to translate the English notion of "economy" as the largely financial skills of arranging for the food, clothing, and shelter of the people.[20] To Chinese observers of Japan in the 1870s and 1880s, this version of "ordering the world and providing for the people" was anathema, because it was the Western idea motivating what they saw as the oppressive tax structure in Japan. Huang's pugnaciousness, in other words, is double-edged; not only should Ōkōchi desist from his joke and maintain a correct attitude toward Huang, but similarly, they would all do well to maintain the distinctions that Liao overlooks, for the sake of defending themselves against a common rival, the West.

The element that most normalizes the participants of the brushtalks, and makes the code impervious to distinctions between Chinese and Japanese identities, is the encoding of names. Although participants may initially be introduced by their personal names, they instead use and refer to each other by their *zi* name—*azana* in Japanese—which is usually translated as "literary name" or "style." This is the Guige of Ōkōchi Teruna, the Gongdu of Huang Zunxian. According to historical accounts, the *zi* was in ancient times a name given by one's family at one's "capping ceremony," that is, when one reached the age of twenty or otherwise "came of age." The zi was typically a privilege of men, and intended to be used by outsiders—one's wife's relations, or those who were otherwise not members of one's patrinomy. Indeed, the peculiarity of the zi is that zi signifies, literally, the proper name as character or word; it is a sign having a formal public status in the written code and was, accordingly, fixed to all pieces of writing and used for public reference generally. In this regard, we can think of the zi as a *code name,* because practically, it provides a persona for usage in the written code; it is a mark of authorship, a name that will "trace," or correspond to, the person in the world. (The critical importance of this persona-as-trace will become apparent in the following chapter, where we look at the analogy proposed between writer and reader.) In other words, the zi is the mark that indicates a degree of maturity and accomplishment and confers on a man the status to participate publicly in the written code.

As a general phenomenon, then, the brushtalks bespeak multiple cultural and historical references—on the one hand, the past worlds of Japanese and Chinese history as they are constituted in and through specific linguistic formulations, and on the other hand, the present world of the 1870s and 1880s in which the participants are embedded and to which they repeatedly refer. Indicative of the power of all language systems, the language of the brushtalks does manage to situate these multiple realities within the same order of signs, but this does not mean that it is a harmonious order. As we have seen, the language of the brushtalks, like all material signs, is multiaccentual. It both reflects and refracts multiple levels of social discourse, bounded at its two extremes by what one philosopher of language has called the "I-experience" and the "we-experience."[21] The brushtalks are an arena in which individuals not only create meaning for themselves, but also assert the social (or ideological) value judgments of their words. In the process, their interaction shimmers with shifting alliances along personal, cultural, and political lines. Nonetheless, as we will continue to see, the very possibility of the brushtalks is an artifact of a long period of Chinese cultural hegemony in East Asia, and in order to participate in the written code, familiarity with both Chinese writing and its textual operations was essential.

Tong Wen: Shared Writing/Shared Civilization

The majority of Chinese scholars who traveled to and wrote about Japan in the late nineteenth century believed that China and Japan shared some common cultural identity, which they most often described as *tong wen*, "shared writing" (or "common code"), by which they signified the potentiality of activities like brushtalking.[22] But "*tong wen*" means much more than "shared writing." "*Wen*," the same character in "*wenming*" or "Civilization," has a basic meaning of "patterns"—the lines in a piece of jade, the grain in wood, the lay of the land, the heavenly images we read as constellations—but it also means "patterned activity"—ritual civility, the cultivated behavior of a gentleman, the visible manifestation of the Way of the Sages.[23] From these two points of reference, then, "*wen*" has come to mean both written characters (zi) as well as the formalized practice of writing. "*Tong*" is both "similar" or "common," and the transitive actions "to make similar," "to make common." "*Tong wen*" is thus a reference to the action of Qin Shi Huang, the first emperor of China, who standardized and unified the writing system in the third century B.C. It was an imperial act, and "*tong wen*" continued to indicate this authoritative regularizing of language during the imperial ages, as well as the fact that the Chinese sphere of Civilization was unified around a common set of written texts and shared patterns of communication.[24] In the words of the Tuan commentary in the *Classic of Changes* (hexagram 22, *Bi*), "Luminous patterning [i.e., Civilization] at its perfection is human patterning [civilized behavior informed by the texts]."[25]

The language community defined by their collective competence with the Chinese writing of the brushtalks shared not only this common writing; it shared a variety of textual practices as well. There was, for the Chinese of course, the primary and administrative activity of diplomacy, which involved the writing of letters, communiqués, and memorials. Outside of the brushtalks, Japanese diplomats did the same. In addition, these Chinese and Japanese scholars were teachers, editors, authors and poets; they taught Chinese language, Confucian texts, writing style, and poetry composition; they edited, proofread, and contributed to various textbooks, histories, and literary journals, composed formal prefaces and afterwords to one another's books, and, most important of all, participated in the quintessential occupation of the scholar's life: poetry gatherings.[26]

Now, it is true that as a description of a common culture, this list of textual activities is a rather limited intersection of the diversity of Chinese and Japanese cultures. Above I argued that, in terms of linguistic activity *inside* the code, neither Chinese nor Japanese had a monopoly on the usage of references and linguistic forms—that a degree of competence was what mattered. But in terms of the persons involved in the activity, the common culture shared by this language community is primarily a sign of the long history of Chinese cultural hegemony in east Asia. I will shortly inquire as to why some Japanese would be willing to participate in this perhaps chauvinistic Chinese arrangement; in the meantime, and looking at the issue from the point of view of China, it is clear that the "shared culture" of textual practices directly reflects certain Chinese cultural priorities. In fact, the training in classicism, poetry, and literature exemplified by this common culture was the basis of Chinese scholars' standing as a political elite in the Chinese imperial state; because the civil service examination required a knowledge of this written culture, writing and poetry were cultural practices allied with the bureaucratic institutions for selecting officials and the educational institutions that prepared one for the exam and such service.

"*Tong wen,*" then, extends beyond shared writing and common patterns of behavior to signify the essence of a shared Civilization.[27] In fact, writing is the preferred mark of Civilization, because it is written language (*wen*) that not only distinguishes man from the animals, but also distinguishes civilized men from the uncivilized. All men, like the animals, manage to "speak" to each other, but only civilized men write to each other, maintaining their collective way of life across space and time. Prior to accepting European linguistic analyses, Chinese were always very clear on this point. *Wen* was to be distinguished from *yan,* or "spoken words," and *yu,* or "speech." According to a classic formulation, "written signs are the formal appearance of words and speech"—but writing is far from being secondary to words or speech, for it is written signs that "make words adequate" for representation in the Confucian classics.[28] Writing thus marks the beginning of history and the claims of a tradition.

According to the Chinese conception of Civilization, *wen* or Chinese writing is the only language. Indeed, it is "language" itself, as distinguished from mere varieties of speech. Historically speaking, in the context of the spread of Chinese hegemony southward and westward between the second century B.C. and the eleventh century A.D., it is not surprising that the written language would become emblematic of Chinese cultural domination over various local speeches, as newer ethnic groups were brought within the territory known as "China." (Even today, linguists disagree about whether regional Chinese languages are "merely" dialects of Chinese or independent languages.) In the nineteenth century, Chinese scholars occasionally referred to the Japanese language in the same way that they still describe the provincial speech of Canton, Jiangsu, or Fujian; it too was a *fangyan* or "regional speech."[29] Since Japanese syllabic writing was so clearly derived from Chinese characters, Chinese scholars typically overlooked its uniqueness and treated it as a modified but aberrant form of Chinese writing. To the degree that Japanese demonstrated their competence with *wen*, or language, Chinese could confidently claim Japan as a *tong wen zhi guo* (or *tong wen zhi bang*), a "country sharing language/Civilization."[30]

What is startling here is this Chinese mistrust of spoken words. Their dim view of speech as an unstable, transient phenomenon quite inadequate for communication contrasts starkly with the Greco-European apprehension of speech as *logos*—language, thought, and the vehicle for truth. Chinese remained unmoved by the immediate presence of speech. Rather than celebrate the fullness of an encounter in the present, they cut human experience differently, across time, and were moved instead by the historical possibility of the past, which, in Stephen Owen's words, "became an absence and an object of desire that had to be earnestly sought, its remains recovered, its losses lamented."[31] Writing thus became the surest and most preferred mark of continuity for the community that defined itself in terms of its inherited language and textual tradition.

Such an explanation for human practice proceeds by way of a metonymic strategy, a maneuver whereby a part, written language, is substituted for the whole, Civilization. By selecting written language as the defining characteristic of Civilization, Chinese ushered in an analogous series of metonymies that structured their perceptions of and relations with other peoples (as discussed in chapter 1). For one, possession and study of the Confucian classics and "Four Books" gave a people like the Japanese access to the Way of the Ancient Sages; accordingly, aside from the question of whether or not Japan was an imperial "tributary," Japanese could still be included within the fold of Civilization. Second, analogous to the way these Chinese texts represented Civilization, a small group of scholars engaged in Chinese studies represented their nation as a whole. Because Japan indeed had such a group of men, it was thus understood to be within Civilization. Its indigenous culture and unique developments were beside the point; what mattered to Chinese scholars was the presence of the written language and other cultural habits that were identified as Chinese. Accordingly, the third metonymy operating here is that this privileged group of Japanese men represents the people—with the deliberate exclusion of lower, uneducated classes of Japanese men, and all Japanese women. Both the "common people" and Japanese women figure merely as objects of the code, never subjects, and accordingly, they cannot and do not participate in the textual activities of the language community. They do not "share language."

Playing the Code: Occasional Poetry

The language community thus defined by the brushtalks inscribed its borders in the space between disparate forms of mere speech and the continuity of Chinese writing. The social activity most expressive of this shared Civilization was the composition of poetry. This is because poetry, since it was first defined as one of the "Six Arts" during the Han dynasty, was long considered the most *wen*, or patterned, of writing.[32] As a generic type within the textual tradition, poetry possesses rhyme and a deliberate rhythmic structure that distinguishes it from prose. As a cultural practice, the writing, reciting or reading of poetry allegedly serves to discipline one's thoughts and emotions, by giving them a form—that is, by creating patterns of correspondence between internal states and the external world.[33] As a form central to communication, self-expression, scholarship, and self-cultivation in the Chinese tradition, poetry incorporates the dual meaning of *wen*—writing as patterned object, and patterned practice as Civilization. As such, it shares the ritual structure underlying so many practices that constitute Chinese Civilization.[34]

In chapter 4, I deal with poetry as an ideological form within this tradition of Civilization; here, the focus is occasional poetry as a cultural practice. Like brushtalking, poetry written on and for selected occasions was a discourse situated ambiguously between conversation and text. It preserves the authentic situation of address, and there is a definite "author" and addressee, but we merely "overhear" their exchange—their words are not expressly intended for us. But unlike brushtalking, poetry is a much more structured (even ritualized) interaction; there are rules of response, involving rhyme, line length, tonal pattern, and so on. Brushtalking in fact frequently breaks into occasional poetry; writers will quote famous poems or lines as consummately illustrative of some point, respond to another's comment with a poem, or challenge each other to express their thoughts or feelings on some topic in a poem.

Examine the following excerpt from a brushtalk that occurred on May 17, 1880; in addition to Ōkōchi (Guige), participants include Zhang Sigui, the Chinese vice ambassador; Oka Senjin (Lumen), a prominent Meiji historian; and Ishikawa Ei (Hongzhai), a Meiji poet and scholar of Chinese learning. The subject has been the development of Tiantai Buddhism in China and Japan; Zhang Sigui has just lamented that in recent years, the monks have turned away from learning to take up martial arts or to fall into the sins of gluttony and wantonness. Ōkōchi follows up this comment on vices with an oxymoron typical of his humor:

Guige [Ōkōchi]: I wonder if you all aren't tired of brushtalking. I don't insist, but perhaps you'd each be willing to close this session with a short poem admonishing our Dwarf Confucians about this sort of good fortune [i.e., gluttony and wantonness].

Sigui [Zhang]:
Seeking spring, I come unto this old and noble house,
The small salon, talk of poetry, guests who clamor not,
A myriad trees of cherry blossoms now in fullest bloom,
Across the river, red exudes from flowers at water's edge.

Hongzhai [Ishikawa]:
A myriad blooming cherry trees at this great scholar's house,
Spring arrives, inviting guests, guests who clamor not
Over leopard womb, unicorn flesh, glasses floating ants,
Regret the lack of gauze-coiffured, lovely, chatting flowers.

Guige [Ōkōchi]:
The atmosphere of this late spring evening at my house,
Climbing floor to floor, view laughing clamorous words.
Changing course, invite some whores, head into the river,
A fantasy of hearts awash on flowers in the mirror.

Hongzhai [Ishikawa]:

> One whole year of spring affairs at, dear sir, your house,
> Never tiring of the whirl, the pleasure of guests' clamor,
> Delight in banquets elegant but without maidens fair—
> You needn't from your pocket pay the singing flowers' fee.[35]

The session was thereupon interrupted by the appearance of Huang Zun-xian and Hê Ruzhang.

As the most honored of the guests here, because of his age and his standing as vice ambassador, Zhang Sigui commences the poetry composition with a poem that determines both the form and the rhyme scheme that the others are obliged to follow. His is a poem of four seven-syllable lines, or a "seven-word quatrain" (*qiyan jueju*), and Zhang has chosen to rhyme the first, second, and fourth lines, with respectively, *jia* (house), *hua* (clamor), and *hua* (flower). (In my translations, I have forsaken end-rhyme in the interests of preserving a rhythm.) Zhang's poem is a rather conservative description of the immediate setting, invoking the springtime and cherry blossoms along the Sumida River, which bordered Ōkōchi's estate on the east (since the 1940s a part of Sumida Park). In his final line, he only suggests the theme taken up by the other three poets, the standard association between flowers, spring, and women. (Is it blushing women he sees on the opposite bank, or another expanse of springtime cherry blossoms?)

In constructing their responses within the confines of the tone structure of quatrains, Ishikawa and Ōkōchi proceed according to certain morphological and semantic choices.[36] In addition to the final characters of lines 1, 2, and 4, "spring" is predictably repeated in each poem; group poems about flower-viewing typically mention the season, and *chun* (spring) here is a reliable "level" tone. Similarly, Zhang's selection of "guest" as a self-reference is repeated in the second lines of Ishikawa's poems, and made a clever point of reference by Ōkōchi in his poem. Ishikawa's first poem replicates several pieces of Zhang's opening poem: Ishikawa's first line ("a myriad cherry trees blooming") reworks Zhang's third line ("a myriad trees of cherry blossoms"); and characters from Zhang's first line are transposed in a new syntax into Ishikawa's second—"seeking spring, I come" becomes "spring arrives."

As we might expect, the third line, which has the fewest formal requirements, is the space for greatest innovation and the point from which the compositions begin to take more individual and alternative directions. Where Zhang's is conventional, Ishikawa's first poem takes a peculiar turn reminiscent of the bizarre imagery of the late Tang poets Li Hê and Du Mu. Presumably, these images of exotic excess—unicorn flesh, glasses aswarm with ants—respond to the preceding conversation about decadent Tiantai monks. At the same time, though, they open the subsequent competition to more vivid and direct references to women—hairstyles, whores, fair maidens, singing girls and their fees. Similarly, Ōkōchi's characteristic twist at the end of his second line, turning the value of "clamor" from negative (tumult to be avoided) to positive (a desirable presence of multiple "floors" of people), is outdone by his colloquial and inelegant third line ("invite some whores . . . into the river"), which is nonetheless matched by an ingenious fourth—his image taken from Bo Juyi, "hearts awash," matches Ishikawa's references to Tang poetry. As a whole, Ōkōchi's poem becomes license for the humorous tone that Ishikawa adopts in his second and the final poem.

One is struck by the degree to which these brushtalkings and related poetry gatherings correspond to the imagined world of China's great vernacular novel, *Dream of the Red Chamber*. In both, the composition of occasional poetry is a social ritual that takes the form of games played in garden pavilions and drawing rooms or more formal settings like banquets. Poets write to appreciate flowers, famous sites, and other literary objects, or to address challenging topics in verse. The ceremonious protocol for selecting the form, subject matter, and rhyme scheme is the same—the most honored guest usually begins the game, but in some of the most formal situations, the host composes his invitation to the most honored guest(s) in the form of a poem in order to offer the latter the advantage of preparing a peerless response before the banquet actually begins. And poems are judged by the quality of their allusions, be they "fabricated," "obvious," or "ingenious."

The novel in fact confirms the inseparable connection between poetic practice and writing. On the most formal of occasions, as when the Imperial Concubine returns to the family for a visit (chapter 18), or Grandmother Jia's birthday party (chapter 94), commemorative poems are presented in writing, from which they are read aloud or recited. At the meetings of the youths' poetry club (chapters 37, 38, and 70), poems are again presented in writing, from which the participants read their offerings. At an auxiliary meeting (chapter 76), one of the heroines emphasizes this fundamental linkage between poetry and writing as she quits the game in consternation, declaring, "I'm done with my brush!"[37] Perhaps the most revealing incident occurs in chapter 78, when the male protagonist, Jia Baoyu, and his clan brothers are brought before his father to be tested on their progress in their studies. The boys are asked to compose poems mentally, and then recite them for their father and his scholar friends, who will judge the winner of this impromptu contest; as they recite, Baoyu's father inscribes the poems on paper, fixing the oral moment as a text.[38]

As just such a test and contest of language, to compose occasional poetry is to play the code of written language, to be able to size up the present moment and to encode it as a linkage between the particulars of self and moment and the universals of language and poetic practice. Such an ability depends, of course, on learning the poetic practice by the reproduction of poetry through reading, memorization, and recitation. What is thereby reproduced and learned is not only a poetic vocabulary and set of poetic forms, which acquire a universality because they have been collectively internalized across generations, but also (and possibly a more critical factor) the ability to *recognize* that certain objects have certain associated meanings. To the degree that an individual is able to size up some object and to recognize it as having certain associated meanings, that individual is able to infuse the personal moment of an "I" experience with the social meaning of a "we" experience. It is this human capacity for recognition that creates the conditions for linking the particular and the universal in games of poetry.

Accordingly, the linguistic linkage of the self and the social in poetry composition is evidence that the individual has learned to recognize in poetic practice a collective activity that requires encoded voices and mutual responses. The literary education of students in China and Japan was precisely intended to teach such recognition and participation in collective language activity. The boys' poetry contest from *Dream of the Red Chamber* demonstrates how children in the eighteenth century were brought into the adult world through poetry. After Jia Zheng and his scholar friends return from their own poetry party, in conjunction with viewing chrysanthemums in the Jia family garden, they propose to see how the younger generation itself is progressing with poetry composition. With the praise

Baoyu receives from the group of scholars, his father reluctantly acknowledges that there may be hope that his discomfortingly frivolous son is progressing with his studies. The ability to compose a suitable poem was, after all, one of the literary talents essential for adult male society.

Celebrating *Tong Wen* : Poetry and History

Given the preeminence of poetry within the practice of Civilization as defined by Chinese writing, it is not coincidental that aside from brush-talking, poetry gatherings were the most common formal social activity joining Chinese and Japanese scholars in the 1870s and 1880s.[39] Some of these poetry gatherings became grand if not extravagant affairs, including some forty to fifty guests; such monumental banquets were actually in vogue during the tenure of the second Chinese ambassador to Japan, Li Shuchang, who served from 1881 to 1884 (and again from 1887 to 1890).[40] But prior to that time, frequent poetry exchanges took place in the midst of Ōkōchi's brushtalks, and contemporaneous with these were still other small poetry gatherings which included many of the same scholars. In fact, one inaugural precedent for the larger Sino-Japanese poetry gatherings was an outgrowth of the connections forged by Ōkōchi and his guests.

This first major poetry gathering occurred in the spring of 1878, on the occasion of a formal visit to the Chinese embassy by Ishikawa Ei—a frequent participant in the Ōkōchi brushtalks (whose occasional poems we have seen above)—and other Japanese scholars. While this particular poetry gathering undoubtedly included a great deal of brushtalking, Ishikawa preserved only the exchange of poems as a volume commemorating the event. This volume, which contains all poems and marginal comments by the participants and onlookers, is entitled *A Laugh on Shiba Hill,* so named after the location of the Chinese embassy at the time, in the Shiba district of Tokyo.[41]

A Laugh on Shiba Hill, like most occasions of poetry exchange, begins with ardent testimonies by both Chinese and Japanese to the long history of warm Sino-Japanese friendship and to the significance of *tong wen*— that China and Japan indeed share common patterns of language and Civilization. Ishikawa's opening poem to Ambassador Hê Ruzhang contains predictable references to the glory of the Qing court, the Tang "system" common to Japan and China, and the legendary beginnings of Japan as a Chinese colony established by Xu Fu, the envoy of China's first emperor, Qin Shi Huang.[42] The theme of *tong wen* appears in Ishikawa's second poem, addressed to Vice Ambassador Zhang Sigui:

Fragrant world, the water sweet, of course we brew our tea,
The garden flowers open full, delight in downing cups;
Fusang from the first has been a country sharing *wen,*
Grateful for a reading of the Chinese emperor's poems.

To this Zhang replies in kind:

In hand I hold the dragon's charge, a royal honor borne
Unto this eastern land of Ying, as envoy and as guest;
A multitude of foreign lands fills this fragrant world,
But I depend for common *wen* on all you gentlemen.[43]

The historical contextualization of *tong wen* here alerts us to the fact that these scholars recognized in the contemporary moment the shared history represented in the textual past of Civilization. The names used for Japan here, "Fusang" and "Ying" (which are explored in detail in chapter 3), are not merely references to early Chinese histories of Japan, but also concretized poetic images habitually associated with Japan. To a certain degree, of course, repetition of these linguistic items reflects both practical politesse in social relations and a standard of erudition in literary matters; at the same time, such repetition becomes constitutive of how the present is to be recognized and understood.

If Ishikawa claims that Japan "originally" shared the *wen* defined by China, he is agreeing with the Chinese understanding that language is essentially the written code of China and that Japanese linguistic culture is best inscribed within that of China. Why he would be willing to make such a move becomes clear from his opening poem to Hê Ruzhang:

The system of the Li clan's Tang is still changing today,
The awesome shadows of Yi and Lo would gradually extend;
I'd hate to tell old Master Xu he crossed the sea in vain—
No, use tradition to defend against the lords of Europe.[44]

The association Ishikawa is proposing here accords with the position of Huang Zunxian discussed earlier; he would define China and Japan as a collective experience in juxtaposition to Europe, which he identifies as a general and foreign other. Ishikawa's images are those of changing world orders: "Yi and Lo" refers to the Neo-Confucian philosophy synthesized by the Cheng brothers and Zhu Xi during the Northern Soong, the dynasty that replaced the Tang (whose emperors were surnamed Li). If Soong Neo-Confucianism modified the Tang version of Civilization that had been appropriated by Japan, Ishikawa understands that it had been expanding throughout the world up until his day, only to be threatened in the present by the alternative order of Europe. Should European ways succeed in displacing those of Neo-Confucianism, such an event would jeopardize the Chinese legacy of Xu Fu—who would have settled Japan in vain.

It is precisely from this point of view that participants in poetry gatherings repeatedly seek to affirm a common history.[45] It is not simply that poets intend to represent the present as continuous with the past; choice is not the crux of the matter. Rather, because poetry is a linguistic form that insists upon repeating specific word associations (based in part on objective morphological properties and in part on internalized meanings), poetry gatherings typically reify the present exchange, with its representations of the present, as a text that *continues* to celebrate this shared history. Shen Wenying, a close associate of both Ishikawa and Ōkōchi, described the poetry gathering at Shiba Hill in this fashion:

These present affairs bespeak sincerity and cultivate harmony, so as to prolong the valuable dividends of people's heroic undertakings and flourishing standards from the past. Certainly, we have moved far beyond the Han and Tang, to a point where wise and great men [now] ride chariots of linked verse back and forth in friendly intercourse, like a single happy team. Toasts of wine, offerings of meat—these banquets of words and laughter are a thing the likes of which have not been seen in the past one thousand years. Those who read these pages in later times will sigh generously, and say, "Can there ever be such a beautiful and congenial mix of the two nations as this?"[46]

Poetry, in other words, is a discourse awash in time, assuming three voices: one speaking the past, another the present, and a third bespeaking the future. He who would engage in poetry places himself at the juncture of the three, recognizing in the present the terms of the past and so perpetuating the code into the future. Because this discourse of poetry is a practice that recombines past and present linguistic material into an utterance that refers to the present—both temporally and spatially—poetry manages to combine language, writing, Civilization, and history; it is the quintessential Chinese code.

Ishikawa's project of using this traditional understanding of Civilization to protest against the West received enthusiastic support from members of the first Chinese embassy. Hê Ruzhang, Huang Zunxian, and Shen Wenying collaborated with Ishikawa on a manual for teaching literary Chinese composition to Japanese students, entitled rather strategically, *Models for Japanese Composition*. In his opening preface, Hê stated the goal of the text with a quite striking metaphor: "Writing is like warfare. The essence of warfare is the selection of crack troops. With writing, it is a matter of eliminating the untidy and uncultivated, and keeping the elegant and clear. This allows the essence of writing to be manifested."[47] The patterned rule of writing, Hê hoped, would offset the growing barbarous interest in military force, and so "arm" the younger generation of Japanese with the means to maintain the borders of Civilization.

The Value of Civilization in Japan

It is this value of Civilization to organize an opposition to the present that best defines the ideological accents of Chinese Civilization in Japan during the first two decades of Meiji. For men like Ishikawa Ei and Ōkōchi Teruna, the tide of Westernization promised to flood Japanese society with immoral and inhuman practices like "economy." This group of Japanese scholars, who so effortlessly mixed with the men from the Chinese embassy, were all born in the 1830s; they had not only come of age under the Tokugawa shogunate, but many of them had served as Tokugawa officials prior to the Meiji Restoration. After the Restoration, they found themselves cast from office and onlookers to a government of upstarts whose ways they viewed with increasing distaste.

This is not to characterize these scholars as simply conservative or reactionary. They did not suddenly take up Chinese-style poetry gatherings in the 1870s as a solace to the present. For this generation of Japanese, the values and habits of Chinese Civilization had long been a part of the upbringing of men of their class. Poetry gatherings and competition at occasional poetry had figured in their own educations.[48] With the Meiji Restoration, these practices continued in the novel settings with Chinese officials and in the new forms of journalism being developed at the time. Indeed, many of these scholars were pleased not merely to associate with the Chinese, but also to include the poetry and essays of these Chinese scholars in their popular journals. Aside from attesting to the friendship and shared Civilization among Chinese and Japanese, writings by Chinese added a mark of authenticity to the indigenous discourse. So it is that we find pieces by Hê Ruzhang, Huang Zunxian, and their compatriots in some of the most popular literary journals of the day in Tokyo—for example, the *Kagetsu Shinshi* (*The Moon and Flowers News Magazine*) of Narushima Ryūhoku, famous for his reportage fiction, which offered an ironic antidote to the pretensions of Western "enlightenment"; the *Tōyō shinpō* (*East Asian News*) of Okamoto Kansuke, geographer and travel diarist; and the *Dōjinsha bungaku zasshi* (*The Literary Magazine of the Society for Common Humanity*) of Nakamura Keiu, celebrated for his early and formative translation of J. S. Mill's *On Liberty*. Given the forum offered by these journals, Chinese scholars occasionally contributed their work to the protest against the present. Huang Zunxian's criticism of economy and the tax system, a poem and commentary from his *Poems on Divers Japanese Affairs*, was reprinted in Nakamura's journal in May 1880, in the heat of the Freedom and People's Rights Movement (see chapter 6 below).[49]

As a number of scholars have pointed out, the historical consciousness of a universal Civilization provided by Chinese poetry was used by Japanese to differentiate the present, with its aspirations to Westernization, from a past that was believed to be more humane.[50] The content of that humane past was fragmented in Japan during the early Meiji, and although this point takes me beyond the intended scope of this chapter, I will close with some borrowed observations.

On the one hand, Chinese poetry offered this network of former Tokugawa officials a discourse that they believed spoke with authority about social justice and addressed the new inequalities of Meiji society, inequalities that were felt immediately and directly because of the disenfranchisement of the former ruling class of samurai. This sentiment was perhaps best expressed during the early Meiji in a Chinese poem by Ōnuma Chinzan, a poet who had extensive alliances among Chinese poetry groups and political parties throughout Japan, and who brought to bear on questions of justice his reputation as the greatest of the Meiji Chinese poets. With reference to disenfranchised samurai, Chinzan wrote:

"Ricksha man, why up so early?"
"To wipe the dust off my ricksha.
The customers still aren't here,
But I get ready at the crack of dawn."
"In the old days what did you do?"
"A shogun's man with three thousand *koku*,
I left my house on chair or horseback,
A proud samurai of high rank.
But these days I forget all that,
I'm quick to carry a merchant around,
I'll pull them east, west, south, and north
All day long for strings of cash.
My wife and children want rice and firewood,
And I'll drink up the change that's left."[51]

Accordingly, Chinzan and other Japanese friends of the Chinese embassy viewed with hope the Satsuma Rebellion led by Saigō Takamori in 1877, which lashed out against the government's insensitivity to the former samurai. These poets, referring to a Chinese discourse about social justice, were consequently saddened by Saigō's demise.

But at the same time, a younger generation of poets, led by Mori Shuntō, a man judged "sycophantic" for his brazen pandering to government officials, used Chinese poetry in opposition to popular movements like Saigō's rebellion. Where Chinzan and his followers saw the defeat of justice in the rebellion, Shuntō and his followers saw the excess of Meiji liberalism represented by the Freedom and People's Rights Movement; their Chinese poetry was a vehicle for reasserting a sense of the moral duties and mutual obligations that bind a society together.[52] If this moral sense had once been defined as the essential practice of civilized behavior, according to the Confucian classics, it became in the 1880s a powerful tool in the argument for establishing the Japanese emperor as a moral paragon who deserved absolute obedience from his subjects.

In both of these ideological programs, and in spite of their differences,

Chinese poetry reified for disgruntled Japanese an understanding of Civilization grounded in historical continuity and attesting to a way of life more common and familiar than that announced by Western ways. But to the Chinese and Japanese participants of the brushtalks in the 1870s and eighties, it was clear that the days of this way of life were numbered, certainly in Japan, and quite possibly in China too.

II Representing Japan

Prologue:

Geographical Knowledge and Forms of Representation

Our experience of the world is necessarily informed by what we see and hear in our encounters. If literate, we have access to still another textual source of knowledge, one abstractly removed from immediate circumstances, that structures our perceptions and informs our judgments. As I described in part 1, when Chinese scholars in the 1870s and eighties encountered "Japan," they did so self-consciously as Chinese—sometimes as representatives of an imperial state, sometimes as representatives of a persisting Civilization—and for them, "Japan" was by turns a reified Japanese state, official representatives of that Japanese state, or private Japanese persons. These reified national identities, "Chinese" and "Japanese," tended to establish partisan guidelines to relationships among official political representatives, for the Chinese and Japanese states were more often than not at odds with each other after 1870. By contrast, personal encounters between Chinese and Japanese scholars in a private capacity could be amicable, even devoted, especially when facilitated by a shared sense of common history and Civilization.[1] In both cases, I have tried to stress, the intercultural encounter from the Chinese side was based upon a knowledge of Japan that was informed by a conception of Civilization that privileged a written language, a set of textual practices, and a conviction about its own historical and universal significance. To be sure, I am not denying the relevance of *individual* factors in relationships between Chinese and Japanese persons, but I do believe that an investigation of such idiosyncratic phenomena is more appropriate to a biography; I am interested, instead, in phenomena that recur among various groups of individuals—that is, I have asked the question, What are the commonly "Chinese" attributes of this range of encounters?

In turning from these Chinese encounters with Japan to Chinese representations of their encounters with Japan, my perspective shifts in order to raise a general question about the status of these encounters as historical events: How did Chinese transform their experience with Japan into a geography and history of Japan, after the fact of encounter? This question points to the same three interrelated areas of inquiry engaged in part 1: language, texts, and knowledge. Language, because it is the material that makes societies and cultures possible, is what grounds both individual and collective representations. It shapes the ways in which societies can and do represent the world. As the material of written texts, language participates in the construction of a textual field, and this textual field, organized into one or another bibliographic scheme, is in turn the material basis (or material remains) of scholarly knowledge. If we read texts as forms of representations, we can construe the epistemological strategy motivating the text. In other words, to rephrase an insightful comment by philosopher of history R. G. Collingwood, we can read the statements in texts as questions that will alert us to the modes of inquiry pursued by the agents of our histories.[2] Consider the following example.

In earlier centuries, Chinese scholars' received knowledge of Japan had largely been contained within the official dynastic histories (with the prominent exception of the independent Ming writings on Japan). Each official dynastic history from the third through tenth centuries contained a "Biography of Wo" (or "Wo Kingdom"), included among the set of "Biographies of the Eastern Outsiders"; after the tenth century, this component was replaced by a comparable "Biography of Japan." (A later modification occurred in the fourteenth century, when, beginning with the *Soong History*, "Foreign Domains" replaced "Eastern Outsiders" as the more general category of biography.) Now, it is remarkable to our contemporary understanding that foreign peoples would be situated textually within the category of biography, especially since a primary historiographical purpose of the biography was to single out the man of virtue and to insure that his fame was handed down to posterity. But we are reminded that a biography could take an inverse tactic—single out the negative example of infamous behavior for vilification and eternal warning. Presumably, outside peoples like the Japanese inclined toward this second example, insofar as they were groups at the periphery of Civilization and in the process of cultivating their virtue. This is certainly true of the *Ming History*, with its biography of Japanese Dwarf pirates attacking the Chinese coast.

But this matter of moral evaluation is, I submit, an intention secondary to the fundamental strategy of the biography. Each dynastic history had four sections; in distinction to the "Chronological Tables" of events that had occurred during a dynasty, the "Court Records" of dynastic activities, and "Treatises" concerning dynastic administration of the empire, "Biographies" were the form given to knowledge of human motive and action. That is, in terms of the *epistemology* of the official dynastic history, the biography undertook a consideration of human action, be it an individual life or a collective way of life of some group, and through its narrative structure, could demonstrate the point at which virtue or error had triumphed. As an epistemological strategy, then, intended to enable the reader to know the workings of human character in the world, the biography was as appropriate a placement for descriptions of the Japanese as were biographies of moral paragons, evil officials, virtuous widows and other subjects of the dynasty. Curiously, these biographies of eastern outsiders and those for foreign domains were typically shunted to the end of the volumes of biographies—in fact, to the end of an official dynastic history—so that a homology was maintained between their geographic marginality and their textual-historical marginality.

By the nineteenth century, several alternative forms of written representation—which we can call genres—were available to Chinese scholars for representing Japan.[3] These were all "local" genres in that they were written by scholars as members of local communities or on behalf of local officials, and not as official history in connection with either the central government's History Bureau or the Hanlin Academy.[4] While the solidification of many of these newer genres can be traced to the Soong period (960–1279), during which China experienced social, economic, and technological advancements that collectively favored an expansion of education and knowledge, our access to the massive number of these newer texts derives from the more recent Ming and early Qing periods, the historical record of which indicates more widespread literacy, printing, and availability of books. In fact, an increasing number of scholars in the seventeenth and eighteenth centuries were privately employed in the writing of *geographical* texts—many of these local geographies of one or another home region. In other words, the expansion of private authorship in late imperial China invited a wider range of genres to be included in the category of "geography," and at the same time, broadened the meaning of "geography" so as to include more kinds of knowledge than had previously been included in the dynastic history treatise on geography and biographies of outsiders. Rather than confine themselves to historical geographies of administrative districts or histories of tributary relations, scholars began to produce new genres that enabled new kinds of knowledge ultimately deemed "geographical." (Some of these found their way into the newer geographic anthologies of the mid-nineteenth century, discussed in chapter 1.) In the 1870s and eighties, the two major genres used for representations of Japan were the *youji*, "travelogue" or "travel diary," and the *zhi* (or *fangzhi*), "treatise" (or "local history").

The travelogue was a form that grew out of two Soong period genres, the *ji* and the *lu*. The *ji*, "memoir" or "record," was a short descriptive prose piece based on one's personal examination of some historic site or object; *ji* typically involved travel to the site examined, and in fact, the titles of many such pieces are "*You* Such-and-Such a Place *ji*" ("A Record of a Journey to Such-and-Such a Place").[5] By contrast, the *lu*, "record" or "jotting," encompassed a range of writings that shared simply a note-like attention to selected, if not miscellaneous, topics. The type of *lu* formalized during the Soong and of interest here was the more extended travel record, in which an official typically described a journey to a distant bureaucratic post or foreign ruler's court. These *lu* record the sights and experiences witnessed along the way, but they are not necessarily in a diary format nor are they necessarily written en route; by the nineteenth century, geographic *lu* took the form of random disquisitions on local peoples and customs, and were more closely related to the treatise genre. By contrast, the travelogue proper, or *youji*, developed as a deliberate chronological and personal diary account of the progress of a journey, and only in the late Ming was it established as a popular genre, with the widely read travel accounts of Xu Xiake (1586–1641), who—according to some—defined the genre.[6] Because the travelogue typically employed poetic devices and included occasional and other poetry, I describe it as a poetic knowledge of geography. That is to say, its epistemological strategy was essentially poetic, in that like poetry, the travelogue as a geographical representation was intended to facilitate the *experience* of an unfamiliar place.

The second major genre used for representations of Japan, the treatise or local history, was a genre with a much older history; its relationship to the body of Chinese texts had changed continually over the centuries. As one of the four major divisions within an official dynastic history, the treatise was reserved for topical discussions of matters intimately involved with administration—waterworks, music, astronomy, and so on.[7] (The "Treatise on Geography" was one of these.) But with the third-century compilation of the *Treatise on the Three Kingdoms*, later designated an official dynastic history, the treatise achieved an independent status as the history of a kingdom or nation—a *part* of the civilized world. As such, it attempted to contain, by way of analogy, all that the official dynastic history included.[8] In time—most scholarly opinion converges on the Soong period—more specialized treatises were compiled, the "Local Treatise" (*fangzhi*), which recorded the history of a province or smaller locality; hence the common translation of "*fangzhi*" as "local history" or "gazetteer."[9] So the treatise, which began as a part of an official dynastic history, came to be used to record the history of a part of the empire.[10] Having borrowed the form and stylistic devices of historiography, the treatise was understood to be a form of historical knowledge. Like history, its epistemological strategy was expository: the treatise was a third-person and abstracted representation of reality that claimed a certain truthfulness as objective knowledge.

The cultural placement of these alternative genres under the classification of "geography" was reinforced in the eighteenth century by the production of the Qianlong emperor's encyclopedia, *The Complete Books of the Four Treasuries* (*Siku quanshu*). Following the emperor's edict of 1771, imperial scholars selected what was to represent the best of Chinese scholarship since the eleventh century, and arrange it into the fourfold bibliographic scheme of classics, history, philosophic schools, and literary collections. The 150-some titles comprising the section for geography included, among other minor genres, local treatises, ethnographic investigations, travel reports, and travel diaries. Because of the long-standing subordination of geography to history, and because the greatest number of these works were local treatises, the entire body of geographical works was placed within the division of history.[11]

While it might seem that the *Four Treasuries* project was a magnanimous imperial tribute to Chinese scholarship (and in part it was), it was nonetheless an *official* classification of books and the knowledge they contained, and as such provoked academic contention among scholars involved in the imperial project.[12] Because the project was directed by scholars identified with so-called classical learning and Han learning, it generated a great deal of dissension among partisans of those two schools and others favoring Soong learning. While I cannot do justice in a few short paragraphs to the complexity of the range of issues, let me briefly sketch two central lines of conflict.

On the one hand, scholarship during the Qing period contended over which set of texts represented the foundations of Chinese Civilization. Both classical learning and Han learning advocated a return to the study of the Five Classics (*Classic of Documents, Classic of Poetry, Classic of Changes, Record of Rites,* and the *Spring and Autumn Annals*), which they believed held the knowledge necessary for a revival of the archetypal Way of the Ancient Sages. Soong learning scholars—so called because they based their views on the teachings of the Soong Confucian scholar Zhu Xi (1130–1200) and his followers—continued to study the Four Books (*Analects, Mencius, The Great Learning,* and *The Doctrine of the Mean*), which, Zhu Xi claimed, represented the true "transmission of the Way" and contained knowledge of the path to "sagehood." Because the Four Books were the official basis of the examination system that selected scholars for the government bureaucracy, this was not an insignificant issue. Followers of Han learning especially hoped to undermine the preeminence of Zhu Xi's Four Books, so as to demonstrate the greater truth and consequent applicability of the more ancient classics, and it is perhaps ironic that some scholars of Han learning were informed by the very Han dynasty (202 B.C.–220 A.D.) commentaries on the classics that had motivated Zhu Xi to redefine the "Way" in the twelfth century.

On the other hand, aside from this choice of authoritative texts and commentaries, scholarship also contended over the appropriate object and method of study. While Soong learning scholars advocated measures of meditation and concentrated reading so as to gain a metaphysical understanding of man's relation to society and the world, classical and Han learning practiced a more straightforward study of the classics so as to gain a knowledge pertaining more to conducting oneself in society and participating in the administration of a changing world. (In the nineteenth century, this took the form of policy recommendation known as "statecraft.") But in addition, because some Han learning scholars felt that a general clearing of the ground was in order—so as to recover the original meaning of texts after so many centuries of Soong learning overlay—they relied on close philological readings of classical texts, a method called "*kaozheng,*" or "evidential research," in order to verify the factual details of texts and, in turn, evaluate texts. In time, as Benjamin Elman has demonstrated, evidential research was generally used among all schools, but at the time of the *Four Treasuries* project, it was the Han learning scholars' primary tool for discrediting the views of Soong learning.[13] Thus the compilation of the *Four Treasuries* was the occasion for contention over which texts were genuine and which spurious, and which were to be included and which excluded.

At the same time, there were scholars who resented that local treatises were "reduced" to the status of geography and not classified as history proper. Because local treatises were composed in imitation of the official dynastic histories, one historian, Zhang Xuecheng, claimed that they should be understood as national histories, or miniature official dynastic histories, and not simply as historical geography. In a revealing dialogue with Dai Zhen, the foremost scholar of the day (and a supporter of evidential research), Zhang outlined his belief that local treatises could make critical contributions to official dynastic histories. He reasoned that because the dynastic histories tend to record recent times in most detail and ancient times only roughly, the local treatise—now sophisticated in the methods of historiography—had the value of preserving much more detail than could the History Bureau of the central government, located as it was in the capital. In his words, a history like the local treatise, in which sixty years ago is a distant time, will prove a better point of reference than the official dynastic history in which distant times are many centuries removed. Had local treatises been compiled for all periods of Chinese history, valuable accounts now lost to the official dynastic histories could have survived the centuries in local (and otherwise uncollected) forms.[14]

In sum, the *Four Treasuries* project and the polemicization of scholarship in the late eighteenth century prompted a pair of issues for scholars involved in potentially any discipline: the credibility of texts and the kind of knowledge appropriate to each. In reflecting upon these issues, attention was necessarily drawn to the fundamental sets of parameters that defined Chinese scholarship; these were, in the first place, traditional objects of knowledge and forms of representation, and in the second place, those new modes of inquiry which not only modified or superseded traditional forms but also potentially produced new objects of knowledge. So, for example, where Soong learning scholars continued to elevate both the Confucian tradition as the Way of the Ancient Sages, and "sagehood" itself, and to represent these in commentaries and anthologies of statements demonstrating the "transmission of the Way," Han learning scholars, by contrast, elevated "antiquity" and relied on evidential research to search the textual tradition for the "original" among conflicting versions of antiquity. In other words, the *Four Treasuries* project drew attention to what I have called above "forms of representation" and "epistemological strategies."

Because Chinese textual representations of Japan in the nineteenth century were classified as "geography," within the larger category of history, the goal here is to elucidate geographical *representations* of Japan as historically determined forms of *knowing* Japan. It is accordingly pertinent to investigate the modes of inquiry available to Chinese scholars at the time, particularly since certain modes of inquiry were used to construct forms of knowledge perceived as more reliable than others. Unlike the predilections of our age and culture, where a scientific or rational explanation is routinely considered most "truthful," a significant number of Chinese by the nineteenth century accorded that preeminent status to history. Historical explanation provided the most convincing knowledge; and this was the goal of evidential research, which, in the nineteenth century, was less the preserve of Han learning than a general mode of historical inquiry. From the evaluative comments and assumptions expressed by Chinese scholars about the texts they read and seriously considered, it is evident that among the texts representing Japan, those that appeared to conform to standards of evidential research received the most acclaim and were considered to provide the most reliable knowledge of that country.

For Chinese scholars representing Japan in geographical texts, the traditional claims of poetry and history promised a knowledge of experience and a knowledge of truth respectively, and located that knowledge in certain poetic and expository forms. These forms had been implicitly questioned by practitioners of evidential research; the travelogue, for example, relied on conventional poetic imagery and first-person narrative to enable its reader to experience "place," and these formal constructions were inconsistent with the procedures of evidential research, which called for an "objective" corroboration of extratextual evidence to get at the truth of the original nature of things. In the context of descriptions of foreign peoples, this truth pursued by evidential research—the original nature of things— was an object of knowledge different from, for example, the moral truth pursued by the historical biography. In other words, forms of representation and epistemological strategies in the nineteenth century interact both to reproduce traditional truths and to seek out new ground.[15] It is for precisely this reason that I pay so much attention here to Huang Zunxian's *Poems on Divers Japanese Affairs,* a text that combines poetry and evidential research in so novel a way that he astonished and delighted many readers in the 1880s.

At issue in this and the following chapters, then, are two interrelated historical questions: As regards forms of representation and objects of knowledge, how did the travelogue, certain poetic forms, and the treatise serve to organize credible representations of Japan? And as regards modes of inquiry, or epistemological strategies, what role did scholarly evaluation, in the form of evidential research, play in validating the credibility of these representations?

3 Journeys to the East

The Geography of Historical Sites and Self

in the Travelogue

Men make their own history, but they do not make it just as they please; they do not make it under circumstances chosen by themselves, but under circumstances directly encountered, given and transmitted from the past.
Karl Marx, *The Eighteenth Brumaire of Louis Bonaparte*

Wherever he went, he recorded the outward form of local customs, the character of the people, and geographic features and scenic vistas; where his inner intention led, his brush followed. For the reader, it's like physically experiencing the scene.
Shigeno Yasutsugu, on Wang Tao's *Travels in Fusang*

The point of departure for Chinese scholars bound for Japan was the textual past. Made conscious of the world through their rich and extended literary tradition, this educated class of men shared a received knowledge of Japan, which in earlier centuries had been largely contained within the official dynastic histories, and then, in the middle of the nineteenth century, expanded to the newer geographic anthologies discussed in chapter 1. This third chapter considers ways in which the textual past served to *familiarize* Japan for Chinese scholars, and moreover, how that goal of familiarization was structured by the epistemological strategy of the travel diary. In essence, we are concerned with three aspects of the travelogue: (1) the poetic use of language (metaphor) to provide a historical continuity of subject matter, linking one's journey to both the past and the future; (2) the creation of a communal memory, linking "I" and would-be travelers; and (3) the role of *place* as a means of linking past and present. Clearly, the first and second aspects here duplicate the epistemological strategy of the practice of occasional poetry described in chapter 2; accordingly, I describe the travel diary as a poetic, or performative, genre. It was ultimately intended to familiarize Japan according to Chinese historical and poetic sensibilities, in a manner comparable to the familiarity produced in brushtalking encounters and poetry gatherings.

Images of the East

When Chinese literati travelers turned to compose their representations of Japan, they frequently made use of conventional images associated with travel to Japan. These images include certain proper names, objects, and events and were culled from historical, geographical, and poetic texts. Because they were persistently reproduced and recirculated as images associated with Japan, they both oriented travel to Japan and asserted a continuity between one's own written record of such travel and the received discourse on Japan. The use of these images is most conspicuous among the travelogues and poetry on Japan written shortly after the resumption of diplomatic relations—in the late 1870s and early 1880s. As a salient component of the received knowledge of Japan, these "images of the east" manifest the substantial claims of literary traditions upon official Chinese travelers. These officials, I believe, were seized by the momentous wonder of their adventures and found a mainstay in images from the past—after all, no Chinese had officially visited Japan in at least three or four generations.

Consider those images frequently used to refer to the place, Japan, in the titles of the travelogues under consideration. The most common image for travel to Japan is *dong you*—an "eastern journey," or "journey to the east"— where *dong* has the sense of "east," the direction, but by metaphorical extension, carries the sense of "East," a proper-noun equivalent for "Japan"— as in *Dong ren* ("Eastern person") for "Japanese." This was a standard usage in the nineteenth century. A second common image is *dong ying*, or "eastern ocean," which can also be understood as "Ying of the East," or "Eastern Ying." "Ying" (or "Yingzhou") is the name of one of the three "Mountains of the Immortals," which were once believed to lie beyond the eastern sea. By the nineteenth century, Ying was thought to be the groundless fancy of an earlier and gullible age, but was nevertheless an accepted literary name for Japan. Another fanciful image is contained in "Fusang," a proper noun, one meaning of which was, likewise, a land long ago believed to lie off the eastern coast of China. Rare indeed is the historical and administrative name "Japan" (Riben), a fact which calls attention to the extensive usage of these other and primarily poetic images in representations of travel to Japan.

The prominent aspect of these images is their *suggestiveness*. In using this word, I draw attention to the degree of difference between what these images denote, and what they connote. The more room for difference, the more suggestive an image. "Riben" ("Japan"), for example, may be said to denote quite literally, "the root [*ben*] of the sun [*ri*]," but as a proper name, it has for over a millenium been used to denote the place, Japan. (By contrast, the pre-Tang name for Japan, "Wo," retained its literal denotation as "Dwarf" as a pejorative.) As standard usage for "Japan" in official correspondence, historical writing, and—if brushtalks are any reliable indication—conversation, "Riben" is a less suggestive image. Unlike "Riben," however, the most common image for travel to Japan, "*dong you,*" is quite suggestive. While "*dong you*" denotes quite literally a "journey to the east," its connotations are several. "*Dong you*" may connote not only "journey in eastern China" with reference to internal China, but also "journey to Tokyo" (the "eastern capital") with reference to internal Japan. Only in the context of overseas Chinese travel does "*dong you*" connote "journey to Japan."

Such a range of suggestive connotations depends on a conspicuous property of images—their natural correspondences. In early Chinese descriptions of poetics and language, images (*xiang*) were understood to be grounded in the categorical correspondences (*lei*) presumed to exist "naturally" among all things.[1] Images of Japan "naturally" share the directional category, "east." The suggestiveness of an image like *dong you* is, in other words, the product of analogical contexts provided by the environment surrounding the image. It is not merely coincidental, for example, that Li Gui, Wang Zhichun, and Hê Ruzhang, en route to the East, all rapturously describe a sunrise at sea.[2] Were one to sail eastward, both the sun (*ri*) and Japan (*ri-ben*) would, so to speak, rise up in the east. Precisely because these images are suggestive and grounded in "natural" correspondences, they not only denote "east," but also connote Japan, the sun, and (we shall shortly see) fantastic travel.

Long before the nineteenth century, however, these correspondences between images and their written representations—between, that is, texts and the world—became conventionalized in poetry and literary texts in general. The case of "Fusang" can be closely documented.

Like the place-name "Ying" or "Yingzhou," "Fusang" was a name long associated with the eastern sea. In some of the oldest Chinese legends collected in the *Classic of Mountains and Oceans* (*Shan hai jing*) and the *Master of Huainan* (*Huainanzi*), "Fusang" designated two legendary objects: (1) a place in the eastern sea, near the Yang Valley of Sunlight, from which the sun began to rise; and (2) a divine tree growing in the eastern sea, in which perched the wondrous three-footed raven of the sun—or, according to an alternate version, in which rested the ten suns that took turns illuminating each day of the ten-day week. During the centuries of disunity between the Han and Tang dynasties (roughly the third through sixth centuries), efforts were made to fix the meaning of "Fusang" to genuine places and trees. Most notable was the tale (recounted in the late-sixth-century *Liang History*) of a Buddhist monk, Hui Shen, who claimed to have sojourned in Fusang—possibly the northern Japanese island of Hokkaidō—where grew the marvelous Fusang tree, a species of mulberry (*sang*) noted for the seven-foot-long silkworms it nourished. Needless to say, the fantastic elements in Hui Shen's story undermined the confidence of later Chinese historians.[3]

Poets in the Tang dynasty fixed the meaning of "Fusang" as we now know it: the imaginary tree mentioned above, and a poetic image connoting Japan. In several of his rhapsodies on the subject of fantastic travel through space and time, the renowned poet Li Bo "sees" the fabulous Fusang tree in the eastern sea. "Sailing the Clouds," for example, includes the stanza

The western sea tends the Ruo tree,
The eastern waters feed the Fusang;
In the few hours since departing, they've
Grown a myriad miles' more leaves and branches.[4]

At the same time that Li was composing such verse, both he and Wang Wei gave "Fusang" a lasting correlation to Japan through their respective poems written to commemorate the departure of Abe Nakamaro, a Japanese student sent to China and befriended by the literary community in the capital Chang'an during the 730s.[5] Where Li Bo gives Abe's homeland as both "Japan" and "Penglai"—yet another of the three mountains of the Immortals—Wang Wei uses "Fusang." The key connotations that associate "Fusang" and Japan in these poems are the great distance separating Japan and China and the great danger in traveling between the two. Ironically, Abe departed for Japan in 753 but was shipwrecked off the coast of south China; rather than venture out again, he remained in China until his death in 770.[6] It was undoubtedly through the circulation of these poems in Japan that Japanese themselves began to use "Fusang" to refer to their own land.[7]

Now, in the accounts of their own "journeys to the east," nineteenth-century Chinese travelers refer to Fusang in the explicit contexts remembered through these texts. The association between "Fusang," Japan, and the sun is based upon a passage in the *Classic of Mountains and Oceans*: "In the upper reaches of the Valley of Sunlight lies Fusang, where the ten suns bathe."[8] Hê Ruzhang and Wang Zhichun echo this in their respective descriptions of a sunrise. Notice the repetitions:

10/24–25 [1877]   Floating upon the great Eastern Sea, the water jet black; about the time we passed in front of the mountains, it appeared turgid. I arose at sunrise to watch the sun. In the ending twilight, it proceeded through the Valley of Sunlight, bathing in Fusang, radiating upward cloudlike wisps of light, then bursting beams of multiple color, to shine brightly. Rising from the sea, it ascended still higher, and from a myriad dragon palaces, reflected spreading purple ripples, until the naked light could no longer be examined closely.[9]

10/22 [1879]   Clear day today. At daybreak I watched the sun rise. In the ending twilight, through Fusang and the Valley of Sunlight, it radiated upward bursts of multiple color; rising from the sea, it ascended still higher, until it could no longer be examined closely. The water first turned a shade of faintest malachite, then gradually a deep blue.[10]

Both Hê and Wang allude to the *Classic of Mountains and Oceans* in their usage of the proper names, "Valley of Sunlight" and "Fusang"—Hê to an even greater degree by reiterating the action of "bathing." But the references are clearly embedded within a conventional description of "sunrise": "in the ending twilight, radiating upward bursts of multiple color," and so on.[11] If the shared language of the descriptions lends credibility to the experience, the very vividness of Hê's expansion of the conventional language makes his description all the more "visible"; and as a matter of style, his rather fabulous mention of "dragon palaces" is quite in keeping with the "fictional" (nonhistorical) status accorded the *Classic of Mountains and Oceans* during the Qing.

Aside from this association between Fusang and sunrise, Wang Tao and others echo Li Bo's poetic association between Fusang and fantastic travel, the locus classicus for which was the ancient *Songs of the South*.[12] Wang Tao records a poem that invokes the mythical *peng* bird (comparable to the European roc), said to have a wingspan vast as the clouds and be able to fly several thousand miles in a moment. (The poem is as well an interesting comment on Chinese and Japanese intertextuality.) Its first stanza reads:

Soaring the seas and beyond, riding aboard the *peng*,
At the eastern extreme, Fusang—Europe in the western;
Will and spirit fly with the wind, travel a myriad miles,
Literature threads the nations, already a thousand years.[13]

In addition to these conventional associations with fantastic travel in such poems, there is the attendant connotation of great distance.[14] As we've seen, Fusang is repeatedly associated with "myriad miles" and "eastern extreme." "Fusang" connotes an image of the eastern edge of the world, where the sun is just below the horizon. Huang Zunxian begins his *Poems on Divers Japanese Affairs* with the line, "The domain Fusang, established near the edge of the sun,"[15] and one Ming poet hyperbolically wrote to a Japanese friend, "Fusang lies already in the offing, [your Japanese home] even further east than east."[16] This would seem the stuff of exaggeration and fantasy, not at all the deliberate recording of a travel experience.

Within nineteenth-century accounts of Japan, then, highly conventional images like Fusang are linguistic antiquities. But insofar as literary Chinese textual practices placed a great value on such references and allusions, it was these images that in part served to establish a writer's credentials and give the text a credible basis (both of which contributed to the persistence of Chinese Civilization over so many centuries). As textual references to the linguistic material of poetry and legend, conventional images serve to maintain intertextual continuity among travelogues, poetry, and other genres. In fact, knowledge of conventional images is an important criterion for admittance to readership—those who will know, for example, the poetic and legendary references to Fusang. For in the end, an image like Fusang depends on its predominantly literary connotations. It is an image of Japan on the basis of a second-order and literary meaning—that is, in connoting Japan, "Fusang" depends on the previous association completed by earlier writers like Li Bo and Wang Wei. In this respect, Fusang—or the East, or Ying—was less a place to be visited than a place to be contemplated. In traveling to Japan, the Chinese official who alluded to Fusang acknowledged his historical placement within a literary tradition, and "celebrated," so to speak, his participation in a long chain of literary remembrances.

Recovering History through Geographical Sites

The Precedent of Xu Fu

When Chinese travelers to Japan referred to Fusang and the like through the sort of literary allusions described above, they engaged in the standard literary practice that Stephen Owen has called a "ritual of remembrance." The occasion of travel to Japan summoned earlier such acts of travel to Japan, and this past served as a commemorative point of reference for the present. These acts of remembering past travel to Japan are highly conventional; there is a routine to them, which takes the form of a rather standardized citation, and which warrents Owen's characterization of such literary practice as "ritual":

A rite is an established form of action, which, as the *Book of Rites* tells us, appears as a natural norm from the communality of human feeling. A rite is always bound to some occasion—a wedding, a funeral, a coming of age—and in carrying out the rite the person is less an individual than a role, a function in the relations of the occasion. In the performance of a rite, everything that is individual is submerged in the normative and collective human response proper to the occasion. The submergence of the individual is what permits repetition, and the possibility of repetition is the very soul of ritual.[17]

Dispatched across the vast and unknown sea, as the first Chinese officials to be sent to Japan in well over one hundred years, these travelers found an anchor in the textual store of historical memories, and recalled an ancient predecessor, Xu Fu. The story of Xu Fu, which is noted in one form or another by nearly every Chinese visitor to Japan prior to the Sino-Japanese War, reads much like an "origin myth" for travel to Japan. Xu Fu, who is sometimes called Xu Shi, first appeared in the model for the official Chinese histories, the *Shi ji*, or *Records of the Historian*, by Sima Qian in the first century B.C. Although different accounts of Xu Fu appear in the *Shi ji* and other early histories, the basic narrative relates that China's first emperor, Qin Shi Huang (reigned 221–210 B.C.), dispatched Xu Fu upon the Eastern Sea in search of the Mountains of the Immortals and the medicines of immortality that grew thereon. A first attempt in 219 B.C. failed, and Xu Fu departed a second time in 210 B.C., in the company of three thousand youths and maidens who were intended to serve, in some versions, as a collective offering to the Ocean Spirit, or, in other versions, as procreators of a Qin colony.[18] It is exceedingly curious that the story of Xu Fu was in time transferred from the records of the first emperor to other sections of the later official dynastic histories. In the *History of the Later Han*, compiled in the third century A.D., Xu Fu appears in the "Collected Biographies of the Eastern Outsiders" under the section for "Wo Kingdom," the Chinese name for Japan at the time. The compilers of the *History of the Later Han* justified connecting Xu Fu and the Wo Kingdom when they explained, "Tradition has it that . . . Xu Fu failed to find Penglai, the land of the immortals, and because he did not dare to return, fearing execution, he settled there [in Yizhou/Tanzhou], generation after generation continuing." The compilers believed that Yizhou (or Tanzhou) was within the Wo Kingdom.[19] Accordingly, in the tenth century, when the compilers of the *Old Tang History* transferred these accounts of the "Wo Kingdom" to the "Japan Biography," the story of Xu Fu remained thereafter an element of the Chinese historiography of Japan.

To the first Chinese literati embarking for Japan in the late nineteenth century, the event of Xu Fu sailing across the ocean is a persistent historical precedent, a point of communal continuity. Wang Tao, in praising the Qing court's decision to send an embassy to Japan, begins: "Among all overseas nations with whom Our Nation early on enjoyed commerce, none is the equal of Japan. During the Qin and the Han, Our officials often claimed that upon the sea were the Three Divine Mountains, which could be gazed at from afar but never attained. Xu Fu was nonetheless the first to reach those shores."[20] Moreover, Chinese travelers interpret their own journeys as repetitions of that of their original predecessor, Xu Fu. Wang Zhichun, for example, claims that he set out to "visit the ancient vestiges of the Mountains of the Immortals," and more specifically, that he "wants to personally search for Xu Fu's descendants."[21] Several of these travelers rehearse a received set of "facts": that Xu Fu was the first man to inhabit Japan, that he settled in the land of Kumano in the province of Kii, that the Japanese people descended from Xu Fu's entourage, and that those Japanese with single-character surnames are the direct descendants of Xu Fu (most Japanese surnames consist of two characters).[22] As the first official visitors to Japan in several generations, they are themselves repeating the first official visit to Japan; they are restoring the interrupted historical bond between China and Japan.

In effect, they are reasserting a claim to what they believe to be theirs. Hê Ruzhang, the first ambassador to Japan, writes in his *Assorted Verse from the Eastern Embassy*:

Boys and girls crossed over—three thousands;
Mirror and seal handed down—a myriad years;
The blue expanse of sea, the new Eastern Office—
And poets themselves laugh at searching for immortals.

About three hundred *li* from Nagasaki is Mount Kumano, where lies the Tomb of Xu Fu; the Domain of Kii additionally contains the Ancestral Temple of Xu Fu. Japan has three [imperial] regalia—a sword, a mirror, and a seal—all of which are artifacts of the Qin system.[23]

In his *Concise Account of the Eastern Embassy*, Hê reiterates these Chinese origins of Japan's people and institutions, adding that many of the names of Japanese offices are those of the ancient Zhou and Qin systems.[24] But Hê is ironic about the difference between present and past. While Japan now has its new eastern capital of Tokyo, as a consequence of the Meiji Restoration, China similarly once had its new Eastern Office of Japan, as a consequence of Xu Fu's journey. Hê points out the irony that although Japan has now broken away from China, and his very office of ambassador is proof of that separation, his predecessor Xu Fu was once proof of the filiation of Japan to China. Accordingly, Hê laughs with the poets at Xu Fu's ostensible commission to "search for immortals." But the scholar Hê remains convinced of the Chinese origins of Japan.

The same "evidence" is recorded by Hê's assistant, Huang Zunxian, in his *Poems on Divers Japanese Affairs,* although Huang is more interested in contesting the Japanese claim that their people descended from gods:

Male and female fled Qin, three thousand crossed over;
Beyond the sea, Penglai and Ying, like another world.
Mirror and seal, eternal transfer, from Kasanui Shrine;
Dare we doubt the imperial line succeeds divine immortals?[25]

The answer to Huang's rhetorical question is yes. His comments proceed nearly verbatim to those of Hê, with the critical difference that Huang cites textual authorities for his interpretation (see chapter 5). He estimates that the formal founding of the Japanese state by Emperor Sujin (reigned ca. 97–30 B.C.) occurred roughly one hundred years after the arrival of Xu Fu. (It was Sujin who established the Kasanui Shrine as a house for the "Three Treasures," the Imperial regalia—an act consonant with Huang's understanding that Chinese feudal states formally begin with the establishment of a temple to house the tokens of investiture and authority.) Huang concludes, "In sum, Japanese today share the same seed as our people, their territory accordingly from the same root." He looks with dismay at Japanese histories in recent centuries, most of which have excised the account of Xu Fu, and laments, "Although Japan desires to cease being our dependency, they need not deceive themselves with this falsification."[26]

Mythos and the Geohistorical Site

This persistent attention to Xu Fu is an example of "mythos," or mythical knowledge, which is typically expressed in ritual acts.[27] But by "mythos," I hasten to add, I do not imply any opposition to "truth" or "history," which historians of religion and anthropologists seem to do. The former understand mythos as the "sacred history" of primitive or premodern man, which serves as a paradigm or archetypal narrative organizing the ritual repetition of mythic acts; these acts in turn provide a mechanism for "mythicizing" history.[28] Similarly, the leading structural anthropologist, Lévi-Strauss, claims that mythical or primal events are used to create structures whereby the present is necessarily interpreted, and that these cultural structures exist by virtue of a rigid system of classification which allows for a "mythical history."[29] There is, in other words, a common attempt to define a basic myth and strip away the excess details of its variant forms so as to establish some enduring cultural significance for the believers of the myth.

In contrast to this analysis of mythos as a static paradigm for "mythicizing" history, mythos in Chinese culture is best described as a performative, if not poetic, form of historical knowledge. Through ritual acts of remembrance, in which one not only remembers but repeats the actions of one's predecessors, Chinese scholars link the historical past to their present—in writing. As a means of supplying historical origins for one's present, this ritual remembering is a way of knowing history—contingent upon a scholarly knowledge of Chinese history and intended to perpetuate that history.[30] If it frequently takes a poetic form, through the use of suggestive or poetic images like Fusang and Ying, and/or through the medium of verse, this is because (as explained in chapter 2) poetry was the primary literary means of celebrating one's present as part of an ongoing history.[31]

The distinguishing aspect of these ritual remembrances is not simply their *literary* form, but the principle according to which they are performed. Unlike rituals typically examined by historians of religion and anthropologists, which involve groups in societies sharing oral traditions, rituals of remembrance are performed as *individual* actions, and their timing is largely at the discretion of the individual rememberer. Indeed, group rituals may take a commemorative form, as with Chinese ancestral sacrifices and many of our national celebrations today, but these commemorative rituals are typically scheduled according to calendar days. The determining aspect of the ritual of remembrance is *place*—one remembers a historical event on the occasion that one travels to the place where the event occurred. It is the place of the event that invokes a literary citation of the memory of the event. This is why *some* travelers to Japan mention Fusang or Ying, places to be intuited in the context of crossing the sea, but nearly *all* travelers mention Xu Fu and his ostensibly more concrete journey to the actual place.

In effect, mythos in the poetry and travel accounts of Japan represents an attempt to efface the intervention of real time by privileging place.[32] Real physical and historical place is presumed to be interchangeable with written representations of that place. Consequently, the occasion of travel to a given place invites references and allusions to others' previous representations of their travels to the place. The point of exchange between the two is the geographical-historical *site*. In the same way that a site can be revisited, so a textual representation of the site can be reread. Stephen Owen has eloquently phrased the matter:

Sites, like texts, are essential for remembrance: they permit rereading, revisiting, and repetition as times do not. Sites and texts are *loci* of remembrance, bounded spaces in which a plenitude of human history, the complexity of human nature, and human experience are concentrated.[33]

Past and present events become interchangeable through the mediation of sites, which for their part facilitate the reassertion of historical claims—like that above, which names Xu Fu as the progenitor of Japan. Indeed, recall that geography was long related to the claims of imperial rule and represented the historical continuity of rule over a certain place.[34]

It would be useful, in this respect, to mention the way in which rituals so dependent on sites can mediate historical change. The historical anthropology of Marshall Sahlins, who seeks to understand the social and historical processes involved in mythos, demonstrates how societies attempt to reproduce cultural structures—what he calls "ritual" or "mythical realities"—in the active work of maintaining cultural continuity. Because this activity is subject to pragmatic innovation, it can result in a revaluation of cultural signs.[35] In his work on Captain James Cook's death in the Sandwich Islands—to the British a brutal murder, to the Hawaiians a divine sacrifice—Sahlins is less concerned with ritual and its repetition, than with ritual as an event and thus open to modifications. An event becomes what it is interpreted to be; it acquires historical significance as it is appropriated in and through cultural experience, and reciprocally, it holds the possibility of refashioning cultural experience in some fundamental way.

Concerning the event of Xu Fu's travel to Japan, Chinese increasingly voiced some skepticism. One traveler, Li Shuchang, who twice served as Chinese ambassador to Japan, went so far as to make a visit to the alleged tomb of Xu Fu in 1890. His "Record of a Visit to the Tomb of Xu Fu" is an example of the *ji* described above: a pilgrimage-like journey to a site potent with historical associations. Li describes in detail the location of the tomb at the foot of Mount Shingū in Kumano, and his journey there from Kobe during the seventh month of the year. But in trying to establish the collective significance of the tomb as a Chinese historical site, his disappointment is profound. The commemorative marker was erected in 1736—

possibly by a Korean; and the site is so neglected that "it is not worth the telling." Although he hears that before the Restoration there were a Fukuoka (Fugang) Heiichirō in Kumano and a "Jo (Xu) So-and-So" in Wakayama, both of whom claimed to be descendants of Xu Fu, these people disappeared long ago. Li feels "left with only ancient legends." If Li's account seems to devalue the Xu Fu story, it is nonetheless compelling as a pragmatic innovation (to use Sahlins's term). He ends his "Record" with a rhetorical question, "How can we doubt this, conclusively?"—which he answers, with some irony: "The present is more than 2,100 years removed, and there is no survivor of the clan or patronym. Past precedes present, and all events proceed in this way. Just the same, men desire wealth [*fu*—a pun on Xu Fu], and do so ceaselessly—why is that?"[36]

While Li humorously equates man's desire for wealth with the Chinese traveler's desire for Xu Fu, the point here, emphatically, is that desire *persists* in the same way that history persists. Human desire for historical origins, like human desire for wealth, is perpetual, and repeats itself endlessly. The Chinese traveler to Japan is bound to compare himself with Xu Fu and seek to validate the comparison, because the historical significance of Japan has already been determined in part by Xu Fu.[37] In other words, journeys to Japan perpetuate the history of Xu Fu by reproducing the event of Xu Fu sailing to Japan, and it is these chains of remembered events that constitute mythos in travel accounts. As we shall see now, travelogues were especially suited to this understanding of geography and history, in that they provide a *textual* site to complement the geographical site that is the object of travel.[38]

Travel Accounts

Overcoming the Unfamiliar

In the same way that this shared body of conventional and history-laden images worked to provide communality among Chinese travelers to Japan and continuity with their literary heritage, Chinese travelogues made use of related devices that provided a measure of continuity for the individual traveler. Chinese travelogues—like travelogues in most national literatures,

I believe—are in part the consequence of an attempt to overcome one's sense of dislocation produced by the mere fact of being in unfamiliar, if not foreign, space.[39] One's sense of self is challenged not only by different physical surroundings, but also—and perhaps even more so—by different social surroundings produced by different "kinds" of human beings with different physical features, languages, and customs. The fact that these unfamiliar people *share* these different features, languages, and so on, is precisely the source of the traveler's sense of dislocation, because, after all, it is the traveler who is objectively different, the unfamiliar one. His sense of strangeness in observing these social others is reciprocated; they too observe and treat him as the stranger. (Of course, there is always the possibility that one could exploit the enticement of the foreign, as an account of exotic encounters, but, as I show below, this is secondary and often ambivalent in Chinese travelogues.) In this context, the Chinese travelogue genre—exemplified by the *youji*—provides the Chinese traveler with some daily means of establishing continuity; the travelogue is, in effect, a defense against the other order of the foreign and serves to guard oneself—one's sense of self—from the estrangement produced by the challenge of another order. Stylistically, two features provide this continuity.

One obvious feature working to establish continuity is the diary format. Travelogues consist of daily entries, which begin with the date according to the Chinese lunar calendar, often followed by a brief note of the weather that day, and then a full description of the day's activities. In some diaries, this initial situating of the self in terms of time and seasonal climate is supplemented by a spatial situating in terms of latitude and longitude—the individuals who cultivated this habit undoubtedly did so after spending extended periods on board ships. Fu Yunlong's *Additional Records from the Illustrated Monograph Based on an Official Tour* (*Youli tujing yuji*) includes a volume of his daily coordinates and distances traveled.[40] This is not new to the nineteenth century—Gu Yanwu included a similar account of a trip to Japan in his seventeenth-century military geography, *On the Gains and Ills of Administrative Domains under Heaven*; but in the nineteenth century, the difference was that Chinese had begun to adopt the European system of coordinates. In a like vein, having spent a few years in Europe, Wang Tao usually supplements the lunar date with the date according to the European solar calendar. This seemingly perfunctory notation of date and weather on the part of the author is in fact an effort to mitigate the difference between familiar and unfamiliar space, by referring both to one set of objective—and hence universal—coordinates and thereby establishing a persistent time-and-place continuum for the journey. Accordingly, the daily entry at least consists of date and weather; often, the weather itself is a reason for having no activities on a given day. Wang Tao's shortest entry, for example, reads: "6/3 (Solar calendar: 7/21) The weather hot as blazes: I sat quite still and didn't go out."[41] Other adverse weather, the rainy season, or sickness occasion similar days of "inactivity" indoors. I take such expressions of "inactivity" as evidence that the travelogue is indeed intended as a geographic record; days of private and sedentary activities like reading or letter writing are not recounted in any detail. Fu Yunlong, whose primary reason for being in Japan was to compile his massive geographic treatise, *An Illustrated Monograph on Japan, Based on an Official Tour* (*Youli Riben tujing*), writes occasional weeks of daily entries consisting of merely "wrote such-and-such a chapter" (of the treatise). In addition to situating the author in terms of a continuous and objective set of coordinates, then, the daily entry conveys active engagements in the new place.

A second feature that maintains continuity with the familiar is the psychological point at which Chinese travel texts begin. Nearly all the Chinese travelogues of Japan for which complete texts survive begin *before* the author arrives in Japan. That is, the author commences his travelogue as an *author*, at a point prior to his becoming a traveler, with an account of the circumstances which led him to undertake a trip to Japan. The effect produced is that the travelogue blurs the distinction between author at home and traveler abroad. Hê Ruzhang opens his *Concise Account of the Eastern Embassy* by briefly recounting the history of Chinese and Japanese diplomatic relations from 1871 through his appointment as the first ambassador to Japan in 1876; it is several pages before he and his entourage board the *Haian* and embark for Nagasaki. Similarly, Wang Tao begins his *Travels in Fusang* by narrating how it was that Takezoe Shin'ichirō, the former Japanese envoy to the Qing court, brought him the invitation extended by a group of Japanese scholars; not until several days later did they sail. As one might expect, most of these travelogues finish *after* the return to China, so that the author, no longer a traveler, is in a position to make his final day's entry as an author at home again.

In terms of a narration of daily activities, the grammatical focus of the travelogue is of course the personal pronoun "I." It is "I" that bridges the conditions of author at home and traveler away; stylistically, "I" provides a center of gravity for the text, a point of reference, and mediates the familiar and the unfamiliar as the trace of "home" in the "away." But "I" is not necessarily the person of the author-traveler. Unlike European travel literature, which has been described as progressively implicated, since the Age of Exploration, with autobiographical genres, the primary intention of the Chinese travelogue is not autobiographical.[42] It is primarily geography, and "I" as the person of the author-traveler is only one of the voices—or values—that "I" can assume in the travelogue. This "I" as self appears in the text only when the author-traveler personally interacts with people whom he meets along his way, or when he engages in reflections upon the significance of what he has seen or heard. "I" as self—as this interacting and reflective consciousness—appears in varying degrees in Chinese travelogues as a group and within any given text. Wang Tao in *Travels in Fusang* and Wang Zhichun in *Diary of an Eastern Journey* often recount their conversations with acquaintances and record occasional poetry from such meetings. Hê Ruzhang in his *Concise Account of the Eastern Embassy* and Li Xiaopu in *Travels in Japan* record nothing of the sort; they instead insert occasional interpretive disquisitions on Japan and its ways. But this self need not be identified with the author-traveler. As the anonymous authors of *A Diary of an Eastern Journey* (different from the text of the same name by Wang Zhichun) and *Copious Notes from an Eastern Journey* demonstrate, personal identity can be irrelevant. "I" in these texts rarely interacts with others, makes no interpretations, and offers no clues as to personal identity. Their "I" is a neutral grammatical subject.[43]

Rather than a narrative of the author himself, the Chinese travelogue is a narrative record of things seen and heard on a travel journey, and accordingly, as I have implied above, most of the text is given to extensive descriptions of scenes, spaces, and objects.[44] "I" serves as the point of reference for the reader who is to "view" these things and who is expected to interpolate himself into the view as it is described by "I." In this sense, "I" is a site provided by the text for the reader; we might say that "I" invites the reader to stand in the place of the traveler. The historian Shigeno Yasutsugu, who participated in the Ōkōchi brushtalks and was instrumental in inviting Wang Tao to Japan, explains in his 1880 preface to Wang Tao's *Travels in Fusang*: "Wherever [Wang] went, he recorded the outward form of local customs, the character of the people, and geographic features and scenic vistas; where his inner intention led, his brush followed. For the reader, it's like physically experiencing the scene."[45] As we will see in the following chapter, Shigeno is reiterating a traditional literary assumption first formulated in Chinese theories of poetry: that authorial intention—an inner force akin to the will—is capable of encoding in writing the outward form of things in the world. According to this assumption, the knowledgeable reader, whose intention is in earnest, will be adequate to the task of recovering authorial intention—and vision—from the outward form given in writing.

As such a junction of self and site, "I" is a device grounding historical knowledge in the travelogue; it is a means of bridging present and past. The author-traveler's "present" experience, as an historical and geographical record, becomes both the record of past events and the possible occasion of a reader's present (or future) recovery. Stephen Owen has quite persuasively argued that this is precisely the historical nature of Chinese Civilization—"chains of remembrance, linking one past to pasts still more remote, and . . . reaching into a speculative future that will remember our remembering."[46] The dual value of "I," as an authorial voice for the traveler/self in a specific and fixed historical moment, and as a historical site for the reader of any time, best distinguishes the peculiar historicity of the travelogue genre in China. The events of travel "unfold on two levels," so to speak: as individual action, in terms of the life history of the author-traveler; and as elements of a collective representation, in terms of the history shared by both author and reader.[47] Because the reader is invited to acquire the subjectivity of the traveler, he has access to both of these levels. When he "fully" apprehends these two orientations for "I," he understands the essentially historical nature of geography.

At the same time, this form of geographical knowledge is as ritual as it is historical. As we saw in the preceding section, ritual acts of remembrance allow a similar exchange of past and present. Past and present events are interchangeable in the same way that author and reader are interchangeable; both depend on sites. The former exchange is a product of geographical sites, the latter a product of textual sites: "I" is the site of interchange, for a self—either anonymous or that of the author-traveler—who is the subject of particular historical events, and a reader who is to recover that history. To be sure, this equivalence between reader and author is on the same order as that between traveler and Xu Fu. A traveler encodes his experiences in writing, and insofar as they can be recovered by a reader, they are the substance of a potential history. But at the same time, the traveler's perceptions of many of those events have already been determined by pre-existing events and are already embedded within a history. In this respect, travelogues too contribute to mythos. As in the example of Xu Fu, journeys to Japan perpetuate the history of Xu Fu by reproducing the event; similarly, readers of travelogues perpetuate the narrative by reproducing—as an act of re-viewing or revisiting—the site of a traveler's remembrance.

Japanese Sites

Japanese sites visited by Chinese travelers include mountains, parks, gardens, palaces, temples, and shrines—all of which can be considered (1) physical landmarks noted for their natural beauty (which may additionally hold an emblematic position in some recorded history), and/or (2) historical landmarks designating the event or individual who imbued the space with its historical aura demanding remembrance. These sites, however, were outside the scope of received Chinese knowledge of Japan, and so travelers had few guidelines as to what ought to be remembered. In fact, aside from Xu Fu and his remains, there was little of immediate significance to Chinese travelers. Accordingly, travelogues can vary markedly as to the reading they provide for Japanese space. Ueno Park in Tokyo, for example, receives various praise: for its springtime cherry blossoms; for its size and variety of landscapes; and for the Tōshōgū Shrine established there as the official shrine of the former Tokugawa shoguns.[48] Similarly, the imposing grandeur of Mount Fuji, which could not have failed to impress Chinese travelers, is described with various emphases. Many note its preeminent height among Japanese mountains and attribute to it an emblematic majesty. Huang Zunxian notes its measured dimensions; Wang Zhichun is more impressed that it is both snow-capped and volcanic. The latter further remembers it in a Chinese context; he mentions a "great copper Buddha" in the vicinity of Fuji, which he believes is a copy of one commissioned by the Latter Zhou emperor Shizong (r. 954–959).[49]

Nevertheless, travelers were predictably interested in one site that had some bearing on Chinese history. Because they had read about the infamous exploits of Toyotomi Hideyoshi, as recorded in the *Ming History*, they found the ruins of his castle in Osaka memorable. (In addition to invading Korea in the 1590s, Hideyoshi was mistakenly thought to be the leader of the Dwarf pirates who ravaged the Chinese coast.) But a visit to the Osaka Castle ruins elicits in one travelogue a description of the wondrous beauty of Japanese gardens, and in another an obituary-like summary of the terrible greatness of both Hideyoshi and Japanese feudalism in general.[50]

Only in cases where Chinese travelers were guided to certain sites by Japanese who explained the Japanese significance of the site, do their descriptions share a common "view." The mountains at Nikkō, for example, on top of which were built the Chinese-style shrines that guard the tombs of the Tokugawa shoguns, prompt both Wang Tao and Li Shuchang to recall past Tokugawa grandeur.[51] In a similar vein, Chinese travelers revisit one or both of a pair of shrines that overtly supported the new Meiji ideology surrounding the Japanese imperial institution. One, the Tenmangū in Osaka, was dedicated to Sugawara Michizane (845–903), an official who had worked to assert the imperial authority of Emperor Uda and so diminish the power of the Fujiwara regents. The other, the Nankōji (or Minatogawa Jinja) near Kobe, was dedicated to Kusunoki Masashige (1294–1336), a warrior and official who had likewise worked to assert the authority of Emperor Godaigo against the Hōjō and Ashikaga clans.[52] During the Meiji period, both Sugawara and Kusunoki served as models for selfless devotion to the emperor; of the two, Kusunoki was the more visible—the Minatogawa shrine was erected in Meiji 5 (1872) near the scene of his death, and he was apotheosized in the highest court rank in Meiji 13 (1880).[53] According to one anonymous Chinese traveler, as early as 1878 the new train line between Kobe and Osaka was making a special stop for the new Minatogawa shrine, evidence that the shrine figured prominently in the growing imperial cult as a site for all visitors.[54] These two sites did, after all, resonate with contemporary Chinese sensibilities; loyalty to the emperor was a virtue that Chinese appreciated themselves, which no doubt prompted their occasional but ardent praise for Kusunoki and Sugawara. Having attained office during the so-called Tongzhi Restoration, which sought to restore the empire in the wake of the devastating Taiping

Rebellion (1850–1864), Chinese officials were keen on the importance of heroic "men of talent" to a powerful central government. Wang Zhichun, for example, praises Japan for honoring these paragons of wisdom and morality.[55]

Another phenomenon I might mention in this context is the participation of Chinese travelogues in the Japanese controversy over whether or not to establish a site in memory of Saigō Takamori (1828–1877). Saigō was the Meiji Restoration leader who, in 1877, committed ritual suicide after leading the failed Satsuma Rebellion against the new government which, in the process of consolidating a centralized basis of power, had deliberately undermined Saigō's samurai class. Japanese government officials were understandably hostile to the memory of Saigō, and their attitude was shared by some Chinese. Hê Ruzhang, for example, vilifies Saigō not only for this act of rebellion, but also for an earlier proposal to "foment rebellion" in Korea.[56] (Saigō had advocated that Japan invade Korea in 1873, as retribution for Korea having spurned Japan's request for a trade treaty.) By contrast, most Chinese travelers, in particular those who shared the brushtalk society of Japanese scholars opposed to the course of the Meiji Restoration, were on the side of those supporting Saigō. This group of Japanese saw Saigō's rebellion as a mark of traditional loyalty to the emperor and opposition to an unfair government with whose policies they also took issue. Chinese travelers, many of whom remarked on what they considered excessive taxation policies of the Meiji government, saw Saigō's act as a righteous protest on behalf of an increasingly impoverished people. For Wang Tao, a trip to Tokyo's new Shōkonsha, the "Summoning Souls" shrine established for martyrs of the Restoration in 1868 (now the controversial Yasukuni shrine), becomes an occasion to commemorate Saigō (in response to an exhibit of Saigō's calligraphy).[57] Wang's travel diary, published in Japan in 1880, gives voice to the Japanese sentiments that would lead to the imperial pardon and apotheosis of Saigō in 1889, on the occasion of the promulgation of the Meiji constitution.

Exotic Objects

In addition to visiting and representing these Japanese sites, Chinese travelers directed their attention to the land through which they wended, and observed and recorded in detail a range of behaviors and physical objects.

Unlike Fusang, for example, which was an image unavailable for viewing, material Japanese culture provided a more conducive occasion for vivid description—in the manner of the sunrise descriptions above. Description was, after all, the major constitutor of travelogues.

Given that most of these scholars express the belief that China engendered Japan, one is struck that they mention so little of their common Chinese culture. (By comparison, this is a significant aspect of Huang Zunxian's *Poems*—see chapter 5.) There are stray identities drawn between Tang Chinese dress and the formal Japanese kimono, and more frequent remarks on the skill of Japanese scholars at Chinese verse and calligraphy as well as their familiarity with Chinese learning. Chinese travelers made a point of visiting Japanese collections of Chinese books, duly noting rare volumes in these collections; in fact, both Huang Zunxian and Li Shuchang compiled extensive lists of such rarities.

For the most part, travelogue descriptions of material culture instead emphasize differences—the unusual, the hitherto unseen, that which constituted what the Chinese understood as "foreign" or even "exotic." Although the Chinese were in some periods repulsed by those beyond the realm of Civilization, they were in other periods—the Tang especially—fascinated with and enamored of the foreign. In this respect, Chinese ideas about the foreign overlap with our notions of "exotic," which not only refers to the alien, that which remains outside, but also refers to the enticing charm of the unfamiliar. We have already seen evidence of official Chinese contempt for "Japanese Dwarfs" on the occasion of the Japanese request for a treaty of trade and friendship in 1871; the travelogues written during the first decade of official relations, by contrast, express for the most part a tolerance and curiosity toward the exotic.

In a history of active Chinese interest in the exotic, no period surpasses the Tang, and as a number of scholars have pointed out, this zenith of exotic charm found its expression in the tradition of *yong wu* poetry, poems "celebrating" or "singing of things." *Yong wu* poetry exemplified the desire that language "embody objects" (*ti wu*); because these objects were drawn from lived experience, they could, when transformed into images, serve as vehicles for historical understanding.[58] The critical device of *yong wu* poetry, so amenable to both history and the travelogue, is "narrative" or "descriptive enumeration" (*fu*), which has been defined as a technique of poetic composition emphasizing the enumeration of units of subject matter—for our purposes, a (narrative) sequence of events descriptive of some object.[59]

In this respect, nineteenth-century travelogues of Japan preserve the association of poetry, exotic objects, and narrative that was formalized during the Tang. One scholar, Edward Schafer, has suggested a causal relationship. If the eighth century was marked by intensive traffic along the Eurasian and overseas trade routes with travelers bearing exotic wares to China, the decrease of these imports in the ninth century was marked by a rise of exotic literature, which Schafer describes as "romantic reminiscence," a literary compensation for objects no longer available.[60] As I described earlier, the ninth century also saw the beginnings of the *ji* or "record" genre of travel account, and it is no coincidence, I believe, that travel accounts incorporated this tendency for "romantic reminiscence," which remains a significant device in nineteenth-century travel diaries. In other words, as *yong wu* poems compensate for lost objects, so the exotic in travel diaries compensates for a lost sense of strangeness—it is what remains when foreign space has become an overly familiar place.

Among Japanese objects, for example, there is one that not only has figured repeatedly as a "celebrated thing" in poetry, but has also persistently captured the attention of Chinese travelers: the Japanese sword. We find at least two Qing *yong wu* poems modeled on the "Song of the Japanese Sword" by the renowned Soong writer, Ouyang Xiu (1007–1072). In each case, the poet recounts how he came to possess the "treasured sword": it was given to Ouyang by a Vietnamese merchant who picked it up in Japan; Liang Peilan (1632–1708) acquired his sword from a merchant who got it from a Dutchman who brought it from Japan; Wang Tao received his as a gift from a Mr. Sagawa in Japan.[61] In each of these poems, the sword is the occasion for historical musings about Japan: Ouyang recalls the archaic times of the Qin "envoy" to Japan, Xu Fu; Liang recalls the last "coming of the sword" when Japanese pirates invaded China during the Ming; Wang ironically recalls the former purpose of the sword in contrast to its future as an ornament in his scholar's library.

In the travelogues, swords observed by Chinese travelers become the occasion for reiterating a related pair of historical narratives. In the first place, travelers (likely following Ouyang Xiu) note in terms of the background of Japanese administration that the "first king" used a great and treasured sword to subdue the domain; the sword thereafter became one of the imperial symbols. (This is a reference to the Prince Yamato-takeru [d. 113 B.C.?], who defeated the "Ebisu in the east" with the help of the divine sword Kusanagi.) Second, in terms of local customs, travelers note the samurai practice of wearing a pair of swords. Only Luo Sen (who visited Japan with Perry in 1854) managed to see this first-hand, but others mention it in passing—the anonymous author of *Random Notes from Japan* remarks that since samurai are no longer permitted to wear their swords, they are selling these heirlooms to foreigners.[62] At issue to all of these travelers and poets—that is, the point shared by the *yong wu* poems and the travelogues—is rule by the sword, or in Chinese terminology, rule by "military might" (*wu*), as opposed to rule by "learning" or "Civilization" (*wen*). Luo Sen asks, "These so-called readers of books and self-styled gentlemen all wear a pair of swords; how can they value learning, and at the same time value military arts?"[63] Rule by military might was anathema to this group of Chinese as was the contemporary Japanese government's militaristic stance over the Liuqiu Islands and Korea, and accordingly, the Chinese condemn the object with a cluster of connotations of barbarism—disorder, violence, and killing—in deliberate juxtaposition to the sword's "treasured" status as the sign of (a restored) imperial rule. In this regard, the Japanese sword as an exotic object is unique—a negative example that resonates with both the rightness of the Meiji overthrow of the Tokugawa shogun's militaristic government (and restoration of the emperor), and criticism of the recent militarist activity of the new Meiji government.

Another element of Japanese exoticism, public baths, was a repeated object of curiosity. Although one might expect that it could have offended Chinese scholars as much as it did American missionaries, the institution was received with tolerance. Where writings of earlier centuries—the *Ming History* for example—condemned the institution of unsegregated bathing as licentious, nineteenth-century travelers to Japan saw nothing offensive in the practice. People were quite well behaved in the bath, and anyway, Wang Zhichun noted, the new government was attempting to enforce a ban against the practice.[64]

On the whole, Chinese travelers repeatedly express delight in the exotic. Their pure fascination with curiosities—"unusual flowers, curious plants, rare birds, and marvellous animals"—was more than gratified in Japan's ubiquitous botanical gardens and the new museums of natural history in Osaka and Tokyo.[65] Wang Zhichun, the Chinese traveler who most gave himself over to exotic experiences, was so enamored of the Natural History Museum in Tokyo that he contrived to make a second trip during his short stay. He was captivated with the Western machinery, impressed with the mineralogical exhibits, awed by a look at the Chinese seal presumably given by the Wei emperor to Empress Jingū in the fourth century, and enraptured by the zoological collection. His observations were astute, and followed from his immediate assessment that the museum was a Confucian-style lesson in *ge wu*, "the examination of things," intended to offer an "attainment of the heights of [Japanese] knowledge." Characteristic of the intelligence that suited him for his mission of investigation, Wang is perhaps unique in focusing on the difference between Chinese and Japanese/Western classification systems. He concluded that "while we know only names, they scrutinize form."[66]

Wang's record of his visit to the museum is indicative of the range of exotics embodied in Chinese travelogues of Japan. A substantial portion of these were characterized as imitations of Western technology: Photographs, trains, telegraphs, bridges, and paper factories reappear in these texts. These included, on the one hand, novelties—many travelers had never seen photographs before. On the other hand, some objects were exotic because they differed from Chinese models: Western-style paper factories churning out reams of wood-pulp paper were considered a remarkable achievement; the amazing iron bridges of Osaka were repeatedly proclaimed the greatest in the world. Hê Ruzhang was stunned to find upon arriving in Kyoto by train that history, so to speak, had preceded the event; in order to make preparations for the ambassador's visit to Kyoto, the authorities had telegraphed the news of his arrival ahead.[67]

Of equal importance are the native Japanese exotics—rickshas, plum and *sakura* (cherry) blossoms, teahouses, and drinking houses—different enough from Chinese models to warrent comment. Chinese from Shanghai, for example, remark that the Japanese ricksha (*renliche*) is what "we in Shanghai call the *dongyangche*," or "Eastern cart."[68] Probably the most persistent exotic in these travel accounts, symptomatic of the gender-exclusivity of Chinese officials, is "Japanese women." Chinese men are delighted by their variety—singing girls, serving girls, geisha, prostitutes, "southern dolls," and the three types of beauties to be found respectively in Tokyo, Osaka, and Kyoto. Their white powder, painted eyebrows, blackened teeth, elaborate coiffures, and splendid robes—Chinese travelers note the enticing charm and mysterious ways of these exotic women encountered in teahouses, wineshops, and restaurants.[69]

In re-presenting these exotics in their travelogues, interspersed with historical sites and personal encounters, Chinese travelers made use of narrative form to facilitate the incorporation of these often unprecedented experiences of Japan within a Chinese history of Japan. It is narrative form, after all, that manages to arrange a diversity of elements into an orderly succession, and as Hayden White has observed, the critical feature of the transaction is "a 'subject' common to all of the referents of the various sentences that register events as having occurred."[70] As we have seen, the narrative "I" is this organizing principle in the Chinese travelogue. It is the subject recording the viewing and the privileged textual site, the consummate correspondence between textual representations and geographical sites—in short, "I" mediates real and represented place. This personal narrative of a self, then, moving through time and place, subdues the two dominant poetic devices lingering in travelogues: the received intertextual images of Japan reviewed above, which were drawn largely from poetry and legend; and the exotic objects recorded as historical and poetic traces of Japan.

Travelogues as Official Knowledge

As a performative strategy for geographical and historical knowledge, the travelogue in the 1870s and eighties recorded (or narrated) *visits* to sites, and enabled its reader to recover the *view*. It is in this sense that the travelogue is first geographical knowledge, but ultimately historical knowledge. That is, the travelogue genre elevated both "place," as a site to behold, and the activity of "replacement," another's beholding the site again. For the inscription of a travelogue set into motion the chain of remembrances— one either recovered earlier inscriptions, or enabled future such recoveries. True, there was always the possibility that one could have a different response to some site or view, but as I have tried to describe with Li Shuchang's account of Xu Fu's tomb above, such differing lacked definitiveness. The alternative response was but one more variation of a ritual defined by its site.

It is this *personal* quality of the travelogue, or rather, the personal idiosyncrasy inherent in the travelogue, that dissuaded some Chinese scholars from producing these texts. (And they may have been simply disinclined to keep a diary.) As a form of scholarship, the travelogue did privilege personal experience and was open to criticism as a rather subjective or undisciplined form of knowledge. We will see in later chapters that a stronger claim was made by scholars working in evidential research and historiography; they were interested in making representations that were more factual, more objective—in short, more true.

Nonetheless, travelogues were accorded some respect as public and official knowledge. The Qing court instructed each of its ambassadors to keep a travel diary of his trip abroad and to return the diary to the Chinese capital upon assuming his official duties at the foreign post. In addition to this status as an official document, such a travelogue was often typeset and printed as a public text. For example, the travel diaries of Zhang Deyi, who had accompanied the first three Chinese missions to Europe (1866, 1868, 1870), were widely read and quoted; as the first personal Chinese accounts of the West available in China, they had a formative impact on officials interested in Westernization and international affairs. As a general rule, travelogues were received as important additions to Chinese information about the world outside.

In some measure, travelogues constituted a degree of "geopolitical" knowledge. To the court in particular, travelogues offered the possibility of an administrative defense against the foreign. Among geographic texts, the travelogue has the unique advantage of being an intentionally first-hand account of things seen and heard. As a "home" account of the foreign, in which the other order of the foreign is subjugated to the home organization of knowledge, the travelogue manages to bypass foreign authorities; Japanese texts that could not be read by Chinese are altogether ignored, and Japanese accounts (referred to only rarely through the medium of brush-talking) are quoted only if the Chinese traveler chose to do so. Aside from the received history, authority and credibility rest primarily in the traveler.

And yet not entirely. Travelogues might have been hailed as contributions to knowledge, but any breach of their defensive uses could be met with swift reprisal. That is to say, as a form of knowledge, the credibility of the travelogue depended upon two sources that could come into conflict. While a large degree of authority was vested in the traveler-author, dominant ideas regarding the "foreign" exerted a measure of force as well. The case of Guo Songtao, China's first ambassador to Britain, stood as a warning to Chinese officialdom after 1877. In addition to Guo's enthusiasm for Western ways—which did not sit well with xenophobic officials at the Chinese court—and his belief that China stood to gain in learning from the West, Guo had stated in his official travelogue that the Europeans possessed a moral order of their own; such claims so angered some members of the Qing court that Guo was in time recalled, cashiered from the bureaucracy, and allowed to retire alive only through the intervention of influential friends. He had dared to contradict the dominant interpretation of Westerners, and his fate undoubtedly persuaded fellow travelers to take care with their interpretations (or, as it seems was more often the case, to refrain from publicly printing interpretations friendly to barbarians).[71] The International Office, too, undoubtedly took care to send less controversial ambassadors abroad. Hê Ruzhang, for example, in his official travelogue from Japan written shortly after the Guo incident, described his official presentation to the Japanese "king," and added as a final interpretive note his dissatisfaction that the ceremonies were "simple and abbreviated, in the Western manner."[72]

From a point of view external to the text, then, the authority and, by extension, the credibility of the travelogue are preserved not only by the traveler-author but also by dominant social beliefs. At the same time, the intertextual credibility of the text is a function of authorial expertise with descriptive language. It is the linguistic description itself that affords a recovery of what Shigeno above called the physical experience encoded by the text. It is perhaps pertinent, as a final note, to emphasize that the travelogue is not a work of imagination; it is intended, rather, to be a close account of a journey. Other related geographic genres, like the *lu* ("records"), the *shu* ("writings"), and the *fengtuji* ("record of local customs"), might be said to be imaginative insofar as they were posttravel representations of information gleaned on such a trip, but the *youji* travelogue undertook to precisely encode the "sights and sounds" of a journey. (Not until the appearance of *Travels in a New Continent*, the 1903 travelogue of North America by the great late-Qing stylist Liang Qichao, did the *youji* genre expand to include thematic divisions.) A telling comparison is the one that can be made between Wang Tao's representative *Travels in Fusang* (*Fusang youji*), his travelogue of Japan, and his *Records of My Distant Journeys* (*Manyou suilu*), which largely recounts his earlier travels in Europe between 1868 and 1870. Unlike the *youji,* the latter text, a *lu,* is arranged topically, from various cities to certain institutions—the British Museum, the Versailles Palace—to specific outings; and each of these short accounts is accompanied by a printed illustration that gives the reader the opportunity to compare the text to a pictorial representation. The travelogue, by contrast, in its most perfect moments of description, was the vehicle for ideally recovering the author-traveler's *presence* before the object of his description.

4 The Historiographical Use of Poetry

For what is knowable is not only a function of objects—of what is there to be known. It is also a function of subjects, of observers—of what is desired and what needs to be known.
Raymond Williams, *The Country and the City*

In the mind, intention; coming forth in language, the poem.
"Great Preface," *Classic of Poetry*

As I described in chapter 2, occasional poetry was the quintessential discourse among participants to Chinese Civilization, a sort of inscribed conversation that on the one hand sought to affirm a shared language and history and on the other hand managed to reify the present occasion as a text. In this chapter, the focus shifts to poetry as a form of literary expression and as a vehicle for historical knowledge. The difference between the former and the latter, between poetry as discourse and poetry as cultural object, is the difference between the historical event of composition and the composition of a historical event. With the former, a historical occasion generates poetry; with the latter, poetry generates history.

The issue is not one of priority; we cannot know which came first. Whenever a fragment of cultural practice—like poetic composition—is pried loose from its practical context and objectified as a thing unto itself, it takes on a normative identity with pointedly ideological trappings; and from this ensconcement in conscious recognition, it defines what might have been, but can no longer be, a naive practice. This is certainly true of Chinese poetry. From the time it was inscribed on both wood and memory as the *Classic of Poetry*, it assumed an identifiable form that thereupon held a certain ideological value within Chinese Civilization. Where there were once ritual advice sung in the presence of the Zhou king and folk song in the mouths of the people, there was now an explicitly Confucian illustration of the people's historical conditions, and this passage from practice to object was just such a normative transformation. Sober Chinese in the second century A.D.—the Han age that saw both the institutionalization of imperial historiography and the beginnings of literary criticism—initiated a style of exegesis of the *Classic of Poetry* that sought to validate the anthology by attesting to its grounding in history. Poetry became identified as having a direct relationship to the circumstances of its production in the world, and in recognition of this certain connection, the event generating the poetry became the goal of subsequent rereadings.[1]

During the Qing period, interest in the historicity of the *Classic of Poetry*, and poetry generally, was expressed in a number of significant practices. On the one hand, the editors of the Qing imperial edition of the *Classic of Poetry*, quite in keeping with the seminal style of Han commentary, proceeded to read the text as a historical document; they read the poems as moral lessons to be remembered, or as advice for future consultation.[2] At the same time, practitioners of evidential research scrutinized the *Poetry* for its traces of historical evidence. One major incentive for this scrutiny was the early Qing classicist Gu Yanwu, whose scholarly eminence was in fact founded on his historical investigations of pronunciation in the *Classic of Poetry*, a body of scholarship that revolutionized the study of phonology.[3] Poetry accordingly came to be valued as evidence to corroborate details of place-names and personal names in historical and geographical texts; similarly, poetry became respected as source material for biography and history.[4]

From the reversibilty of this understanding was born a powerful and productive homology: in the same way that a reading of poetry imparted an understanding of its historical production, the writing of poetry could be considered a similar inscription of history. Future others could read in the present what would look like past history to their unborn eyes. In short, poetry could record events. Such deliberate composition was of course in imitation of utterances in poetic discourse; as an unoccasional poetry unmoored from any pragmatic context, it presumed the historicity of an event that it may not have possessed.[5] Nonetheless, as an ideological and epistemological position, this understanding of poetry received a substantial hearing. As we will see in this chapter, a number of eighteenth-century scholars showed interest in this theoretically homological relationship between poetry and the historical event. But even more important, a number of poets developed a form of poetry-as-history in order to free themselves from the conventions of official historiography and its strict attention to chronology. They created, in effect, a new form of historiography.

The *Poems on Divers Japanese Affairs*

As "counselor" to the first Chinese embassy in Japan, Huang Zunxian proved himself not only a skillful diplomat and an observant scholar but an innovative poet as well. In a position to examine Japan in more thorough detail than any of his countrymen at any previous time in Chinese history, he wrote the first widely read, first-hand description of Japan available in Chinese, the *Poems on Divers Japanese Affairs*. This text was received most favorably by both Japanese and Chinese scholars—the former were flattered by the work as an erudite tour de force, the latter valued it as an accumulation of information unprecedented in previous Chinese texts on Japan. Unlike the travel diaries, with their more personal idiom, Huang's *Poems* was widely praised as a contribution to Chinese *knowledge* of Japan, meeting the standards of one dominant method of scholarship at the time, evidential research.

The *Poems on Divers Japanese Affairs* was printed first in 1879 by the imperial Tongwen Guan (Office for Unified Language) in Beijing.[6] This first edition contains 154 poems; each is an untitled *shi* poem having four heptasyllabic lines—in the terms of Chinese poetics, a seven-word quatrain. Each poem is followed by a set of notes that elaborate upon the themes, and explain those Japanese names and allusions used in the poems that Huang knew would be obscure to the Chinese reader. (In fact, to most nonspecialist Chinese, the Japanese names written in Chinese characters would be gibberish without these notes.)[7]

Huang had planned a revised edition as early as 1890, in order to make the work accord with his finally completed masterpiece, the *Japan Treatise*. In the wake of the Sino-Japanese War, when his *Treatise* was at last published, its popularity and the contemporary vogue for reform prompted another reprinting of the first edition of the *Poems on Divers Japanese Affairs* in 1897, which was followed immediately by the first printing of the second edition in 1898; both of these printings occurred in Changsha, as part of the reform movement under way in Hunan. For the second edition,

Huang added fifty-five poems of identical style and deleted nine of the original poems, making a total of two hundred poems. Although this second edition is the text reprinted today, I will instead concern myself here with the first edition of the *Poems*, because, in the first place, the first edition enjoyed a greater contemporary popularity and aroused more scholarly interest, and in the second place, would-be reformers in Hunan turned first, between 1896 and 1898, to this first edition of the text for information about Japan.[8]

An Alternative Use of Poetry

Consider the following set of examples that contrast Huang's *Poems* to elements of the larger poetic tradition. Like the set of brushtalk poems in chapter 2 that juxtapose cherry blossoms (*sakura*) along the Sumida with springtime and women, the following is also an occasional poem, a hepta-syllabic and eight-line regulated verse, written and addressed by Wang Tao to the great Japanese poet of the Meiji period, Ōnuma Chinzan, on May 22, 1879:

Follow tracks of crowds bound for the mouth of the Sumida,
An expansive view, together ascending to this highest floor.
In March, *sakura* banks grow to a fresh green,
Half a river of peach water gushes a flow of spring.
I'd leave to future ages a thousand years of brush,
And not extend the heart on some thousand-mile roam;
Today, those ancient vacant names in substance a mere glance,
If it's feelings you would quiet, I'd ask the vagrant gull.[9]

We know that Wang and Ōnuma and their friends had been brushtalk-ing, but that interchange has not been preserved. Consequently, we have no immediate context for Wang's theme of quietude; aside from it being a recurring theme in poetry, it contrasts here with the bustle of cherry-blossom viewers and the cherry blossoms themselves, swirling into the river toward the sea. In fact, the poem is constructed from contrasts; there is a clever reversal of colors in lines three and four—green where we would expect red; peach-colored petals in a river normally green—and this is followed by a more typical reversal of the allegiance of human feelings—let inscribed papers carry the burden so that the heart's feelings might dissipate like the cherry blossoms into the river. The poem underlines the fragility of a human lifetime: where cherries bud green in March, they vanish peach in April; if poems may be inscribed for a thousand years, their authors long afterwards receive only a cursory glance—it would be better to soar above it all, Wang concludes, like the vagrant seagull.

What we learn from this occasional poem is the structure of a human feeling, which is grounded in the analogical correspondence between the world and man. The flower and the human life—the latter as a heart and name—correspond in that they are both subject to the ravages of time. In terms of the analysis of the Qing critic Weng Fanggang (1733–1818) outlined below, the poem manages to represent this feeling insofar as it crystallizes the nexus of the poet, his times, and the event circumscribing him. This is not deliberate historiography; rather, it is poetic knowledge of the human condition, as perceived, intended, and inscribed by Wang Tao.

The following, rather lengthy, "*Sakura* Song" by Huang Zunxian offers an alternative poetic understanding. The rather liberally defined "song" form (*ge*) was not considered an element of the *shi* poetic tradition, and accordingly, it is quite different from Huang's own *Poems on Divers Japanese Affairs*. In the "Song," Huang's historical presentation of the subject of *sakura* takes the form of a rather straightforward *narration* in the service of a poetic metaphor, and the result is more a commentary on the present, from a historical perspective, than historical knowledge as practitioners of evidential research would have preferred it. The first section reads like a description of an Edo woodblock print, an archaicized portrait of a pair of lovers riding horseback through the cherry blossoms; the lady (*Okugata*) carries a delicate parasol—is it her man (*Dannasama*) that carries the lacquer box inlaid with mother-of-pearl?

Gold-dusted treasured saddle, gilt pillion,
Lacquered box, nacre-inlaid, containing ancient goblet;
Parasol opens like butterfly, cloth quivering,
This one's called the *Okugata*, that's the *Dannasama*.

Every blossom on every tree fluttering, fluttering,
Those sitting, those strolling, all singing song;
Those climbing, those plucking, gently stroking hands;
Those coming, those going, their shoulders rubbing.

The Sumida splashes green water rippling,
A myriad flowers hide reflections of river's tears.
The tragic beauty in viewing flowers—what can flowers do?
One and all in unison sing the *sakura* song.

Having introduced in this first section the conventional comparison between fragile love and cherry blossoms, Huang turns to the tradition of *sakura* viewing during the preceding Tokugawa age. Like the cherry blossoms, the Tokugawa has passed from the world of men, and Huang sets up the force of that decay by spending a great deal of space on images of ascendence: the shogun's emblematic sunflower overpowering the imperial chrysanthemum; the shogun defeating aristocratic rivals, the Minamoto and Taira; and the Tokugawa shogun creating a capital in Edo settled with the hostages of his potential rivals, who proceeded to create a lush if not decadent urban culture.

Huang then turns in the final section to describe the grave danger that the West has recently begun to pose to a people who, like the Japanese, fritter away so much time in pleasures like flower viewing, or who, like the Chinese, drift through their days in an opium-induced fog. Then comes Huang's pointed analogy. In the same way that the inhabitants of the mysterious land beyond the mouth of the cave in Tao Qian's (365–427) "Peach Blossom Spring" have long lived apart from the rest of the world, so too the Japanese have isolated themselves in a "Buddhist blindness" and "Shinto stupidity." Huang uses these images for both their repetition of "flower" and their stark contrast to the destructive force employed by the West. It is as though the simple Japanese can only fight back with balls of mud:

In this time, from over the seas, high waves reel in,
Dragons, demons of Buddhist heaven all in thunderous fright;
The great of Western Europe rely daily on brute force,
Gradually destroy the black slaves and the yellow race.

Opium's poison fog expansive like the sea,
We close ourselves off, our eyes we do not move;
The day of steamships, sounds of cannon fire come—
Alarm and crush the dreams of flower-viewing masses.

The Historiographical Use of Poetry   113

I hear the tale of "Peach Blossom Spring";
Cloud confusion at cave's mouth:
Among mankind, those ignorant of Han and Wei
Have heard of Buddha's Pure Land where flowers fall four inches thick,
And each has read the "Flower" Sutra, spiritual unto stupidity,
And burned flowers in another offering to the goddess of the "Flower of the
    Wood that Opens the World,"
Of old called the "Country on the Plain of Abundant Flowers" of the Heaven-
    honored human emperor of the hundred heavenly and earthly spirits,
So willing, armed with balls of mud, to close itself up for a thousand years.

With Heaven's rain, a fresh delight in flowers;
So enduring, this time of flower viewing.[10]

The formal departure from regular stanzas of four lines in the penultimate segment emphasizes the breakdown of order and impending crisis, and the last brief couplet finalizes the pessimism of the poem: men will renew their interest in flower viewing, and so through eternity they will be forced to jump from their pleasures to face the outside that threatens unawares.

The significance of the poem for our purposes is the way in which Huang "reads" the event of flower viewing in a very conventional and moralistic manner: it is a historical lesson from which men should take note in order to change their behavior for the better. As with Wang Tao's occasional poem, this is not a piece of historiography in accord with the designs of evidential research. Aside from an indifference to the disciplinary standards of evidential research—the lack of an objective view, textual corroboration, and notation form (discussed below)—one explicit difference between this reading of flower viewing and one that would be more compatible with evidential research is the poetic usage of analogy. In the "*Sakura* Song," the sets of analogies draw comparisons for the sake of an *external* point that the poet hopes to establish *within* the intuitive powers of the reader. The opium-induced daze in China is similar to the flower-viewing craze in Japan, because both practices distract one from seeing the danger at hand. Japan's oblivion of flower-minded religions recalls the seclusion of "Peach Blossom Spring," with both places removed from the imperial Civilization founded by the Han emperors. Huang has a moral-historical point to make—to shore up the defenses of Civilization against the West—and the analogies serve his purpose. In this regard, his use of

analogy in "*Sakura* Song" is the quite conventional practice of metaphor—
to allude to one thing by means of another.

Compare this usage of analogy to that of my final example, poem 83
from the *Poems on Divers Japanese Affairs*, which also treats the subject of
sakura:

View from early dawn until the setting sun's aslant,
Flowing river—soaring dragon: compete with royal carriage.
Dinner banquet ends as red clouds sing of crimson snow,
The Eastern Emperor was first to love *sakura* above all.

Sakura are a thing lacking on the five great continents. There are the deep red, the
faint pink, and the white varieties, in both single and double blossoms. They are
brilliant, luxuriant flowers. *Sakura* are classified as a kind of cherry, but the blossom
is far superior to that of the cherry. It may very well be a graft of [the cherry and]
some other tree, which would account for its altered appearance. March is blossom
time. Of old, the Court and its ministers would arrange a holiday to appreciate
the flowers; today as well, the boys and girls of wealthy families pursue similar
pleasures—it's as if the entire country is mad. Japanese call *sakura* the "King of
Flowers."[11]

The most immediate point of difference is the emotional distance here
between poet and reader. The reader is invited not to recover something of
the poet's emotional response to the event of *sakura*, nor to intuit some
larger metaphor for which flowers are the ground, but to recover both the
poet's view and understanding of *sakura*, laid out as an initial sequence
of images and statements in verse and discussed in the notes in prose.
Huang's motive here is that the poem purely record the event of *sakura* in
Japan. In the understanding provided by traditional criticism, which I will
discuss shortly, the poem mediates the poet's interior, responsive state and
the external world of the event.

Now, some critics charge that the *Poems on Divers Japanese Affairs* is
prosaic and labored, and does not make for good poetry. Although my
interest here is not aesthetic value, there is indeed some literary play at
work. This is perhaps one of Huang's most generous poems, in that he
seems to acknowledge something unique about Japan: its *sakura*. Perhaps
for this reason he makes the extraordinary move of granting the Japanese
"king" his presumptuous self-designation as "emperor"; or perhaps he calls

the Japanese king "emperor" because *sakura* is "king" and an appropriate hierarchy must be maintained. In either case, his respect is qualified—the Japanese emperor in his royal carriage must compete with the celebrated carriage and team of horses driven by the Han empress Ming De, so fast and mighty as to be compared to a "flowing river and soaring dragon." The use of metaphor here, compared to the earlier examples, is localized and specific to individual images.

Of greater interest is Huang's self-conscious use of this combination of poem-and-note as geographical knowledge. Huang intends to place Japan's *sakura* within a systematic knowledge of Japan; he defines *sakura* objectively as a thing in the world of the familiar, and so he resorts to analogies with Chinese things. It is like the cherry; it may very well be a grafting of the cherry and another tree. As we will see in other examples in this chapter, one major ideological effect of Huang's *Poems* is analogical—to propose an equivalence between two items, one Chinese and one Japanese. Always the Japanese is coordinated to the Chinese point of reference, and Huang maintains the two at tension, because the analogy is not to be collapsed like a metaphor for the sake of an external point.

Like the travelogue, then, Huang's *Poems* are a performative expression of a personal view of Japan. Also like the travelogue, the choice of sites to view and events to record is largely idiosyncratic—although there is a much more externally defined structure to the arrangement of the *Poems*, which I describe below. And ultimately, like the travelogue, one of Huang's implicit ideological moves is to familiarize Japan in Chinese terms. But aside from these similarities, Huang's text differs from the travel diaries in a fundamental and categorical way—the *Poems on Divers Japanese Affairs* was considered by contemporaries to be historical knowledge, a serious and valuable contribution to Chinese understanding of Japan. This claim is all the more remarkable since the *Poems* is neither a narrative nor a chronological representation. It is a nearly unique, hybrid genre—in part poem, benefiting from certain assumptions about poetry; and in part history, benefiting from other assumptions about historical and textual research. In other words, Huang's text moves from poetic form and typically poetic devices like imagery and metaphor to engage larger questions about epistemology—what are the formal requirements of securely grounded knowledge, and how can poetry represent such knowledge? My purpose in this chapter is to explain how such an unusual understanding of poetry was possible in the nineteenth century.

Placing the Poems in the Chinese Tradition

Huang's contemporaries were moved by his attempt at a "new" form. Wang Zhichun, who was traveling in Japan in 1879 and saw a copy of the *Poems* just after its publication, expressed such a reaction in his travel diary.[12] He compares Huang's "new poetry" to the work of earlier poets known for their unconventional uses of poetry—Bo Juyi (772–846) and Yuan Zhen (779–831), who were responsible for popularizing a new form that Bo may in fact have invented, the "new *yuefu*" (discussed below); and Yuan Mei (1716–1798), who composed poetry enlivened by an interest in the humorous, the worldly, even the erotic, and combined poem and anecdote in a manner unique among Qing poets, ranging from the "purely learned" to autobiographical sketches of contemporary eighteenth-century poets.[13]

What Bo Juyi, Yuan Zhen, and Yuan Mei share with Huang Zunxian is the daring to expand poetic boundaries in the interests of engaging worldly affairs. To Huang and his readers, the true novelty of the *Poems on Divers Japanese Affairs* lies not in their poetic form per se—which, as I stated above, is the quite conventional seven-syllable quatrain. Rather, it is Huang's expansion of poetic boundaries, and especially his motives for doing so, that distinguish this work from those of his contemporaries. By incorporating notes and corroborating evidence into the structure of the work, Huang links his *Poems* to the major methodology practiced by Qing scholars, evidential research. By employing the *shi* poetic form, and leaving the *Poems* individually untitled and largely impersonal, Huang harkens back to the *Classic of Poetry*, in which poetry served to record contemporary affairs and popular customs.

These motives, however, are only implicit in Huang's *Poems on Divers Japanese Affairs*; he was never identified with any "school" of poetry or poetics, nor did he contribute any writings to the voluminous Qing discourse on poetics. Consequently, in order to examine the epistemology underlying this remarkable text, we must turn to the nexus of texts and poets that Huang and his admirers acknowledged as Huang's antecedents.[14] These are three: (1) the early Qing poet You Tong (1618–1704), whose *Waiguo zhuzhi ci* (*Bamboo Stalk Lyrics on the Foreign Domains*) attests to both a Qing deemphasis of "high Tang" poetic form and style as the proper model for composition, and an appreciation of the geographic ends of the *yuefu* poetic genre; (2) the poets Zha Shenxing (1650–1727) and Li E (1692–1752), respectively mentor and member of the Seven Masters of Wulin, a group of poets active in Hangzhou in the mid-eighteenth century and responsible for the *Nansong zashi shi* (*Poems on Divers Affairs of the Southern Soong*), the text that Huang's *Poems* most resembles; and (3) the late-eighteenth-century poet and scholar Weng Fanggang (1733–1818), who more than anyone during the Qing period elevated the concerns evident in earlier poets like Zha and Li—both the general importance of scholarship for poetry and the specific theoretical linkage of poetry to the Soong learning concern for *li* ("principle," "reason," or "order"). It is telling that these earlier Qing poets, like Huang Zunxian, are most often described in surveys of Qing poetry and poetics as "independent"; they are either unaffiliated with the major schools of poetics or said to have founded their own schools.[15]

In general, then, Huang Zunxian is an heir to two broad trends in poetics during the Qing period. In the first place, a number of Qing poets underwent a shift in sensibility regarding the preeminence of "method" (*fa*) and "form" (*ge* or *ti*). Where their Ming predecessors, the Earlier and Later Seven Masters, stressed "poetic method" in terms of modeling one's form, style, and diction after one or another Han or high Tang master, these Qing poets revived an interest in Soong poetry—and the diversity and experimentation exemplary of Soong poetry—and did so with a keen awareness of *change*: a refrain among scholars and poets in the late seventeenth and eighteenth centuries (which many historians attribute to the fall of the Chinese Ming dynasty and its replacement by a Manchu Qing dynasty) is the claim that forms evolve, meanings change, standards shift— in short, that each age differs from its predecessor, and that consequently, the forms, styles, and standards of each are appropriate to each alone.[16] (For many poets, this was a protest against the Ming goal of *fugu*, "reviving antiquity," which I take up in chapter 6.) For Huang Zunxian's *Poems on Divers Japanese Affairs,* the most important consequence of this shift in favor of Soong poetry was an acceptance of the *ci*, or "lyric" form, as a legitimate development within the *shi* poetic tradition.

In the second place, some Qing poets engaged in what has been described as an "intellectualization" of poetry—in effect, the writing of "scholarly poetry." Where some stressed personal expression and focused on the poet's intuition, inspiration, or emotion, others insisted that book learning was central to poetic composition. Li E put the issue succinctly: "As fir is material for rooms, so books are material for poetry."[17] In both his own *Song shi ji shi* (*Recorded Affairs in Soong Poetry*) and his collective work with the Seven Masters of Wulin, Li demonstrated a use of poetry both informed by scholarship and intended to contribute to research and scholarship. Weng Fanggang took the issue further; he developed a theory of poetic "texture" (*jili*), which connected personal expression and scholarship, and linked "word" (associated with poetry) to "event" (associated with history). It is this pair of developments, I will show, that participate in the epistemology informing Huang Zunxian's *Poems* of 1879.[18]

The Epistemological Basis of the Poetry-History Homology

Over a century before Huang Zunxian wrote his *Poems on Divers Japanese Affairs*, Yuan Mei had asserted, "Writing poetry is like writing history—talent, learning, and understanding in suitable proportion."[19] That this understanding of poetry was accepted among some of Huang Zunxian's contemporaries is clear from the prefaces to the *Poems on Divers Japanese Affairs*. In one of these, Hong Shiwei recalls the essential relationship between poetry and historical affairs proposed in antiquity; in the same way that the ancients actively gathered the folk songs comprising the *Classic of Poetry*, so too the poetry of later generations is necessarily worthwhile for the historical knowledge to be gleaned therefrom:

Because we admire the composing of poems and songs, there have been people who carry on the practice in every generation. Among the ancients, the lightweight carriage was chosen . . . [to search out poems and songs] in order to examine the waxing and waning of popular custom, and the gains and losses of administrative affairs. Since that time, writers have rivaled each other at flowery composition and chased after elegance. . . . This has been of course an expression of the new and an emulation of gracefulness; after all, each [style] came from a reputable school. Nonetheless, if we examine how each represented events and outline them in an orderly way—as a contribution to evidential research—we will not lose the received ideas of the ancients, which abound therein.[20]

Wang Tao, too, in his own preface to Huang's *Poems,* reiterates this description of poetry's connection to history. Because Wang understands that poetry is inherently suitable for recording historical events, he unequivocally commends Huang's intentions to record Japanese affairs in verse—a motive he finds preferable to the mere "composition of elegant phrases."[21]

It is the ideological and epistemological pretensions latent in these statements that concern us here—particularly as they figure in the *perceived* intentions of Huang Zunxian's *Poems on Divers Japanese Affairs.* Although Huang was for the most part his own teacher, and was never associated with any of the literary "schools" of his day, his own view of his craft reiterates the widespread sensibility that the writing of poetry bespoke an unmediated connection to the historical circumstances of its production.[22] In a rare pronouncement on the subject of poetry, he maintained:

From ancient times to today, the associative stimulus of poetry has undergone transformations of definitive magnitude. Although there have been scholars of unusual talent, extraordinary capability, and heroic stature . . . not one of them has been able to step outside his surroundings. In this sense, poetry is neither "ancient" nor "contemporary." Even if one could feel what they experienced, see what they saw, hear what they heard, and transcribe it into poetry, would it necessarily be the work of the ancients? I myself am in the midst of the poetry I write. . . . The times I experience today, the circumstances I encounter, the people I think of, and the ideas I bring forth neither existed in the past nor will exist in the future. They exist only within me. If people before me looked to the ancients, people after me will look to those still to come; there is no one in a position to compete with me. . . . So in my poetry I write what I experience, what I see, and what I hear.[23]

There is a provocative alliance here between Huang's staunch individualism and his equally stringent historical particularism. He belittles those who would presume to "revive the ancients" by imitating their poetic style; like his predecessors You Tong and Li E, he does not believe that some anterior historical reality could be recovered through an imitation of language or style alone.[24] But in criticizing such a claim, and insisting on individualism in poetic composition, Huang elevates his own historical particularity and invests his own experience with absolute knowability. Although he may relegate language and form to the status of attendant phenomena in his quest for knowledge, his choice of form for his *Poems on Divers Japanese Affairs* was nevertheless the one that traditionally privileged individual perceptions of the world—the *shi*, epistemological assumptions of which grew out of the canonization of the *Classic of Poetry*.

"Poetry Verbalizes Intention"

As numerous scholars have repeated, the "Great Preface" to the *Classic of Poetry* asserts an inherent connection between mind and world in the *shi* poem: "In the mind it is intention; coming forth in language it is the poem." That is, an external event (or scene) prompts an internal stirring of intention (or emotion), which is then manifested externally in the poem.[25] To follow the process to its conclusion, a reader is thereafter stirred by the poem, and reflects upon the original event as manifested by authorial intention.[26] In the third and fourth centuries A.D., in conjunction with the theory of "analogical correspondence" (*lei*), the *shi* underwent a further epistemological development; it became a new form of poetic knowledge, capable of revealing insight into the enduring pattern of things.[27] If Tang poets perfected this aspect of *shi* with their elaborate rules for parallelism, which reified the *formal* fusion of interior intention and exterior event as an act of personal expression, then we can see here an available theoretical basis for the pretensions of Huang and other Qing poets who invested their personal compositions with the larger significance of "historical events." As Huang phrased the assumption in his foreword to his collected poems, "Outside the poem is the event, within the poem is the man."[28]

The difficulty with a long-term view of this epistemological posture is that it overlooks the historical contingencies of formal changes for the sake of the common category. Changes in form were, after all, always possible within the rubric of *shi* poetry. The poetry of the great Tang poets was a formal modification of the ancient *shi* of the *Classic of Poetry*, from lines of four syllables to lines of five and seven. Between the ancient *Poetry* and the Tang masters, the *shi* form incorporated clearly defined rules of tonal patterns, rhyming, and parallelism of the regulated poem (*lüshi*) and its shorter variant, the quatrain (*jueju*). When Chinese poets and theoreticians, in other words, attributed to the *shi* a special capacity for linking mind and world, this linkage was less dependent on formal specifications than on the reified category of *shi*. As we shall see, Huang's *Poems on Divers Japanese Affairs* undertook a similar incorporation of external devices tangential to the *shi* form.

The primary epistemological pretension of *shi* poetry, then, is not poetic form but is instead the elevating of the person of the poet, and in particular his "intention" or "meaning" (*yi*) as inscribed by his choice of "wording" (*yan*). More so than form, the poet is the point of mediation between language and world, and this is because, I believe, the deliberate selection and arrangement of images (explained above in chapters 2 and 3) was the activity integrating the conventional and the novel in such a way as to textualize the present occasion in terms of an ongoing history.[29] Of Huang's antecedents, both You Tong and Zha Shenxing understood that the "self" of the poet mediated language and a collective entity larger than the self. You Tong, who acknowledged that "poetry verbalizes intention," settled on *zhen* or "genuineness" as the criterion that determined how a poet selected form, style, and theme from the received tradition; according to Guo Shaoyu, You specified that a poet's "genuine intention" authorized the choice of poetic elements that linked his own poetry to the historical tradition.[30] Similarly, Zha Shenxing noted that the principles of all the things in the world were present in the poet's "feeling," and that it was the poet's "intention" more than his choice of words that afforded poetry its profundity.[31]

The Principle Uniting Words and Events

In the eighteenth century, some Qing scholars working in history, literary theory, and textual studies proceeded to examine more fully the process suggested by "Poetry verbalizes intention." This was, in the first place, a consequence of Han learning scholars' renewed interest in Han dynasty commentaries—they turned away from Zhu Xi's Soong learning interpretation of textuality, "Texts are bearers of the Way" (*wen yi zai dao*), in order to devote more attention to the alternative based on Han commentaries. At the same time, they were attempting to renovate the Chinese textual tradition by reworking what they took to be an unfortunate, if not false, distinction encouraged by scholarly trends. Earlier I described the Qianlong emperor's project of *The Complete Books of the Four Trea-suries,* the animosities thereby generated between Soong and Han learning scholars, and the resentment of one scholar, Zhang Xuecheng, over the classification system. An important consequence of these developments was a set of efforts at what has been considered "syncretism" or "eclec-ticism," namely, attempts to reconcile Han and Soong learning and to rework the long-standing distinction made between "words" (*yan*) and "events" (*shi*).[32]

Implicitly at issue in these arguments is the question of a standard or cri-terion of truth. Soong learning scholars maintained a metaphysical dual-ism of *li* and *qi*: *li* was "principle," the standard of order, above the phe-nomenal world but immanent in all things; *qi* was an etherlike material force that constituted all things. Han learning scholars, who rejected this dualism, were troubled that principle, which ought to serve more con-cretely as a standard of order and guarantor of truth, was *outside* the clas-sics, and so they contrived to to locate principle in materiality, and more importantly, within the textual tradition of the classics. Rather than main-tain, as Soong learning scholars did, that study was a spiritually transform-ing process (ultimately called "Transmission of the Way") whereby princi-ple accrued to the student in the same way that it had to followers of the ancient sages, Han learning scholars rather straightforwardly maintained that principle was *in the texts,* and that study enabled the student to under-stand the workings of principle in the world.[33] One goal of these efforts, to theorists of poetics, was the possibility of effacing any distinction between poetic voice and the voice of prose—in other words, to unify the truth inherent in poetry with the truth inherent in the descriptive prose of history. Just such an epistemological strategy underlies Huang Zunxian's *Poems on Divers Japanese Affairs.*

The distinction between "words" and "events" was historiographical, first formulated in the *History of the Han,* and based on the stylistic differ-ences between the ancient *Classic of Documents* and the *Spring and Autumn Annals*; traditionally, the former was considered a record of words, the latter a record of events.[34] The radical contention of Zhang Xuecheng was that the distinction was artificial. In his view, the two histories were part of a single tradition, which had yet a third companion history, the *Zuo zhuan.* In comparing and contrasting the three, he concluded that their words were themselves events, and that their events were constituted by words, so the two could not be so simply distinguished. Worse, the distinction was pernicious, because it authorized the separation between, on the one hand, philosophic schools and literary collections—as the "words" of scholars—and on the other hand, classics and history—as recorded "events."[35]

With these revisionist remarks, Zhang was overtly attacking the rigid fourfold classification of texts employed by the *Four Treasuries* project, and at the same time, proposing an expanded understanding of texts and history. He believed that by disregarding the content and motivations of writing, the traditional classification not only imposed ill-conceived divisions between texts, but also ignored the historical connections between writing and events. Not only was the distinction between word and event artificial, but so was the distinction between poetry and prose—which, he believed, had historically authorized the further separation between, respectively, literary collections and philosophy. Both literary collections and philosophy ought to be used as historical evidence; they themselves constituted a history of their own. And rather than segregate poetry and prose on the basis of some distinction between writing motivated by feeling and writing motivated by factual or practical content, Zhang maintained that the good literary critic was not bound by considerations of form.[36] The textual tradition defined as *wen* encompassed *all* classes of texts, and insofar as texts were carriers of principle, they stood in the same relation to the Way of the Ancient Sages.[37]

Although Zhang Xuecheng had rather programmatically established this set of associations between words and poetry, and events and prose—in order to formulate an understanding of textuality in opposition to the received divisions among genres—the nexus of his ideas was implicit in the production of poetic texts like the *Poems on Divers Affairs of the Southern Soong,* You Tong's *Bamboo Stalk Lyrics on the Foreign Domains,* and Huang's *Poems on Divers Japanese Affairs.* At the same time, the epistemological implications of the *shi* poem—in particular the sympathetic linkage of "word" and "event" in the *shi*—facilitated a similar reconsideration of mingling poetic and prose voices. In the traditional exegesis, the *shi* poem was a receptacle for intention, and was "sung out" as a consequence.[38] At the same time, on the basis of the ancient graphic association between the characters for poem (*shi*) and intention (*zhi*), the poem has been repeatedly considered as a remembering, a recording, or a cherishing in the mind.[39] To some Qing theoreticians of poetics, this relationship between word and event was expressed as a concern with how poetry could best record the "event."

Central to the issue of Qing poetic interest in the "event"—or, as I have translated the word in the context of Huang Zunxian's work, the "affair"—was the matter of principle. (Although I have referred to *li* as "principle," which is appropriate in a philosophical context, I will also refer to *li* as "order" in the context of poetry—by which I mean to stress the "orderly" or "patterned" correspondence between poet, poem, and world.) The most common precedent for Qing poetic considerations of principle is the Soong example of Su Shi (1037–1101), whose stylistic intent was to develop the "principle" or "core" of an event. That is, rather than offer a series of images in the manner of the Tang masters, Su and other Soong poets poeticized in an orderly, logical, and discursive manner to explicate the experience of the poet in the event.[40] Where many Ming poets found this intolerably prosaic, some Qing poets not only found this style of "voice" compelling, but also proceeded to theorize about the manner in which principle linked intention or emotion and the poem. Both Zha Shenxing and Wang Fuzhi (1619–1692) made principle central to their understandings of poetry; for Zha, following the manner of Han learning scholarship, principle was located in the material of human feeling and patterned the fit between poem and world.[41] For Wang, principle was both the object and the ordering principle of poetic feeling; when principle accomplished such a fit between the poet's feeling and the world, the poem had an obvious "dynamism" or "liveliness."[42]

The Qing critic who devoted most attention to this matter was Weng Fanggang. Like Zhang Xuecheng, Weng was interested in restoring a wholeness to seeming oppositions, but his syncretism was motivated by a desire to safeguard the preeminence of Soong learning. While Wang appreciated the research techniques of Han learning and evidential research, he worried that such research would fail to undertake its logical "next step"—to reground the Way in the textual tradition—and thereby undermine the moral leadership of Soong learning.[43]

As a poet, Weng found the Tang poets' elaborate images to be empty words, and was more persuaded by Su Shi's plumbing of principle and the corresponding concreteness of his poetry.[44] Weng admitted in a very conventional manner that poetry was indeed based on feeling and objects, but he added that it incorporated both a systematic ordering and an awareness of origin and development.[45] This ordering in poetry, when properly executed, granted the poem a truthfulness about its origins and development—an understanding implicit in Weng's mature theory of "texture" (*jili*). Weng maintained that in the same way that evidential research gives learning its accuracy, "texture" gives poetry its accuracy.[46] By "texture"— literally, the "arrangement of muscles and skin"—Weng made use of an anatomical metaphor to describe the written poem as a beautiful, well-ordered surface dependent upon some underlying skeletal framework. This framework supporting the poem was the triad formed by the self, the times, and the event, each of which had its "solid ground" and respective mode of principle or "order" (*li*). In composing a poem, the poet restructured the three into a new unity.[47]

When he analyzed "ordering" (*li*), Weng was most specific about the event. In discussing the differences between the canonical *Classic of Documents* and *Classic of Poetry,* Weng stated:

Li, or "order," includes "synthetic order" [*zongli*—of the self], "consecutive order" [*jingli*—of the times], and "reasoned order" [*tiaoli*—of the event]. In the *Classic of Documents,* prose directly lays out the events; the *Poetry,* however, uses "ordering" to do the same. To "directly lay out an event" is *not* to directly put into words that which can assume some order; [poetry] must instead "elegantly beautify" and only then can it order events. "Elegance" is exactitude; to "beautify" is to flower.[48]

Notice that Weng's point of reference is the traditional understanding of the *Documents* as directly quoted "words." Poetry is, by contrast, a mediated form. Wu Hongyi reminds us that Weng's statement is not only a description of literary style; rather, there are two senses of *li*: *wenli,* ordered composition (or "principle in writing"); and *yili,* ordered meaning (or Soong learning "principle accrued in study").[49] The key word here is "exactitude" (*zheng*), often translated alternatively as "orthodox" or "correct." Weng means that poetry maintains the same exactitude toward events that the direct recording of prose maintains. The two voices speak with equivalent accuracy, or truthfulness.

But additionally, poetry beautifies. Through the intuitive selection of images, it makes events flower into a history of associations. Here, however, I cannot overemphasize the stress placed on events, over and above beauty in Qing poetics. Qing scholars like Weng Fanggang, the authors of the *Poems on Divers Affairs of the Southern Soong,* and the associates of Huang Zunxian, all took the *Classic of Poetry* as the unadulterated foundation of the genre. As the *Poetry* was a truthful record of ancient events, so too contemporary poetry should proceed to record events. An event skillfully recorded in poetry would give later generations a clear understanding of the author and his times. The point is stressed in Hong Shiwei's preface to Huang's *Poems,* quoted above: when poets rival each other at flowery composition, they are distracted from their categorical imperative—to represent events. In recent centuries, if poets had deliberately ignored their true vocation, scholars like Hong Shiwei and Wang Tao in the late Qing decidedly praised Huang for returning to the canonical nature of poetry—and moreover, with an eye to contributing to evidential research.

Shi poetry that remained true to its essence was marked by an obvious formal element—the absence of titles. A poem without a title—that is, a poem designated by its first line or first words—was a poem more faithful to the original example of the *Classic of Poetry.* Such poems were presumably not created to fit fixed notions or preconceived purposes of the writer, which were signaled by the choice of a title. In short, the title was a mark of artificiality, and compromised the poem as a direct or "exact" record of an event.[50] In composing such a set of individually untitled poems, Huang Zunxian (as well as the authors he names as antecedent) was attributing an explicit connection between his *Poems on Divers Japanese Affairs* and the *Classic of Poetry.*

This association was stated outright by the would-be reformer of 1898, Kang Youwei. In yet another preface to Huang's *Poems,* Kang makes the significance of the *Poetry* and its emphasis on events most explicit. In describing the ancient varieties of "writing that records events," Kang commented on the superiority of the *Classic of Poetry* in comparison to the classical history, the *Spring and Autumn Annals.* The latter depends significantly on the former for its "descriptions of domainal administration, outlines of popular custom, and the ideas of the sages." In praising the *Poetry* for its noteworthy breadth, Kang commends Huang's *Poems on Divers Japanese Affairs,* which similarly "covers land and territory, popular custom, produce and manufactures, domainal administration, human talents, successive transformations, and developments and declines—all clearly and straightforwardly."[51]

Moreover, both Kang and Hong Shiwei praise Huang for his use of supplementary notes. Kang observes that by "using both phrases and notes, the details and outlines complement each other, so that this style is a compound one."[52] Hong states that the transformation from poetry to history is evident in Huang's text, wherein "poetry is used to record events, and annotations are used to render the poetry detailed."[53] Through this complex use of poetry and notes, designed to give a full record of Japanese affairs, Huang managed to resuscitate the classical purpose of poetic form, and do so as a contribution to evidential research.

Before turning to a discussion of the two specific innovations in the poetry of Huang Zunxian, the use of poetry for geography and the inclusion of evidential research method, let me offer what I hope is a helpful comparison. More than anyone in a European tradition, W. B. Yeats parallels the pretensions operating here. His collection of 1899, *The Wind among the Reeds*, bears a striking resemblance to Huang's *Poems* in that in some poems Yeats too arrays sequences of images that are incomprehensible unless the reader is provided with the poet's supplemental notes. Consider, for example:

Do you not hear me calling, white deer with no horns?
I have been changed to a hound with one red ear;
I have been in the Path of Stones and the Wood of Thorns,
For somebody hid hatred and hope and desire and fear
Under my feet that they follow you night and day.[54]

Where Yeats's images are the vehicle through which the poet would associate himself with some universal and mythological experience, in order to gain a poetic knowledge of the self, Huang's images are the vehicle through which the poet associates his experience of Japan with a Chinese history of Japan, in the interests of a more critical and objective knowledge of Japan. In both cases, the poet mediates the language of self and a greater history. In Yeats's symbolist language of the time, these images "take upon themselves an independent life," becoming part of his mystical language.[55] In the same way, Huang's and his contemporaries' images function as points of convergence between an ongoing discourse on Japan and historically determined repetitions in the present. The difference, however, is that Huang and his contemporaries were working within specific Chinese conventions of genre, for which we must account.

Poetry and Geography

As I stated above, Huang Zunxian benefited from a revival of interest in Soong poetry during the early Qing. Both You Tong and Li E participated in a movement to legitimize the dominant Soong genre, the *ci* or lyric, as a natural development within the *shi* poetic tradition.[56] In the first place, because they justified their activity on the grounds of historical change and development, the movement had the effect of equalizing all received poetic forms, leaving poets free to write whichever genre(s) they chose. At the same time, their minimization of form had the attendant effect of elevating voice or "wording" as the more significant aspect of poetic composition. It is these two issues that we explore here.

The Yuefu *Poem*

In terms of formal structure and the intentionality that actualized it, Huang Zunxian's *Poems on Divers Japanese Affairs* took advantage of an ambiguous form, the *yuefu*, which in the early Qing developmental scheme lay between the Tang *shi* form and the Soong *ci* form.[57] Huang, we know, modeled his work after You Tong's *Bamboo Stalk Lyrics on the Foreign Domains* (an example is quoted below in the section on "The Note"). You's poems, although nominally "lyrics," are indistinguishable from "seven-syllable quatrains"; the same is true of Huang's *Poems*. Although scholars have observed that early "literary" *ci* were modeled after Tang quatrains, and only in the late Tang evolved into different formal structures, the "bamboo stalk lyric" (*zhuzhi ci*) continued to double as a quatrain, because of its specific value as a *yuefu* poem.[58]

The "bamboo stalk lyric" was invented by the Tang poet Liu Yuxi, as a "new *yuefu*," a ballad form popularized by Liu and his more celebrated eighth-century contemporary Bo Juyi. These "new *yuefu*" were composed in imitation of Han "Music Department" (*Yue Fu*) ballads, which were themselves Han-period imitations of still earlier folk ballads. To a large extent, this subgenre of *yuefu* was characterized by the convention of posturing the voice of an historical figure; in the Tang, *yuefu* were often used for describing contemporary events and for voicing social protest—safely under the guise of another persona. As a form, then, the *yuefu* was associated with both an artificiality of construction and a pretension of imitating history.[59] Stephen Owen has stated that the *yuefu* was, from the Tang period,

the form most strongly divorced from occasion . . . [and] a literary experience that was *repeatable* in a way that occasional poetry was not. [The *yuefu*'s] referents were general; it was not bound to the circumstances of its composition; and usually the personality and biography of the author were not the primary contexts for understanding. It was a form with whose fictional personae the reader could identify by the various forms of transference that occur in fictional modes.[60]

Liu Yuxi's "bamboo stalk lyrics," as imitation *yuefu* ballads, mimicked folk songs of southwestern China; Liu wrote them as a series of love lyrics, romantically impersonating popular stereotypes of the region.[61] As it evolved in later centuries, the title continued to reflect an ambiguity of form; it was both *yuefu* and quatrain, and poets proceded to write this lyric according to the rhyme and tonal patterns of quatrains. But at the same time, the content borne by the form underwent an innovative shift; in the hands of You Tong, Liu Yuxi's "bamboo stalk lyrics" no longer related the fabricated experience of a fictionalized historical persona, but became the vehicle for carefully selected images attesting to an objective knowledge of history and geography.

This change from fictive voice to geographical or historical description was not absolute, however. Although You Tong wrote utterly impersonal geographic descriptions in his *Bamboo Stalk Lyrics on the Foreign Domains* (the style which Huang Zunxian chose to copy), Huang's contemporary, Wang Zhichun, included in his travel diary of Japan a consciously narrative set of "Bamboo Stalk Lyrics on Tokyo," which describes his experiences— or the fabricated and romantic experiences of someone like himself—in Tokyo teahouses and drinking establishments. Below is an excerpt from Wang's "Lyrics," where the narrator is in erotic pursuit of dancing girls:

With slender bow and short arrow, I wait to take the stage,
Left and right they flee and run, these lovely maidens.
The chosen one who hits his mark, dead center, like a drumbeat,
Will delight in anecdotes recalling Sui and Tang.

When all depends on play and games to make a livelihood,
A dozen colleagues as a group can let the party start.

To come and play with lovely ladies, you'd want to play at love,
Wait till curtain's close to couple on the Phoenix terrace.[62]

The explicit eroticism of the narrator's tale here makes use of only the most oblique of references to China's past—if he is successful with one of these girls, the narrator will be able to compare his conquest to similar anecdotes of the Sui or Tang; but in the meantime, he is reticent about any specific reference. This is a striking contrast to Huang's treatment of the subject. His poem 118, concerning geisha, is a much more impersonal, even objective, account:

Shamisen in hand, ascend the painted hall,
Low-voiced, hands keep time, decline gratuities;
Day on day of song and dance in the springtime breeze,
Only speaks of happiness, never speaks of sorrow.

Those who perform song and dance for a living are called *geisha*. They serve wine at dinner parties in a most dignified manner. Among musical instruments, they play only the *shamisen*, the strings of which they pluck with ivory picks; their songs sound like those of India. They also play a small, narrow-waisted cane drum, which they beat with their hands. They have a large marching drum that they strike with two mallets; it makes the full ringing sound of bells or stone chimes. Dancers use fans to mark rhythm, weaving with their waists and swinging their hands in many different poses. They are truly like the women who entertained the troops and the official prostitutes of the Tang and Soong. When officials gather for drinking parties, they usually summon such women, and no one thinks it strange.[63]

If Wang Zhichun narrates an engaging—even titillating—scene, he means to evoke his experience, so as to impress upon the reader a vicarious feeling of the scene. Accordingly, Wang's reference to Sui and Tang is oblique because it is a similarly vicarious happenstance; having such an experience in Japan may lead one to think of similar experiences recorded in Sui and Tang history. Huang, by contrast, is interested in describing a phenomenon, the geisha, and so his reference to the Chinese past is direct; his point is to establish an equivalence between Chinese and Japanese things. Where Wang narrates with impressions, Huang describes with details and precedents; nonetheless, their intention is similar: to establish an analogy between their own experience (as Chinese experience) and phenomena in Japan, and thereby unify the two.

The "bamboo stalk lyric," in other words, manages by the 1870s to convey not only Tang presumptions about described experience in poetry, based on the representational value of the *shi*, but also the textual factualness sought by Qing practitioners of evidential research. It is not at all accidental that in all of these examples, what is being represented is some people and/or geographic area at the periphery of "China." In a preface to another of Huang's acknowledged precedents, the *Poems on Divers Affairs of the Southern Soong*, Zhao Diancheng (fl. 1720) noted that the "bamboo stalk lyric" was typically used for recording regional customs.[64] Liu Yuxi's southwest China was a distant, exotic land to which officials were sent as punishment; You Tong's subject was the outlandish "foreign domains"; Wang Zhichun's was the fascination and intrigue of Tokyo pleasure quarters. Geographic interest, then, was the common element bridging fictive "history" more typical of the Tang *yuefu* and forms of historical representation more typical of the pretensions of *shi* poetry during the Qing.[65]

Poetic Voice and Description

At the same time, a second element remains common to the earlier *yuefu* form, Huang's precedents, and Huang's own poems of the 1870s: All of these poems share a poetic language more willing to diverge from the usual poetic syntax so as to incorporate a syntax akin to those of both classical prose and spoken language.[66] Hans Frankel has shown that from the genuine folk ballads of ancient times to the imitations composed during the Tang, the *yuefu* consistently employed forms typical of speech, and particles of prose or spoken language habitually avoided in the *shi* form.[67] The same is true of Huang's *Poems*. Many lines include particles or "function words" normally dispensed with in poetry.[68] Line two of poem 61 reads, "[They] afterward intermixed even more horizontally printed books" (*houlai geng za xiexing shu*); the directional complement *lai* is rather incongruous—*hou* ("afterward") alone would have been sufficient, although it indeed does not work as well prosodically.[69] Other lines include word choices unusual for poetry. Poem 77, which expresses Huang's skepticism of the Shinto incarnation of the "Eternal Bug," ends with the line "do not know which bug is the eternal [one]" (*bu zhi changshi shi he chong*); the copula *"shi"* is rare in poetry, and normally dispensed with—*"changshi he chong"* ("the eternal [one]—which bug?") would have been acceptable.[70] Poem 12 begins with "Xi Hê has her domain in Barren Mulberry" (*Xi Hê you guo zai Kongsang*), a line unusually unpoetic for its directness and inclusion of both the rather vernacular *zai*—"to be located in/at"—where the more literary *yu* could be expected, and the verb of possession *you*, which could be eliminated altogether.[71]

Now, this usage of syntax more appropriate to spoken language might be interpreted as a movement toward greater verisimilitude. Stephen Owen, for example, implies in the quotation above that the process at work in both *yuefu* and fictional modes of discourse is transference—an identification with the fabricated personae. Indeed, in much of European literature at least, the stylistic technique motivating transference has been mimesis, the attempt to fabricate a copy of reality in the interests of verisimilitude. The Chinese tradition, however, never formulated the same kind of distinction between truth and fiction (until its encounter with European literature in the twentieth century); rather, history and fiction were both included within the larger category of "writing." History was the model of true writing; recorded events were presumed to be true, and fabricated stories comprised a subgenre judged accordingly as "unofficial history" (*yeshi*), "fabricated history" (*baishi*), or "trivial tales" (*xiaoshuo*).[72] The inherent truthfulness of writing (*wen*) was based on its capacity to pattern the correspondences in the natural world—in the same way that *shi* poetry was alleged to do.

In fact, the more significant opposition (from the Soong period) in Chinese literature was that between prose and poetry; and for our purposes, a critical difference between the two was that while the true forms of prose were official or public histories, and the ficticious forms of prose were exclusively "unofficial" or "private," poetic forms expressed truth or fiction independent of public or private dimensions. Poetry was primarily a public practice; the traditional evaluation of *shi* poetry was based on the exegesis of a public text, the *Classic of Poetry*, and the *shi* evolved as a public form invested with the same kind of public truth as the *Poetry*. Insofar as the poem was a linguistic and external manifestation of inner intention, the reader was capable of retrieving an adequate knowledge of the poet on the basis of the poet's authorial voice in the poem.[73] Bo Juyi put the matter succinctly in a verse addressed to his contemporary Zhang Ji:

The Word is the sprout of intention,
The Act is the root of writing;
And so, as I read your poems,
I know the man you are.[74]

In distinction to some sort of European mimetic efforts at verisimilitude, then, the use of syntax common to spoken language in poetic texts like Huang Zunxian's *Poems on Divers Japanese Affairs* represents instead, I believe, a widespread Qing enthusiasm for poetic voice or "wording." This was, in the first place, a reaction to Ming emphases on the preeminence of form and method. Urged on by the example of Gu Yanwu, who emphasized "change" as a natural given and the fact that each age spoke with its own voice, a widespread movement against those who would "revive the ancients"—by imitating the forms or voices of earlier periods—took various theoretical groundings.[75] Early Qing theorists of poetics, like Wang Fuzhi and Wang Shizhen (1634–1711), who understood poetry as personal self-expression and intuitive vision respectively, dislodged voice from its subordination to form; in examining how feeling or vision was best verbalized so as to fuse the "inner" and "outer" aspects of the poem, they relegated form to a secondary status.[76] Ye Xie (1627–1703) was perhaps the most outspoken early Qing critic of "formal rules" or "method"; to him, rules absurdly restricted the implicit freedom of the poetic voice, whose purpose was to express the personality of the poet and to do so as a natural response of the heart-mind to events.[77] Weng Fanggang went so far as to describe the concern with "formal style" as a "poet's sickness" and "poetry's ruin."[78]

In the second place, the Qing enthusiasm for "voice" was one aspect of the recovery of Soong poetic traditions. In addition to an interest in forms like the lyric, Qing poets also experimented with Soong diction—what has been described as "plain," "direct," or "continuous" poetic syntax.[79] Yu-kung Kao and Tsu-lin Mei have convincingly shown that imagery and "poetizing" in Tang Chinese poetry depends on nondirect or "discontinuous" syntax—that is, the juxtaposition of nouns and noun phrases. They postulate that a poem typically proceeds from discontinuous to continuous syntax—or, as they put it alternatively, from the juxtaposition of (noun) images to a propositional statement—at a relation of six lines to two in the eight-line poem, or a ratio of three to one in the quatrain.[80] Typically, a seven-word line of "discontinuous" syntax would be broken up 2/2/3, as either three images or two images followed by a comment. A ready example is You Tong's line from a poem on the geography of Japan, "Five principalities, seven departments, dependent domains as well."[81] A seven-word line of "continuous" syntax exhibits no such subdivision or juxtaposition, but is a complete and direct "proposition" of seven words. Now, the examples of such direct lines quoted above from Huang's *Poems* are not only final lines, but first, second, and even third lines. We find analogous examples in the texts he names as his precedents. You Tong's poem on Vietnam begins with the straightforward statement, "In February always blooms the *xian'ai* flower" (*eryue chang kai xian'ai hua*).[82] One of the *Poems on Divers Affairs of the Southern Soong* includes the third and fourth lines, "Who's to say the lotus [merely] adorns the river bank? / A beautiful face in any age harbors some danger" (*Shei shuo furong jiang shang mao? / Hong yan yidai you weiji*).[83]

It is clear that Huang, following the example of earlier Qing poets, has moved beyond the syntactic regularities typical of Tang poetry and in the direction of a syntax like Soong poetry—variously direct, proselike, and colloquial. In relaxing particularly the received Tang rules governing parallelism (which produced discontinuous syntax), Huang and other Qing poets understood themselves to be transcribing a voice more responsive to the world and more true to experience. As Huang proclaimed in his youthful celebration of feeling, "My hand writes my mouth" (*wo shou xie wo kou*).[84] But apart from such interest in expressiveness, this poetic voice was well suited to *description,* and at the hands of You Tong, the Seven Masters of Wulin, and Huang Zunxian, it proved to be quite compatible with a concurrent interest in inventing a poetry that took upon itself the recording of events and did so with the historical veracity attributed to evidential research methods.

Evidential Research

In composing the *Poems on Divers Japanese Affairs,* Huang was intentionally adding to China's knowledge of Japan. In his only public statement at the time—a brief afterword to the first printing—he indicates his concern for historical accuracy:

The evidence for these poems draws from Japanese texts. I had to make use of their chronologies of reign titles, since there are so few accounts of Japanese history in China's biographies [in the official dynastic histories]. Only in recent times do we have Li Zhaolo's *Dictionary of Reign Names* and Young J. Allen's *Chronologies of the Four Frontiers,* which—aside from occasional errors—are still worth consulting. Since I have constructed a "China-Japan Chronological Table," which will be contained in my *Japan Treatise,* I've declined to reannotate the reign titles and genealogies in these poems.[85]

At issue here are the *formal* requirements of geographical and historical knowledge: how was it that contemporaries understood Huang's text—a work of poetry—as an example of knowledge proper, and in that respect, a text much more worthwhile than either the more common travel diaries or the *yuefu* poem by itself?

Intertextuality and Observation

It is clear that Huang planned his *Poems* as an intertextual project; he cites not only others' texts, but also his own work in progress. At the same time, his motive in mentioning these other texts is to account for his research sources—by way of indicating corroborating evidence for what he has written. Such an attitude toward texts was, by Huang's time, firmly institutionalized in the practice known as evidential research.[86] Although Huang acknowledged only elsewhere that he subscribed to this method of scholarship, the prefaces to the first printings of the *Poems,* by his friend Wang Tao and acquaintance Hong Shiwei, explicitly endorse the work as an example of *kaozheng* scholarship.[87] Wang Tao praised Huang in this manner:

He took his leisure amid administrative affairs, so as to inquire after Japanese customs, and wrote these *Poems on Divers Japanese Affairs* in two volumes of altogether 154 poems. In this work, he describes local areas, records regional speech, intertwines and synthesizes affairs and their earlier traces, and painstakingly recollects the ancient and contemporary, at times recording one affair in a single poem, at other times gathering several affairs into one poem. Altogether, they suitably contribute to evidential research. The overall intention is primarily to record affairs, not to compose elegant phrases.[88]

This expression, "a suitable contribution to evidential research" (*zu zi kaozheng*), is found frequently in evaluations of texts during the middle and late Qing, when *kaozheng* became the major mode of scholarly inquiry practiced during the Qing period. (Although historians variously translate this term as "investigation of evidence," "critical philology," or "textual collation,"[89] I here use "evidential research," following the example of Benjamin Elman.)[90] Generally, in practicing *kaozheng*, Qing scholars scrutinized anew the received texts, critically evaluated the traditional historical accounts, vigorously gathered corroborating evidence so as to evaluate or supplement these received histories with nontextual materials like bronze inscriptions and commemorative steles, and frequently, redefined fields of inquiry.

The single most important event bearing upon our understanding of Huang's *Poems* as an example of evidential research was the compilation of *The Complete Books of the Four Treasuries* in the eighteenth century, a project that one line of scholarly interpretation identifies as the institutionalization of evidential research as an orthodox practice.[91] Significantly, the language used in the *Annotated Catalogue* to describe and evaluate each of the thousands of works considered for *The Complete Books of the Four Treasuries* matches the above language used to preface Huang's *Poems*—in the editors' words, a work either did or did not "suitably contribute to evidential research." This new critical attitude toward texts is evident from the fact that certain long-standing "classics" were "demoted"—removed from categories of "genuine" histories and relegated to categories of the "spurious." The *Classic of Mountains and Oceans*, for example, was removed from its long-standing position under "Geography" in the "History Division," and relegated to "Spurious History" (or "Trivial Tales") in the "Philosophy Division"; given the incredible quality of many of the "legends," the editors concluded that nothing justified keeping the text in "History" proper.[92] Other texts were excluded altogether. The remnants of the Ming discourse on Japan (discussed in chapter 1), like Xue Jun's *Concise Investigations of Japan*, were considered for inclusion in *The Complete Books of the Four Treasuries*, but were ultimately rejected because—according to the editors—the authors had indiscriminately recorded what they had heard, and had consequently failed to distinguish between truth and falsity.[93]

We do not know all of the criteria that informed the editors' conclusions, but based on the two extant collections of "draft reviews" from which the editors in part worked, R. Kent Guy has instructively demonstrated that in evaluating some "classics," "histories," and "philosophic schools," scholars criticized texts on the basis of textual errors, literary quality, proper moral interpretations of events, and the problem of forgery.[94] Evaluations of geographic works exhibit similar concerns, and in addition, reveal that evidence of firsthand observation was another criterion that supported textual validity.[95] This is clear from the editorial praise given to Chen Lunjiong's *Recorded News of the Sea Kingdoms*. The editors approved of the work, which was based on the travels of the author and his father, because "although a short work, it gathers together the first-hand examinations of two generations. In their inquiries and evaluations, [the authors'] words certainly possess demonstrable evidence, because they have inspected and eliminated hearsay, and have described the new and unusual."[96] Although the *Recorded News of the Sea Kingdoms* was not considered an example of evidential research, this comment nonetheless alerts us to one overriding concern among *kaozheng* practitioners—the connection between scholarship and firsthand experience. This understanding of scholarly practice was accepted widely enough by the mid-nineteenth century that Huang Zunxian absorbed it quite early in life; he wrote in a verse composed at the age of seventeen:

The Confucian scholar who stays indoors
Says nothing about the affairs of the age.
Understand the times and you will know the present;
Sympathize with others and you will experience society.[97]

Engagement with the world for the sake of knowledge and experience is a sensibility with a long history among Chinese scholars, so we cannot simply and abstractly ascribe this concern with firsthand experience to the "influence" of evidential research. (Indeed, there is little that is new about evidential research in terms of method and form; what is novel is this specific combination of elements.) From the Soong period especially, Chinese scholars have emphasized a relationship between writing and experience; Zhu Xi's slogan, "writing bears the Way," was meant to stress the effects that writing properly read and understood would have on behavior. Unfortunately, this history has never been studied systematically, but for our purposes of understanding Huang's *Poems* as an example of evidential research, three likely antecedents should be kept in mind: (1) the Soong tradition of *ji*—"memoirs" or "records" based on one's *in-person* examination of some historic site or object;[98] (2) the Ming tradition of *shixue* "practical" or "actual learning"—which emphatically interpreted "the investigation of things" (*ge wu*) as a critical *observation* of things;[99] and (3) the popular travel accounts of Xu Xiake, who, in the course of his travels, noted his discovery of nontextual materials which could corroborate received texts.[100] Huang Zunxian himself praised travel and travel diaries for their value to in-person examination and "evidential research" of traces of antiquity.[101]

In the words of scholars engaged in evidential research, this concern with first-hand investigation was translated into the principle that one should "search for the truth in actual affairs" (*shi shi qui shi*). For the scholar working in geography or "local history," it was critical that he personally observe the actual terrain and people he intended to represent in writing; and yet to have such a work conform to the standards of evidential research, it was not enough to simply record what one observed—as in the manner of a "travel memoir." Huang and his contemporaries were well aware of this limitation. Wang Zhichun, for example, discusses the difficulties of turning travel notes into respectable research in the introductory note to the third volume of his travel memoir of Japan, entitled *Random Notes on the East*. This volume, I should point out, was meant to be read as evidential research, and Wang deliberately distinguished it from his poetry and travel diary:

Like a wild goose leaving tracks in winter slush, I'd occasionally pause while passing through, my ears and eyes unable to completely assimilate my all-too-narrow surroundings. When my wheels rolled to a stop, and I had a leisurely day, I'd pick up my brush and note what I could. I toured those places I could personally experience; I observed and made inquiries but was deficient in detail; I examined maps and books but couldn't synthesize them completely; I used the records of friends. One by one I selected topics; I discussed them with others, and laughed about those that had never been recorded before. Which were the ones I'd overheard? Which were the ones I'd seen somewhere? I wanted to use them to plumb the source and its deviations, to penetrate the sincere and the false, and to arrange everything neatly and record it all in a detailed volume—as a humble contribution to evidential research.[102]

Wang's rather sympathetic apology is colored by his poetic sensibility; contemporary readers would not have missed the opening reference to the Soong poet Su Shi's famous simile:

Do you know what it's like?—human life everywhere?
It must be like a wild goose flying, then treading slush of melting snow.[103]

The alleged shortness—if not ephemerality—of a human life powerfully challenges Wang's aspirations to enduring scholarship. The restless activity of travel does not lend itself to rigorous research, and Wang is left laughing over his confusions as to when and where he picked up certain evidence. It is his description of a method that interests us most: personal observation, verbal inquiry, examination of texts, and sensitivity to other individuals' personal accounts. The ideal result of this activity was a neat, detailed volume that gave a historical account of phenomena—their successive divergences from some original source—and did so discriminatingly, by determining which aspects were genuine and which spurious.

For the purposes of turning travel records into suitable evidential research, the key component of Wang Zhichun's method is the examination of texts. Wang himself specifies the connection between *kaozheng* and texts when he describes Huang Zunxian's *Poems on Divers Japanese Affairs* as having "multiple volumes on the development of administrative affairs, the succession of reigns, and the mountains and waters, landforms, costumes and arts. [Huang] 'evidentially researches' the accuracy of the literature, transcribing [affairs] one by one."[104] Huang's successful molding of his travel experience into a scholarly work was contingent upon this activity. Wang Tao noted that with Huang's work "it's as if Japan now has a 'historical treatise' . . . written in the manner of a travel diary, and suitably contributing to evidential research."[105]

Significantly, Wang compares the *Poems on Divers Japanese Affairs* to a "history" or "treatise"—the name Huang chose for his subsequent work, the *Japan Treatise* (*Riben guozhi*). The "treatise," recall, was a genre long established in the series of official histories, and its variant, the "local history" or "gazetteer," was an exceedingly widespread form of scholarship during the Ming and Qing dynasties. From the fourth century, when treatises became independent works and each typically concentrated on all aspects of a single kingdom or province, authors of treatises imitated the overall form of an official history. So both the treatise and the local history include accounts of the administrative history, geography, educational institutions, scholars, local customs, and local crafts and products of the region in question. Treatises on foreign nations, by comparison, include additional accounts of a nation's ruling classes, foreign relations, and legal, educational, and military systems.[106]

Huang's *Poems* includes all of these features. Although Huang did not divide the text into any subsections, the entries do correspond to the typical set of topics included in the local treatise. Poems 1 through 50 constitute what can be called "national conditions," which encompass national administration and its history, heaven's signs (the calendar and weather, useful for administration), geography (the territory administered), and specific institutions. Poems 51 through 77 cover "learning," including schools, scholarly traditions, and books. Poems 78 through 135 comprise "local customs"—social relations, pastimes, habits of daily life, festivals, entertainments, and so on. And poems 136 through 153 include "local products" and "crafts and manufactures." Poem 154 summarizes and concludes. (I analyze this series in greater detail in chapter 5.)

Like most forms of official history, an obligatory stylistic element of the treatise was the citation of other texts—often, the "veritable court records" of a given dynasty. The distinctive purpose in evidential research was to evaluate the factualness of such received texts.[107] Indeed, one of the earliest models for evidential research scholars was the eminent Gu Yanwu, who engaged in a lifelong series of wide-ranging trips during which he gathered obscure historical source materials—rare texts, forgotten inscriptions, and the like—for the express purpose of evaluating the received histories.[108] Gu's great work of military geography, *On the Gains and Ills of the Administrative Domains under Heaven,* was praised by the eighteenth-century historian, Quan Zuwang (1705–1755), precisely for its textual expertise:

He read in detail the twenty-one Histories and the thirteen Veritable Court Records; he collected maps of All-under-Heaven and all manner of essays of the previous generations, from the *Shuo Bu* [companions to the classics] to official documents and proclamations. He recorded whatever had to do with the advantages and disadvantages of the lives of the people, investigating collateral documents and mutually authenticating all, so as to evaluate contemporary wisdom, and still avoid becoming a slave to the empty words of ancient days.[109]

In coordination with firsthand observation, then, a scholar must demonstrate that he has thoroughly examined the related textual tradition in his own process of scholarly research. What is wanting in both the *Classic of Mountains and Oceans* and the Ming texts mentioned above is such an intertextual or "second-party" point of view. That is to say, a text was approved as a "suitable contribution to evidential research" to the degree that its author offered corroborating evidence for the facts.

In establishing his work as an example of evidential research, Huang makes many such references to other texts. His citations vary in manner, from extended quotation to mere mention, and also in purpose. Some confirm an observation; in poem 98 (which is translated and discussed later in this chapter), Huang uses the *History of the Han* and *Treatise of the Three Kingdoms* to corroborate Japanese sitting habits. Some support or contradict a historical interpretation; in poem 7, the *Classic of Mountains and Oceans* corroborates the rule of women in early Japan. A few textual references develop poetic allusions, while others are only names in a list of examples of the phenomenon in question. Poem 70 includes a list of Japanese "Masters of Chinese Classical Prose"—the followers of Ogyū Sorai and Rai San'yō—and their works; poem 71 includes a list of Japanese writers of "Chinese poetry" and their collections.[110]

Given the dominant position of literary Chinese texts in evidential research concerns, very few of the group of texts cited by Huang are Japanese. Similarly, only two "Western" works are cited—the book of Genesis in poem 2, and in poem 52, a *Concise Discussion of German Schools* by the German missionary Ernst Faber (1839–1899).[111] The Chinese text cited most often is the *Classic of Mountains and Oceans*; one of Huang's persistent interests is the accuracy of this ancient but recently demoted record. In fact, much of his work serves to reiterate—albeit in the specific detail of Japan—the negative conclusions drawn by the editors of the *Four Treasuries*.

And statistically, 72 of the 154 poems in the first edition make references to other texts—47 percent. (By comparison, 88 of the 200 poems in the second edition include such references—a smaller 44 percent.) We might conclude, then, that the work contains slightly more poems that treat subjects hitherto undocumented in those Chinese (and Japanese) sources of which Huang was aware. In other words, the slight majority of the *Poems* is given to descriptions of Huang's in-person observations of Japan, those sites and affairs that charted new ground in Chinese geographical representation.

The Note as Research Convention

Because scholars hoped to amass a plenitude of documentation and to recover and examine firsthand whatever evidence earlier scholars may have missed, works of evidential research scholarship became elaborately detailed. As scholars proceeded with the search for evidence to substantiate their interpretations of history, they cultivated the practice of the "note" (*biji* or *ji*), which became a dominant writing style of scholars engaged in evidential research.[112] Quite simply, a "note" was the individual record of an observation or a textual citation. Scholars typically collected notes in "notation books" and later reworked them into finished, publishable texts.[113] Gu Yanwu's celebrated *Record of Knowledge Gained Daily* was compiled in this way and allegedly served as the model for later evidential research texts. As with the *Poems on Divers Japanese Affairs*, these works typically contain comments on a variety of subjects, and each comment is intended to complement, correct, or supplement traditional historical accounts.[114]

An extended example will clarify the complexities of Huang's evidential research and particularly his usage of "notes." In poem 7, Huang expresses admiration for Jingū, the powerful consort of Emperor Chūai [r. 192–200?], but criticizes the scholarly interpretation that makes her a divinity:

Fox cage and cattle coffin—will stupefy the people;
In Paekche and Silla—lords and ministers all
Rocks in girdle, bows in hand, in person take up arms;
A reckless claim—the "Queen Domain" begotten by divinities!

Japan appropriated the laws of the Han system, which came to them by way of [the Korean domains] Paekche and Silla. Empress Jingū was the first to establish communications with these two domains; she is known as "Himiko" in the *Wei Treatise* and the *History of the Han* [wherein is recorded her enfeoffment as "Friend of Wei"]. Histories relate that during Chūai's campaign against the Kumaso [of Kyūshū], a spirit advised the empress to first subdue Silla. The emperor opposed this plan, and shortly thereafter died. The empress assumed the regency, and forthwith began the Western Expedition. On crossing the sea, she prayed, saying,

"I receive the commands of the spirits of heaven, and cross the sea to embark upon this distant expedition. If my victory is indeed to be achieved, let the waves rise to part my hair in two." She went into the water, and it was as she had prayed. Thereafter, she wore her hair in two coils, like a man, and took upon herself a great crossbow. The empress occasionally felt a movement in her womb for ten months running; she concealed a stone in her sash [to delay the birth of the child], and prayed again [to the spirits], saying, "Grant that I give birth when I return in triumph." She reached Silla; the king of Silla raised his hands in surrender, and she sealed his treasury, removed all charts and books, and returned [to Japan]. After fourteen months, she bore [the Emperor] Ōjin. These events were the founding of the Shinto teachings, intended to stupefy the common people. Treatises state that she used sorceresses to beguile the masses, and a thousand or more palace maidens who were never allowed to see her face.

China's entire involvement with Japan begins here. Empress Jingū called the domains of Silla, Paekche, and Koguryō the "Western domains," and sent her embassy to the Wei court. Histories accordingly speak of the "Queen Domain." Guo Pu's annotated *Classic of Mountains and Oceans* records a land called Wo to the east of Daifang, which has a woman for king. Later generations have considered that Empress Jingū used all these women to dominate the domain; so how can her success be called the work of the gods?![115]

Although this poem-and-commentary focuses on historical events—most of which are narrated—the piece as a whole is not composed as a historical narrative, but as an inventory. The poem establishes the themes to be treated: administration, the conquest of Korea, and a traditional interpretation of the "Queen Kingdom." The notes then address the themes by way of textual references: (1) the *Wei Treatise* and the *History of the Han,* in which China records its first references to Wo (in time, "Japan"), and through which Japan first acquires information about Han administration (through the mediation of the Korean kingdoms); (2) unspecified Japanese histories and treatises, in which the exploits of Jingū are narrated; (3) and finally, subsequent references to her alleged affairs in terms of the "Queen Kingdom" in Chinese histories and the *Classic of Mountains and Oceans.* Huang then returns to the theme of administration—in particular, Jingū's successful administration of her kingdom. Those who would mystify the story of Jingū—as an account of either the divine origins of the "Queen Kingdom" or the Shinto teachings—are themselves benighted, missing the fact of a very shrewd administrator who knew how to control the masses with a set of techniques that in time were established as the Shinto teachings.[116]

Notes vs. Annotations

Huang's combination of poetry and notes in the *Poems on Divers Japanese Affairs* is a conscious expansion of the practice of poetry in the interests of evidential research. In the first place, the notes that constitute the major part of his work differ from the more typical notes that describe the circumstances surrounding the composition of a poem. Examples of this "conventional" usage of notes abound in the *Assorted Verse from the Eastern Embassy* by Huang's superior, Ambassador Hê Ruzhang. Hê's notes are often biographical and begin with the date of composition or some temporal context for the poem, much in the manner of poetic diaries like those by Wang Zhichun and Wang Tao. Hê's first poem, for example, reads:

Like receiving a proclamation to go colonize frontiers,
Gaze afar, aboard a raft, to bore through space and return,
What compares—to have in hand the Son of Heaven's orders?—
To clear the clouds, pointblank, and arrive in this Eastern Sea.

In the seventh month of the *ding chou* year [June 1877], I received my diplomatic credentials, which I accepted with reverence, and set forth. During the ten-odd days on the seas, there were no overpowering winds; our group of voyagers were safe, knowing that the sea too appeared to serve and safeguard the ethereal majesty of the Son of Heaven.[117]

Aside from the fact that Hê's note evokes a curious temporal dissonance with the poem (the poem becomes "here and now" as a consequence of its final word "arrive," and the note abruptly shifts to an anterior past), the note is clearly not a textual citation in the manner of evidential research. Rather, the note reinforces the historicity or actual occurence of the event which the poem records; it is an example of the use of poetry to record events *without* any engagement of evidential research methods.

In the second place, Huang Zunxian's notes are a significant modification of the more typical "annotations" (*zhu*) that figure in the seventeenth-century poetic texts he names as the antecedents of his work.[118] In two of these texts, You Tong's *Bamboo Stalk Lyrics on the Foreign Domains*, and the *Assorted Verse on Japan* (*Riben za yong*) by Sha Qiyun (17th c.?), the authors' annotations do little more than explain the references and allusions in the poems. For example, the first of You Tong's poems on Japan reads:

Emperor of the Rising Sun, designated "Most Venerable,"
Five principalities, seven departments, dependent domains as well;
A vainglorious record of historical ages in the *Mirror of Azuma*,
The Taikō, in the end, was the man Kinoshita.

During the Sui Dynasty [seventh century], the Japanese ruler sent a letter in which he called himself the "Son of Heaven where the Sun Rises." Within his domain he was designated "Emperor," and known also as "Mikoto" ["Most Venerable"]. His domain includes five principalities, seven departments, three main islands, and more than one hundred dependencies. The *Mirror of Azuma* records the affairs of Japanese lords and officials; "Azuma" is the name of an island. The man Kinoshita was Taira [Toyotomi] Hideyoshi; during the Ming dynasty Wan Li reign [1573–1619], he usurped control of the Dwarf Kingdom and called himself the "King of Taikō."[119]

Stylistically, You's poem and annotations proceed as a rather mechanical juxtaposition of themes quite similar to that seen in Huang's *Poems*. Each annotation corresponds to a line of the poem. Furthermore, You cites the Japanese text *Mirror of Azuma* not out of any concern for historiographical method, but simply to reinforce his readers' awareness of a Japanese text with the quite poetic name, "*Azuma*" (*wu qi*), literally "my dear wife." (I say "reinforce," because You's celebrated contemporary, the poet and scholar Zhu Yizun [1629–1709], wrote a short expository description of the *Mirror of Azuma*, which was familiar to scholars writing on Japan.)[120]

By contrast, Huang's use of notes is most similar to the third seventeenth-century poetic text he names as his precedent, the *Poems on Divers Affairs of the Southern Soong* (*Nan Song zashi shi*). This work is the result of a massive research project undertaken by the Seven Masters of Wulin—led by Shen Jiache (fl. 1720), and most famous of whom were the poet and historian Li E, and the pair of poets and bibliophiles, brothers Zhao Yu (1689–1747) and Zhao Xin (b. 1701). The program for this work was directed explicitly at the historical record—"to substantiate with evidence its flaws, and to supplement its omissions."[121] An example will demonstrate the degree to which Huang imitated this work. The eleventh poem in the first set concerns the twelfth-century calligrapher and musicologist Jiang Kui (Jiang Yaozhang, 1163–1203); I translate, at some length:

In calligraphy, Shen or Han—which style outshoulders which?
Of ancient marches, the "Drums and Pipes"—a sage leading;
At Great Constancy, "Brocade Zither" still surprises:
The twelve tones of antiquity no longer passed on today.

In the *Divers Treatises on Yan Bei*, Zhao Zigong views Jiang Yaozhang as a calligrapher of the Shen and Han styles. Zhou Gongjin adds that Jiang Yaozhang's martial song, "Drums and Pipes Melody," follows the patterns of Lu Shiyin.

According to the *Essay on the Zhouhe Flute*, Jiang Kui offered a letter begging that music be rectified, and proceeded to the Office of Great Constancy to have officials there emend the musical scores [so as to reestablish ancient practices]. The Music Master showed him the [medieval] tune "Brocade Zither." Jiang exclaimed, "What sort of music is this!?" All the officials, already having more than enough work, sighed and requested of the Music Master, "Tell him it's called 'Drum and Zither,' a piece no one has ever heard played." The officials all laughed and went back to their individual places.

Wu Xingzhang relates that Yaozhang was a master of tonality and once composed a "Critique of Grand Music" in hopes of rectifying Confucian temple music. In the third year of Blessed Origin [1197], officials at the Bureau of Decrees and Orders received a copy of the work, and ordered the Office of Great Constancy to consult among themselves and to evaluate the state of grand music. At that time, those officials were jealous of Yaozhang's talent and did not fully comply with the proposals in his "Critique"—a great pity for the man!

Note that Jiang Kui, whose courtesy name was Yaozhang, completed a five-volume work entitled *White Stone Lyrics*.[122]

In gathering details concerning the life of would-be music reformer Jiang Kui, Shen Jiache has related them here as an inventory of activities, incidents, and consequences; the first two lines of the poem refer to Jiang's commendable achievements as calligrapher and musician, the third line to his blighted efforts to reform music, and the last line laments the consequences of his failed ideals—China has lost its ancient music. Each of these elements is corroborated by a textual reference. It was this style that Huang consciously imitated in attempting a poetic work in the manner of evidential research.

However, a critical difference between this combination of poem and notes and that in Huang's *Poems on Divers Japanese Affairs* is the way in which they are printed. As with most annotations (*zhu*), those in the seventeenth-century texts are printed in double rows of smaller-size (subscript) characters. (This was a practice established during the Han period in order to distinguish a text proper from an editor's commentary.)[123] By contrast, Huang's notes (*ji*) are printed in full-size characters. They are clearly not a secondary phenomenon, especially since they contain annotations of their own (see poem 98 in the next section). While this difference may seem minor or mechanical, Huang's notes were in fact considered such a valuable and plentiful source of information on Japan that the editors of the late-nineteenth-century geographic anthology, the *Collected Reprints on Geography from the "Little Square Hu" Studio*, reprinted them without the poems as *Divers Affairs of Japan* (*Riben Zashi*).[124] Clearly, the difference in printing technique is evidence that some of Huang's contemporaries perceived his notes as equal in importance to the poems, if not the essential portion of the work.

Chinese References and Cultural Precedents

One immediate limit to the breadth of Huang's research was his inability to read most Japanese (*wabun*) texts. He was restricted to Japanese texts of the literary Chinese form, *kanbun,* and during his stay, he seems to have had trouble finding resources. Aside from Rai San'yō's well-known *Nihon seiki* (*Administrative Records of Japan*) and *Nihon gaishi* (*Unofficial History of Japan*), he mentioned only the Mito school's incomplete *Dai Nihon shi* (*Great History of Japan*), in the process of compilation since the 1650s, and Iwagaki Matsunae's (1774–1849) *Kokushi ryaku* (*Short History of Japan*).[125] When Huang was in Japan, only the "Basic Annals" and the "Arrayed Biographies" of the Mito text were available, and it seems that he unfortunately had only a *kanamajiribun* copy of the *Kokushi ryaku*, in which the Chinese characters had been rearranged for Japanese syntax. He complains of his lack of sources in the brushtalks, but expresses his gratitude that his friend Ishikawa Ei was helping him read the *Kokushi ryaku*.[126]

Accordingly, as we have seen in the example of poem 7 ("Fox cage and cattle coffin—"), Huang does not typically specify Japanese references. That he is aware of this deficiency is clear from his afterword to the *Poems* (quoted above), where he describes his research as "drawing from Japanese texts for evidence" and emphasizes that he does so because there are few *Chinese* alternatives. From statements in the Ōkōchi brushtalks, it seems that Huang acquired most of his knowledge from conversations with assistants who did read other Japanese texts, and from brushtalking with his professional historian friends, Shigenobu Yasutsugu, Aoyama Nobutoshi, Miyajima Seiichirō, and Oka Senjin.[127] He acknowledges in poem 154 that he solicited the advice of these Japanese scholars, "so that some errors were thereby corrected."[128] In any case, it is difficult to trace the sources of his information for Japanese history.

By contrast, his erudition and breadth of research excels when he is concerned with Chinese sources, and particularly when he is intent on showing the Chinese antecedents of some Japanese customary practice. Poem 98, for example, makes twenty-two references to nineteen Chinese texts in an attempt to demonstrate that Japanese habits of sitting on the floor originated in Tang China. I quote this piece at length in order to indicate the extent of Huang's historical, cultural, and linguistic knowledge, and to offer a sense of Huang's style of poetry as evidential research. Huang constructs his argument in the methodical manner suggested above, moving from observation to research of textual and pictoral evidence for both his descriptions and his interpretation of the development of furniture for sitting. He begins with ancient equipment for reclining—the *ji*, a stand or stool, and the *chuang*, a platform bed—and moves to the "outlandish seat" (or "barbarian bed": *hu chuang*) of foreign origin, which he identifies as the chair:

Floral cushions piled in layers of shining splendor,
Guests bow prostrate, sleeves arrayed, fill the chamber;
Except the phoenix bearing imperial decree,
None may sit tall on the "outlandish seat."

Sitting and standing are both done on the floor, with the two knees against the floor, the back straightened to a solemn sitting position, and the feet supporting the buttocks. Although there are also those who sit cross-legged, squat, or sit with legs outstretched, none of these are respectful. Cushions are necessarily arranged for sitting, as a ceremonious expression of respect for one's guests. Of old, the practice was to use several layers of cushions. When orders arrived from one's lord, a *ji* [stool/stand] was arranged [to seat the messenger], and after he proclaimed the edict, he immediately sat on the floor.

This is all ancient ritual, and accords with research into the *History of the Han*. The "Jia Yi Biography" records that Emperor Wen "unconsciously stretched out his legs on the mat." The "Guan Ning Biography" in the *Treatise of the Three Kingdoms* contains "in sitting, don't squat on your haunches; make sure clothing covers your knees." The *History of the Later Han* records that Xiang Yu sat on a plank, and after sitting for a long time, the plank left indications of his knees, ankles, and feet. Zhu Xi adds that "there is today a place of learning in Chengdu, the Wen Weng Ceremonial Hall, which has stone carvings of various scholars, all sitting solemnly with their knees on the floor, but the soles of their feet can be secretly seen beneath the tapestry robes covering the back of the area where the figures sit." From the Japanese I've observed today, I understand how men of former days sat for a long time in the same manner.

Hence, the ancients were without *ji* and could not dangle their feet as they sat. Furnishings for sitting upright sprouted with King Wuling of Zhao [during the Warring Kingdoms], grew in the Six Dynasties Period, flourished in the Northern Soong, and became widespread in the Yuan. Prior to the Three Dynasties of antiquity, there were *ji* for leaning upon—as references attest in the *Classic of Poetry*, "offering *ji* with shuffling steps," and in the *Mencius*, "leaned upon the *ji* and fell asleep." For sleeping there were *chuang* [platforms]. The *Classic of Poetry* speaks of "now, platforms for sleeping"; the *Classic of Changes*, "the platform is split at the edge." In sum, platforms and *ji* were originally for leaning or reclining, for placing things down, or for sleeping—but neither item was for sitting. Not until the *Comprehensive Customs* of Ying Shao do we read that King Wuling of Zhao had constructed an "outlandish seat" [*hu chuang*] which he used for sitting. During the Han, everyone still sat upon the floor. . . . At the end of the Eastern Han, there were wood pieces hewn to serve for sitting, which some called platforms, and some called *ta* [couches]—like those upon which Guan Ning and Xiang Yu sat. These may have been planks upon the floor, but they could not have been more than a short distance off the floor. After the Wei and Jin, we read in the "Su Ze Biography" of the *Wei Treatise* that "Emperor Wen rested upon the platform and drew his sword." In the *History of the Jin*, "Huan Yi rested on an 'outlandish seat,' took out a flute, and played three tunes." The *History of the Southern Dynasties* records that when Ji Sengzhen paid a visit to Jiang Xiao, he climbed upon the couch and sat down; Xiao ordered his attendants to "move my platform to make way for the guest." . . . A guest who was not respectful was not allowed to sit. Moreover, sitting upon a couch or a *ji* was done kneeling. The "Hou Jing Biography" in the *History of the Liang* records, "ascending the hall to occupy an 'outlandish seat,' with feet dangling while sitting down." History deliberately records that this was an unusual custom and views it with shock, so we know that even though men in the past had platforms or *ji,* they did not use them in a manner like our sitting down today.

In the Tang, people altered wooden platforms with rope, which they called a "rope *chuang*" or "hammock." Cheng Dacheng's *Yan fanlu* reports all the officials in the Purple Imperial Hall on great hammocks. Nevertheless, these are not called "chairs" [*yizi*]; not until the Soong is this word used. Ding Jingong's *Tan lu* includes "Dou Yi carved two chairs in a floral design." . . . (Note: In all these texts, "chair" [*yi*] was originally written with the character for "recline," but in time "paulonia-wood chair" was simply written with the character for "chair.") After these texts, one repeatedly sees [our contemporary word for] "chair" [*yizi*]. . . . Zhu Bian's *Quwei jiuwen* includes "embroidered backs of chairs." Particularly during the Soong period, there was decoration for show—already so widespread then! But if we observe ancient drawings and paintings before and during the Tang, neither people nor things rested on chairs. Not every scene in Soong paintings necessarily shows chairs provided for figures. I venture to suspect that the "outlandish seat" was originally a Western custom, which King Wuling of Zhao first studied and constructed, which entered China during the Yuan, and which—because of long usage—has become widespread. The Japanese system was in a large part modeled on the Tang; since the Tang still sat upon the floor, the Japanese were originally without chairs. Only in the last ten years has the chair become widespread.[129]

Of course, most of Huang's evidence is what we would today term "circumstantial," marshaled in support of a problematic historical argument. His proof that Japanese sitting customs are modeled after those of ancient China hinges, in the end, upon two potentially controversial and interrelated assumptions: (1) that Japanese culture as a whole was modeled primarily on that of Tang China; and (2) that an equivalence exists between present Japanese practices and descriptions of past Chinese practices. Now, there is certainly a great deal of historical evidence documenting the Japanese borrowing of many Chinese practices during the Tang dynasty, but as I described earlier, Huang and his contemporaries habitually see Japan as a variant of China. He is indifferent to the possibility of independent Japanese cultural evolution; rather, his manner of argument shows a marked preference for correspondences between his own observations and intertextual historical evidence. He chooses to comment on those aspects of *Chinese* culture most visible in Japan—administrative institutions, schools, language and learning, music, clothing, and various Chinese arts (calligraphy, medicine, painting) and crafts (rice, tea, silk, ceramics, and laquerware production)—because these, including the example above, have documentation in Chinese texts.

In poem 98, Huang further links China and Japan by singling out the "West" as a mutual bearer of differences—that is to say, Huang implies that China and Japan are the same insofar as they both differ from the West. Huang makes the curious claim that the chair is a Western import for *both* China and Japan, albeit in different historic periods. While it may be that chairs came to Japan through contact with Europeans in the seventeenth, eighteenth, or nineteenth centuries, it is not at all certain that Chinese obtained chairs through similar contact with Europeans in a much earlier age. The fourth-century northwestern Hu tribe(s)—to whom I refer with the adjective "outlandish"—were far different from the Europeans in the nineteenth century.[130] But the precise history of the cultural diffusion of the chair is not the issue here; rather, at stake is Huang's ability to subordinate observable Japan within a pattern of Chinese intertextuality. In observing Japan, Huang represents Japan in terms of Chinese texts and according to the mode of inquiry practiced by evidential research; this, after all, was largely a practice of verifying one's interpretations of the past on the basis of evidence found in texts from an earlier time.

Critical in this enterprise was the *truth* of one's interpretations, which one demonstrated through such erudition in corroborating evidence. Yan Ruoju (1636–1704) put the point most strongly when forced to justify his initially shocking analysis of the *Classic of Documents*:

Someone may ask: "Concerning your study of the *Documents*, you accept Han [authorities] and suspect Jin [317–420] and Tang [authorities]. That is fine. But then you proceed to give credence to the histories and the commentaries and suspect the classics. Is that permissible?" I reply: "What classics? What histories? What commentaries? My concern is only with what is true. If the classic is true and the history and commentary false, then it is permissible to use the classic to correct the history and the commentary. If the history and the commentary are true and the classic false, then can it be impermissible to use the history and the commentary to correct the classic?"[131]

Dai Zhen (1724–1777), the great eighteenth-century scholar who served for a time as a senior editor in the *Four Treasuries* project, reiterates the point in a passage that nicely—and metaphorically—reinforces the connection between observation and research:

Some of my works are based on thoroughly conclusive views; others are not yet so based. By conclusive views, I mean that the text must be verified by antiquity in every particular; the work must be in such complete accord with the truth as to leave nothing debatable. . . . If we rely on hearsay to determine the meaning of a text, to choose the best of a variety of interpretations to point out its strengths, to express its arguments with empty words, or to use random proofs to verify it, then although we are moving upstream to determine the source, we won't see the original spring with our own eyes.[132]

The understanding of truth asserted here elevates an examination of origins. At issue in Huang's project, accordingly—insofar as the *Poems* were a contribution to evidential research—was the very truthfulness of Japanese origins, which Huang necessarily understood in terms of Chinese textual antecedents. In fact, Huang begins the *Poems* by recounting the origin of Chinese contact with Japan—the infamous incident during the Sui, when "His [Japanese] Majesty Suiko sent a communiqué to Emperor Yangdi, in which he called himself 'Son of Heaven where the Sun Rises.'"[133] Poems 2 and 3 then go on to recount the two most famous Japanese stories about their origins, the creator divinities, Izanagi and Izanami, and the birth of the father of the first emperor Jimmu, Ugayafukiaezu-no-mikoto. Huang calls these "marvellous tales," clearly not the stuff of history.[134]

So even if the origins of Japanese antiquity were subsequent to those of Chinese antiquity, and ancient Japanese texts were nonexistent or inaccessible to Huang, Huang noted that those *kanbun* texts of the Edo period to which he did have reading access habitually and deliberately suppressed any inquiry into the truth of origins. Huang complains in his notes to poem 5 that Japanese historians wrongly eliminate the story of the second-century-B.C. envoy, Xu Fu, from their histories of Japanese antiquity:

[Tokugawa] Mitsukuni rejects [this story], saying, "As soon as we mention this honorable man of Qin, he becomes the means for our being a satellite state; so I've cut it out." When Rai San'yō wrote his *Administrative Records of Japan*, the matter of the Qin envoy Xu Fu coming to Japan was screened off and not recorded. These are the views of Confucians who would control the legacy of the past, and not the words of historians who would record the truth. [The story of Xu Fu] is a good example of points that need to be explored.[135]

In distinction to those who would "screen off" or "control" the textual past, Huang is motivated intellectually to investigate Japanese origins and determine the extent to which Japanese culture originated in China. Huang understands his activity as that of a historian, tracing the sources of Japanese customs and recording their truth as he finds evidence to corroborate received interpretations. In chapter 6, I will show that Huang treats Japan's Westernization in a similar manner: as a search for the origins of Western practices in Japan, which can ultimately be traced to Chinese antecedents.

To summarize: If Chinese early on established a homology between occasional poetry as a historical record, and the recording of history through *shi* poetry, the force of this epistemological move took a new direction during the Qing period, when some scholars and poets challenged the categorical division between poetry and a prose exemplified by historical narrative. In the first place, the effort to equalize the *wording* (syntax or voice) appropriate to poetry and prose had, as one consequence, the perhaps weak claim that there was no difference in truth value between the two, but that poetry might be a better form since it additionally beautified the language of "events" (or "affairs") with its usage of imagery. In the second place, the effort to equalize the *content* of poetry and prose resulted in the strongly ideological claim that from the point of view of history, *shi* poetry was as adequate to the task of recording historical affairs as was narrative prose— and in fact, poets might insist, the *shi* was a superior form since in addition to linking words and affairs it also incorporated—by way of authorial intention—the position of the individual doing the recording.

This amounts to a significant innovation, if not revolution, in Chinese textual practices. In the attempt to efface a distinction between historical narrative and a poetic discourse, Huang (and his predecessors) called into question the difference between what observers of language activity have described as the "subject of the enounced" (the "objectivized" subject of historical narrative) and the "subject of the enunciation" (the speaking subject of discourse).[136] In other words, this is a striking transformation of historiography, precisely because it is mediated by the author-subject of the poetry. Through such an involvement in the representation of events, the poet Huang no longer has to obey the conventions of official narrative history—particularly chronology and didacticism. Accordingly, as we have seen, Huang prefers to represent events in poetic juxtapositions, based on the harmonizing of events as images. That is, his use of word-images is meant to comprehend historical events in such a way as to generate a knowledge of history. This method, I have concluded, is based in a homology established between poetry and history.

It is this motive that explains the adaptation of certain features of the *yuefu* by Huang Zunxian and the poets he names as his predecessors. In their attempts at something novel, the recording of historical affairs in poetry, the "informal" wording of the *yuefu* and its pretensions at representing other times and places provided the wherewithal sufficient for expanding the *shi* form in the interests of such an end. Note, however, that only the results of their *research* labors received attention as serious works of historical scholarship. The *yuefu* was on its own insufficient. The reason for this—that is, the reason why only certain texts like the *Poems on Divers Affairs of the Southern Soong* and Huang's *Poems on Divers Japanese Affairs* were singled out as evidential research contributions to historical knowledge—is that aside from the questions of observation, experience, and textual collation, when poetry claimed to represent a knowledge of history, it depended on the epistemological assumptions of the *shi* form. To express objective historical evidence, poetry had to structure historical images so as to invite an explanation and corroboration in notation form.

Huang's experiment, which so caught the attention of his readers between 1879 and 1898, was to my knowledge never repeated. The *Poems* became a mere overture, an eccentric precursor, to his forty-volume *Japan Treatise*—more a source of information to peruse than a style of poetry to imitate. We will return to his text in the last part of this essay, because, apart from its novel use of poetry for historiography, Huang's *Poems* offers an imaginative reading of Westernization that bears directly on the issue of Chinese perceptions of a changing Japan reflecting a changing position of China. If Huang's analogies in the *Poems* served to familiarize Japan in Chinese terms, the same was true of Westernization: its origins were Chinese, and Chinese could follow Japan's precedent in the legitimate business of reviving the Way of the Ancient Sages.

5 The Utility of Objectification in the Geographic Treatise

Japan has been established for two thousand years, but has been without official history. Private schools have recorded and narrated all variety of unseemly stories, without regard for reason. Among their Chinese learning scholars, rare are those who can thoroughly examine the roots and branches of words and things. Why then should scholars of our land translate books from their shores? A distant land of uncommon customs, having different writing and another speech, New Year's Day color of dress, names of things, measurements of distance, area, and weight—none of it is similar. Who can follow and connect the whole?
Liang Qichao, in praise of Huang Zunxian's *Japan Treatise*

To observe, then, is to be content with seeing—with seeing a few things systematically. With seeing what, in the rather confused wealth of representation, can be analysed, recognized by all, and thus given a name that everyone will be able to understand.
Michel Foucault, *The Order of Things*

 The 1880s witnessed the production of the six geographical treatises on Japan compiled by Chinese scholars in the nineteenth century. As a form of representation and contribution to knowledge, the local treatise, unlike diplomacy, was beyond dispute. Unlike brushtalking, it did not elevate metonymic strategies, and unlike travelogues and poetry, it dispensed with personal orientations. Where diplomats elevated a history of tributary relations to contain Japan, where the language and poetic practices of personal encounters in brushtalk assimilated Japan, where the travelogue deployed poetic images, personal narrative, and geohistorical sites to familiarize Japan, and where Huang Zunxian's *Poems* employed poetic technique and textual practices of evidential research to corroborate Japan—in short, where these other textual practices and genres foregrounded personal experience with Japan, the geographic treatise could forgo a preference for any of these strategies. It presented factual knowledge of Japan in a manner entirely compatible with common sense.

The six geographic treatises of the 1880s served to *objectify* Japan, both in order to produce true representations of Japan and to afford readers useful information about Japan. The truth of these representations lay in the form of the treatise. Because so much of the content of the geographic treatise is an effect of its form, and because this nexus of form and content was so established in Chinese scholarship, the treatise was a form of representation so reasonable as to be above controversy. It confirmed not only a structure of perceptions that had centuries earlier ceased to require any logical consideration, but also a conceptual framework that was "natural." Put simply, it was the most "truthful" form of geographical representation.

In a corresponding manner, the utility of the treatise lay in its objectifications. The categories into which Japan was analyzed grew out of the ancient encyclopedic techniques that informed literate knowledge. In time, these categories were adopted by the local treatise in an effort to facilitate governmental administration of local areas. The utility of the treatise was thus defined in conjunction with its relations to this structure of knowledge and practices of administration. The facts contained in the treatise confirmed not only the scholar's perceptions and habits of analysis—the foundations of his education—but also the official's strategies of administration. In assuming that a geographic treatise had a utility in and of itself, Chinese authors and readers, scholars and officials, confirmed the inherent sensibility and usefulness of information contained in a treatise.

The Decade of Geographic Treatises on Japan

Although Huang Zunxian's *Poems on Divers Japanese Affairs* was an exceptional text, a number of fellow officials shared the motive that prompted his work: the Chinese court and bureaucracy urgently needed to know more about Japan. This interest was typically stated in one of two ways: in terms of Japan's growing aggressiveness off the Chinese coast, as demonstrated by the Taiwan Incident of 1874 and the subsequent Japanese incorporation of the Liuqiu Islands as Okinawa Prefecture in 1879, or in terms of the applicability of knowledge about Japan toward China's own efforts at self-strengthening. In both cases, it was Li Hongzhang, Prince Gong, and other officials affiliated with the International Office and various "self-strengthening" projects who pursued the cause of better information on

Japan. As Li stated in a memorial to the throne in 1875, "The various European powers are strong, but they are still seventy thousand *li* away; Japan, however, is near at hand—on the threshold, and peering into our empty courtyard."[1] This uncanny prospect of a proximate adversary, and one seemingly better adept at Western ways, prompted Chinese officials to proceed with the work of gathering information on Japan. Once an embassy had been established in Tokyo in 1877, with affiliated consulates in Yokohama, Kobe, and Nagasaki, Chinese were in a position to begin; Huang Zunxian's idiosyncratic *Poems* of 1879 was followed in the 1880s by the series of six geographic treatises on Japan published in the nineteenth century.[2]

First of these geographies was that by Yao Wendong (b. 1852), *The Military Essentials of Japanese Geography* (*Riben dili bingyao*), published in 1884 by the Tongwen Guan of the International Office in Beijing.[3] Yao served as an attaché in the Chinese embassy between February 1882 and January 1888, and produced his monograph in rapid time, translating and adapting material—even his title—from a text by the Meiji scholar Nakane Shuku (1839–1913), *A Short Treatise on the Military Essentials of Japanese Geography* (*Heiyō Nihon chiri shōshi*).[4] Yao was perhaps the Chinese diplomat most outspoken about Japan's aggression in Taiwan, the Liuqiu Islands, and Korea.[5] His express purpose in *The Military Essentials* was to prepare Chinese troops for a possible military invasion of Japan; after all, Japanese army and navy personnel had already compiled an analogous text for their own use, *A Geographical Treatise on the Military Essentials of China* (*Shinkoku heiyō chiri shō*).[6] Accordingly, Yao focused on the geographic layout of each of Japan's nine "circuits," one per volume, and used extensive tables to minutely analyze Japan's topography, roads, locations of cities and landmarks, and access thereto. Although only the first volume of the ten-volume work treats the more typical subjects of geography—administrative structure, local customs, manufactures, and so on—the entire work has a historiographical cast since Yao presents each geographic region with a section on "successive administrative changes" (*yan'ge*), the history of local rule.

The second of these six geographies was Chen Jialin's *A Record of Things Seen and Heard on the Eastern Mission* (*Dong cha wenjian lu*), published in four volumes in 1887.[7] Chen served on the staff of (and was from the same home town as) the third ambassador to Japan, Xu Chengzu, from December 1884 to January 1888; although he did not claim to be producing a work of evidential research, his *Record* conforms to standards of the discipline—he uses Chinese points of reference, cites Chinese texts as corroborating evidence, and organizes the work as a series of specific notations on one topic after another, roughly sixty in all. In this regard, his text is more like a typical geographical treatise than is that by Yao Wendong, and as the pair of these monographs most available to Chinese until the Sino-Japanese War of 1894, the two texts nicely complement each other. Chen's work was well received, for sections of it are quoted and reproduced in later writings on Japan. Readers were perhaps responding to Chen's endorsement of Westernization, or to the novelty of a comprehensive geography of Japan. Nonetheless, the *Record of Things Seen and Heard* never attained the popularity of Huang Zunxian's *Poems on Divers Japanese Affairs*.

In 1887 the International Office acted on a proposal to send a small number of officials out on a world mission of investigation.[8] Of the twelve selected, Gu Houkun and Fu Yunlong (d. 1901) made extensive tours of Japan, and from their research compiled the third and fourth in this series of geographies.[9] The two of them arrived in Nagasaki in November 1887; Gu toured Japan during the first three months of 1888, and returned to Tokyo in early April to compile *An Examination of Japan's New Administration* (*Riben xinzheng kao*), before sailing on to North America in May. From all indications, it seems that Gu's text was published in 1888 in Japan, with the encouragement of Ambassador Li Shuchang.[10] Although Gu benefited from the research initiated by Yao Wendong and Chen Jialin—in fact, he quotes lengthy sections of Chen's *Record*—Gu's *Examination* differs substantially from the works of his predecessors. It is primarily a description of the new Japanese government's progress in major areas of administration—fiscal, military, industrial, educational, and organizational—with an emphasis on Westernization, but Gu also includes surveys of Japanese history and physical geography. What especially distinguishes Gu's work from that of his predecessors is the novelty of statistical tables, which constitute the greatest part of Gu's geographical representation.

By contrast, Fu Yunlong's *An Illustrated Monograph on Japan, Based on an Official Tour* (*Youli Riben tujing*) is a far more ambitious work.[11] Fu spent a total of eleven months at travel, research, and writing in Japan; in addition to the first stay between November 1887 and May 1888 (with his colleague Gu), he returned in 1889, from late May through October, during which time he completed both the writing and the printing of his massive thirty-volume monograph on Japan (as well as his prolific corpus of diaries, poetry, and geography from his two-year soujourn). The breadth of Fu's *Illustrated Monograph on Japan* is indicative of his wide investigations: astronomy, physical geography, political history, local customs, production and political economy, military and administrative systems, and so on. Although it is clear from certain details that he was guided by Chen Jialin's *Record of Things Seen and Heard* (examples below), he treats his range of geographic topics in greater detail than any of his predecessors. Moreover, as a self-conscious work of evidential research, Fu's monograph contains extensive cross-references on many of these topics, and displays a critical engagement with Japan unsurpassed in some respects to this day. Attempting to understand Japanese representations of themselves, Fu was the first Chinese official to investigate, for example, Japanese interpretations of Neo-Confucianism and Japanese "nativism" (*kokugaku*). In addition to these discussions of Japanese philosophy and language systems, Fu included bibliographies of Chinese books in Japan, and extensive rubbings of Japanese inscriptions and examples of Japanese belles-lettres in literary Chinese. Moreover, as indicated by the "Illustrated" in his title, he added a set of surveyors' topographical maps of Japan, the first such magnificently detailed representations (from copperplate etchings) available to Chinese eyes (map 1). Although the work was received favorably by some members of the court when Fu presented it to the throne in November 1889, it does not seem to have circulated widely.[12]

Far more obscure is the fifth geography, *Random Pickings from a Dragon Ride (Ce ao za zhi)*, by Ye Qingyi and Yuan Zuzhi (1827–1898), published privately in Shanghai in 1889. *Random Pickings* was not the product of an official commission, although its two authors had multiple contacts among Chinese and Japanese officials. Ye was the "younger brother" (or cousin) of Ye Songshi, a private scholar who had taught Chinese at the Japanese government language school in Tokyo sometime after the Meiji Restoration until 1876; in 1880 he returned to Japan and during this second stay, he arranged for his relation Ye Qingyi to spend two years in Japan, between 1881 and 1883.[13] Ye apparently took the materials gathered in Japan back to Shanghai, where Yuan Zuzhi later assisted him in the writing of the monograph. Yuan was the grandson of the celebrated poet Yuan Mei, and himself accompanied Tang Tingshu on the 1883 tour to investigate mining

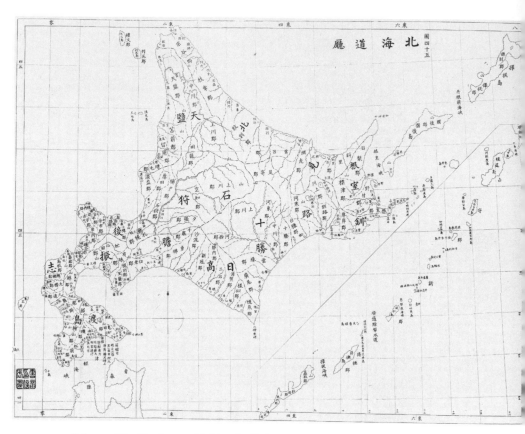

Map 1   The Prefecture Hokkaidō, Fu Yunlong, *Youli Riben tujing* (1889).
Reproduced by courtesy of the Harvard-Yenching Library, Harvard University.

technology in Europe.[14] Their eight-volume geography is indeed a somewhat "random" set of topics, more limited than most geographies but
nonetheless an effort at evidential research; they examine eight areas from
a historical perspective and cite textual corroboration whenever they can:
names for Japan in Chinese historiography, Japanese history, historical
geography, government administration, military organization, physical
geography, famous sites, and "unorthodox names"—names of Japanese
things that allegedly required explanation for Chinese. In addition, the
work is prefaced by an extensive collection of woodblock maps (map 2),
less fine than Fu Yunlong's but equally unprecedented in Chinese works on
Japan.

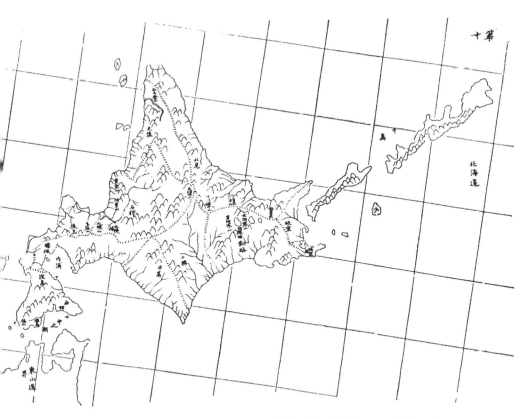

Map 2　The Circuit Hokkaidō, Ye Qingyi and Yuan Zuzhi, *Ce ao za zhi* (1889).
Reproduced by courtesy of the Harvard-Yenching Library, Harvard University.

　　The sixth and final geography to appear was Huang Zunxian's *Japan Treatise* (*Riben guozhi*). Although Huang began writing the work during his stay in Japan (1877–1881) and concurrently with his *Poems on Divers Japanese Affairs,* he did not finish it until 1887, nearly ten years later. The *Japan Treatise* is impressive, not only for its monumental size of forty volumes, but also for the care and reflection with which Huang interpreted his data. It covers much of the same material that Chen Jialin and Fu Yunlong covered contemporaneously, but Huang's work especially seeks to represent the historical significance of its information. Like Chen and Fu—and Ye Qingyi and Yuan Zuzhi as well—Huang generally reproduced the genre of local treatise, but like Yao Wendong and Gu Houkun, Huang included numerous tables and statistics; one might say that Huang's *Japan*

Objectification in the Geographic Treatise　163

Treatise, in terms of both form and analysis, is the most comprehensive of these geographies. Nonetheless, when Huang sent his *Treatise* to the International Office to be considered for publication, with Li Hongzhang and Zhang Zhidong's recommendations, the Office declined to print it. Only because of the crisis generated by the Sino-Japanese War, a time during which Huang's information gained the attention of the court, was the *Treatise* finally printed in 1895 and then reprinted thrice in 1898, so that it remains the best known of these texts today.[15]

The Local Treatise as a Model

As I explained at the beginning of this study, geography was early on affiliated with the claims of imperial rule. A branch of learning subordinate to historiography, geography undertook an account of the historical constitution of the territories subject to the administration of the Chinese emperor. E. Balazs has suggested that the prototypical genre in which geography was first represented, the *zhi* or "treatise," was from its inception in Sima Qian's *Shi ji* intended not only to serve as an aid to practical governing but also to deliberately mark an increased use of "rational" institutions in governing the empire—including laws, fiscal policy, education, and the civil and military bureaucracies.[16] While I do not endorse Balazs's (Weberian) assumption that the Chinese imperial bureaucracy was from early on a primarily rational form of government, certainly accurate is his observation that the treatise (and official history itself) was an innovation less dependent on the imperial family than on the imperial state, and, unlike earlier chronicle forms of historiography in China, was designed to transmit not merely the activities of the ruler but the general experience of statecraft and administration.[17]

In fact, the later, commonplace manifestation of the treatise as local history or gazetteer (*fangzhi*) was especially intended to offer a district magistrate the information that would help him govern his assigned district.[18] From the appearance of this "local treatise" during the Soong, district magistrates were periodically asked to compile or update local treatises, not only for their own use and that of their successors at the district office, but also for their superiors at the provincial and circuit levels. Several scholars have observed that the massive production of local treatises in the eighteenth century followed from the pair of official orders in 1672 and 1729 that each province compile a gazetteer; these would necessarily be based on the data provided by local, district treatises.[19] Given the promise of posterity that accompanied the compilation of such a local document, local degree-holders and landowners frequently cooperated in the work and financing of these texts in the eighteenth and nineteenth centuries.[20]

The six geographic representations of Japan produced in the 1880s were modeled after this genre of local treatise. To the degree that the local treatise had become a standard form for representations of local places subordinate to imperial centers (the imperial capital, the provincial capitals, and so on), it was a logical point of departure for geographers of Japan in the 1880s.[21] The attentive reader of examples of this genre will notice immediately three significant differences between, on the one hand, the local treatise, and on the other, the travelogue and travel poetry discussed earlier.

Characteristic Uses of Language

In the first place, local treatises and these geographies of Japan forgo poetic practices. With the sole exception of the metaphors in the two titles, *A Record of Things Seen and Heard on the Eastern Mission* and *Random Pickings from a Dragon Ride,* none of these authors deliberately reproduce the poetic images of Japan and overseas travel—Fusang, Xu Fu's journey, and so on. Only in two prefaces to the latter geography do we find poetic imagery; but these are pieces by poet associates of the authors, and made possible because this prefatory space is typically the only place within the geographic monograph that allows the authorial "I" a position from which to engage in representation, poetic or otherwise. Instead, these geographies all quite soberly inscribe the "objective" voice of history, emphasizing not connotative (or "suggestive") uses of words as in poetry but denotative uses of words to refer as explicitly as possible to things in the world (the so-called referential or first-order function of language). Interestingly, *Random Pickings* includes an entire section examining the facticity of names for Japan in Chinese histories, one purpose of which is to minimize their poetic status as images. The authors trace the appearances of names like "Fusang" and "Wonu" through Chinese texts, and based on existing philological and textual evidence, evaluate the appropriateness of such names. "Wonu" ("Dwarf"), for example, they conclude,

> was the name of a racial type, and not the name of a state. These people lived on the remote edges of northeastern Japan, and later moved to Hokkaidō, where they mingled with the Xiayi people, and from that point became a different people who are today known as the Aina or Ainu. Japan was early on called the "Wo Kingdom," until the Tang period, when Japanese traveled frequently to China [and Chinese learned of the name "Riben" for Japan]. During the Tang, many people called Japan the "Wo Kingdom," and Japanese became used to the name; but later, for a name that sounded better, the character was changed from "wo" to "huo."[22]

This quotation attests to the elimination of the first-person "I" from the local treatises and these geographies of Japan, in favor of the conventional and declarative third-person voice of historiography (the "enounced"). The official or impersonal voice of historical geography here reflects a conscious effort to absent the speaker; the author invisible in the text assumes a distanced, omniscient, and transparent position, as if inviting the reader to assume the position of transcendental ego. This is not the complex dialogue of poetic practice, where voices of the present and past recombine in a discourse affirming a common history. Rather, facts are "simply" presented as they are supposed to occur, and we are to understand this impersonal voice as inscribing the objective truth of historical fact.

Only in prefaces and colophons do authors speak of the individual will responsible for producing the text; this is usually an account of the circumstances under which the author(s) undertook the project of writing the text. Friends, relations, teachers, or bureaucratic superiors may also write such pieces, which are typically commendations of the author and his work. In short, prefaces and colophons in the geographic monograph are no different from prefaces and colophons to travel diaries and poetry. Like virtually all Chinese textual genres, the geographic monograph permits the addition of personal statements relating text and authorial experience. But in the geographic monograph, "I" is restricted to this prefatory or appendant position.

It is remarkable, in this regard, that Huang Zunxian invokes an archaic persona in order to make room for a personal voice within his *Japan Treatise*. In the previous chapter, I discussed the ingenuity with which he synthesized poetic and historiographical forms in writing his *Poems on*

Divers Japanese Affairs; similarly, his *Japan Treatise* modifies the geographic monograph in order to introduce his own modest evaluations of the information he presents. As Huang explains in his "Prefatory Remarks," the office of "counselor" (*canzan*), which he held at the Chinese embassy in Japan, corresponds to the ancient Zhou positions of both (1) "junior messenger" (*xiaoxingren*), who was to compile information on the conditions of the people within the four directions, particularly rites and customs, administrative affairs, and punishments; and (2) "outer historian" (*waishi* or "external scribe"), who was supposed to compile treatises on the people within the "four directions."[23] As a representative of the sovereign, Huang took it upon himself to inquire into Japanese affairs so as to faithfully report to the court information that would assist its deliberations and policies. Accordingly, each of his topical volumes begins with the declaration, "The Outer Historian states," which we are to read as a sign that the commentary and information that follows is a report by the "outer historian."[24] Huang's objective voice is an assumed disguise, and it is a testament to his preference for and conviction about the genuineness of poetry that he so curiously adopts the persona of "outer historian." He places himself outside of his preferred poetic discourse in order to represent Japanese history and geography in an expository mode.[25]

The Content of the Form

In addition to this characteristic use of language in the local treatise—the denotative or objective use of words and the impersonal or official voice—there is a second and even more generic element that both distinguishes the local treatise and these geographies of Japan from the travelogue and poetry, and identifies what I have described as an *expository* epistemological strategy. This is the sequence of information given by the form of the local treatise itself. The local treatise represents geographic space objectified in terms of administrative units—most commonly (in the Qing structure of government) the district (*xian*), the department (*zhou*), or the prefecture (*fu*). The geographic and administrative unit is represented as an inventory of topics, and each topic is substantiated with appropriate and specific facts, examples, and other such details. In this regard, my designation of "expository" becomes quite literal: this form of knowledge is a "setting forth" or "display."

Since the set of topics was not fixed absolutely, and since the filling in of a given topic depended upon local circumstances, the contents of a local treatise vary slightly from one to another. But in general, each local treatise draws from a rather circumscribed set, and consequently its contents are much more predictable than the more personal geographic genres.[26] Consider the following list, a composite of various representations of the "typical" contents of the local treatise.[27] I have indicated repeated items among these representations of the "typical" with italics:

1. Prefatory remarks
2. Maps and city plans
3. *Historical development of the district borders*
4. *Mountains and rivers*
5. *Famous or ancient sites*
6. *Official buildings, city walls, schools*
7. Buddhist and Daoist temples
8. *Bridges, canals, irrigation systems*
9. *Officeholders*
10. Examinations
11. *Census and taxes*
12. Markets, tolls, and barriers
13. *Local products*
14. Local customs
15. *Local worthies, officials, virtuous women*
16. Exorcists, magicians, Buddhist and Daoist monks
17. *Local inscriptions and tombs*
18. *Local writings and bibliographies*
19. Chronicles of disasters and omens
20. Miscellaneous records

As we see, the local treatise moves from the historical and "natural" geography of the district and its landscape (2–5) to descriptions of the physical infrastructure of the district (6–8), and then to the contributions of district personnel to the system of imperial administration (9–10). This is the place and material of administration. The treatise then turns to the objects of administration—household censuses, taxes, markets, and local products (11–13). Finally, it examines local customs (14) and the local written record so as to record what I might call evidence of a history of civilizing administration: biographies of celebrated individuals (15–16) (in the manner of official history); local evidence of history, learning, and erudition (17–18); and a history of manifestations of Heaven's signs (19). This pattern is generally followed not only by the Ming geographers of Japan, but also by the Qing geographers of the 1880s, with some important additions and modifications: treatises of "foreign domains" include histories of both the domain and its relations with the Chinese court; and they treat with greater specificity the means of administration—in addition to "examinations" and "census and taxes," they include topics like military systems, laws and punishments, and so on. In this regard, we might say that the geographic treatise on Japan comes full circle, in that it begins with the model of the local treatise but emulates the scale of an official history, the very form that had earlier engendered the local treatise.[28]

Two observations regarding these formal contents are in order. In the first place, this conceptual framework of geographic analysis in the local treatise is an outgrowth of one of the earliest Chinese examples of *leishu* or "encyclopedia," the *Explanation of Names* (*Shi ming*) by the second-century-A.D. scholar Liu Xi. Liu Xi's classificatory scheme reflected the ancient Chinese conception of kingship; as the king was the "Unique Man" who united Heaven, Earth, and man, so the *Explanation of Names* and many later encyclopedias divide all things into those three basic divisions.[29] Although this structure was modified over time and is less evident in the local treatise, where Heaven's signs (if included) are treated as local history and placed toward the end of the text, the basic tripartite division of phenomena is pronounced in the geographies of Japan: Chen Jialin, Fu Yunlong, and Huang Zunxian place "Heaven's patterns"—time zones, calendrical practices, climate, and so on—near the beginnings of their respective representations of Japan; physical geography ("Earth") and man's activities follow. In short, the set of categorical divisions into which the geographical object of scholarship was to be analyzed was highly conventional, roughly as long-lived as the imperial state and official history, and grounded in the imperial ideology of rule.

In the second place, this inventory of topics was ideally a *comprehensive* representation of its geographic object. Unlike the travelogue or poetry, the unity of which was personally determined by the itinerary of the traveler or the idiosyncratic selectivity and inspiration of the poet, the form of the local treatise imposed an external and predetermined structure onto its object. In the local treatise, geographic place is not a chronological sequence of geohistorical sites, but an abstracted set of topics. In this regard, it is a much more "orthodox" or "standard" representation of geography than these other personal and performative genres. As a mode of analysis closely associated with the imperial state, the local treatise was a *bureaucratic* form of knowledge, a standardized and disciplined practice that would facilitate the state's management of its localities.[30]

Useful Information

The third specific characteristic of the local treatise, then, is this putative utility of the genre. Clearly, a travelogue could record useful details, but making use of such details was an activity secondary to the primary purpose of recording one's journey. Similarly, poetry could record historical events, but making use of those historical details was an activity secondary to inspired expression. Indeed, these genres could be *made* useful—Gu Yanwu's important innovation was to use poetry for philological research— but the local treatise was *intended* to be useful. In short, the representation presented in the local treatise was to serve some practical use, and in two environments: the more immediate interests of district administration; and the more general interests of historiography.

To begin with, the utility of this series of topics appropriate to the concerns of district administration has been contextualized in a well-known statement relating utility and the objects of representation in the local treatise. Huang Liuhong (17th c.), known to many readers of Chinese history through Jonathan Spence's imaginative *The Death of Woman Wang*, compiled in the 1690s what was reportedly a quite popularly used and frequently reprinted administrative manual for district magistrates in the eighteenth and nineteenth centuries.[31] The third volume of the lengthy work, on the general subject of "assuming office," includes the following exhortation to "Study the Local Treatise":

> Mountains and rivers, noted inhabitants, tributes to the Imperial Court, local products, communities, temples, bridges, and so on are clearly recorded in the

local treatise. When the magistrate makes a thorough study of the local treatise he will be able to have a clear picture of the district's geographical layout, the amounts and rates of taxation, and the vital statistics and degree of prosperity of its population. This information is indispensable in planning his administration.

The temples and tombs of local celebrities and sages are places for people to worship; they should be kept in repair and sacrifices offered at proper intervals. Ancient relics and sacred places that have been obscured with the passage of time should be decorated with elaborate ornamentation. Centers of study must be graced with students who can write elegant compositions. All these sundry matters should receive the minute attention of the magistrate. Some magistrates may say that their time is consumed in reading documents and meeting deadlines; they wonder how they can afford to consider [these secondary matters]. But such an attitude risks resigning oneself to being a mediocre and indifferent administrator.

When I assumed the magistracy of Tancheng, it was considered a busy and arduous post. After having finished my official duties, I frequently found time to ride to the suburban areas. I paid respect to the Yu Tomb and issued an order prohibiting people from gathering firewood there. I paid a visit to the Youwu Grotto to enjoy its extraordinary beauty. I repaired the Wenguan Temple so that it looked like new, and restored the Qinggai Shrine to its original grandeur so as to revive our deep respect for the ancient sages. In addition, I repaved the street in front of the Jiebei Temple with flagstones and built the guest house at the Ten-mile Hamlet, so that travelers and visitors could enjoy comfort and ease. Although such matters are not a magistrate's first priority, magistrates who undertake them might avoid being labeled mediocre and indifferent administrators.[32]

Striking here is the attention paid to matters allegedly low in "priority"; only one statement has to do with business that one would initially assume to be at the heart of local administration—taxation, vital statistics like the census, and the general prosperity of the district. Huang instead places a greater stress on the issue of *ming,* the name and reputation of the magistrate, which will favorably accrue in proportion to his personal involvement with the historical sites native to the district. To Huang, lest one be considered mediocre and indifferent, the geographical layout of the district is a minimal degree of understanding that one should gain from the local treatise; it is more important that the magistrate take the treatise as a guide to how he can best experience and renew those elements of the district that share in the Civilization that he represents as magistrate. As an imperial official learned in the textual tradition of the ruling class, the magistrate ideally does more than the routine activities of maintaining schools, overseeing the examination system, reading imperial edicts, exhorting the wayward to remember their duties, and so on.[33] He safeguards the history of his district, so that under his tenure the sites of Civilization recorded in the local treatise continue to figure as memorable local sites for future revisions of the treatise. If he does this well, he may in turn be remembered favorably—and, incidentally, receive a promotion. The local treatise, in other words, was an account of the degree to which Civilization was manifested in the district; therein lies much of its utility to both the imperial Chinese state and local literate society. In addition to offering information useful to imperial administration, the local treatise confirmed the value and encouraged the success of that very activity—"rule by enlightening," or civilizing.[34]

At the same time, because geography was fundamentally motivated by a historiographical impulse, the local treatise was useful in a manner appropriate to historiography. It recorded information for future study and consultation. As the basic unit of official cultural production in imperial China, the local, *district* treatise assembled a range of information from which—as Zhang Xuecheng had envisioned—future and greater geographies and histories would be constructed.[35]

The term that most often figures in this context of utility is the commonplace sign *yong*—"to use," "use," and "useful." *Yong* does not represent any particular philosophical or historiographical position; it is but one manifestation of what A. C. Graham and other scholars have called China's long-term concern for the useful.[36] To use a thing for a tool, to use an encyclopedia to prepare for an examination, to use a local treatise for government administration—these are all common precedents to the widespread sense during the Qing period that scholarship could and should be useful. In the same way that Gu Yanwu and other early evidential research scholars demonstrated that the classics could be useful to hitherto unexplored branches of history, so Zhang Xuecheng declared that historiography, and the compilation of local treatises specifically, should produce texts that are useful. It was not enough to delve into the past. The historian's proper task was to show how the present diverged from the time of the ancient sages; this would ensure that a local treatise was not only useful to men in the present, but would be useful to future generations.[37]

Utility as Means and End

It is this potential utility to scholarship and other future purposes that is most pronounced in the six geographies of Japan. As the set of regulations and injunctions to the members of the 1887 mission of investigation specified, officials

should record in detail for future study the following: general topography, strategic passes, natural defenses and distances; and local customs, government administration, naval forces, fortifications, factories, steamships and railroads, buoyant mines, and arsenals.

In addition,

All officials who have the mind for investigation and study of the speech and writing of the various countries—as well as astronomy, mathematics, chemistry, mechanics, electricity, optics, and all sciences of measurement and the physical world—may turn their notebooks over to the International Office for future reference.[38]

"Future study and reference" is the purpose proposed for readers of the texts that may result from the mission, but precisely how a text is to be used for such an end is not specified. From the point of view of everyday or scholarly experience, this is a moot point—one opens a historiographical or geographical text and finds useful information therein. On the one hand, then, utility is deferred; it is a potential that is available when the appropriate reader appears, and indeed, grammatical forms reflect such a deferral: *ke yong,* the text "can be used" by an implied but unspecified reader at an unspecified time; or *you yong,* the declaration that the text "is useful" generally, without regard for reader or purpose. Utility may be a deliberate intention in the geographical treatise, but the actualization of that attribute of the text depends upon the future reader and his or her own specific motives.

But on the other hand, some texts specify uses more goal-oriented than "future study and reference." Yao's text will aid in planning an invasion of Japan; Huang's text will assist the court in its deliberations; both Chen and Gu hope to inspire Chinese with the example of a strong and independent Japan. Given the added complications of methodology—that Fu and Ye, for example, claim to offer "substantive learning" about Japan; that Huang,

Fu, and Ye claim to undertake evidential research of Japan—the question arises: how are we to relate the conscious variety and seemingly multiple purposes of the information in these texts to the putative utility of this *form* of geographic representation?

This is not an idle question, because at least two scholars who have previously evaluated these geographies have criticized them for a fundamental *uselessness*. In their estimation, motivated by the analysis of diplomatic history, these texts failed to alert the Chinese to the inevitability of the Sino-Japanese War of 1894, and so failed to prompt Chinese leaders to take the necessary measures that might have prevented the war from happening.[39] Such an interpretation, which foregrounds the authors' position of hindsight, does not seriously consider the Chinese intention to produce useful knowledge of Japan in the 1880s. The confusion here, I believe, is due to mistaking utility as an end for utility as means.

Historians have not yet considered the transition between the practical and the representational in the texts they examine. How do we begin to interpret a writer's intentions for his text to be read and used, a reader's abstractions from a text so as to make it useful, or a text's ability to effect movement from its representations to its practical utility? To claim that a text is useful raises the issue of *agency*—not who might use it (agent), nor why it is useful (purpose), but how it is used: *the text as a means* for some agent with some purpose.[40] In other words, the claim that a text is useful specifies both a property of the text itself and some action that a reader may undertake with a text; the text harbors a potentiality and an instrumentality.

Consider first the more straightforward case, the text that represents a series of procedures for the reader to follow—the cookbook, the computer software manual, or those sections of Yao Wendong's military geography that instruct one on navigating Japan. The author of such a manual represents a level of competence that is presumed to be recoverable by the reader. But as anyone who has tasted a failed recipe or called software support in confusion knows, there is often a significant gap between the representation and the use to which it is put. That is, there often exists a level of abstraction or experience that remains invisible to any effort to provide practical information in a textual representation. Either an acclimated writer fails to account for some level of abstraction or experience that he has overlooked, or the ignorant reader fails to abstract that prerequisite information or experience from the representation he attempts to put to use. Yao Wendong may begin his geography with a description of nine routes for penetrating Japanese waters, but that representation presumes both a vast knowledge of handling a ship and, more specifically, correct identification of the places one is supposed to take as landmarks.[41] While one may glean such information elsewhere in his text—much of Yao's geography describes passages through the landscape of Japan—Yao's representation does not instruct the reader as to securing provisions in Japan, dealing with the natives, and the host of potential contingencies that could affect one's progress through the landscape. Moreover, his representation runs the risk of obsolescence; the Japanese were building new bridges, roads, and railroads during the 1880s, all of which modified the landscape. The aspiring Chinese invader of Japan could certainly have used, for example, Fu Yunlong's updated information on lighthouses, a subject that Yao Wendong omits.[42] This is all to say, for even the most instrumental a text, such instrumentality is at best potential; the text *as a means* does not guarantee its applicability for some user's purpose.

Now consider the more problematic second case, the text that claims to be useful but does not signify its applicability. It offers no series of procedures nor indications of how it is to be used. Since the instrumentality of such a text is not identified, the agency of such a text remains potential; how it is used depends upon the agent and his or her purpose. In other words, to claim that such a text is useful is to say that the text is useful *in and of itself*.

This, I submit, is the case with Chinese histories and geographic treatises. Although Chinese early on offered an explanation as to the utility of history, in a metaphorical statement to the effect that history is like a mirror, reflecting our present distance from a golden age of antiquity, this was not a description of a process, as with "poetry verbalizes intention." Aside from a serious interest in drawing analogies from the past (see chapter 6), Chinese did not much philosophize as to precisely *how* history was to be used, or what aspect of it lent a reader its utility. Accordingly, histories and geographic treatises maintain a deliberate ambiguity of agency and purpose. The distinction between *how* and *why* such a text is used collapses into the concept of "useful." When Huang Liuhong urges a magistrate to study the local treatise, or when Huang Zunxian anticipates that his geography will assist the court in its deliberations, each confirms the assumption that a text's objectifications convey knowledge that is useful to administration, which is by definition its own method and purpose. Utility, in other words, is both means and end in the geographic treatise.

This administrative context of the production of geographic treatises helps to better explain the profoundly conservative documentary ideal of the Chinese geographies of Japan. Unlike a performative text, in which writing and reading were understood to be complementary aspects of the representation itself, and understood to be in a homological relationship to inner intention producing the writing and the external scene prompting the writing, the geographic treatise was an effect of the bureaucratic organization of government and knowledge. Because the point of contact (or observation) was removed from the point of application (or utility), the *form* of the geographic treatise was its most pertinent aspect. When geographers reproduced the categories of the local treatise, they were assured of the "obvious" utility of their text. The documentary ideal—to record facts as found and according to prescribed categories—served to guarantee that a fact would find its place in a reader's subsequent characterizations.[43]

Strategies of Objectification

This is not to say that the compilation of a geographic treatise was reduced to being an exercise in mere "technique" (*jishu*). On the contrary. Chinese denigration of technique, as when "historicist" officials dismissed Western science for its overemphasis on technique at the expense of moral principle (see chapter 1), was a criticism of utility as means alone. As an instance of historiographical method, the geographic treatise interested nineteenth-century readers as means and end in two ways, both of which were key attributes of the author's exposition of the facts: his strategies of objectification and his organization of the whole.

In the first place, the grounding of this form of knowledge is the deliberate work of *objectification*, that set of procedures executed by the observer-geographer in constructing a representation of Japan. Foremost among these procedures, or "strategies," are the habits of abstraction and analysis, which are among the sensibilities one acquires in the course of initiation into literate society. In that regard, abstraction and analysis operate at the points of both observation (or perception) and inscription (or representation). What best characterizes objectification in the geographic treatise is that the knowledge so produced is both abstract and concrete. It is "abstract" in that it is removed from experience and all evidence of personal connections to its object is effaced (or, more accurately, is restricted to preface or colophon). In being abstract, the knowledge of Japan represented in the geographic treatise is removed from its social context: it is not performative.[44] At the same time, this knowledge is concrete. One main goal of objectification is to delineate the constituent elements of Japan, and this is best accomplished by presenting concrete detail. In this regard, "concrete" is comparable to the Chinese conception of *shi,* often translated as "substantive" or "actual."[45] In fact, two of the six geographies of Japan— the one by Fu Yunlong and the other by Ye Qingyi and Yuan Zuzhi—are praised for their "substantive learning" (*shixue*). In any case, Chinese readers of all these texts were especially interested in concrete detail of Japan, and evaluations of the six stress that the texts are informative and useful; Huang Zunxian's *Japan Treatise,* according to Zhang Zhidong, should be mandatory reading for all diplomatic personnel sent to Japan.[46]

In addition to praise for the considerable efforts of these authors at objective representation—as well as their skills at evidential research or substantive learning—we find among commentators a pronounced attentiveness to *organization.* The preponderance of critical acclaim focuses on the Chinese word *tiao,* meaning "orderly"—from a neatly branched tree, to the orderly contents of a book, to properly organized branches of learning. In other words, *tiao* connotes a degree of satisfaction resulting from a systematic and well-proportioned organization. Four specific terms predominate in praise of these geographies: (1) *tiaolie,* to "arrange" or "array" the material in an orderly manner; (2) *tiaofen,* to "delineate" or "analyze" the material in an orderly manner; (3) *tiaoli,* to order the material "with suitable proportions"; and (4) *tiaoli,* to arrange the material "reasonably" or "according to principle." Many instances of these expressions are accompanied by the words *xiang* or *xi,* both of which mean "detailed." Apparently, Chinese readers of geographic treatises were quite absorbed by the variety and presentation of facts. In the absence of argument, personal narrative, poetic language, and other such experiential approaches, the interest of the Chinese reader was engaged by a text's "strategies of objectification," those procedures by which geographers determine and enumerate the features and characteristics of the central object, Japan. For it was these strategies, I am convinced, that constituted the utility of the treatise form.

Patterns of Abstraction

A first and perhaps most obvious strategy of objectification is abstraction, which refers most simply to the placement of things in the geographical representation. Insofar as abstraction is the groundwork of classification (the work of identifying similarities and differences among abstracted qualities of objects so as to arrange and classify objects), the received inventory of topics in the local treatise is the basis of abstraction for the geographies of Japan. But, as I mentioned earlier, the items included in any treatise depended in part upon local conditions; in the case of Japan, a given geographer's placement of things in his representation was mitigated by the conditions under which he sought to gather information: what he was specifically looking for; what he had access to; and what he happened upon. In other words, patterns of abstraction in a geography reflect a compromise between received categories and the contingencies of choice and availability.

Consider the example of "learning" (*xue*). Although "learning" is a matter central to Chinese Civilization and easily identified in Japan by Chinese geographers, there is little consensus among these six geographies as to the placement of learning. Yao Wendong ignores the subject entirely. Neither Gu Houkun nor Ye Qingyi treats the subject as an independent item; both divide the civil school system—as "administration" and "bureaucracy" respectively—from military schools, reflecting a traditional understanding of learning as an activity essentially preparatory for the more important matters of central government administration. Their classification accordingly assumes that higher-level point of view.[47] Chen Jialin, by contrast, treats the subject in two sections, "schools" (*xuexiao*) and "writing" (*wenzi*), each of which is primarily a historical account of the development of Japanese institutions, from Chinese models to recent Western models.[48] Only Fu Yunlong and Huang Zunxian objectify learning as an independent unity: Fu presents the history of Japanese schools of learning, the background of Japanese writing and various theories of language, and extensive data on the contemporary school system in his two-volume section, "textual learning" (*wenxue*);[49] Huang includes even more in his own two-volume section, "scholarship" (*xueshu*), organized methodically into Chinese learning, Western learning, writing, and the school system.[50] As is so often the case in comparisons of these six texts, Chen, Fu, and Huang are most intent on reproducing the form of the local treatise and so their inventories of topics most carefully parallel that system of abstraction.

Be that as it may, these strategies of abstraction reflect authorial evaluations, which place material according to one or another intellectual convention. Consider an item especially "Japanese" to the Chinese geographer: Shinto ("Way of the Gods"), the indigenous religious tradition for which a Chinese model is not readily apparent. Neither Gu Houkun nor Ye Qingyi mentions Shinto specifically, even though aspects of the religion are present in their accounts of the genealogy of the Japanese gods and their lists of governmental offices within the Imperial Household Ministry and Home Ministry that oversee (Shinto) shrines and ceremonies.[51] Shinto as an object does not fit within their systems of abstractions. Yao Wendong and Chen Jialin, by contrast, simply note the existence of—not Shinto (*shendao*), but—what they call the "Shin teaching" (*shenjiao*) in their respective sections on "local customs"; it figures with Confucianism, "Westernism," and Buddhism as one of four important teachings in Japan.[52] At issue, then, in the objectification of Shinto are two matters: whether it is indeed a (moral) "way" or merely a sectarian teaching; and whether or not it qualifies as an element of learning. Fu Yunlong uses the designation "Shin teaching" but treats it is an element of learning; he explains this placement by claiming that Shin teaching is a Japanese adaptation of two Chinese teachings, Buddhism and Daoism.[53] Huang Zunxian, by contrast, agrees with Yao and Chen that Shinto is a "custom," but he uses the Japanese appellation, "Shinto," in spite of its inherent universalistic claim as a "Way."[54] If Fu's account is rather far-fetched by our contemporary understanding, and Huang's fuller and more accurate, the two nonetheless reproduce the claim that Shinto was brought to Japan by that original predecessor, Xu Fu. In both cases, Shinto confirms the precedence of Chinese Civilization.

Although some evaluation is evident in the abstracting of phenomena like learning or Shinto, the primary concern of these geographers is not to evaluate a phenomenon, but to simply name it, so as to place it within the pattern of abstractions that composes Japan. Consider the placement of a novel object, the newspaper. Some geographers cite newspapers as the source of certain information, but do not abstract the newspaper as a singular phenomenon.[55] Chen Jialin treats newspapers under "local customs," described as mandatory reading for those interested in knowledge of contemporary affairs.[56] Gu Houkun and Huang Zunxian, by contrast, treat the newspaper as an element of "Western affairs" and "Western learning" respectively; it is a recent introduction to Japan from the West that disseminates knowledge of contemporary affairs far and wide, and both Gu and Huang present extensive lists of the major newspapers in Japan.[57] What is interesting here is that as the Chinese geographers began to abstract the newspaper as an object, they located it according to different conceptions. To Chen, the newspaper is yet another Japanese curiosity, like Shinto or smoking or bathing habits; to Gu, it is a major Western institution like the railroad or postal system; and to Huang, a handmaiden to Western learning like the library or museum. It is the conception informing each such abstraction, and not the implicit evaluation per se, that confirms the utility of the representation. For insofar as the fact of "newspaper" has been abstracted as one or another kind of thing, that very conception in itself demonstrates one useful characterization of "newspaper." Given more information about the newspaper, another useful quality may be abstracted.

Historical Depth

A second strategy of objectification is historical depth, the degree to which a geographer treats the historical constitution of an object. At one extreme is a "presentist" approach; the geographer like Gu Houkun represents only contemporary phenomena. At the other extreme is a "historicist" approach, in which the geographer not only describes the historical background of the phenomenon but cites Chinese and Japanese texts by way of substantiating this history. Fu Yunlong is the geographer most consistently given to this technique.

One central factor guiding the geographer's degree of historical depth is of course the degree to which he both perceived and attempted to represent historical change under way in his object. The example of administrative geography especially demonstrates repeated ways in which history figured in geographical representation. During the time that these men were in Japan, the Japanese government was finalizing a change in administrative structure, begun in 1871, that disbanded the former domains (*han*) of the Tokugawa lords and created the system of prefectures (*ken*) still used today. Accordingly, to observe and to represent the system of administrative districts in Japan during the 1870s and eighties was to negotiate two sets of representations. On the one hand, there was the older organization of Japan into nine circuits and eighty-two provinces, a process begun in 645 and most recently revised in 1869 with the incorporation of the northernmost island and circuit of Hokkaidō.[58] Insofar as many Japanese geographies of their own land were organized in this manner, such a geographical representation was strongly historicist. On the other hand, there was the evolving administrative structure of forty-some prefectures (with a few municipal districts), which constituted the basis of government-sponsored education, economic, and political policies, and generated an increasing quantity of statistics. This afforded a strongly presentist representation. When Chinese geographers determined to represent this shift from domains to prefectures, they objectified the process as *yan'ge,* or "successive changes." Although only Yao Wendong, Fu Yunlong, and Huang Zunxian represent the process in such a way, most of the geographers included some of the historical background of administrative geography, by referring either to the circuit and province system or to the domainal system of Tokugawa.[59]

In addition to the geographer's perceptions of historical change, a second factor guiding historical depth is his engagement with evidential research. The item "official corps" or "bureaucracy" (*zhiguan*) is a telling example, since it discloses familiar motives related to this representation of history. Yao Wendong, Chen Jialin, and Ye Qingyi contextualize the recent changes in Japanese governmental institutions as a shift from a feudal (*fengjian*) to an administrative districts (*junxian*) system, after which they describe a range of past and present offices and officials, along with their functions and ranks.[60] This context of feudal and administrative districts systems is an analogy from Chinese history, connoting the shift from the pre-imperial Zhou kingship to the imperial state inaugurated by Qin Shi Huang, the first emperor. Such use of history is by now familiar—it establishes the precedence of Chinese experience. A similar usage of history is the observation, by Chen Jialin, Fu Yunlong, and Huang Zunxian, that the establishment of government in Japan was based on the Tang dynastic system (618–906).[61] Both of these precedents are quite limited in scope; the shift from feudal to administrative districts applies narrowly to the shift from the Minamoto, Ashikaga, and Tokugawa shogunates to the modern Meiji state, while the Tang precedent applies to the attempt to create a Chinese-style imperial state in the Asuka and Nara periods (552–794). Neither precedent accounts for indigenous and long-term Japanese developments in any detail; each locates Japan in terms of some Chinese experience. But Fu Yunlong goes further and takes a different approach—that of evidential research; in his disquisition on the "official corps," he quotes passages on the subject of Japanese government from China's official histories, beginning with *The Wei Treatise* (see chapter 1), thereby generating a Chinese history of Japanese government that serves to introduce his discussion of past and present offices and officials.[62] Fu's goal is similar to that of Huang Zunxian in the *Poems on Divers Japanese Affairs*—to account for the origins of Japan from the perspective of Chinese textual practice. Only Gu Houkun neglects the history of central government administration in Japan; he is content to describe the structure of the current central government.[63]

It is curious, in this regard, that the geographers most committed to evidential research—Fu Yunlong, Ye Qingyi and Yuan Zuzhi, and Huang Zunxian—include what are in effect two histories of Japan. One is based largely in Chinese texts and recounts the history of Chinese interactions with the places successively known as Japan. Fu, and Ye and Yuan, array extensive quotations from Chinese texts in chronological order to construct this history, while Huang produces a less ethnocentric account by extensively quoting Japanese documents.[64] The second history reflects imperial Japanese history, beginning with the age of the gods and following the genealogy of the Japanese emperors.[65]

Representing the historical constitution of the object, in sum, becomes the occasion for introducing multiple accounts into the geography that tries to be complete. In the first place, the availability of multiple points from which to perceive the object—be they presentist or historicist—permits geographers to sequence a number of representations. In the second place, the disciplinary standards of evidential research encourage geographers to segregate those elements of Japan that are amenable to evidential research; these segments are then developed as individual topics or sections within the overall pattern of abstraction. In both cases, the issue is not as much synthesis (or a lack thereof) as it is *distribution*. Given the formal structure of the geographical treatise, historical depth enriches a representation by diversifying its object—that is, by increasing either the quantity of detail or the number of scholarly approaches to the object. Ironically, it is the objective and official stance of the author in the geographic treatise that makes such a multivocal representation of Japan possible. Where the poet Huang Zunxian could skeptically dismiss Japanese stories of the gods, the geographer Huang Zunxian duly records the Japanese history of their gods and emperors. "Objectivity" in historical representations means recording as factual some details that critical thought might otherwise ignore.

Degree of Analysis

Technically, analysis is a set of procedures for resolving a whole into its parts. As a third strategy of objectification, analysis refers to the degree of detail represented in the objectification. With respect to the organization of the geographic treatise into topical "systems," two issues are pertinent: (a) whether or not the constituent parts of a general system are further represented as constituting units of a lower order; and (b) the simple quantity of specific detail substantiating features or characteristics of the object. So, for example, representations of the central government "bureaucracy" or "official corps" may present the various ministries either as details substantiating the whole, as do Yao Wendong, Chen Jialin, and Gu Houkun, or as details which in turn constitute a second order of units described in further detail. Obviously, this is a matter of degree, and this second case—which we find in Fu Yunlong, Ye Qingyi, and Huang Zunxian—is the more extensive and detailed treatment. Regarding the Ministry of Agriculture and Commerce, for example, Chen Jialin reports in a footnote: "The Ministry of Agriculture and Commerce, in the manner of the preceding ministries, has a minister of agriculture and commerce, a vice minister, a secretary, a consultant, and a legal officer. In addition, it has the following departments: General Affairs, Agriculture, Commerce, Industry, Marine Production, Forestry, Geology, Mining, and Accounting."[66] Huang Zunxian, by contrast, spends three pages on the Ministry of Agriculture and Commerce, relating the historical background of the ministry and describing in detail its officials and departments and the responsibilities of each; elsewhere, in an extensive comparative table of the entire government, he displays the number and ranks of positions in the ministry.[67]

Similarly, representations of Japan's military system differ in their degree of analysis. Given that this was a matter of intense interest to Chinese committed to "self-strengthening," it is curious that only Gu Houkun and Huang Zunxian reproduce the bifurcation central to the Japanese system, the division between army and navy. The others represent the military as it existed in China, a monolithic structure in which "water forces" were but another subdivision within the army.[68] Generally, these representations of the military system are given over to data in tabular form—the number of armies and units, their size and location, their numbers of officers and enlisted men; the number of reserves; the number, locations, and size of fortifications; the kind, quantity, and size of ships, when and where each was made; and so on. Fu Yunlong includes even a statistical table entitled "Height of Army Recruits," which informs the reader of the number of army recruits for 1886 by regional division and body height in increments of one "inch."[69] Clearly, detail used to substantiate features of an object can become excessive if not absurd quantification, but this is an effect of the Chinese realization that the Japanese enthusiasm for government maintenance of statistics—a new "Western method"—served an eminently useful purpose.[70]

At the same time, we might consider the degree of analysis in light of patterns of abstraction: a geographer may perceive some phenomenon as being a unity or constituting a "system," and so abstract it as a topic. Take, for example, the matter of "personal qualities" or "human feeling" (renqing). This was both an issue central to Neo-Confucianism and a subject of long-standing provincial stereotypes among Chinese. To the former, a question was formulated as to whether or not feelings were grounded in material force (qi) and therefore opposed to rational principle (li); to the latter, it was merely a series of useful generalizations—that the Hunanese were hot-headed, the Cantonese avaricious, and so on.[71] The latter information was arguably pertinent to a geographer, and in the context of Japan, some of our texts include the topic renqing, so as to give the reader a stereotypical understanding of the respective regional characteristics of the Japanese people:

The people of the Tōkaidō are insightful, quick-witted, and straightforward; the people of Kai strong and fearsome. Inhabitants of Tokyo are chivalrous but super-ficial. The people of Kazusa and Shimoosa are gentle, even friendly, while those in Hitachi are warlike and stubborn. In Kinai, people are creative and precise. In Kyoto, refined but frugal; in Osaka, entrepreneurial if not vulgar.[72]

And so on. Yao Wendong, Chen Jialin, and Fu Yunlong borrow this representation directly from Nakane Shuku's *A Short Treatise on the Military Essentials of Japanese Geography*; they find it worth repeating as an element of "local customs."[73] The others, by contrast, do not perceive "personal qualities" so systematically; they instead make stray references to this sort of stereotype in the context of "geography." Ye Qingyi and Yuan Zuzhi note in their discussion of Kyoto that the scenery is delicate, the people elegant; Huang Zunxian notes in his description of Kōchi that its people are pure and innocent, and as for Kai, its people ferocious.[74] But as "outer historian," Huang also explains in his introduction to "local customs" that he is at a loss as to how to account for "personal qualities." Given that all people are the same the world over, and differ only in the matter of their customs, he would think of people as learning habits from their parents and rulers, and not as having some essential "qualities" determined by geography.[75] Analysis, in other words, may potentially modify the system of abstractions.

Modes of Presentation

As a fourth strategy of objectification, presentation refers to the mode or *form* in which information is presented. The three such modes most common in the geographic treatises of Japan are prose, the list, and the table.[76] There are long-standing precedents for these modes of presentation in standard historiography. Most of the contents of official histories are in prose form, and lists figured in the treatises from early on. The table is a relatively recent development. Although the majority of official histories include chronological tables, which synchronize multiple dating systems or coordinate events in the lives of imperial rulers and their family members, the use of tables in official histories to represent other kinds of information did not occur until the fourteenth century. According to Lien-sheng Yang, tables were an innovation in the *History of the Liao* and *History of the Jin,* where they were used to coordinate, respectively, imperial visits over time and diplomatic envoys over time.[77] Not until the eighteenth century were tables extensively used in geography for presentation and explanation.[78] Although Huang Zunxian does begin his *Japan Treatise* with the earlier and standard variety of table, a "China-Japan Chronological Table," the use of tables in the geographies of Japan accords more generally with these later developments. As I have mentioned, Chinese geographers were encouraged by the Japanese enthusiasm for statistical tables.

There is no determinate relationship between mode and object of presentation. Certainly personal idiosyncracy is a factor, as well as the form in which information was received by Chinese geographers from Japanese sources. Yao Wendong and Huang Zunxian use primarily prose and tables, Chen Jialin and Ye Qingyi prose and lists, and Gu Houkun lists and tables; only Fu Yunlong moves frequently among the three modes. Since the three are used interchangeably among the six geographies, it would seem that the deciding criterion is a threshold of quantity (and its attendant complexity). "Latitude and longitude," for example, is not abstracted as an independent topic in the works of Yao Wendong and Ye Qingyi, but figures as a detail within the topic of "territory" (*jiangyu,* or "borders and perimeters"). Accordingly, they have a rather easy time of describing Japan's latitude and longitude in prose: "Japan lies at the eastern edge of the Asian continent on the eastern half of the globe; its latitude is from thirty to forty-six degrees north of the equator, and its longitude, measuring from Tokyo, is eastward ten degrees and westward eleven degrees."[79] The other four geographies include separate sections on latitude and longitude, and so resort to other modes for their increased quantity of data. Chen Jialin lists the main islands and their latitudes and longitudes; his representation is quite difficult to follow, since each island name and numerical figure is qualified by a footnote, which together eliminate the independent coherence of each item.[80] Gu Houkun converts Chen's data for islands into a more readable table, Huang Zunxian includes a table of figures for all provinces, and Fu Yunlong a table of coordinates of all prefectures, which he prefaces with an unusually discriminating discussion of the problem of selecting a standard point of reference.[81] The quantity of information here makes the table a more accessible mode of presentation; where one must read through all of Chen's list, line by line, in order to have a grasp of the whole, one need only read place-names across the top of the others' tables and find the values for latitude and longitude arrayed below.

And yet accessibility is not from the viewpoint of the detail. Geographic treatises are organized from the top down, so to speak; the systematic inventory of topics and their respective subjects is the point of reference. As Wolfgang Bauer has observed, there are two fundamental forms of encyclopedic arrangement: the phonetic, determined by the particulars of language and culture; and the material, which mimics the "natural order" given by culture.[82] Chinese geographies are of the latter sort, and although they attempt to provide a comprehensive representation of the world, they do not facilitate location of specific information. To repeat, utility lies in the overall organization. One might be hard pressed, for example, to quickly locate Mount Fuji in any of these geographies. Do you turn to "Mountains and Rivers" first, or to "Famous Sites"? Chen Jialin and Ye Qingyi turn out to be relatively straightforward, as Mount Fuji is the first item in each of their sections on "Mountains and Rivers."[83] In Yao Wendong's geography, Mount Fuji is soon found in the introductory section, "Mountains and Rivers."[84] Fortunately, Fu Yunlong mentions Mount Fuji in his introduction to his "Table of Mountains"; otherwise one would have to hunt through his fourteen-page table, arranged by prefecture.[85] Huang Zunxian has no section for either "Mountains and Rivers" or "Famous Sites"; one can only begin reading his three volumes on "Geography" to discover a mention of Fuji, and a fuller description later on in the section on Suruga Province.[86] But Gu Houkun is most abstract; one must search through his tables of mountains before finding Fuji listed under Suruga Province in the table of "Celebrated Mountains Taller than 1,000 Feet above Sea Level."[87] From such a representation, so utterly at odds with the notion of geohistorical sites central to the travelogue, one would never realize the cultural preeminence of Mount Fuji among Japanese mountains.

A mode of presentation, then, is largely selected not according to content per se, but in the interests of systematizing the information at hand. Clearly, some sets of subject matter are more amenable to certain modes than others; "Local Products" are usually presented in list form, and "Genealogical Records" in prose form. But as Gu Houkun demonstrates with his "Genealogy," one can eliminate or reduce narrative detail to annotation and simply present a chronological list of emperors.[88] Modes of presentation are a matter of *process,* the conforming of information to the form of the geographical treatise, or, more specifically, the systematization of objectified details that constitute the range of topics and the central object, Japan. Unlike a reference text with a convenient index, the Chinese geographical treatise presumes a reader who will peruse long sections of the text and gather what detail he will. The utility of the text, to repeat, lies not as means alone—as information providing an answer to one or another question—but as an end in itself as well—as a comprehensive representation of the whole, Japan.

Maps

Another pertinent but minor mode of presentation, which only Fu Yunlong and Ye Qingyi include in their geographies of Japan, is the map. Maps were a relative latecomer to geographical representation, and maps of Japan were apparently not readily available before the sixteenth century.[89] During the sixteenth through eighteenth centuries, Chinese produced a number of coastal maps, the earliest of which were allegedly based on the work of the fifteenth-century explorer, Zheng Hê.[90] These are narrow strip-maps in which a long stretch of the coast is represented as running in a horizontal direction from right to left irrespective of its true direction; typically, the ocean appears at the bottom of the map, and the reader looks from the water to the land.[91] They are thought to have been route maps. The late Ming examples available to Wei Yuan—like Mao Yuanyi's *Treatise on Military Preparations* (1621) and Hu Zongxian's *Illustrated Collection on Coastal Defense* (1562/1624), which were produced as aids in combatting the Dwarf pirates—include crude maps of Japan, the style of which is reproduced by Wei Yuan in his *Illustrated Treatise on the Sea Kingdoms.*[92] Wei's map of Japan (map 3) exhibits little detail, irregular scale, no interest in topography, and makes only the simplest stylized divisions among departments (*zhou*) and offshore islands.

Largely contemporaneous with the production of these coastal maps was the introduction of European Renaissance cartography to China through Matteo Ricci and his Jesuit comrades.[93] Although Ricci's world map was first printed in 1602, prompting the imperial-sponsored production of considerably more precise maps of the empire, accurate maps of Japan were not available to Chinese until after the renewal of diplomatic relations in 1877.[94] It is remarkable that as late as 1880, Wang Zhichun's *Records from Overseas* included maps of Japan that improve little upon that of Wei Yuan. One of these (map 4) displays Japan, Korea, and the eastern coast of China. The inaccuracies of Japan's geography are startling: what ought to be the island of Shikoku is marked as the southernmost end of Honshū; Osaka is indicated as being north of Tokyo—in fact, most place-names are misplaced—and the northernmost island of Hokkaidō is marked "Xia Outsiders." Information is both out of date and incorrect.

Accordingly, the contrast presented by the map collections of 1889 is striking. In their respective geographies of Japan, both Fu Yunlong and Ye Qingyi include maps borrowed from unnamed Japanese sources. Ye's were cut on woodblock in Shanghai, Fu's are copper etchings reproduced in Japan. Since Ye's are maps of the circuits (map 2), and Fu's maps of the prefectures (map 1), I have used their maps of Hokkaidō—both a circuit and a prefecture—for the sake of comparison. The general outline of the two is similar; scale is quite regular, and coastline detail comparable to present-day maps. Where Ye's map contains the traditional grid structure unrelated to latitude and longitude values, Fu's is a surveyor's map deliberately marking latitude and longitude (in graticules) as a frame of reference and border for the map. Both maps represent topography; Ye's map contains stylized mountains to indicate their location, Fu's map indicates them with the Chinese character for "mountain." Rivers are similarly drawn in. Clearly, Fu's map contains more detail—districts and towns (the latter with some distinctions of size), and harbors, marshes, and other geological features are indicated. The two maps have in common only the prefectures and the names of a few stray mountains and cities. Even then, the precise location of an important city like Hakodate is not given in Ye's map. Be that as it may, the map collections substantially improve upon others available in China.

The question remains as to why the majority of these geographers (and travelers) were indifferent to the inclusion of maps in their works. Clearly, the iconic representations provided by maps were a secondary concern, and this in spite of the fact, as Wang Yong points out, that the local treatise developed in tandem with the Soong period desire for maps of local areas and borderlands.[95] By the late eighteenth century, Zhang Xuecheng was insisting that local treatises include maps of the area represented in the text.[96] It may be, then, that the geographers of Japan simply lacked the

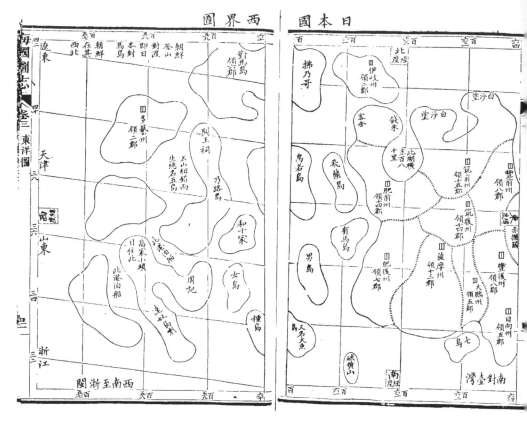

Map 3 (*above and opposite*) Japan, Wei Yuan, *Hai guo tu zhi* [1852]. *Reproduced by courtesy of the Harvard-Yenching Library, Harvard University.*

wherewithal to reproduce and include maps; or, since Japan was not an administrative district of China, they were less motivated to include maps of Japan. A scholar like Huang Zunxian, who saw himself so much within the tradition of Chinese historiography, was perhaps content to exclude maps since histories per se did not usually include maps.

Only Yao Wendong makes a reference to this absence. His "Prefatory Remarks" close with the comment:

The two best maps of Japan are the "Comprehensive Map of Japan," printed by the Ministry of Education, and the "Complete Map of Japan." There are also three excellent sets of maps: (1) "Municipal and Prefectural Maps of Great Japan" printed by the Geographical Department of the Home Ministry, which includes

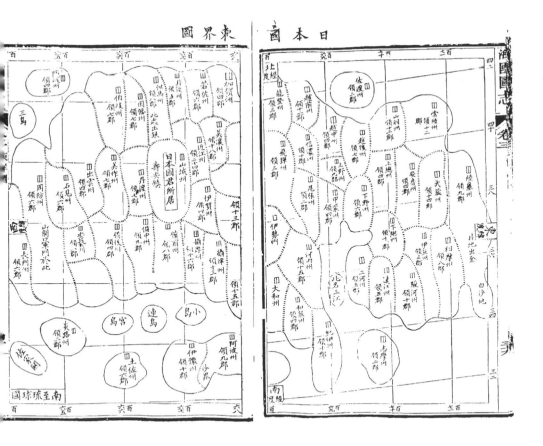

three municipal and thirty-six prefectural maps; (2) "Comprehensive Regional Maps of the Territory of Great Japan" by Sakai Takemitsu, which includes over forty maps of the eighty-five provinces; and (3) "Naval Charts" printed by the Department of Ocean Routes in the Ministry of the Navy, consisting of over 150 leaves, each detailing the coastline of Japan. These can all be used with reference to this volume.[97]

It is certainly possible that Yao secured a set of these maps for the International Office—we do not know—but one wonders how the interested reader of Yao's geography in China was going to acquire these maps. He likely wasn't. Yao's decision to omit a set of maps underscores the persisting *textual* nature of geography in China, for it is Yao's text, more than others,

萬里長城
寧河 樂亭 關海 遼東 灣

九連城
鐵嶺 義州
金州
旅順
勃海
大沽
天津
黃河口
登州
威海衛

京北

運河

東山

楊子江
上海
崇明

珍島

巨文島

浙江

福建

臺灣

澎湖

宮古島
石垣島
入安島
與邦國島

Map 4 (*above and opposite*) Eastern China, Korea, Japan, and the Liuqiu Islands, Wang Zhichun, *Tan ying lu* (1880). *Reproduced by courtesy of the Harvard-Yenching Library, Harvard University.*

that single-mindedly attempts to mediate human intention and the physical geography of Japan. With extensive lists and tables that locate cities, towns, mountains, bays, and so on, and specify paths of approach, Yao means to instruct his reader in navigating the landscape of Japan. The assumption that such a task could be accomplished *without maps* corresponds to the assumption at work in travel diaries: physical space could be sufficiently transformed into textual space; as Chinese conceived geography in the treatise, maps were not essential.

Yet some of Yao's contemporaries behaved otherwise. Wang Zhichun, Fu Yunlong, and Ye Qingyi and Yuan Zuzhi include maps in their works on Japan. These are not idiosyncratic decisions; these men share, along with the sixteenth- and seventeenth-century makers of coastal maps, experience in navigation and interest in technology. Wang, Fu, and Yuan all participated in missions of investigation—Wang and Yuan to Europe, Fu to North and South America—and likely came to appreciate the value of maps to the traveler and geographer. Such a personal sensibility, reinforced

Objectification in the Geographic Treatise   193

by the personal wherewithal to arrange for printing both maps and geographies, explains how these maps of Japan came to take a place alongside the more essential textual representation.

A question remains: why did the International Office and its Tongwen Guan fail to appreciate the utility of these texts? As the institutions most occupied with international relations, one might expect more attention and support, but of all the texts considered in this study, the Tongwen Guan published *only* Huang Zunxian's *Poems on Divers Japanese Affairs* (1879) and Yao Wendong's *Military Essentials of Japanese Geography* (1884). Although the disinterest may in part reflect financial limitations, I believe that the priorities of the institutions lay elsewhere. By the late 1870s, the Tongwen Guan under the leadership of W. A. P. Martin was vigorously pursuing "Western learning"—those mathematic, scientific, engineering, legal, and economic textbooks that would prepare Chinese scholars for Westernization.[98] Geography of a conventional sort was not suitable; Westernization demanded texts with the overtly pragmatic and pedagogic emphases of Western learning. Consequently, the six geographies of Japan were of marginal concern and remained minor texts until the Sino-Japanese War in 1894. Knowledge useful to Civilization would not necessarily prove to be useful to Westernization, just as the day of idle poetry gatherings among gentlemen was soon eclipsed by the cool resolve of acrimonious conflict.

III Representing Japan's Westernization

6 Negotiating Civilization and Westernization

Today each of the overseas barbarians is like one of the arrayed states of the Spring and Autumn period. It is not so much that the arrangement of power is the same; the habits and attitudes are similar. The force of each is roughly equivalent, so their words must express principles; each respects the capacity for treachery, so their mouths voice trust. When two armies engage each other in battle, they do not dispense with diplomats. But in the event that peace is betrayed, states become friends and acquiesce as the great invade the small, the strong conquer the weak, and each of course stands by its own excuses. No longer does it matter that none discuss principle, that none discuss trust—as the warring states of old.

Feng Guifen, "On the Importance of Directness"

If analogy is not a method of demonstration in the true sense of the word, it is nevertheless a method of illustration and of secondary verification which may be of some use. It is always interesting to see whether a law established for one order of facts may not, *mutatis mutandis,* be found to apply elsewhere. This comparison may also serve to confirm it and give a greater understanding of its implications. In fact, analogy is a legitimate form of comparison, and comparison is the only practical means we have for the understanding of things.

Emile Durkheim, "Individual and Collective Representations"

In the movement from Chinese encounters to Chinese representations of Japan, I shifted from behavioral expectations to strategies of knowledge. Chinese Civilization—conceived as an expansive and hierarchic motion of "enlightening through patterning"—anticipated that Japanese would draw close to the light of Chinese cultural hegemony and, in so doing, participate in the linguistic, poetic, historical, and tributary practices of Civilization. At the same time, the historical development of Chinese Civilization promoted specific forms of representing the peoples in the borderlands beyond Civilization. Travel diaries, geographic and travel poetry, and the geographic treatise were in the nineteenth century the primary and generic ways of knowing such peripheries. These were the received forms that contained Japan as an object of knowledge; or, to put it another way, it was the reproduction of these genres that enabled a Chinese scholar to contain Japan within familiar forms of geographical knowledge.

However, each of the scholars examined here noted the introduction of new and specifically Western elements in Japan during the 1870s and eighties. To varying degrees and consistencies, they praised or disdained the changes under way in Japan. While one might perceive a general apprehension at this "barbarization" of Japan, such a conclusion wrongly minimizes the intense ambivalence among these Chinese scholars. Chen Jialin, for example, criticizes the Japanese for discarding Chinese learning and altering age-old law, but he prefaces his geography with the brave hope that knowledge of Japan's new trends will inspire China to "stand up tall."[1] The introduction of Western elements to Japan, in other words, *destabilized* the position from which Chinese scholars perceived and represented Japan. Chinese Civilization, as a frame of reference for Chinese scholars, was challenged by this new content of Westernization in Japan, and a recurring effort in all of these texts is the work of condemning, legitimizing, or otherwise containing the new Western aspects of Japan.

Many of these elements were of course already familiar to these scholars; to reach Japan, they all had to board ship from Shanghai or another of the treaty ports, those points in China to which elements of Westernization had been transplanted since the 1850s. The newspapers discussed in chapter 5, for example, were certainly to be seen in China's treaty ports during the 1870s and eighties, and yet some Chinese geographers were so surprised by the ubiquity of newspapers in the major cities of Japan that they made a place for this new Western element in their geographies. It is significant that these geographical representations of Japan provided their Chinese authors with a forum in which to confront the Westernization under way in their world. As we will see, those genres more engaged with historiography—Huang Zunxian's *Poems on Divers Japanese Affairs* and the six geographies of Japan—were also more engaged in negotiating some workable relationship between Civilization and Westernization.

But Chinese scholars did not identify these contemporary changes as "Westernization"; in the nineteenth century, they spoke in terms of "imitating Western ways" (*mofang xifa*) and "studying Western learning" (*xue xixue*).[2] Accordingly, when I write of "Westernization," this is a heuristic device intended to summarize the contents of "Western ways" and "Western learning." Chinese did not perceive the West as a cultural totality, as a complete and alternative form of civilization peculiar to the West. The fixed and central position of China in the world was such a well-established "fact" that Chinese had neither need nor cause to identify some Western "other" as distinct from some universal Chinese Civilization.[3] The cultural strength of China was that it assumed it could incorporate anything—the Son of Heaven presided over all the earth; his domain included everything, and all peoples came to him. Some Chinese scholars understood, from their own readings of Westerners' reports, that the West was a geographic unity beyond the seas and far overland, but they did not perceive this geographic unity—symbolized by means of cartography—as some other cultural totality. Because these Westerners sailed to Chinese shores on ships, simple artifacts of the West not unlike Chinese models, the Chinese did not immediately construct a whole from such an aggregate of national fragments. Rather, beginning from their encounters with the Jesuits in the late 1500s, they observed the Westerners who came to China in shiploads, one or several at a time, and noticed a sufficient quantity of Western behavior so as to construct, in time, the pair of categories which were used to identify and discuss the West, and which remain in the writings of Huang Zunxian and his contemporaries: Western ways and Western learning.

Accordingly, we find Chinese scholars confronting Westernization in the three areas implicit in the model of Civilization: learning, practice, and world order. In each of these negotiations, Chinese scholars relied on the logic of analogy to account for Westernization. Huang Zunxian's poetic vision of a new unity of Civilization and Westernization is certainly original and imaginative, but ultimately impractical. Similar efforts to contain the West within analogies drawn between elements of the West and China's antiquity were ultimately unsuccessful, and worse, such an engagement with Westernization promised to undermine Civilization. The expectations of "shared language" and "shared Civilization" were in time foreclosed, and Chinese Civilization would lose its universality, becoming but one voice offering its own particular version of reality.

Analogy and Containment

As a means of understanding what is outside our immediate experience, analogy is a commonplace and useful technique. To begin with, it does lead to some sort of understanding, and in that sense it is a technique of reasoning.[4] As scholars repeatedly point out, reasoning by analogy—like reasoning by example—is closely linked to explanatory uses of language.[5] When Huang Zunxian proposes an analogy between transformations in the ancient text *Mozi* and the Western science of chemistry, he has indeed just such a deliberate purpose—to explain that which is outside of his experience, chemistry, in order to bring it within his experience, to understand it as an extension of the *Mozi*. That such an analogical explanation for Western learning appealed to Chinese scholars in the nineteenth century may be due to the fact that the *Mozi* was the primary text in antiquity to take up the issues of logic and analogy.[6]

In terms of the intercultural contact at issue in this study, I have shown in my discussions of poetic language that the primary way by which analogy leads to understanding is to bring the unfamiliar within one's own linguistic order—to name in familiar terms what might at first appear different. Given that the practitioners of Chinese Civilization constituted themselves in a language that privileged history, as representations of continuous chains of remembered events and images, it is not surprising that Chinese officials after the 1860s enlisted an analogy from ancient Chinese history to define their historical circumstances as a "Restoration"; they responded sympathetically when Japanese did the same. In fact, the use of historical analogies was a standard practice over the centuries, both in Chinese education and as an examination technique for entry into a bureaucratic post.[7] A similarly long-established practice was the application of analogy in juridical decisions.[8]

The habit peculiar to scholars in the late nineteenth century was their looking back to ancient Chinese history—to the time prior to the establishment of the empire—as a way to understand the tumultuous present. The analogy that dominated their imaginations, when they considered the persistent and perplexing changes upsetting China's relations with foreign powers, was that the present corresponded to the periods comprising the Eastern Zhou: the "Spring and Autumn" period (ca. 771–481 B.C.), during which the various states arrayed themselves with increasing independence from the Zhou court, and the "Warring States" period (ca. 453–221 B.C.), when all pretense of loyalty to the Zhou kings was dispensed with and the states fought each other for ultimate domination. It was, I believe, the suggestiveness of this analogy between antiquity and the present world situation that prompted the wide-ranging references to the entire Zhou era among Chinese scholars from the 1860s on—including the "Restoration," "Renovation," and "Joint Rule" discussed later in this chapter.

What specifically distinguishes analogy in the representations of Japan, however, is a pair of usages corresponding to the performative (poetic) and expository epistemological strategies characteristic of the Chinese representations of Japan outlined in the preceding section. On the one hand, when Huang Zunxian and other scholars compare Western learning to Chinese knowledge, in order to identify Western learning with something Chinese, this is a *performative* use of analogy: the analogy is meant to extend meaning across present and past through texts. By contrast, when Hê Ruzhang, Feng Guifen, and others seek to guide court policy by identifying the present with the Warring States period, this is an *expository* use of analogy; these scholars use the analogy as an appeal to historiographical truth. In fact, they defer meaning and evade the present, consoling themselves within a historical narrative that is no longer appropriate.

But Chinese scholars and officials did not consider Japan's Westernization (and Westernization generally) only in terms of analogies. I have already described (in chapter 1) the work of pragmatic officials involved in treaty arrangements with Western powers. There were certainly Chinese who reacted to Western ways and Western learning with both the ability and perspicacity to engage things Western on their own terms; among the Chinese visitors to Japan, Wang Tao and Wang Zhichun most often responded in such a manner. But in my own examination of Chinese representations of Japan, I have instead been struck by Chinese scholars' habit of employing analogy when Japan's Westernization is at issue.[9]

The Precedence of Learning Before Action

That Chinese began to consider the West in terms of Western ways and Western learning was not a random choice. In spite of their being open to differing interpretations, two of the Four Books—which formed the basis of the examination system curriculum in China long before the Qing dynasty—begin with references to the priority of learning (*xue*), from which proceeds practice (*xi*), the following of "models" or "methods" (*fa*).[10] The Confucian *Analects* opens with learning, asking the rhetorical question, "Is it not a pleasure to learn, and to practice from time to time what has been learned?" The well-known beginning to *The Great Learning* goes even further in linking learning to the practice of moral leadership:

The extension of knowledge is the investigation of things. When things are investigated, knowledge is extended; when knowledge is extended, the will becomes sincere; when the will is sincere, the mind is rectified, when the mind is rectified, the person is cultivated; when the person is cultivated, the family will be regulated; when the family is regulated, the domain will be in order; and when the domain is in order, there is peace throughout the world.[11]

Because these and other such passages from the classics were interpreted quite differently between the eleventh and nineteenth centuries, the dominant moral considerations here sanctioned several programs of learning. Nonetheless, the model was widespread and instructed to all: men properly proceed from learning to practice.[12]

Accordingly, when Chinese scholars confronted Western learning and Western ways, beginning with Jesuit skills in astronomy and mathematics in the late 1500s, many concentrated on undermining Western learning. Those who were determined to "drive out the barbarian," first, and rather ineffectively, claimed that the Christian teachings were preposterous and that Western learning should not be believed either.[13] But in the nineteenth century, when Chinese were absolutely unable to deny the effectiveness and superiority of Western armaments, "anti-Western" officials argued that Western learning was inappropriate because in failing to address moral considerations, it produced bad practices; this was obvious to them when they considered the opium trade and Britain's willingness to engage in warfare in order to protect that trade.

Nevertheless, in attempting to discredit Western learning—and by sequential association, Western ways—these officials did not claim that Western learning was immoral; rather, they sought to deny the originality and independence of Western learning by claiming that Western learning had, after all, originated in China.[14] In making such an argument, "anti-Western" officials inadvertently aligned themselves with other "pro-

Western" scholars who hoped to incorporate Western learning into Chinese knowledge. Both groups of officials claimed that China had originally possessed Western learning, but that the ancient sages had deliberately chosen not to pursue that path. Where the former group of "anti-Western" officials then used this "road-not-taken" argument to forestall all attempts to introduce Western science and language into official educational and examination curricula, the latter group of "pro-Western" officials argued that, on the contrary, to incorporate Western learning into China would be a pious act of "reviving ancient ways."[15] Both arguments used the point of "origin" to effectively encompass Westernization within Chinese Civilization.

The most interesting example of this argument is that of Zeng Jize. In a disquisition included in his official diary of his ambassadorial duties in Europe (1878–1886), he maintained that Heaven had changed human affairs, so that even though Western learning had existed in ancient times, the sages hadn't discussed it thoroughly, and later generations had lost it, not realizing the value of such learning for still later ages—the present! Accordingly, when Zeng combined the West and China into one path of development, he reached the startling but no doubt satisfying conclusion, "When we observe the West today, we see a China of ancient times; when we observe China today, we see the West of a future time."[16] A return to ancient times, so as to revive a body of learning left as an open possibility by the sages, provided the means whereby China could both modify its own development, and in the process, put the West on its proper course.

Western Learning and Western Ways

A similar realignment of Civilization and Westernization occurs in Huang Zunxian's *Poems on Divers Japanese Affairs*. Like the experiences of his contemporaries Wang Tao and Zeng Jize in Europe, Huang's experience in Japan provided an occasion to imagine a new combination of Civilization and Westernization; and like Zeng, Huang links this recombination to a notion of "reviving ancient ways." Insofar as Chinese ancient ways and Chinese texts are understood as points of origin for observed Japanese practices, Huang's realignment of Civilization and Westernization is consistent with his evidential research concerns; Huang proceeds by explaining the origins of Japan's Westernization—both Western ways and Western learning—and in the process, corroborates their Chinese origins. But this combination of Civilization and Westernization is not without dissonances, and Huang's solution, I will demonstrate, is primarily "poetic" in that he situates present Japanese policies by citing Chinese historical references, and these poetic allusions and deliberate usages of analogy thus reconcile his ambivalence toward Japan's Westernization.

As I described in chapter 4, Huang's *Poems on Divers Japanese Affairs* was in part a hybrid of two familiar genres, *shi* poetry and the geographic treatise. If we examine the contents of Huang's *Poems* in this context, it becomes clear how Huang understood the relationship between, on the one hand, Western ways and Western learning, and on the other hand, Japan and its (Chinese) Civilization. I offer here my own analytic "table of contents" for the work, which parallels the contents of the typical local treatise: the superscript *C* indicates that roughly 50 percent or more of this set of poems include textual references to Chinese antecedents of Japanese practices; and the superscript *W* indicates that roughly 50 percent or more of this set of poems include statements referring Japanese practices to Western ways or Western learning:

1–11^{cw}	History: origins of Japan and its administration
12–14^{w}	Heavenly signs: calendar and weather
15–27	The land: famous cities and mountains
28–30	Heroes
31–35^{w}	Palaces, parliament, and imperial ceremonies
36–50^{cw}	Administrative institutions: taxes, laws, Fire Department, hospitals, museums, and the like
51–57^{cw}	Schools
58–77^{c}	Learning, language, scholars, and books
78–80	Clans, sons-in-law, and warriors
81–86	Pastimes: sightseeing, sakura, gardens, drinking
87–98	Habits of daily life: food, living quarters, shops
99–104^{c}	Music
105–106^{w}	Photography and the telegraph
107–113	Festivals and ceremonies
114–122	Japanese women
123–125	Tattoos and family crests

One can see that Huang's references to China and the West overlap in three important areas: administration, schools, and local products. (The other area of Chinese precedents is local customs—music, clothing, and traditional Chinese arts—in which the West is largely ignored.) Of the three, the first and third are areas in which Huang observes a Japanese engagement with Western ways—new administrative institutions, concentrated in poems 1–14 and 31–50; and new techniques in communications and manufacturing, concentrated in poems 105–106 and 136–153. The second area, schools and learning, contains Huang's references to Japanese adoption of Western learning (concentrated in poems 51–57).

We might expect these three areas to be sites of tension between Civilization and Westernization, but of the three, the third—local products— poses the least difficulty for Huang. In a quite matter-of-fact manner, some of poems 136–153 mention either Western trade with Japan—tea, for example, in poem 143—or Japanese adoption of Western ways of manufacturing—weaving, mining, and paper, for example, in poems 144, 145, and 149 respectively. We see here not only Huang's personal disinterest in trade and production, but also the pronounced bureaucratic habit of relegating trade and manufacturing to "mere technique." In much the same way that the previous generation of officials like Zeng Guofan, Li Hongzhang, and Zuo Zongtang believed that China could "self-strengthen" by copying Western techniques for manufacturing weapons, so too Huang sees this process of "imitation" as uncomplicated and undeserving of more extensive comment. In time, Western ways would simply supersede obsolete or less efficient ways, in much the same manner that any improvement serviceably supersedes an extant process; Japan has demonstrably incorporated such changes.

By contrast, administration and learning are the areas where Huang does observe a problematic alignment between Civilization and Westernization, and makes a point of elucidating the relationship. Unlike trade and manufacturing techniques, which can be supplemented or replaced, learning and administration—in the Confucian analysis of social practice outlined above—work their effects at a level of social organization more fundamental than that of production techniques. Learning determines not only the textual, intellectual, and moral foundations for the leaders of a state, but also the very ways of administration by which those leaders order a state. Because Huang does have reservations about the effects of Western learning and Western ways on the Japanese social order, he makes a point of containing, redefining, and moving to legitimize the processes of Westernization under way in Japan. But this activity, as I have stated, is limited by the logic of analogy.

The Chinese Origins of Western Learning: Containment by Analogy

Like many of his contemporaries, Huang Zunxian repeated the belief that Western learning had originated in China. He was among the majority in the nineteenth century who traced Western learning to the *Mozi*, a text dated to the fourth century B.C. and believed to be the work of Mo Di, a philosopher condemned by Mencius and later Confucians for two ideas which they found particularly anathema: (1) "universal love" (*jian ai*), which advocated a type of mutual regard and equality that threatened to cancel hierarchic relations and attendant duties between people, as understood in the Confucian *Analects*; and (2) "utility" or "benefit" (*li*), which declared that the criterion for action was whether or not action benefited the common good, a position contrary to the Confucian emphasis on "benevolence," "righteousness," and "propriety" in action. Huang, we will see, felt that these two ideas were characteristic of Western learning and traceable to the *Mozi*.[17]

Huang's primary discussion of Western learning appears in poem 51, the longest piece in the work and one that critically bridges his discussions of administrative institutions and those of learning; it is ostensibly on the subject of schools:

Wood-carved yet able to fly, it boasts the magpie's living spirit;
A ladder prepared, a secure guard; practice the *yangling* pillbox.
One doesn't know if all are "methods originating in the East";
I would we discard Confucian books and read the *Mozi* canons.

Schools have proliferated, and are the sole monopoly of teachers of Western learning. I have examined Western learning [and conclude that] it is the learning of Mo Di. Quite similar to Mo Di's notions of "universal love," "the discerning soul," and "serving Heaven" are [the principles of] Jesus' Ten Commandments: to honor and serve the Lord of Heaven, and to love mankind as one's own self.

Other similarities are as follows: "Transformations are evidenced by [external] changes, as when the frog turns into the quail." (Note: the transformations of animals); "Of the five elements, water, fire, and earth counteract each other; but in addition, fire melts metal, decomposes water, and destroys wood." (Note: the transformations of metal, stone, grass, and trees); "Similarity is a matter of weight, substance, composition, and type; difference takes two forms: substances may have different compositions, or they may be of different types." These statements are all precursors of [Western] "chemistry."[18]

Huang goes on in this vein, discussing in turn mechanics, mathematics, optics, electricity, machine production, magnetism, and astronomy, by citing passages in the *Mozi* (and other ancient texts) that putatively corroborate both facts and principles in those respective branches of Western learning.[19] He then concludes:

Now, not all the profound and subtle truths [of Western learning] can be derived from our books. We merely introduce the groundwork, which Westerners carry through to the end. But it is precisely here that we can learn from their superior techniques. These days the Japanese admire Western learning; they want to abandon what they own and pursue what they lack. Surprisingly, there are those who say Chinese learning is useless, so this [examination] has been provided in order to shut those mouths who would claim that [Chinese learning] is as pointless as an ant trying to shake down a tree.[20]

Huang, in the end, is providing a defense of Chinese learning in the face of an overwhelming shift to Western learning in Japanese schools, but his argument follows a peculiar logic. He begins the poem in the realm of fanciful allusion, but moves to quite serious citations of textual precedents in the notes. Lines 1 and 2 in the poem contain three allusions to incidents portrayed in the *Mozi*; the first is utterly fantastic—the bird carved by Gong Yu, so lifelike that it actually flies away—while the second and third are genuine but long-forgotten weapons of defensive warfare—the scaling ladder and the pillbox. If the bird serves as a striking and direct image for the later discussion of the amazing transformation of animals (and yet another example of fantastic flight), the ladder and pillbox are mundane and tangential examples of machines known to the ancients. Huang questions, with a pun in the third line, whether or not he can know if Western ways (to which he will refer) all came from China. The pun is that "method originating in the East" (*donglaifa*) was a faulty etymology for the European word for "algebra"; based on what the Jesuits had told them, Chinese thought that algebra had gone to Europe from China (by way of Arabia). This sort of explanation, common in Huang's day, could only rely on inconclusive evidence; Chinese claimed that ancient Chinese books, lost to China, had been transmitted to the West, either during the flood unleashed by the (legendary) Huang Di or through Roman and Han contact (and so on).[21]

Huang's solution to this problem of origins is analogical. Insofar as a statement in the *Mozi* can be characterized by—or reduced to—some fundamental phenomenon, Huang can then identify that statement with the branch of Western learning associated with that phenomenon. So, in one of the above examples, because *Mozi*'s statement "fire melts metal, decomposes water, and destroys wood" is characteristic of "transformations of metal, stone, grass, and trees," the statement is taken to be evidence of Chinese precedents for the Western science, "chemistry" (*huaxue*), which in Huang's day was understood to be the study (*xue*) of transformations (*hua*). The character *hua* is the point of mediation here, between the Chinese text, *Mozi*, and the Western science, chemistry.[22] (Frogs changing into quails and "transformations of animals" in general are undoubtedly references to contemporary notions of evolution.)[23] If the analogy is true, which Huang thinks it is, then Chinese and Japanese are completely correct to pursue branches of learning known to but neglected by the ancients.

The difficulty with the analogy is that in the transaction, a revaluation of great consequence takes place. Huang constructs his analogy after the formal analogy of four terms, "A is to B as C is to D" ($A : B :: C : D$); that is, the *Mozi* is to Western learning as Mo Di's "transformation of metal" is to chemistry. If this is true, one would expect that the corresponding parts would also form a true analogy; that is, the *Mozi* is to Mo Di's "transformation of metal" as Western learning is to chemistry ($A : C :: B : D$).[24] This second analogy, however, is not true; the parts do not correspond analogously. Chemistry is an exemplary branch of Western learning, but random comments taken from the *Mozi* do not constitute any such "branch" of the *Mozi*. While one may ostensibly go to the Mozi to find out about Western learning, one cannot very well go to random comments from the *Mozi* to find out about chemistry, for chemistry attempts to do more than cite transformations—it attempts to *analyze* and systematically *describe* them.

The problem lies in Huang's metonymic substitution of the *Mozi* for statements about transformations.[25] In raiding the *Mozi* and other ancient texts for passages adequate to this sort of analogical construction, Huang effects a critical displacement of the Chinese text; he shifts it from the subject position to the analogue position in the analogy. To explain: if a second criterion of a truthful analogy is reversibility, one would expect that the simple analogy, "Mo Di's transformation of metal is like chemistry," be reversible—that is, it should be true to say "chemistry is like Mo Di's transformation of metal." However, in the context of Huang's project, it is precisely this second analogy that is the more accurate. Accordingly, the subject of the original analogy, "Mo Di's transformation of metal," becomes dependent upon the analogue "chemistry," and because neither these random statements nor the *Mozi* can substantiate the science of chemistry, the preferred analogy becomes "chemistry is like Mo Di's transformations of animals." The priority of the terms of the analogy is reversed—chemistry becomes the subject, and Mo Di's transformations the analogue. Chemistry comes to take precedence.

It should not surprise us, then, that Huang boldly approves the comprehensive overhaul of education that he observes in Japan. He follows poem 51 with a confident description of the curriculum of the new Tokyo Imperial University, wherein Chinese learning has a place among the other branches of learning:

Schools are under the jurisdiction of the Ministry of Education. Tokyo Imperial University has over one hundred students, and is divided into three divisions— Law, Science, and Literature. The Law Division includes English law, French law, and both current and ancient Japanese law. The Science Division includes chemistry, mechanics, optics, climatology, mathematics, mineralogy, drafting, astronomy, geography, engineering, biology, and botany. The Literature Division includes history, Chinese literature, and English literature.[26]

Huang is not troubled by the consequent reduction of Chinese learning to merely one among several disciplines; he accepts it as a necessary policy of Westernization. He holds his ground, however, against certain Japanese who would eliminate Chinese learning altogether. In spite of its diminished status in the context of a Western education, Chinese learning is nonetheless pertinent, not only because it accounts for the origins of Western learning, but also because, as we will see Huang argue, it continues to provide the fundamental principles of Civilization.

Accordingly, Huang welcomes the corresponding reorientation of the education process, in the interests of pragmatism and expertise. He explains in his notes to poem 52, regarding the school system, that

Tokyo has both middle schools and teachers' schools. After completing their courses, students are allowed to become the teachers of others. The teaching method for these students is to divide them into seven ranks. . . . Divided by years to receive instruction, they proceed in succession from the seventh to the first rank. . . . Their books and written materials all confer some practical utility; the courses of study all have a fixed schedule. . . . Students are assembled together according to their professional interests, and one teacher instructs a few dozen students; when a teacher is skilled, the students' accomplishments quickly double. This entire teaching method was acquired from the West; I myself have observed it in action, and am awed by its excellence. . . . His excellency Guo Songtao has said, "Human talent in the West is entirely a product of schools." Alas—how true![27]

As Huang represents it, the acquisition of Western learning depends upon this teaching method of graded instruction. While a student is initially self-selected on the basis of his interests and presumably advances according to his abilities, Huang here appraises teachers in terms of their effectiveness—as he does textbooks and materials. The importance of *utility* to Western learning, which Huang and his contemporaries trace to the *Mozi*, is here justified because it contributes to the production of "human talent." The teacher is no longer a moral exemplar, but an effective instructor and dispenser of knowledge. Huang's commitment to this idea is expressed in his final comment—"Alas, how true!" Having witnessed China's recent failures at "self-strengthening" in the wake of the Opium War and the Taiping Rebellion—that is, the building of effective ships and guns on Western models—Huang here, recalling the cashiered ambassador Guo Songtao, concludes that these were due to a shortage of human talent.[28] If only Western learning had accompanied such efforts!

What does disturb Huang, as he contemplates Western learning in Japan, is that a number of Japanese scholars describe these developments as "Civilization" (*wenming*). To Huang, *wenming* denoted specifically the dynamic and transformative spread of an imperial Chinese administration informed by Chinese learning. Westernization was clearly not *wenming*.

This point is raised in Huang's poem about newspapers, poem 50. Along with Western schools and overseas students, newspapers were a third vehicle for the dissemination of Western learning. The issue here is whether newspapers spread information or Civilization, and in either case, to what end? Huang dwells on the problematic relationship between private and public information, emphasizing the value of public access to government but cautioning against potential private misuse of the new public newspaper:

A newspaper appears in the imperial city;
Transmitted decrees of the sovereign—more civilizing.
Sun-basking, village elders converse in private,
Dare not correct errors nor criticize careless mouths.

Whether remote mountains or distant seas, there is no place a newspaper does not reach. They inform [readers] on current affairs and publicize truth and falsity— a truly excellent enterprise! And so Westerners take advantage of newspapers to spread news of all manner of affairs. They have accordingly established laws against slandering government and spreading rumors of personal misconduct, in order to guard against deliberate recklessness. For a light offense, they propose a fine; for a grave offense, incarceration. Japan has imitated these procedures in toto.

That newspapers discuss current political affairs is not "civilizing"; rather, it is "enlightening."[29]

Huang contrasts the old Japanese ways of village elders, who controlled politics privately, and the new Western ways of representative government, sustained by public dissemination of information through newspapers. If the former ran the risk of error through local ignorance, the latter run the risk of slanderous misinformation. Better—"more civilizing," that is—than either of these alternatives is the Chinese habit of transmitting decrees, from imperial lord, through officials, to the people.[30] At the heart of this matter is the unspecified relationship between Western learning and government administration; with Chinese learning, there was always the ideal of an explicit continuity between the examination system and bureaucratic office, but Western learning bears no such direct relationship to government—it takes the form of a popular movement, involving groups that had never before been educated on so wide a scale. And although Huang applauds, for example, the education of women in the new women's colleges (see poem 56), he is at times bothered by the uncontrolled dissemination of information through newspapers; they contribute to social unrest. This discord is evident from Huang's final but initially puzzling observation, "That newspapers discuss current political affairs is not civilizing; rather, it is enlightening."

The context of Huang's comment is an event of 1873, when the educator Fukuzawa Yukichi outlined his argument against the participation of scholars in government. The duty of scholars, Fukuzawa maintained, was to lead the advance of civilization in Japan, by cultivating the independence of spirit that was responsible for the progress of civilization; if scholars sought government office, they would be unable to take any independent stand.[31] He was roundly criticized by his associates, the group of self-styled "enlighteners" who presumed that it was their privilege and duty, as men of talent (very much in Confucian terms), to use the offices of government for the guidance of the people.[32] The significant result of this incident was to split in two what had been a movement organized around the rallying slogan, *bunmeikaika* (C: *wenming-kaihua*), a neologism used to translate the English word "civilization." Curiously, this split between intellectual elites both confirmed and identified itself with a parallel split in the language of the movement—henceforth, *bunmei* and *kaika* assumed ideologically opposed evaluations.[33] Although both terms should be translated as "civilization," I here follow convention and translate *kaika* as "enlightenment."[34] The critical difference is that *bunmei* became the word preferred by Fukuzawa for indicating that state of universal civilization grounded especially in Western learning and to be cultivated privately by scholars, and *kaika* became the term used by his opponents, the "enlighteners," to indicate the active and public cultivation of such civilization through government policy.[35] ("Enlightening" thus has a strong connotation of "development.") Huang Zunxian sided with the enlighteners, not simply because one of these men, Nakamura Keiu, was his friend, but also because he supported their position: when he diagnosed the situation in China, his vision of a solution necessitated government management by "civilizing" officials.

Nakamura, who stressed moral cultivation and the teacher as model in his pronouncements on enlightenment, was among the first to use *kaika* for the process of Westernization; Nakamura moreover shared Huang's concern for the fate of Chinese learning.[36] In addition to teaching and government service, Nakamura and the other Meiji enlighteners were involved in writing, translation, and newspaper and magazine publication, which they understood to be central to the enlightening process. In conjunction with this activity, and on the basis of their experiences in Europe, many of these men were emphatic in declaring that in order for enlightenment to succeed, it was essential that Japan preserve the freedom of the press. With the curtailment of that freedom in 1875, the government prompted agitation and resistance among that segment of Japanese society who had used the newspapers to call for the establishment of a representative legislature. The most active years of this Freedom and People's Rights Movement coincided with Huang's tenure as counselor at the Chinese embassy, and the social unrest that he witnessed made him very apprehensive about this consequence of Western learning.

In the first two lines of poem 50 above, then—

A newspaper appears in the imperial city;
Transmitted decrees of the sovereign—more civilizing

—Huang is reserving for *wenming* the notion of a people civilized by the Son of Heaven by means of Chinese Civilization, and denying its Japanese extension to some newly formulated universal (Western) civilization. Hence the final comment of the poem, where Huang prefers to use the Japanese enlighteners' term for their project, *kaika* (C: *kaihua*), or "enlightening," which advocates that active, governmental policy of "transforming" the people for the sake of developing the nation. Public newspapers, Huang insists, have nothing to do with "Civilization."[37]

The problem, as Huang observed Japan from 1877 to 1881, was that Western learning in practice tended to stimulate the popular political movement, but at the same time, it had no necessary relationship to administration. He concluded from the point of view of the administrative class that there was something amiss with Western learning in Japan. This view is expressed in poem 6, which occurs in the set of poems about the history of Japanese administration and, conspicuously, includes the only mention of Western learning outside of those poems on schools and learning. I translate in full:

The sword flashes, restroked again; the mirror polished anew;
After a long six hundred years, the "renowned blade" is restored.
Just when one sun returns, adorning the upper branches,
Helter-skelter—the people call for a "republic."

In the time of Middle Antiquity, clairvoyant lords and excellent ministers devoted themselves ceaselessly to the writing of history; the Outer Relations [the queens' families] ignorantly meddled in administration; and the tyrants rose in succession. After rounds of the Minamoto and the Taira, it was like the Zhou lord in his eastern capital, hanging on to an empty throne. In the founding year of Meiji, the Tokugawa family and their kingly administration were cast off, and for the first time, there was a return to the ways of antiquity. Is it not splendid?—the success of this restoration! And then recently, Western learning has been greatly promoted, and some are even advocating the people's rights and the freedom of the United States of America.

In the chapter called "Eastern Meridians of the Outer Oceans" in the *Classic of Mountains and Oceans,* in the upper reaches of the Valley of Sunrise, lies Fusang, where the ten suns bathe. In the north of this land of the Black-toothed People, dwelling in the water, there is a great tree; nine suns rest in the lower branches, and one sun rests in the upper branches. In Japan, "lord" is called "the sun," as in "Ohirume-no-muchi," "Nigihayahi-no-mikoto," and other such expressions.[38]

Thematically, this poem-and-commentary concerns light, the Light of Japan (the absent emperor), referred to by two of three symbols of his regalia, the sword and the mirror, and his "ancestor(s)," the sun. In opposition to these sources of light, we see the tyrants—Minamoto and Taira samurai administrators of the medieval period—and the people currently advocating Westernization. Huang is describing certain sociopolitical changes in Meiji Japan, and tactfully eliding that lasting difference of opinion between Chinese and Japanese on the status of the Japanese "king" or "emperor."

But in addition, we see a conventional Chinese analysis based on Zhou dynasty moral-political categories. Within the motif of lordship, tyrants are distinguished from kings, and that set of predicates is contrasted with "ways of antiquity." There is one explicit comparison of Japan to the Zhou dynasty, and two significant allusions: (1) the "renowned blade" Tai e, a specific heirloom of the Warring States period; and (2) "restoration" (*zhongxing*), first used with reference to the Zhou court restored by King Xuan in the eighth century B.C. (and most recently, from Huang's point of view, with the Tongzhi Restoration [1862–1874]). This is followed by the only coordinating conjunction in the commentary, "and then . . . even" (*er . . . nai*), which both connects the recent trends in Western learning to the preceding discussion of history, and also differentiates the two temporally. This structure is duplicated in the poem as well, the "just when" (*fang*) introducing the third line has the same function of creating a temporal division between the sun and the people: the definite history suggested by ancient ways as the object of a restoration, and the ambiguous present observed in association with the popular repercussions of Western ways.

I use the word "ambiguous," because there is a difficulty here. In the commentary, the force of *nai* suggests that "even" advocating rights and freedom is excessive. Similarly, in the poem, the "people in their profusion-confusion" (*fenfen min*) suggests disorder, and has an accordingly negative nuance. What then is the status of the neologism, *gonghe,* or "republic?" In its Zhou historical context, it is an action taken by one of the great sages of Chinese history, the Duke of Zhou, as he set up the kingly institutions of Zhou; as a word used for the regency of "joint rule," "*gonghe*" has a positive nuance (see next section). As "republic," in "call for a republic," the term is compromised. Its immediate context, the signified "republic," has this negative tone. But the signifier *gonghe* includes both the positive memory of a prior meaning, and the sound "gonghe," a poetic utility. (Along with "polish" and "renowned blade," it completes the rhyme structure of the poem.) Such a reading of the piece reinforces its theme of light, contrasted with both tyranny and "en*light*enment" (Western learning), the former clearly bad, the latter compromised.

Reviving the Ancients through Western Ways: Legitimization by Analogy

If Western learning approaches the limits of its utility in this context of administration in Japan, poem 6 is at the same time one of several pieces celebrating the success of the Meiji Restoration. As Huang understands recent developments in Japan, the Restoration was the watershed event that fostered Western ways.[39] But the very terms that Huang and his contemporaries use for "Restoration" are well-known allusions to analogous events recorded in Chinese and Japanese histories. Huang's interpretation of the Restoration as an event, in other words, is performative and has the appearance of convention; he refers to textual precedents that provide both understandings for action in the present and the criteria with which to justify or condemn action. Administration, after all, is the arena for action; and action, we recall, follows from learning.

Huang's representations of the activities of the Restoration, however, are not completely conventional, for he often describes them as a "return to ancient ways." Now, this idea of *fugu*, "recovering antiquity" or "reviving ancient ways," was a concept with a long history by Huang's day; the issue it raised perenially was the continuity of the traditions of Chinese Civilization, or in other words, the question of how Chinese were to maintain a connection to their past.[40] In the Tang and Soong dynasties, scholars focused their attention on ancient poetic form, the literary style of the ancient classics, and the ideals of ancient institutions; during the Ming, "reviving antiquity" was a major force in the many poetic movements to recover the poetic style of ancient masters.[41] All of these movements, in one way or another, were related to attempts to link the universal and eternal *Dao* or "Way" of Chinese Civilization to its material manifestation, its *wen* or "writing" ("Civilization") that existed in human, historical time. During the Soong, Zhu Xi had already challenged these conceptions by claiming that not *wen* but the Way itself was the more appropriate focus for self-cultivation; during the early Qing, as I mentioned earlier, scholars like Gu Yanwu challenged the idea of "reviving antiquity" by asserting that human existence was *inherently* subject to change and that there could be no return to the past.[42]

Huang Zunxian at least shared the belief that an attempt to recover ancient literary language or style was a pointless undertaking (chapter 4), but he was nonetheless susceptible to the Qing period interest in returning to the classics—not only to better understand antiquity, but also to perhaps begin to reform the present according to the models of antiquity.[43] It is in this context, then, that he describes the Meiji Restoration as a "return to antiquity." In the same way that he validates Western learning by claiming that it originated in the classics of Chinese antiquity, he likewise legitimizes Western ways by associating them with a "return to ancient ways."

Huang first describes the "Restoration" and its sweeping force in poem 11:

The jade-ringed ancient country records a Restoration—
The myriad ways follow the winds, an abrupt turn of the wheel;
The shuttle weaves in empty space, yet the finished cloth shines—
Eastern man succeeds at imitating Western man.

Since [the Japanese] knew they couldn't expel the barbarians, they sent off high officials and ambassadors to all the countries of Europe and America in Meiji 4 [1871]. When they returned, Japan was forthwith firmly committed to studying and disseminating Western ways, as the foremost order of the day. This was called the "Restoration," a superior and beneficial administration of extreme diversity.[44]

Huang's word for "restoration" here is *weixin*, the word by which the Meiji Restoration is known today—*ishin* in Japanese. It is, literally, a "weaving anew," a complete reorganizing of the administration of the state.[45] In addition to this term, Huang sometimes uses *zhongxing*—as in poem 6, quoted earlier in this chapter—another word used by Japanese during the inception of the Meiji Restoration. *Zhongxing*, additionally, was a term current among Chinese at the time, used to characterize the reign of the preceding Chinese emperor; the so-called Tongzhi Restoration (*Tongzhi zhongxing*) had followed the Opium War and Taiping Rebellion, from 1862 to 1874. This term is, literally, a "revival of the center," a revival of the central administration after a period of decline.

Now, both of these terms are potent historical allusions for not only Huang, but also the Japanese. Both are derived from the early history—if not legends—of China found in the *Classic of Poetry*. The *weixin* remembered in Chinese history was the reorganization of government undertaken by King Wen in founding the Zhou kingship during the twelfth century B.C. King Wen began the conquest of the corrupt remnants of the previous dynasty, the Shang, and his work of establishing a new form of central administration was completed by his younger brother, the Duke of Zhou, acting as regent for his son, King Wu. (This was the period of regency called the *gonghe*—the joint rule of court and officials, as mentioned above.) In this context, the *weixin* represents a break with the aberrant past and the promise of a new order; we might translate it "reorganization" or "renovation." By contrast, the *zhongxing* occurred about four hundred years later; rebellions and barbarian invasions had brought the Zhou into a period of decline, and by virtue of the strength, wisdom, and charisma of King Xuan (r. 827–782 B.C.), order was restored and the authority of the Zhou court extended as far south as the Yangzi River.[46] The *zhongxing*, then, represents a resurgence of central authority, a rekindling of an eclipsed radiance, an idea not unlike our idea of "restoration."

The restoration that occurred in medieval Japanese history, and which figured prominently in the discourse surrounding the establishment of the Meiji Restoration, was the Kemmu Restoration (*Kemmu chūkō*). This was proclaimed in 1333 by the Emperor Godaigo, who consciously modeled and deliberately named his action after the Chinese precedent of Han emperor Guangwu's Jianwu Restoration of the later (Eastern) Han dynasty beginning in A.D. 25. (Han Guangwu was in turn consciously imitating King Xuan's archetypical restoration of the Zhou.) In proclaiming the short-lived Kemmu Restoration, Godaigo was intent on eliminating the Kamakura shogunate and restoring his personal imperial rule; in this respect, it represented a "return to ancient ways" for early Meiji leaders, and was accordingly alluded to as a precedent authorizing their actions.[47] Moreover, the Kemmu Restoration had in common with its earlier references the participation of loyal and talented officials—what Huang and his contemporaries refer to as "men of talent." Godaigo's military commander, Kusunoki Masashige, was posthumously promoted to high court rank in early Meiji and enshrined at Minatogawa in 1872 near the site of his 1336 demise, becoming thereafter a paragon of loyalty to the emperor for Meiji ideologues.[48]

This overlay of allusions to the Zhou king Xuan's Restoration converges upon the aspect that we have seen Huang Zunxian stress in poem 6 above: a return to ancient ways. All of these sovereigns—King Xuan, Han Guangwu, Godaigo, and by analogy, Meiji—overthrew what they claimed was an interim and aberrant administration by men outside the proper sovereign authority, and returned to the ways of their august ancestors; in all cases, the salient features of these "ancient ways" were land tenure and taxation, and bureaucratic position (features consistent with the economic and political stakes of the sovereign and his supporters).

Precisely this focus of the Restoration—as *zhongxing* (J: *chūkō*)—is indicated by Huang in poem 36, which recounts the land tax reform promulgated in 1873. After describing the tax-in-kind (rice) levied by the Tokugawa shogunate—which, he adds, was modeled after the Tang Chinese system—and the hardships suffered by the peasants during the civil wars preceding the Tokugawa, Huang concludes with the Meiji tax in cash:

With the Meiji Restoration, all the provincial lords submitted their land charts and census registers, and yielded their fields to the public domain; whereupon, in conformity with ancient ways, all of these public lands were rented according to their local value, and taxed at a rate of 3 percent. Although the yearly interest on taxes due could not exceed 10 percent, the common people could little afford even this 3 percent. The present sovereign is humane and generous; on the first day of the tenth year of His reign [1877], He repealed the law and reduced the land tax to 2.5 percent. Yet even this is greater than Our Nation's tax of one-fortieth [1.2 percent], which still causes Our People to sigh in distress.[49]

This discussion points out the tension in the conception of restoration as a return to ancient ways, as an event both new and timeless. The striking issue is not whether or not the Meiji land tax reform was truly a return to ancient ways,[50] but rather, how it is that the sovereign may authorize modifications of ancient ways. As Huang represents the Restoration, a humane and generous purpose permits innovation, presumably because administrative justice and excellence justifies its own end—peace throughout the realm. Through just such a rationale, Western ways could be worked into the fabric of the Restoration.

But Western ways were new, and had at best tenuous, if any, precedents among the ancients. Accordingly, Japanese advocates of restoration came to abandon the use of *zhongxing* (J: *chūkō*) in the first years of Meiji, and in the interests of more comfortably incorporating Western ways, increasingly preferred the term *weixin* (J: *ishin*). *Weixin*, "reorganization" or "renovation," we recall, alluded to the Zhou king Wen's founding of a new administration, and to Japanese, this resonated with two such earlier renovations: (1) the first emperor Jimmu's system of laws founding the imperial line in the seventh century B.C.; and (2) the Taika reforms initiated by Emperor Kōtoku (r. A.D. 645–654), which were finalized in the Taihō legal code of 701 and intended to provide Japan with a Tang Chinese style of administration. The analogy suggested through this allusion—that Jimmu's and Kōtoku's ancient precedents prefigured a contemporary systemic renovation—took hold by 1871 and was refocused in the overwhelming popularity of the idea of a Meiji *Ishin*.[51]

Huang's *Poems on Divers Japanese Affairs* acknowledges this motivated shift in vocabulary. In his words, the "Renovation" (*weixin* or *ishin*) eliminated the Tokugawa shogunate (poems 11 and 29) and the *han* system of domainal control (poem 30), opened the new northern land of Hokkaidō (poem 4), introduced legislative government (poem 32), and worked other major administrative changes. And additionally, the Renovation not only represented a return to ancient ways, but also introduced Western ways. Huang describes the process in poem 31:

The Domainal Princes' offices assigned per former codes—
Of glorious things, none more so than Confucians' official hats;
Today's orders issued to "all respectful ministries,"
While affixing seals depends alone on the Dajōkan.

The feudal landholders in ancient antiquity were called the "Domainal Princes" [Kuni no Miyatsuko]; [Jimmu] enfeoffed them as local officials and in time, there were 144. Subsequently, the Domainal Princes were abolished, and the Domainal Governors [Kuni no Mikotomochi] were established; this transformed the feudal order into the prefectural system.[52]

After describing the major offices and listing the official ranks in the central administration of Kōtoku's prefectural system—which he calls the Dajōkan administration—Huang turns to the matter of the Renovation:

Nevertheless, from the time the Shogun's warriors seized the administration and revived the feudal system, the power of the Dajōkan became merely nominal. With the Meiji Renovation, there has been a systematic return to ancient ways; [Japanese leaders] have carefully considered the matter of accomodating the Chinese and the European systems, and made substantial preparations. They call the new administration the Dajōkan; it is controlled by preeminent ministers and counsellors, who aid the sovereign in administering his rule through the ministries, of which there are nine: Foreign Affairs, Internal Affairs, Treasury, Army, Navy, Education, Industry, Justice, and Imperial Household. In addition to these, the new administration has established three municipalities and thirty-five prefectures.[53]

We have, then, both Restoration and Renovation considered as a revival of ancient ways, and additionally, the Renovation as a means of introducing Western ways into the new administration. In one sense, Huang's characterization of the new administration as a "revival of ancient ways" is purely nominal and utterly a figure of allusion: the Meiji Dajōkan ("Supreme Imperial Council"), aside from its name, had little in common with that established as a final feature of the Taika reforms in A.D. 702. But this is not an idle allusion; it invokes the promise of historical precedent for the hope of a brilliant future. And in terms of Huang's working analogies of Restoration, the breadth of vision, innovation, and administration validated by the actions of earlier emperors recurs with the Meiji Restoration. As Huang implies with his praise of the Meiji government in the poem above, the credibility of the dynamic new administration is maintained through the continuity of Confucian participation, on the model of an exemplary officaldom, in combination with the newer institutions of Western origin.

But as we have seen with Western learning, Huang is not completely comfortable with the integration of Western ways into the Japanese order that he observes. His sense of apprehension is clear in poem 32, which follows the piece we have just been considering and concerns the new legislative assembly. I translate in full:

Assembly members, when elected, took jubilantly their seats;
The Imperial Elders follow along, in talk behind closed doors.
How can it be—all these lords enjoy a parade of power?
The Court, without remiss, lacks all remonstrant advice.

The authority of the Dajōkan [est. 1869] is weightiest; the Genrōin [Senate of Elders] was established later [1875]. When the country faces some major affair, a collective body is assembled to deliberate it. Prefectures first selected [prefectural] assembly members in Meiji 11 [1878] to discuss local affairs. The intention was quite likely in imitation of the Western manner of upper and lower assemblies, and was done precisely because the people so desired. The organization of these [governing] bodies has not yet been finalized. Of old, there was the Danjōdai [High Court of Justice], in time abolished. With Western ways, a greater number of people produce administrative guidelines, but the sovereign executes administration. Authority is held by the Assembly, so there is no office of censor [whose function is to remonstrate with the ruler]. Japan is a monarchy ruled by a sovereign king, and still there is no censor.[54]

The problem Huang contemplates is not an excess of Western ways in Japan. He is not alarmed that the people become involved in administration; rather, it is a welcome innovation precisely because legislative assemblies create a formal space for popular participation, and so eliminate popular movements in the streets. The difficulty Huang does foresee derives instead from a specific *insufficiency* of Confucian ways in the new Japanese administration; missing is the traditional post of censor, which was designed in ancient wisdom to safeguard against the excesses of individuals, and Huang is concerned because administrative management still lies in the hands of an individual king, without formal channels for remonstration. The admirable quality of a legislative assembly is that it is comprised of many, who accordingly will guard against the potential excesses of any of their fellows. The sovereign, by contrast, is one; and his formal independence from the legislature remains yet unchecked in the Japanese administration.[55]

With this, Huang's representation of Westernization comes full circle. It is proper learning that produces moral individuals, and if Western learning is inattentive to moral behavior, Chinese learning supplies the necessary and appropriate program of study. The classics not only illuminate the way to public virtue, but they also point toward the benefits of science. Similarly, proper administration produces peace Under-Heaven, and if Western ways are deficient in limiting the excesses of individuals who administer, Chinese ways supply the appropriate model for enlightened rule. It is the example of the ancient sage who, precisely because he managed to restore a failing age and to carry it to new heights of glory, demonstrates the value of innovation and vision.

Alternative Approaches to World Order

In addition to this effort to contain Japan's Westernization within analogies to Chinese precedents, Chinese scholars also engaged these developments within the larger framework of world order. There were really two ways in which world order was conceived by the 1880s: on the one hand, there was the international system of states, managed by the Western powers and in which Chinese participated with growing sophistication; on the other hand, there was the model of Civilization, which promised a world unified under the moral guidance of the Chinese emperor. As I have remarked already, where the former proposed equality and differentiation, the latter proposed hierarchy and unity. But in the course of the 1880s, I am convinced, it became increasingly difficult to entertain both of these possibilities. What we observe in Chinese representations of Japan is a progressive infiltration of Civilization by Westernization; Chinese geographers acknowledge disunity, both at the level of official state relations and within the common language and Civilization (*tong wen*) shared by China and Japan.

To a large degree, this growing acceptance of equivalence and disunity in the relationship between China and Japan is an effect of the *form* of representation itself. Performative genres like travel diaries and poetry manage to include Japan within Civilization because the author of such a text experienced Japan as an extension of Civilization.[56] The unity of content in travel diaries and poetry—and the unity of a worldview—are grounded in the author inscribing his experiences. The geographies of Japan written in the 1880s, by contrast, impose an abstract and objective organization upon Japan—a set of topics—the validity of which, recall, is grounded in the ideal unity of a world defined by imperial administration. That is to say, the geographic treatises take their principle of unity from a structure (of Civilization) *external* to their object. Because they represent a piece of the world in a manner independent of either the geographer or his subject, such representations readily reflected the fragmentation of the world. Accordingly, the production of the six nineteenth-century geographies of Japan in the 1880s reinforces the progressive differentiation of China and Japan precisely during that decade.

An Analogical Frame of Reference: Warring States

But there was in the 1880s one formulation in which both approaches to world order could be considered, and it was analogical. When Chinese scholars considered the persistent and perplexing changes upsetting China's relations with foreign powers in the late nineteenth century, many proposed that the present corresponded to one or the other half of the Eastern Zhou, the Spring and Autumn period (ca. 771–481 B.C.), when the feudal states stridently challenged each other in the name of defending the Zhou court, and the Warring States period (ca. 453–221 B.C.), when loyalty to the Zhou kings was dispensed with, and the states fought amongst themselves for ultimate domination.

Feng Guifen has been credited with the first such comparison of the present and the Eastern Zhou, in an essay written in 1861 (widely known but unpublished until 1884, a full decade after Feng's death).[57] Central to Feng's analogy with the Eastern Zhou is his concern over the danger that could arise if the present situation of China and the Westerners were to turn from resembling the Spring and Autumn period to being more like the Warring States:

Today each of the overseas barbarians is like one of the arrayed states of the Spring and Autumn period. It is not so much that the arrangement of power is the same; the habits and attitudes are similar. The force of each is roughly equivalent, so their words must express principles; each respects the capacity for treachery, so their mouths voice trust. When two armies engage each other in battle, they do not dispense with diplomats. *But in the event that peace is betrayed,* states become friends and acquiesce as the great invade the small, the strong conquer the weak, and each of course stands by its own excuses. No longer does it matter that none discuss principle, that none discuss trust—*as the warring states of old.* [Emphasis added][58]

Implicit in the analogy is a concern about unity and division in the world. Feng expresses the growing sense that China is but one in a world of rival and independent states, but his analogy serves to affirm both the centrality of Chinese Civilization as a point of reference as well as the Western-inspired "international consciousness" under formation. The analogy is especially pertinent because it raises certain questions of procedure that Chinese had debated time and again over the centuries—in situations of potential political conflict, did one act according to principle, or according to power? In this essay, Feng recommends that China safeguard a clear understanding of events and future agreements by directly and candidly discussing matters with the other states. The unconscious irony here is the fact that the analogical frame of reference is a period prior to the unification of China as an imperial form—and indeed, later scholars at the end of the nineteenth century would take up the unspoken possibility in the analogy, that China, like one of the warring states (excluding victorious but unprincipled Qin), would emerge triumphant as the leader of a new world order.

In contrast to Feng's use of the analogy, other scholars who figure in this study—Wang Tao and Hê Ruzhang, for example—wrote as though the time of the Warring States were already at hand. To them, the analogy served as a warning about the impending danger of Russia, which, like the state of Qin (in time the first empire), was plotting world domination and threatening to invade China from the west. These analogies drawn between the contemporary nations and the various ancient warring states are often remarkably detailed. Hê, for example, stated in a discussion of diplomatic protocol,

The great powers of Europe are like the warring states: Russia is Qin; Austria and Germany are Yan and Zhao respectively; France and Italy are Han and Wei; and England is the Qi and Chu of today. As for Turkey, Persia, Denmark, Switzerland, and Holland, they are comparably equal: like Song, some will be protected; like Xue, some will be conquered. In recent years, they all make military alliances out of fear for some day of vulnerability. Each state talks of war and builds defenses, and makes administrative preparations like the telegraph to speed written reports and roads to convey supplies. Their hearts are hardened for combat; they fear only some future day.[59]

The curious aspect of these analogies is the utter absence of China. In a move similar to the way that Western learning was analogically reduced to a text from China's past, so the present world of politics is reduced to a moment in China's antiquity. But in this case, the Chinese scholars who propose the analogy absent themselves from its specific structure; it is the Westerners who are like the warring states. The historical analogy addresses Chinese insecurities in a violent and changing world, but it also serves to keep the present at bay—a present the outcome of which is too uncertain to face directly.

This analogy, drawn between the contemporary world of the late nineteenth century and the ancient Eastern Zhou, thus managed to serve two purposes: a more pessimistic signification of imminent danger in the world; and a more optimistic vision of principled conduct among states. Its primary historical importance is that it directed the attention of Chinese scholars to the world of antiquity, which, since the classical formulation in the Confucian *Analects,* had held the promise of perfection for human society on earth. If only one could return to the Way of the Ancient Sages. It is of course difficult, if not impossible, to describe laws of the imagination, but it is likely that because of the perceived similarity between the Eastern Zhou and contemporary times, some Chinese scholars began to locate change and the possibility of new arrangements in images from the ancient Zhou texts. As we have seen above, for example, Huang Zunxian understood that the combined work of restoration and renovation in Japan constituted a new arrangement that incorporated Western ways, and this overall process was sanctioned by the examples of the Zhou king Wu's renovation in the twelfth century B.C. and King Xuan's restoration in the eighth century B.C.

There were scholars who did in fact imagine a novel order of the nations, one that did not reflect official imperial ideology; and these were, without exception it seems, among the members of the diplomatic corps who had the experience of world travel. Zhigang, for example, who was the Chinese (Manchu) minister leading the "Burlingame Mission" to the United States and Europe from 1868 to 1870, perceived the new world order in terms of division.[60] He recalled the ancient philosopher Zou Yan's claim that the world was divided into eighty-one parts, of which China was only one, and testified that his travels corroborated not only this fact, but also the sage king Yu's description of the world as divided into nine "circuits" (*zhou*), of which China was again only one. Zhigang implied at the end of his travel diary that this piece of information verified the possibility of a new interconnection (*tong*) among all peoples; he prudently left open the critical question of what the basis of the new order might be.[61]

By contrast, Guo Songtao, China's first ambassador to Britain (1875–1878), approached the issue as one of unity. He saw that the description of flags and pennants in the ancient *Rites of Zhou* was corroborated by his world travels, a fact which testified to Heaven and Earth's spontaneous and inherent unity; Guo accordingly claimed that China and the other nations were one, and that through negotiations based in principle—which both China and the West shared—all sides would attain a mutual and truthful point of view.[62] As stated earlier, Guo's vision of unity, which so outrageously granted China and the Westerners an equivalent moral standing, was denounced most harshly by the court.

Signs of a New Unity

Among the Chinese representations of Japan, a far less controversial vision of a new arrangement linking Civilization and the West was Huang Zun-xian's unique poetic vision. As we have seen, Huang's writings on Japan share the analogical frame of reference relating the present and the Zhou period. As he candidly admitted, he had pursued these studies of Japan because he believed that his diplomatic duties included those of the ancient Zhou "outer historian" and "junior messenger"—to gather knowledge of areas outside one's lord's domain while traveling in the company of his diplomats.[63] For Huang, the point of correspondence between Japan and the analogy of the Eastern Zhou was precisely this timely theme of unity and division.

Huang mentions a "new arrangement" specifically in poem 52, where, in the process of acknowledging the Japanese shift from Chinese to Western models of education, he alludes to the possibility of a new "interweaving" of civilizing and Western ways:

Chemistry books, strange machines—question the new arrangement.
Sail the seas, search far and wide for the sagely Gui Gu.
From Western lands learn a legacy of beneficial dazzle.
Encourage all acquaintances to speak out on world affairs.[64]

While we earlier looked at the notes to this piece in the context of utility—which warrants one's "questioning the new arrangements"—the critical point to gather from the poem is that the "new arrangements" are rearranging the world as Huang knows it. Lines 2 and 3 introduce allusions that evoke lost opportunities and potential models from Chinese history. What I have translated as "Western lands" is an ancient word that in the Han dynasty became a proper name, "Libian," the great empire to the West that scholars identify as Rome. As I mentioned above, some Chinese in the nineteenth century believed that Chinese learning had been transmitted to Rome during the Han; recovering that knowledge would provoke the "dizzying, dazzling disorder" (*xuan*) that Huang here believes is nonetheless beneficial. The allusion to Gui Gu in the second line provides a familiar, if radical, context for understanding the new, if confusing, arrangements. Gui Gu, an obscure figure from the Warring States period, is considered one of the *Zongheng Jia,* "specialists of the horizontal and the vertical," or political strategists, whose business was to plot alliances among the states in order to further the (re)unification of All-under-Heaven. The associations between horizontal and vertical, and the warp and woof of weaving, are underscored by the word in line 1 that I translate as "arrangement" (*bian*), which can also be thought of as an "interweaving." It is important to note that Huang's horizon for the new arrangement, beginning with education, is beyond the seas—and Western learning, through its teaching method and encouragement of overseas students, provides the basis for a new international order.

But in the *Poems on Divers Japanese Affairs,* he does more than merely observe or advocate a new synthesis of Civilization and Westernization. By introducing a set of terms that give his Chinese readers a vocabulary for describing the practices of this new order, he begins the actual linguistic labor of integrating Chinese writing and Westernization. This was possible, I believe, because Huang approached Japan with the assumption of *tong wen*—that China and Japan shared a common language and Civilization.

To begin with, Huang's *Poems* incorporate a range of new terminology that describe the process of Westernization in Japan and that we find in other contemporary Chinese accounts of Western countries. Chinese who read such accounts, had traveled abroad, or lived in the growing treaty port cities would have been quite familiar with these things and their names: *renliche,* the ricksha; *huoche* (or its expanded form *huolunche*), the steam locomotive; *tielu* or *tiedao,* the railway; *huolunchuan* (or the simplified *huochuan*), the steamship; *dianqibao* (and its variants *dianbao* or *dianxin*), the telegraph; *xinwen,* the newspaper; and of course the names of Western sciences—chemistry, physics, mechanics, and so on.[65] Another such object familiar to Chinese, but for which Huang uses the Japanese name, is the daguerrotype (in time, photograph), which Japanese call *shashin* (C: *xiezhen*), but Chinese know as *zhaoxiang.* As signs of Western ways and Western learning, Huang notes their novelty in Japan, and their contribution to the new society of the Meiji Restoration. (Remember that the ricksha had been introduced to China and was a ubiquitous domesticate in the treaty port cities.)

But in addition to these names of material things, Huang mentions a number of terms describing the new Westernizing administration under way in Japan. This is not surprising, given the scrutiny with which Huang examined administration. Because these are words that I have not found in other contemporary travel accounts or geographies, I conclude that Huang's *Poems* was the first popular presentation of these terms. Some of these were words that Chinese readers would have encountered in other Chinese texts—significantly, from the Zhou period: (1) "*gonghe*" (J: *kyōwa*), or "republic", which was the metaphorical extension of the Duke of Zhou's system of joint rule; (2) "*ziyou*" (J: *jiyū*), or "freedom," which the Tang poet Du Fu coined from a still older expression (in the ancient work of philosophy, the *Zhuangzi*), "*ziyouzizai*," meaning "to wander where one will"; and (3) "*falü*" (J: *hōritsu*), or "law," which the ancient philosopher Guanzi used as a collective term for those measures by which a ruler prevailed over others through fear or violence (*fa*), and fixed people's ranks so as to prevent competition among them (*lü*).[66]

In the context of law, Huang introduces other terms unprecedented in Chinese texts. Because these are names, his readers could likely understand them from their context. "*Xianfa*" (J: *kenpō*), or "constitution," which means literally something like "supreme law," had been first used by the Japanese in the seventh century to describe the new legal order borrowed from China and promulgated by Shōtoku-taishi (572–621) in 604. Clearly, the call for a constitution in Meiji Japan was in remembrance of that first such legal innovation. Similarly, two other novel terms are names of proposed texts: the *Minfa* (J: *Minpō*), or "civil law," and the *Xingfa* (J: *Keihō*), or "criminal law." (The Japanese government began compiling these in the 1870s, but final forms were not enacted until the 1890s.) In the context of "superior law" (qua "constitution"), Chinese readers could undoubtedly understand these in terms of analogous bodies of law in China—as "laws governing people," not unlike clan codes of behavior, and "laws prescribing punishments," quite similar to such laws in China.

All of these carry references to the political situation in Japan during Huang's sojourn there, dominated as it was by the debate over the choice of political and legal forms brought on by the Freedom and People's Rights Movement. Like "freedom," two other unprecedented terms in the *Poems* refer directly to this movement: "*minquan*" (J: *minken*), or "people's rights," and "*yiyuan*" (J: *giin*), meaning literally "court of debate" or "parliament," which were specific goals of the movement.[67]

By contrast, other new vocabulary items had to do with administrative matters of keen and growing interest to the Chinese. "*Shuchu*" (J: *yushutsu*), or exports, and "*shuru*" (J: *yu'nyū*), or imports, were for many officials the main purpose of China's treaty with Japan, and Chinese diplomats followed very closely the growth of Japan's trade as both a source of state revenue and a foundation for military strength. They studied Japan's exports and imports through the novel practice of "*tongji*" (J: *tōkei*), or statistical tables, a practice the Japanese had learned from the West. A related term concerning fiscal matters that Huang notes is "*zhengquan*" (J: *shōken*), meaning "paper securities," an extension of the practice of paper currency.

Now, the curious fact is that Huang does not bother to gloss the above terms. Unlike the specificity with which he indicates that tobacco, for example, is an exotic thing brought to Japan from the Philippines by Western traders, and that the very Japanese word for the item, "*tabako,*" is a transliteration of Western speech, the new terminology typically receives no explication.[68] With the sole exception of "paper securities," he does not call attention to them as new or unusual practices. They are unproblematic, if not familiar, and he anticipated that his readers would read them as such.

The fact that we find this body of seemingly new terminology in Huang's *Poems*—nearly all of which is treated as familiar—points to the actual practice of *tong wen* ("shared writing/Civilization") as Chinese represented Japan during this period. Accordingly, I do not think it is appropriate to treat these terms as evidence of "language borrowing." Linguists who have examined the phenomena of vocabulary building through various kinds of loanwords, and who have done a great deal of work on the Chinese incorporation of such "new" Chinese-character words, have compiled extensive lists of primarily two kinds: those which already existed in Chinese, but were given new meanings in Japan and thereafter recirculated in China (like "*gonghe,*" "*ziyou,*" and "*falü*" above, or "*jingji*": see chapter 2); and those invented by Japanese during the Meiji period (like "*xianfa,*" "*minfa,*" "*minquan,*" and so on).[69] Even though this work, based as it is on a principle of hindsight, might help us to locate such words in any random text, what we see in the *Poems on Divers Japanese Affairs* is that this terminology is undifferentiated from the rest of Huang's language. It is, in fact, shared language—with all the implications of that relationship that were described in chapter 2.

In this respect, the question of language origins and the problem of who borrowed what from whom becomes a moot point; these are, finally, not genuine historical questions since they address only idealized words ("types") abstracted from their actual, material usage ("tokens"). We have no way of knowing, for example, if Huang's readers read "*xianfa*" as "constitution" or as "supreme law," but this becomes an issue only if the problem of meaning is understood as a problem of translation (as with "*tabako,*" for example), or when theories of language are grounded in a practice of translation rather than usage.[70] (And bear in mind, in light of my previous discussion concerning the inferior status of speech vis-à-vis [written] language, that the transliteration of a word like "*tabako*" is an operation preformed on speech, mere ephemeral sound.) Huang Zunxian was engaged not in translation, but in a poetic practice—a performative epistemology—with deliberate aspirations to evidential research; because he believed that Japan and China actually did "share language," when he encountered some unprecedented or uncorroborated phenomenon in Japan, he accordingly represented these signs of the new administration with the assumption of and in the terms of *tong wen*.[71]

As we know, Huang was favorably impressed with much of the Westernization that he observed in Japan; he had reservations about the way in which Western learning contributed to political activism, and the absence of Confucian controls on imperial rule, but he was generally optimistic that Japan was successfully synthesizing Civilization and Westernization into a new unity. As I described in chapter 4, his choice of poetry was intended to represent this unity undifferentiated from his own perceptions of it and in such a way that unity was not sacrificed for the sake of received conventions of geographical and historical analysis. In this respect, his "new" terminology is a sign of that new unity. If we recall the metonymic relationship existing between language and Civilization, we might say that in the *Poems*, Huang is reasserting the metonymic relationship, but supplying a new linguistic content for Civilization.[72] We know from the brush-talks that he was interested in an alliance between Japan and China so as to safeguard Civilization from certain disruptive forms of Westernization; his representation of the new administration in Japan imagines a new order of Civilization, one that would begin to include aspects of Westernization, and one that would continue to be shared by China and Japan. The new terminology is thus an expression of that possibility. Under the sign of the ancient Zhou, the Westerners would continue to behave as warring states, but China and Japan, following Japan's lead, would undertake a renovation of Civilization, not only maintaining continuity with the past, but also preserving their moral superiority over the West.

This aspect of the *Poems,* that is, this capacity of the text to represent a new order in the actual terms of both Civilization and Westernizing practices—more than any other attribute—conclusively sealed its appeal to the imaginations of Japanese and Chinese readers alike. Appearing amidst the political controversy over the sovereignty of the Liuqiu Islands (which China ultimately abandoned to Japan, although the issue was never formally settled until the Korean controversy violently intervened beginning in 1882), it was both the first and the last text that represented Japan as a prodigal son returned from a long absence and received with much hope for a common future.

In the 1880s, such a point of view was no longer taken, and poetry as a form of historical representation was neglected out of a preference for the more conventional style of historical geography. Huang himself was relocated in the United States, as consul in San Francisco, and there he completed his own historical geography, the *Japan Treatise,* the opening line of which testifies to the shift taken in Huang's own perception of the world situation:

The Outer Historian states: Circling the earth are one hundred and some domains. With a domain, you have of course a people; with a people, you have a ruler. Now, of those one hundred and some domains, there are some where one man rules alone; these are called autocracies. In others, the common people discuss administration; these are called democracies. When these higher and lower elements divide responsibilities and privileges, this is called the joint governing of ruler and people. . . . [Japan] has planned to inaugurate its National Assembly within ten years, and so its autocratic administration, which has endured for over 2,500 years, is heading today in the direction of what some say will be a joint rule, and what others say will be a democracy.[73]

Where the *Poems* of the late 1870s facilitate a unity of Civilization and Westernization, through the unity of the poet's experience, the later text begins by asserting the existence of a world composed of arrayed states, each with its own type of administration. Japan is not situated in the poet's perception, which provides the context of Chinese Civilization, but in the international context of a set of alternative administrations. The very form of the geographic treatise situates Japan vis-à-vis other similar administrative units—differentiated, of equivalent types, and disunited. As a vision of the world as a whole, Huang has employed the figure of division, a point of view standard among those Chinese diplomats who replaced him in Japan.

What is so striking about this process of differentiation is that we can witness it taking place as a fragmentation of the "shared language" of Civilization: what was once ostensibly familiar and could be claimed effortlessly as China's own became within a decade a space most decidedly foreign. This development, along with the deterioration of official Chinese and Japanese relations, undoubtedly accounts for the objectified representations of Japan among Chinese scholars in Japan during the 1880s. This shift, in other words, occurs as a dual negation—of both the analogy of the "warring states" and the reality of "shared language/Civilization."

Rejecting Analogy and Confronting Division

More than anyone, Yao Wendong embodies the trends and contradictions of the decade of the 1880s. Yao, recall, accompanied the second ambassador to Japan, Li Shuchang, in 1882, with the specific assignment to compile a geography of Japan. They and their associates moved into the same brush-talking and literary circles, where Li and Yao enjoyed a popularity more remarkable than that of Huang Zunxian—if only because the numbers of Japanese scholars involved in Chinese poetry had markedly increased during 1881 and 1882. But additionally, Yao learned to speak Japanese and could communicate with his hosts outside of brushtalking. In the numerous records of poetry gatherings that remain, Yao is witty, warm, and erudite—but he never mentions *tong wen*.[74]

Official Chinese attitudes toward Japan shifted sharply because of the failure of negotiations over the Liuqiu Islands, which had followed too closely after the Taiwan Incident, and many Chinese were increasingly suspicious of Japan. Yao's official reports and personal correspondence reiterate accusations that the "Dwarfs" are plotting treachery, and he urges his superiors to begin arranging defensive measures.[75] Accordingly, his *Military Essentials of Japanese Geography* is intended to give China some basis for gauging military preparations, "in case of some unexpected emergency."[76]

As poetry gatherings among Chinese and Japanese in Tokyo during the

1880s became grand social affairs of the major poetry societies, it is significant that their ideological value became more pronounced among the Japanese. It may be that when confronted by both the irrelevance of Chinese learning and the Genbunitchi Movement (Movement to Unify the Spoken and Written) that valorized spoken Japanese as a written form, the Japanese saw poetry gatherings as their last connection to a Chinese heritage. Or they may have been trying to contain uncomfortable diplomatic hostilities in friendly social situations. But by contrast, Chinese only rarely referred to Japan as a *tong wen zhi guo*, "a country sharing Civilization." Where Japanese continued to celebrate "shared language" in their poetry to Yao, he never acknowledged such a relation. On the contrary, he avowed the opposite. In a letter publicly reprinted a number of times, he declared:

I'm about to submit the geography of Japan that I was sent here to complete. At first I was uncertain about my accomplishments with the Japanese language—this land has eliminated the Chinese language—and only later did I slowly discuss things in a grammatical manner without daring to simplify my meaning to the point of losing its truth. . . . As for the Liuqiu affair, things are stuck at emphatic declarations, and my humble opinion, I fear, is not appropriate for writing or speaking. These days most people are saying that the nations of the world are in a situation like that of the warring states at the end of the Zhou, but that only shows how little they know about general affairs. Actually, it's not like the Warring States period at all, when discussions of political strategy were transferred to the professional strategists. These days we may have a hundred Su Qin's or Zhang Yi's [successful "hard-line" Warring States strategists], but how can we use them? And why is this? In the first place, the speech and writing of each nation is different, and translation so twists the tone of words in the transmission that they go awry. In the second place, nations rely on power and not on principle. The powerful start with crooked principles and try to straighten them; while the weaker start with straightforward principles and make them crooked. Only if we have warships and the best troops can we prevail over the world.[77]

What is striking here is that as Yao dismisses the prevalent analogy with the Warring States period, he reintroduces China into the world order in terms that reverse what we have seen above. It is a world that disregards principle, where each state does its best to prevail over others by military force alone, and if China is to triumph over that order, its weapons will decide. Such a world is, after all, a world where Civilization cannot work its effects. Military subjugation would be more appropriate than transformation through patterning. Without principle, behavior has no patterns; and without a common language, patterned words no longer convey truth. Worse, given the context in which Yao was placed, Japan has discarded Chinese language and the present difficulties consequently seem unresolvable.

Not only does Japan *not* share the language or Civilization of China, but Japan has removed itself so far from civilized ways since the Meiji Restoration that according to Yao, it has undergone what he termed a "singular transformation" (*yibian*) or "transmutation" (*biange*).[78] The reason for this, of course, is its comprehensive program of Westernization. As one of his associates wrote, "Never before has a people so believed in and imitated Western ways as to totally transform their old customs."[79] In 1879, Wang Zhichun and Huang Zunxian had noted that Japan was sending growing numbers of students to the West in the same way that students had been sent to China during the Tang, and that Japanese trade with China still matched that with the West, but in the 1880s—especially beginning with Yao's *Military Essentials*, a mere five years later—Chinese perceptions of Japan would imply that by and large, Japan had so inundated itself with Western ideas and things that it had remade itself into a "Western" nation.

Westernization, in and of itself, was not a reprehensible undertaking; what Chinese so strongly objected to was the indiscriminate and generalized Westernization of Japan, which dispensed with proper moral proprieties. Even Yao, for example, admitted the potential value of Western learning; in a letter outlining his plans for a "Society for the Study of Geography," he wrote:

Westerners say that the exchange of knowledge transforms the pattern of commerce into a single road of learning. The collective thought of all the brilliant men from the five continents would be a great advantage to our country as a whole, and after several decades, we would be able to see the nature and conditions of Europe and America as clearly as looking at a fire.[80]

Yao is not urging a wholesale Westernization of China similar to that of Japan, but imagining a new synthesis of knowledge and culture in a worldwide context. The difficulty with Yao's and others' representations of Westernization in the 1880s geographies of Japan, however, is that they are largely conventional and descriptive; aside from the use of statistics, they contain little evidence of Western ways.[81] In the context of Chinese problems with foreign aggression, the six geographies offer little in the way of practical solutions to the actual problems of division.[82] Instead, we have this hopeful but abstract projection of the possibility of unity onto a grander but more removed stage of activity—the "five continents." In this larger world context, Japan comes to be perceived as a rival more on the side of the Westerners than on the side of Civilization.

From Shared Language to Signs of Difference

This retreat from analogy on the part of officials like Yao, whose work in Japan necessitated perceiving the world with an eye to the intrusions of practical politics, coincided with the retreat from acknowledging *tong wen*. With the same gaze that observed the overall Westernization of Japan during the 1880s, Chinese scholars noted Japan's accessory and comprehensive abandonment of Civilization. This was in part, of course, because Chinese officials were better prepared to engage the Japanese in matters more pressing than brushtalking and poetry; they had the experience and contacts of their predecessors, and many of them, like Yao, became proficient with the Japanese language. They perceived Japan as having, in addition to its respective regional speech, a written language of its own, different from Chinese and hence outside the domain of Civilization. In this respect, we observe in the geographies of Japan written during the 1880s a progressive distancing of Japan, which is expressed most clearly in respective sections on language and learning. They discussed this change in terms of three particulars that defined the metonymic relationship between language and Civilization: the unitary and moral "Way" of Chinese Civilization; *hanwen* as "Chinese texts and learning"; and *hanwen* as Chinese (written) language.

The first abandonment was seen as implicit in the desire to imitate Western ways. To forgo the models of the past was to depart from propriety, and Chinese became especially condemnatory of Japan on this point. Reminiscent of earlier denunciations of "Dwarfish deviousness," Gu Houkun attributed Japan's departure from the Way to an inherent perversity: "Japanese adore what is different and take pride in the strange, and have accordingly undertaken a singular transformation, leaving nothing unchanged." He questioned, "Truly, what Way is this?"[83] Elsewhere, however, Gu expressed a more optimistic tone; Japan may adopt Western ways, but in time all Western(ized) nations would come to learn the superiority of Chinese Civilization:

There is nothing outside of the Way of the Sages, in antiquity and today, and so outside of China, nothing is flawed. Since Western ways proliferated [in Japan], there are those who slander Our Way, assault Our Way, and repudiate Our Way, who enter into heterodoxy and betray moral relations. But who can know if Western teachings and Our Way are incompatible? Each learns what he is taught. As for those who slander, assault, and repudiate Our Way—why is that? Western ways locate the foundation of the nation in military drill, the opening of mines, trade, the manufacture of guns and cannon, the establishment of telegraph lines, and so on. . . . In the future, the nations of the earth will each have great military capabilities, and government coffers will overflow—and conflict will be inevitable. Those who are willing to turn from military might and cultivate Civilization will delight upon entering the kingly design of old; and the greatness of the Way of the Ancient Sages will inevitably spread to all the edges of the earth.[84]

If Gu imagined the possibility of Japan's penitent return to Civilization, his hope was uncommon and admittedly foreclosed by the momentous marginalization of Chinese learning in Japan. In keeping with Huang Zunxian's greatest fears, the Chinese textual tradition became not merely one course in a student's program of study, but was taught for only one year at that. The senior high school visited by Gu Houkun offered Chinese learning as part of the third-year curriculum; the girls' school offered it in the fourth year. The vocational high school offered no Chinese learning per se; rather, students were taught *kanbun* for composition purposes.[85] Older students already prepared for advanced study under the old system could still follow a course of Chinese learning at Tokyo University in the 1880s.[86] But by and large, as Fu Yunlong lamented, Chinese learning had been abandoned in favor of Western studies.[87]

In fact, "Chinese learning" existed only as a university course of study by the 1880s. In Japanese middle schools and normal schools during the 1880s and nineties (as standardized respectively in the 1880 and 1883 education codes), "Chinese literature" constituted part of the "Japanese and Chinese literature" course in all grades. Excerpts from Chinese and Japanese *kanbun* texts were used simply to familiarize students with the *kanbun* tradition in Japan, and students were expected to be capable of rudimentary composition in *kanbun* by their fourth year. Aside from this textual study, students in both middle and normal schools were taught short courses in Chinese history, which bridged their studies of Japanese and world history.[88] In comparison to the regular course of study by samurai during the Tokugawa age—Huang's and his colleagues' brushtalking partners—this was paltry and superficial exposure to Chinese learning.[89]

In addition to lamenting Japan's abandonment of the "Way," Chinese scholars drew increasingly sophisticated boundaries between the Japanese and Chinese languages. As I have indicated, the most sweeping development in the 1880s is the elimination of claims to *tong wen*. Rather than "sharing language," Chinese acknowledge that Japan has a written language of its own, historically based upon but currently different from Chinese language. While most of these geographers begin discussions of Japanese learning or language by explaining that Japan borrowed Chinese characters during the Tang dynasty, they tend to focus on different aspects of the relationship between the two linguistic spheres.

Chen Jialin and Gu Houkun, for example, dwell on the physical appearance of Japanese writing. To Gu, it is an erratic mixture of Chinese and Japanese; to Chen, it is a distortion of Chinese. Chen quite literally takes Japanese *kana* (C: *jiaming*) to be "false" (*jia*) characters used to "name" (*ming*) Chinese characters. As he explains it, the Japanese took parts of Chinese characters and transformed them into their *I-ro-ha* system of *kana*. These they insert into Chinese writing, which they then proceed to read in a reverse order.[90]

In addition, Chen, Fu Yunlong, and Huang Zunxian discuss the complex system of multiple pronunciations for Chinese characters in Japanese: the *Go'on* (Wu or Six Dynasties), *Kan'on* (Tang), and *Kun* ("native") Japanese pronunciations. These are of course historical accounts of the development of these different pronunciations, which were the result of Japan's borrowing Chinese language material at different points in China's own linguistic history. Again, this is the kind of subject matter we would expect, given the historiographical requirements of evidential research.

This sense of difference with the way Japanese pronounced Chinese characters was further explored by Huang and especially Fu, both of whom include discussions of Japanese "nativist" and philological theories of language. In general, these theories sought to differentiate a pure and hence preferable (spoken) Japanese from the alien (and "unnatural") Chinese overlay of (written) characters. Although Fu would agree that Chinese characters indeed registered a regional set of sounds [those of north China], which inherently differed from those of Japanese, he could not accept the Japanese nativist argument that the Japanese language "naturally" combined signs and sounds in a one-to-one relationship, while the Chinese language combined multiple sounds with each written character in an accordingly unnatural way.[91] The Japanese argument sought to distinguish languages along these lines of written signs and sounds: "For the most part, the Chinese language takes the written sign as the pattern of language, while Sanskrit takes the sound as the pattern of language. Japanese is like Sanskrit; its sounds come from nature, while its written signs come from man. That which comes from nature is the same for all nations."[92] Fu responded, based on Chinese theories of language and its origins, that past history showed that the sounds of Chinese characters were not fixed, but changed over time, and that the essence of sound was the four tones of Chinese characters, which were in fact grounded in nature and which Japan lacked altogether.[93]

If Chinese awareness of Japanese arguments like these may have enhanced the Chinese sense of difference when confronted with the written Japanese language, it was the use of Chinese characters—and certain characters themselves—that most impressed Chinese with the difference of Japanese. In the first place, they noted the presence of "different" or "unorthodox" characters (*yizi*) in Japan, lexical items alien to Chinese. Both Chen Jialin and Fu Yunlong include lists of these, and interestingly, they comment on this unusual material in a number of ways. Chen supplies either a commonly recognizable substitute—in effect, a Chinese translation of the Japanese character—or an expanded description of the meaning of the character.[94] Fu does the same, but in addition, resorts to the Ming practice of *jiyu*, or "transmitted vocabulary," which involves roughly transliterating the Japanese pronunciation of the character into Chinese characters of comparable sound value.[95]

What these practices indicate is that by the 1880s, as an alternative to brushtalking, Chinese had begun *translating* between Japanese and Chinese writing. In a world where the two no longer shared language, such a practice was needed. Of course, from the time of the first embassy, there were professional Chinese (and Japanese) translators of Japanese *speech*, but in the space of a decade, the same techniques were being commonly applied to *writing* as well. This technique of translation, more than anything, emphasized the difference between China and Japan, a difference, bear in mind, that Chinese represented as a Japanese departure from Civilization.

It is no coincidence, I believe, that the last major geography of the decade, *Random Pickings from a Dragon Ride,* includes an entire volume of *yiming,* "different" or "unorthodox" names. The authors provide an expansive list of Japanese names for "affairs and things" in Japan that would appear unusual to the Chinese reader; each item, like the *yizi* or "unorthodox characters" of Chen and Fu, is explained and given a translation. As a collection of the names of things, this volume certainly bears the signs of exotica; but their purpose is not to represent the ambiance of the foreign. Rather, they intend to define terms, to delimit meaning, in accordance with evidential research style and the authoritative voice of history. Expressions that Huang Zunxian used in his *Poems on Divers Japanese Affairs,* and that required no explanations for his readers—from new affairs like "post office" to common things like the edible seaweed "laver"—are now given definite descriptions, and placed as objects of knowledge within a geographic representation.[96]

What we are witnessing here is the passage of "shared language" from practical reality to historical fossil. Like the living tree buried through centuries, whose cells one by one petrify into a substance more permanent, so the language of Civilization, that once brushed its designs among otherwise mute strangers, was consigned to print, the lexical fragments of its patterns to be examined for the truth that each might hold. More than anyone, Fu Yunlong mourned the passing of *tong wen* from Japan. With scholars of Chinese learning reduced to a mere faction among the politically conservative, Chinese learning itself abandoned, Chinese books discarded and all their knowledge devalued, Fu set about gathering a representative collection of Japanese works in Chinese belles-lettres, inscriptions, and scholarship. He devoted an entire third of his geography to this project because, he wrote, he hoped to save for future generations of Japanese what was on the verge of being lost.[97]

For China itself, the passing of *tong wen* held implications of even greater magnitude. In a world without principle, where force alone mattered, and where language itself had been replaced by a conflicting congeries of incompatible speeches, communication became a fragile, ethereal thing. Through the tortuous twists and turns of translation, meaning itself threatened to escape words. In the late 1870s, confident in a shared language informed by the universality of poetry, Huang Zunxian could name signs of the new that not only he, but other travelers and inhabitants of the new treaty ports saw as unproblematic—as straightforward a practice to him and to us now, for example, as all that was meant by "post office." A decade later, others would follow him and feel the need for an explanation. In that deliberate attempt to translate some difference of meaning into language inexplicably no longer familiar, something had changed most profoundly. Chinese were demonstrating that they had become different to themselves; and this monumental disorientation within the very possibility of representation, I maintain, startled China far more than any "response to the West."

For China, I believe, was always safe from the West, since the West could be contained within analogies. The Western nations were as strong as they were barbarian, and as advanced as they were locked into a moment in China's past—a way of life that, like the proposals of the *Mozi*, China had long ago rejected. Chinese scholars could always explain the West, because they knew its location and motivations. Their usage of historical analogy to place the West managed to keep both China itself and the West familiar. What they could not explain was Japan's so suddenly becoming like the West; aside from disparaging remarks about Japanese character, they could not comprehend the remarkable transformation. They could measure it statistically, but that ultimately was no help. They simply had no analogies for such a phenomenon, and that, I am convinced, is why the Sino-Japanese War in 1894 made such a profound impression on the Chinese government and ruling officialdom. It was the clearest and most forceful indication that, as a world order, Civilization had failed. And there would be no restoring it except at the cost of redefinition, by incorporating into practice the very terms of change.

Afterword

I remember, as a student in Japan, that many of my fellows were reluctant to study either written or spoken Japanese. When I asked them why, they had generally two responses. One was that both written and spoken Japanese were useless, not nearly as useful as English upon returning to China. The other was that Japan itself had little of value to study—apart from civilization imported from China, India, and Europe, Japan had nothing of its own that merited study. I thought that the first response erred from utilitarianism, the second, from egotism. . . . I would urge Chinese henceforth to diligently study Japan. What is the character of the Japanese? What are their ways of thinking? What is the nature of their customs and habits? What is the basis of their nation and society? On what is their way of life grounded? Study these questions diligently! . . . In the words of an ancient saying, "Know thyself and thy opponent, and a hundred battles will be a hundred victories." Whether you oppose or attack him, you must understand him!
Dai Jitao, *An Essay on Japan*

It is 1971, and Mirek says that the struggle of man against power is the struggle of memory against forgetting.
Milan Kundera, *The Book of Laughter and Forgetting*

History, we understand, is a record of the past, an explanation of the past, an analysis of the past. But history is equally a forgetting of the past. In the act of choosing a theme, we necessarily cut through the fabric of past lives, much as we reap words from the pages of a book; we attend to some, as we forget others.

In my effort to explain a Chinese response to the changing world of the nineteenth century, I have had to foreground an obscure moment in China's past that has been minimized or overlooked by the modernization narratives common in the historiography of China. Rather than represent the history of late imperial China as a progressive series of failed attempts to modernize in the manner of the West, I have attempted to address developments in Chinese intellectual history at their textual basis. While this may seem to be no less arbitrary a decision—indeed, one might rightly insist that the Chinese culture appreciated here is but the pretensions of an elite minority in Chinese society—my selection of nineteenth-century Chinese texts concerning Japan does allow me to control my subject matter in the manner of a scientific experiment and to observe things Western as they intrude into an otherwise coherent set of representations. Suspended in the background of this study, after all, is the rise of Westernization in Japan, which, I have argued, destabilized Chinese representations of Japan and necessarily altered the ways in which Chinese perceived and represented Japan after 1890.

To borrow another's words, I have not attempted to *reconstruct* a series of events in China's past, to represent a period in the past "as it really happened," but have tried to *construct* a history of Chinese representations of Japan at a critical moment in Chinese and Japanese interaction. My model in this effort has been Walter Benjamin, who explained in a discussion of the cultural history of ruling classes,

The historical materialist must sacrifice the epic dimension of history. The past for him becomes the subject of a construction whose locus is not empty time, but the particular epoch, the particular life, the particular work. He breaks the epoch away from its reified *historical continuity*, and the life from the epoch, and the work from the life's work. But the result of his construction is that *in* the work the life's work, *in* the life's work the epoch, and *in* the epoch the course of history are suspended and preserved.[1]

Here, Benjamin urges us to reject our habitual perspective, in which the past inevitably leads to the present and, as an alternative, proposes that we dwell on particular details that will reflect or refract the epochal history. Accordingly, I began by analyzing a specific linguistic community in Tokyo and the forms of representation that in part determined the Chinese participants' constructions of those experiences at the borders of their world. Following a lack of official contact for nearly one and a half centuries, the Chinese diplomats and travelers who journeyed to Japan during the critical years from 1877 to 1890 found themselves in the midst of a momentous transformation. Where the first of these men, Ambassador Hê Ruzhang and his staff, arrived with expectations of commonality, those who came later, in the company of Ambassador Li Shuchang, could no longer sustain such a sense of unity. What I have examined is the coherence of their worldview, a geographical and historical problematic informed by a pair of concepts, *wenming*, or Civilization, and *tong wen*, or "shared writing/ Civilization." By analyzing the textual remains of this group, I have attempted *not* to recover a phase of ongoing Sino-Japanese relations, but to illuminate first, Chinese understandings of Civilization, Japan, and the West; and second, the hitherto unexamined relations among the literary Chinese language, geographical texts, and a worldview. *Tong wen*, I have tried to show, was much more than the usual truism that "Japan borrowed Chinese characters in the seventh century A.D." *Tong wen* was a vision of the world, and if I have located it at a moment when Chinese scholars were abroad and engaged with Japanese scholars in the pleasantries of brushtalking and poetry writing, that choice, I maintain, does not minimize the validity of my construction. For this essay, in the end, concerns the "borders," the practical limits, of that nineteenth-century Chinese worldview. When Chinese scholars in Japan rejected the linguistic and behavioral basis of Civilization, *tong wen* was no longer a credible model for understanding Japan. Accordingly, Chinese after 1890 were faced with the project of constructing newer, more "truthful" representations of Japan.

In other words, Chinese geographical knowledge of Japan changed after 1890, and generally as the imperial period drew to a close. Chinese continued to travel to Japan for diplomacy, official investigation, pleasure, and especially study, as thousands of students pursued "Western" educations there between 1896 and 1919. From the extensive research into the activities of those Chinese students in Japan, we know that they transferred into Chinese society a wide range of new, Western culture and behavior, from the educational disciplines to specific practices of journalism, literature, and politics.[2] These practices spread among Chinese students abroad, by and large, as new modes of experience, which underscores what I have called the performative approach to Japan and helps to explain, in a preliminary manner, the huge number of Chinese travel diaries of Japan which continued to be written until the end of the long "Anti-Japanese War" (1937–1945). For it is clear from the textual record that of the imperial geographic representations examined here, the travel diary became the dominant form after 1890, as the genre of geographical treatise disappeared, its place in part taken by new and rudimentary textbooks on geography—the first of which were Chinese translations of European and Japanese textbooks.[3] This new expository genre, the "modern" textbook, exposed Chinese students to an epistemology of "geography" informed by European concepts, which, by Dai Jitao's time, would become a primary intellectual construct.[4]

In addition to this preference for the performative strategy of geographical knowledge, we see the scope of utility restricted to a pragmatic sensibility in the three main scholarly works on Japan published after 1890 and prior to the Anti-Japanese War. The first of these, Kang Youwei's *Riben bianzheng kao* (*An examination of Japan's political changes*), was presented to the Guangxu emperor in 1897 as part of the reform effort Kang and other scholars advocated in the wake of the Sino-Japanese War.[5] Taking the form of a traditional chronicle and covering the reign years Meiji 1 through 23 (1868–1890), it explains the Japanese construction of a new administration and includes Kang's advice to the Guangxu emperor on how to implement institutional reforms and which historical precedents to cite in justifying such change. In a similar manner, the second text, Wang Xianqian's *Riben yuanliu kao* (*An examination of Japan's origin and development*) of 1902, outlines a chronology of Japanese history from its beginnings to Meiji 26 (1893), in an effort to explain how this powerful Eastern nation came to "reform" itself and incorporate Western ways.[6] Both of these texts, which relied heavily on Huang Zunxian's *Japan Treatise,* serve as exercises in what we might call applied history. In the language I used in chapter 5, they imply a preference for utility as means insofar as the information contained in them is meant to be deliberately used to inform policy.

Such an orientation is emphatic in the third of these texts, Dai Jitao's *Riben lun*—as I have indicated in the above epigraph. Dai's *Essay on Japan,* published in 1928, examines the administrative and religious background of Japan's "body politic" (*kokutai*) in an effort to explain political and ideological developments since the Meiji Restoration.[7] Dai would have his Chinese readers study Japan in preparation for political conflict between the Chinese and Japanese nations. Here, geographical knowledge assumes its now familiar form as an accomplice to a rather deterministic use of history and politics. No longer approaching geography in the once conventional form of imperial administration, Dai understands that geographical boundaries define a national people, whose character, customs, habits of mind, and way of life constitute knowledge useful for informing international political relations.

This epistemological transformation of Chinese geography, accomplished in two generations, was surely motivated by the new concept of the nation. One has only to read, for example, the diary of Xue Fucheng, Chinese ambassador to England, France, Italy, and Belgium between 1890 and 1894, to see intellectual change under way. From his offices in Europe, where one of his major goals was to negotiate a Burma-China border with the British, Xue painstakingly generates histories of relations between the Qing emperors and several Southeast Asian chiefdoms—*and maps them*—to produce an international border representing the limits of British and Chinese territorial claims. Xue comes to understand that the contemporary state is defined not by the civilizing influence of ritual protocol but by the military maintenance of territorial integrity.[8] This new space, "China," was by Dai Jitao's time being conceived as a nation, which, according to recent scholarly work, was repeatedly constructed around the trinity of a people, a spoken language, and a mapped territory.[9]

In tandem with this shift in geographical representations that followed the rejection of *tong wen*, Chinese after 1890 had to reconsider the relations among writing, behavior, and the larger world. Although the notion that China and Japan "shared Civilization" was not to return, a greatly reduced version of *tong wen* was revived optimistically at the turn of the century—the simple acknowledgment that China and Japan shared a measure of writing. Zhang Zhidong, as leader of the conservative reform movement that proceeded cautiously after the aborted Hundred Days of Reform in 1898, urged Chinese students to go to Japan to study the new Western learning that would bring China wealth and power. Since the Japanese language shared Chinese characters, Zhang felt that Chinese students would have an easier time studying there. Many did, like Dai Jitao, and among the new terminology they brought back to China was Fukuzawa Yukichi's Japanese translation for the English word "civilization," *wenming* (J: *bunmei*), which he had used to refer to that universal civilization grounded in Western learning and toward which the entire world was progressing. Such a usage of *wenming* gained a youthful currency in the first decade of this century in China, where it served to indicate Western phenomena that differed from their Chinese counterparts; among the most widespread usages were "*wenming* drama"—the European spoken drama that differed significantly from Chinese opera—and the "*wenming* marriage"—the Western-style marriage in which one chose one's own mate apart from family or matchmaker preferences.[10] Accordingly, it is this version of *tong wen*, announced by Zhang Zhidong, that is remembered in China and among Chinese historians today. China and Japan share Chinese characters, in spite of all their attempts to reform, simplify, or efface these signs. And they share them in the precise context of the practice of translation—what is pronounced *X* in one language is pronounced *Y* in the other; what means *A* in one language means *B* in the other—the very practice that Chinese students learned from Japan when they went to study at Zhang's bidding.

For both *tong wen* and *wenming*, the metaphorical extension from writing to patterned behavior and imperial Civilization was severed. *Wen* has been reduced to mere "writing," and *wenming*, as we see in the above epigraph by Dai Jitao, abstracted to refer to one or another historicized form of human civilization, whether Chinese, Indian, or European. The space between those two poles—the present written word and the civilizations of the past—has been filled by a second Japanese translation word, *wenhua*, or "culture," the patterned behavior that defines one or another people's distance from a "natural" state of man. Japanese themselves had begun to use *wenhua* (J: *bunka*) around the turn of the century to stress the need for a more Germanic and spiritual *Kultur*, as a deliberate alternative to the objectionably materialist "civilization" (*wenming*) advocated by Fukuzawa and other enlighteners of the early Meiji period. As a result of the Chinese language having incorporated European ideas in a Japanese idiom, the former breadth of *wen* has assumed a fragmented and more localized meaning, on the one hand, as "writing," and on the other hand, as "patterned behavior."

In the 1930s and forties, the hegemonic connotations of *tong wen* returned with a vengeance as the Japanese army invaded China in the name of "same culture and same race" (*tong wen tong zhong*).[11] As I mentioned in chapter 2, Japanese continued to celebrate *tong wen* with Chinese in poetry gatherings of the 1880s, and such an attitude figured in early pan-Asian associations established in Japan, like the Kōakai (Revive Asia Society), for example, which advocated the preserving of shared Civilization and cooperation between China and Japan in the face of Western influences.[12] But after Chinese participation in societies like the Kōakai declined in the 1880s, as a result of the conflict with Japan over Korean sovereignty, they were eventually absorbed into Konoe Atsumarō's Tōa Dōbunkai, or East Asian Common Culture Society, which directed Japan's activities of cultural imperialism in China.[13] Underlying this Japanese version of *tong wen* was the intellectual project undertaken in Japan to achieve a self-respecting parity with the West; as Stefan Tanaka has convincingly argued, Japanese first established the historical equivalence and difference of Europe and Asia, and then the cultural superiority of Japan over China.[14] In addition to fragmenting Fukuzawa's notion of *wenming* as universal civilization into the multiple and equivalent forms we see in Dai's usage of "civilization" above, a second consequence of this project was that in the 1930s, the Tōa Dōbunkai could justify Japan's cultural tutelage over China in the interests of Asian unity against the West.

Apart from whatever "factual objectivity" has accrued to Zhang Zhidong's understanding of *tong wen*, it is remembered today because it is the last official Chinese diagnosis of the disposition of *tong wen*, for Zhang uttered his injunction at the close of the era defined by a comfortable correspondence between language and the world. In the reduction from Civilization to language, and from language to various written forms of speech that require translation, the relationship between language and life was radically rearranged. Chinese students returned from Japan at the beginning of our century with new descriptions of reality, and these descriptions were at odds with each other in that they informed the pursuit of differing political and economic agendas—from nationalism and revolution to industrialization and socialism. If the 1989 events in Tian'an Men square are any indication, Chinese have still not arrived at an acceptable unity between language and the world.

Civilization has been forgotten, a historical artifact replaced by "culture" and the nation-state. The former points to the variety of material practices like translating, the latter to the absolute sovereignty of and over the people—both are elements of the "new arrangement" several times removed, to recall Huang Zunxian's terms. If Chinese scholars once celebrated history as an affirmation of Civilization, they still celebrate it, but for quite different reasons—as proof of progress in newer material practices.

This is pronounced in the way Chinese scholars now approach Japan. In September of 1983, for example, a group of Chinese scholars operating through the auspices of the International Problems Section of the Beijing

Social Science Research Institute issued the first of a series of symposium volumes entitled *Chinese-Japanese Culture and Interaction*. In introducing the volume, the editors issued a statement, which included the following:

China and Japan, as the saying goes, are "separated by a mere belt of water," and close neighbors daily looking across the way. Between the two nations exists an exceedingly long, two-thousand-year history of friendly interaction. They have, moreover, several similar elements of cultural background. The two peoples are both industrious and wise.

Amidst the vast years and months of times past, Japan once imbibed from China the forefront of Civilization. Nowadays, Japan has already absorbed an astonishing expertise in economic and scientific culture. As a whole, Japan's understanding and analysis of China is considerable. Our own people's study of Japan, although getting off to a slow start, has made significant developments only in recent years.

During the past century, the encroachment of Japanese militarism created a man-made obstacle between the two peoples, and forced both to suffer tremendous calamities. But men draw lessons from bitter experiences, as deep sorrow leads to enlightenment. The Chinese and Japanese peoples need only continue in harmony, generation after generation, in order to keep in step with the course of history.

The friendly relations between the Chinese and Japanese peoples have their origin in the progress of history, and become even more important as they continue into tomorrow. In order to fully introduce the two nations' cultural and amicable relations, and to further mutual understanding between the two peoples, we have edited and published this collection of articles.[15]

The tone of hopefulness and nostalgia here is as pronounced for an innate Chinese and Japanese commonality as it is for a past moment when relations between people were unmediated by state governments. Given the expression of confidence in a better future, which is a sign of both historical determinism and the degree to which Chinese state institutions centrally manage representations, what are we to make of the self-conscious use of historical analogy—"a mere belt of water" (*yi yi dai shui*)? A tentative reference to normative conditions of peace? The locus classicus for the expression is the seventh-century *History of the Southern Dynasties,* which records that the Sui emperor Wendi told his vice director of the Left, Gao Ying, at the crossing of the (Yangzi) River during the campaign to pacify Chen, "I am the father and mother of the people; how can I be restrained by this mere belt of water, and fail to assist those in trouble?"[16] As the sign of a proximity that lent itself to imperial claims of hegemony, "a mere belt of water" has long figured in representations of relations between China and Japan. It is commendable that these Chinese scholars would minimize the hegemonic claims put forward by emperors and nation-states, in the interest of affirming the hope of a revived sensitivity between peoples. But behind their enthusiasm for economic and scientific progress, which indeed promises to efface borders between people, lies a hegemony of another order. The struggle of man against power requires, if nothing else, an attempt of memory against forgetting.

Notes

Abbreviations

BTYG	*Huang Zunxian yu Riben youren bitan yigao*, ed. Zheng Ziyu and Sanetō Keishū (Taibei: Wenhai chubanshe, 1968)
CAZZ	*Ce ao za zhi*, Ye Qingyi and Yuan Zuzhi (Shanghai: n.p., [1889])
DCWJL	*Dong cha wenjian lu*, Chen Jialin (n.p., [1887]; reprinted in *XFHZ, zhi* 10: 371–407)
ECCP	*Eminent Chinese of the Ch'ing Period (1644–1912)*, ed. Arthur Hummel (Taipei: Ch'eng Wen Publishing, 1970)
FSYJ	*Fusang youji*, Wang Tao (Tokyo: Kunten shuppan, [1880])
HJAS	*Harvard Journal of Asiatic Studies*
JAS	*Journal of Asian Studies*
QWPZH	*Qingdai wenxue piping ziliao huibian*, ed. Wu Hongyi and Ye Qingbing (Taibei: Chengwen chubanshe, 1979)
RBDLBY	*Riben dili bingyao*, Yao Wendong (Beijing: Zongli yamen, [1884])
RBGZ	*Riben guozhi*, Huang Zunxian, 2d ed. (Shanghai: Tushu jicheng, [1898]; reprinted Taibei: Wenhai chubanshe, 1981)
RBXZK	*Riben xinzheng kao*, Gu Houkun (n.p., [1889], reprinted in *Xizheng congshu*, vols. 25–26. n.p., [1897])
RBZSS	*Riben zashi shi*, Huang Zunxian, 1st ed. (Hong Kong: Xunhuan baoguan, [1880])
RJLSC	*Renjinglu shicao jianzhu*, Huang Zunxian, ann. Qian Zhonglian (Hong Kong: Zhonghua shuju, 1963)
TYL	*Tan ying lu*, Wang Zhichun (n.p.: Shangyang wenyi zhai, [1880])
XFHZ	*Xiaofanghuzhai yudi cong chao*, comp. Wang Xiqi (Shanghai: Zhuyi tang, [1877–1897])
XFHZBP	*Xiaofanghuzhai yudi cong chao bupian*, comp. Wang Xiqi (Shanghai: Zhuyi tang, [1877–1897?])
YLRBTJ	*Youli Riben tujing*, Fu Yunlong (Tokyo: n.p., [1889])
ZRYW	*Zaoqi Riben youji wuzhong*, ed. Wang Xiaoqiu (Changsha: Hunan renmin chubanshe, 1983)

Introduction

1 Kristin Ross, *The Emergence of Social Space: Rimbaud and the Paris Commune* (Minneapolis: University of Minnesota Press, 1988), 9.

2 The *Han shu* was of course modeled after the celebrated *Records of the Historian* (*Shi ji*) of Sima Qian (145?–90? B.C.), but the earlier text is technically *not* a "dynastic history." Incidentally, there is an exception to the tradition of the "Treatise on Earth's Patterns": the second dynastic history, *History of the Later Han* (*Hou Han shu*), substitutes a "Treatise on Districts and Domains" (*Junguo zhi*).

3 See Joseph Needham, "Geography and Cartography," in *Science and Civilization in China*, vol. 3, *Mathematics and the Sciences of the Heavens and the Earth* (Cambridge: Cambridge University Press, 1959), 497–590; and Cordell D. K. Yee, "Chinese Maps in Political Culture," in *The History of Cartography*, vol. 2, bk. 2, *Cartography in the Traditional East and Southeast Asian Societies*, ed. J. B. Harley and David Woodward (Chicago: University of Chicago Press, 1994), 71–95.

1 Civilization from the Center

1 See the analysis of Janet Kate Leonard, *Wei Yuan and China's Rediscovery of the Maritime World* (Cambridge, Mass.: Harvard University, Council on East Asian Studies, 1984), especially the section "Regional Overlordship and Tribute," 121–141.

2 See Suzuki Shūji, *Bunmei no kotoba* [The vocabulary of enlightenment] (Hiroshima: Bunka hyōron, 1981), 33–68; and Joseph R. Allen, *In the Voice of Others: Chinese Music Bureau Poetry* (Ann Arbor: University of Michigan, Center for Chinese Studies, 1992), 15–24.

3 In this regard, the point made by James Hevia in his study of imperial guest ritual is well taken: Those who did not participate in Civilization, like the English, were not so much "uncivilized" or "barbarian" as undifferentiated—without a place in the hierarchy of the moral universe understood as Civilization. See his "Guest Ritual and Interdomainal Relations in the Late Qing" (Ph.D. diss., University of Chicago, 1986), 246. More recently, Hevia has pointed out the particularity of Manchu lordship, which I do not take into account here. See his *Cherishing Men from Afar: Qing Guest Ritual and the Macartney Embassy of 1793* (Durham: Duke University Press, 1995), 29–49, 116–33.

4 Under the rule of the Qing dynasty, the Manchu emperors corresponded with their Tibetan, Mongolian, and Manchu allies in those respective languages; a series of official bureaus was established to accomodate these special groups, foremost of which was the Lifan Yuan (Office of Frontier Affairs).

5 Chinese officials in the nineteenth century did not consciously refer their diplomatic interpretations and recommendations to a "principle" of *jin*; rather, they invoked Japan's "proximity" in the context of trade, moral expectations, and the dangers of war. Hence my use of "proximity" here is an effort to explicate the complex discourse on Japan's position with regard to the Chinese empire and Chinese Civilization. In addition to the documents concerning the Taiwan Incident from the *Chouban yiwu shimo* (cited below), I have also examined the many memorials in response to the Liuqiu Incident. See, for example, Li Hongzhang's memorial on the Taiwan Incident in *Li Wenzhong Gong quanji: Zougao* [Complete works of Li Wenzhong: Memorials] (Nan-

jing: n.p., 1908), 24:26a–28a; and Chen Baochen's memorial on the Liuqiu Incident in *Qing Guangxuchao Zhong-Ri jiaoshe shiliao* [Historical materials on Sino-Japanese relations during the Qing Guangxu court] (Beiping: Palace Museum, 1932), 2:10–12.

6 See Hevia, "Guest Ritual," 104 105; and *Cherishing Men from Afar*, 50–52. See also the several anecdotes about Korean envoys' participation in Chinese guest ritual by Ŏ Sukkwŏn, *A Korean Storyteller's Miscellany: The P'aegwan Chapki of Ŏ Sukkwŏn*, [trans.] Peter H. Lee (Princeton: Princeton University Press, 1989), 85, 150f., 182f., 235f.

7 I might emphasize here that this study is *not* a contribution to diplomatic history or to the history of foreign relations, but an examination of cultural history. Those interested in the former should consult the more extensive interpretations of John K. Fairbank and his colleagues in *The Chinese World Order: Traditional China's Foreign Relations* (Cambridge, Mass.: Harvard University Press, 1968). By way of a methodology in that volume, Fairbank reifies "Sinocentrism" and a "Chinese World Order" (p. 2), and although my interpretation is not incompatible with his, it is somewhat different. By developing the concepts of "Civilization" and "proximity," I am providing Chinese terms (*wenming* and *jin*) to fill the lack of "an indigenous term" that Fairbank recognized in his work (p. 5). Of special importance are his introduction, "A Preliminary Framework" (pp. 1–19), and concluding essay, "The Early Treaty System in the Chinese World Order" (pp. 257–275), as well as the second introductory essay by Lien-sheng Yang, "Historical Notes on the Chinese World Order" (pp. 20–33). An earlier and worthwhile statement that takes a similar approach is Immanuel C.Y. Hsü's *China's Entrance into the Family of Nations: The Diplomatic Phase, 1858–1880* (Cambridge, Mass.: Harvard University Press, 1960); his "Prologue" more extensively treats Chinese ideology as "stereotyped thinking" concerning barbarians (p. 12). See, however, the important criticism of the Fairbankian approach to China's tributary relations in Hevia, "Guest Ritual," 1–66.

8 Andrew L. March treats this ideal protocol in more specifically geographic terms in *The Idea of China: Myth and Theory in Geographic Thought* (New York: Praeger, 1974): 12–22.

9 Pierre Bourdieu, *Outline of a Theory of Practice*, trans. Richard Nice (Cambridge: Cambridge University Press, 1977), 120.

10 Angela Rose Zito, "Re-presenting Sacrifice: Cosmology and the Editing of Texts," *Ch'ing-shih wen-t'i* 5, no. 2 (12/1984): 47–78.

11 See Xu Gongsheng, "Fuzhou yu Neishuang guanxishi chu tan" [Preliminary investigations into the history of relations between Fuzhou and Naha], in *Zhong-Ri guanxishi lunji: Di er ji* [Collected articles on the history of Chinese-Japanese relations, 2d ser.], ed. Dongbei diqu Zhong-Ri guanxishi yanjiuhui [Manchuria Research Group on the History of Chinese-Japanese Relations] (Jilin: Renmin chubanshe, 1984), 23–38 passim. See also Ta-tuan Ch'en, "Investiture of Liu-ch'iu Kings in the Ch'ing Period," in *The Chinese World Order*, 135–164.

12 Ren Hongzhang, "Cong *Zhupi yuzhi* kan Kang-Yong shiqi de Zhong-Ri jiaoshe" [Chinese-Japanese interactions during the Kangxi and Yongzheng reigns, as seen in *Imperial Comments in Vermilion*], in *Zhong-Ri guanxishi lunji: Di er ji*, 38–53. A rare

account of Li Wei's diplomacy is now available in reprint: Wang Zhichun, *Qingchao rouyuan ji* [Records of Qing dynastic grace to distant peoples] ([1876]; reprinted Beijing: Zhonghua shuju, 1989), 71–77. The 1715 incident over "passes" is also discussed from Japanese sources by Ronald P. Toby, *State and Diplomacy in Early Modern Japan: Asia in the Development of the Tokugawa Bakufu* (Princeton: Princeton University Press, 1984), 198–201; and Marius Jansen supplies an informative summary of trade and piracy issues in *China in the Tokugawa World* (Cambridge, Mass.: Harvard University Press, 1992), 25–33.

13 Ren, "Cong *Zhupi yuzhi* kan Kang-Yong shiqi de Zhong-Ri jiaoshe," 46. For a concise discussion of the various Chinese active in Japan, see Jansen, *China in the Tokugawa World,* 54–64. It is curious that Chinese merchant accounts of Japan are so rare in the anthologies compiled during the Qing period. The one account that seems to have had any circulation was that of Wang Peng, *An Essay on Ocean Passages* (*Xiu hai bian*), which recounted his trip to Nagasaki in 1764; the one reputable early Qing geography was Chen Lunjiong's *Recorded News of the Sea Kingdoms,* published first in 1730 and the only noteworthy geography written prior to that of Wei Yuan—a hiatus of more than a century.

14 The last official Japanese tribute mission(s) to the Ming court arrived between 1547 and 1549. The *Ming History* is unclear as to the actual dates of the mission's arrival and presentation of tribute; compare relevant sections reprinted in *Zhong-Ri guanxishi ziliao huibian,* ed. Wang Xiangrong and Xia Yingyuan (Beijing: Zhonghua shuju, 1984), 281–292, 301–304. Ronald Toby gives the year of the last mission as 1547 in *State and Diplomacy,* 24, 57; but Wang Yi-t'ung maintains that a final mission arrived in Beijing in 1549; see his *Official Relations between China and Japan, 1368–1549* (Cambridge, Mass.: Harvard University Press, 1953), 80. The first two Tokugawa shoguns, Ieyasu and Hidetada, expressed interest in reopening relations with China between 1611 and 1625, but gave up the attempt in opposition to Ming Chinese claims of superiority, and the Manchu invasion of Korea and China was cause to forgo further attempts. See Toby, pp. 59–64, 91–95.

15 See the helpful discussion, especially regarding Wei Yuan, by James M. Polachek, *The Inner Opium War* (Cambridge, Mass.: Harvard University, Council on East Asian Studies, 1992), 194–200.

16 Suzanne Wilson Barnett surveys these Chinese-language geographies written by Europeans in "Wei Yuan and Westerners: Notes on the Sources of the *Hai-Kuo T'u-Chih,*" *Ch'ing-shih wen-t'i* 2, no. 4 (November 1970): 1–20.

17 Xu Jiyu apparently completed the work in 1848, published it privately in 1849, and reprinted it in the better-known "second edition" of 1850. See Fred W. Drake, *China Charts the World: Hsu Chi-yü and His Geography of 1848* (Cambridge, Mass.: Harvard University, East Asian Research Center, 1975), 220–221n8.

18 I cite these texts as they appear reprinted in the third edition of Wei Yuan. Where significant textual variations occur, I cite independent editions. My own copy of the text is an 1895 "supplemented" edition, which is itself a reprint of the third edition of

1852 and continues with twenty-five additional *juan* by various authors: Wei Yuan, *Hai guo tu zhi* (Shanghai: Shanghai Shuju Shiyin, [1895]); reprinted as *Zengdu hai guo tu zhi* (Taibei: Guiting chubanshe, 1979).

19 Wei's title here, *Huang Qing tong kao*, is an abbreviation for the work entitled *Huangchao wenxian tong kao* [Imperial compendium of documents], also known as the *Qing wenxian tong kao* [Qing compendium of documents]. The Qianlong emperor commanded that it be compiled in 1747, as a continuation of Ma Duanlin's *Wenxian tong kao* [Compendium of documents] of 1224.

20 I have not seen a first edition of this work, but Paul Cohen has dated its first printing to 1751 in his *China and Christianity* (Cambridge, Mass.: Harvard University Press, 1963), 29.

21 The earliest edition of this work that I have found is the reprint in the *Shuo ling* collection of 1825. Fang Hao states that prior to this reprinting, the work was called *San'gang zhi lue* [A brief account of San'gang], which includes a preface dated 1738; see his "Qingdai jinyang tianzhujiao suo shou Riben zhi yingxiang" [Japanese influence on Qing suppression of Catholicism], in *Fang Hao wenlu* [Writings of Fang Hao] (Beiping: Shangzhi bianyiguan, 1948), 47–65. Dong Han is mentioned in the biography of his poet brother, Dong Yu, in *Qing shi liezhuan* [Biographies from Qing history] (Shanghai: Zhonghua shuju, 1928): 70: 45b–46b.

22 Scholars dispute the authorship of the *Xing chao lu*. Passages in Huang's chapter on Japan are identical with passages in the *Notes on Japanese Manners* (*Riben fengtu ji*), written around 1700 by the renowned Tongcheng stylist, Dai Mingshi. Dai also was said to have written a history of the Ming pretenders, but such a work is not extant. Compare Wei Yuan, *Zengdu hai guo tu zhi*, 351–352; and Dai Mingshi, *Riben fengtu ji*, reprinted in *Xiaofanghuzhai yudi cong chao bupian* [Supplement to the collected reprints on geography from the "Little Square Hu" studio], compiled by Wang Xiqi (Shanghai: [1877–1897?]; reprinted Taibei: Guangwen Shuju, 1964), vol. 10, [unpaginated]. I hereafter refer to this collection as *XFHZBP*.

23 The excerpts from Wang Yun in Wei Yuan's *Illustrated Treatise on the Sea Kingdoms* appear to have been derived from versions incorporated by Xu Jiyu in his *A Short Treatise on the Ocean Circuits*. Compare Wei, *Zengdu hai guo tu zhi*, 353, and Xu Jiyu, *Ying huan zhi lue* ([1850]; reprinted Taibei: Huawen shuju, n.d.), 1:71–73.

24 James Polachek discusses the pertinence of Gu Yanwu to official opponents of the Opium War settlement in *The Inner Opium War*, 205–231.

25 The "Japan Biography" in the *Ming History* is the primary synthesis of the Ming accounts of the Japanese pirates. See Wei, *Zengdu hai guo tu zhi*, 345–347. Two other major Qing accounts are Gu Yingtai, *Ming shi jishi benmo* [Highlights of Ming history, beginning to end], vol. 8, *juan* 55, *Yanhai wo luan* [The Dwarf rebellion along the coast] ([ca. 1658]; reprinted Shanghai: Shangwu yinshuguan, 1933); and Gu Yanwu's *Tianxia junguo libing shu* [On the gains and ills of the administrative domains under Heaven], reprinted in *Si bu cong kan: San bian* (Shanghai: Shanghai shangwu yinying, 1936), *han* 17, *juan* 48: 48a–58b.

26 Accounts of anti-Christian activity include the *Guisi lei gao, Aomen ji lue,* and *Chunxiang zhui bi,* as well as Morrison's *Waiguo shi lue,* all of which are included in Wei, *Zengdu hai guo tu zhi,* 348, 349, 349–350, and 350–351 respectively.

27 Wei, *Zengdu hai guo tu zhi,* 345.

28 See Wei, *Zengdu hai guo tu zhi,* 349 [*Aomen ji lue*] and 350 [*Chunxiang zhui bi*]. I should note that Wei either misread or had in his possession an erroneous copy of the *Aomen ji lue*—other versions of the text read not "Japanese" but "Javanese." See, for example, the *Zhao dai cong shu* edition of the text reprinted in *Zhongshan wenxian* (Taibei: Taiwan xuesheng shuju, 1965), 8:143. This error does not, of course, erase the "facts" as received by Wei's readers.

29 The background of Chinese usage of *Wo* and *Wonu* is obscure, but the primary theories emphasize the sound value of the term. *Wo* may have referred to an island people off the coast of China or Kyūshū, or to the ancient Japanese name for their land, "Yamato"; in any case, scholars claim that the name was extended to refer to Japan by the late Han period. The resurgence of *Wo* in the 1500s has been explained as a reference to the fact that these pirates were Japanese convicts, or "slaves." See Wang Xiangrong, "Gudai Zhongguoren de Riben guan" [Ancient Chinese views of Japan], in his *Gudai de Zhongguo yu Riben* [China and Japan in antiquity] (Beijing: Sanguan shudian, 1989), 312–325; Wang Xiangrong, "Zhongguo zhengshi zhong de Riben zhuan" [The "Japan Biographies" in Chinese official histories], in his *Zhong-Ri guanxishi wenxian lunkao* [Critical examinations of documents for the history of Chinese-Japanese relations] (Changsha: Yuelu shushe, 1985), 7f.; and Shen Ren'an, *Wakoku to higashi Ajia* [The Wo Kingdom and east Asia] (Tokyo: Rokkō Shuppan, 1990), 18–35. Although "slave" is a better translation for the pejorative use of *Wo,* I will continue to use the rather erroneous nineteenth-century translation of *Wo* as "Dwarf" when it refers to the Ming-period pirates and nineteenth-century Japanese; otherwise, I use *Wo* in references to the early Chinese accounts of Japan.

30 The exception to this usage is Yu Zhengxie's anti-Christian narrative in *Guisi lei gao.* It is curious, however, that Wei's excerpt alters what was originally "Japan" (i.e., "Riben") in Yu's text. Compare Wei, *Zengdu hai guo tu zhi,* 348, and Yu Zhengxie, *Guisi lei gao,* reprinted in the *Anhui cong shu* [Collected works from Anhui Province], *juan* 9: 2a–3a.

31 In his survey of these early and mid-Qing writings on anti-Christian activity in Japan, Fang Hao traces the titles in Wei Yuan and others to a seventeenth-century (late Ming?) text, *Feng shi Riben ji lue* [A short account of ambassadorial service to Japan]; all of these use "Riben." See his "Qingdai jinyang tianzhujiao suo shou Riben zhi yingxiang," 47–65. Moreover, Morrison, the only European who wrote during the Qing period about anti-Christian activity in Japan, mentions in passing the "Japanese pirates" (*Riben haidao*), a usage independent of Chinese histories of the Dwarf pirates, and the only reference to pirates that omits "Dwarf" (and makes use of an alternative word for "pirates"). See Wei, *Zengdu hai guo tu zhi,* 350 [Morrison].

32 Wei, *Zengdu hai guo tu zhi,* 348 [*Hai guo wenjian lu*].

33 This is Jerry Dennerline's conclusion as well, based on the work of Li Guangbi and

Tanaka Takeo; see *The Chia-ting Loyalists: Confucian Leadership and Social Change in Seventeenth-century China* (New Haven: Yale University Press, 1981), 127.

34   Ralph C. Croizier, *Koxinga and Chinese Nationalism: History, Myth, and the Hero* (Cambridge, Mass.: Harvard University Press, 1977), 17–28.

35   The Chinese dynastic histories from the third through tenth centuries include a set of treatises "on the eastern outsiders" (*Dong yi zhi*), which contain biographies on the "Wo" or "Wo Kingdom" (*Wo guo*). Beginning with the tenth-century *Old Tang History*, these reports are replaced by comparable reports entitled "Japan" ("Riben"). This transition from "Wo" to "Riben" represents a shift in name that was rather simply accomplished, in that Chinese historians and geographers transcribed the earlier accounts of the Wo Kingdom within their reports on Japan. The compilers of the *Old Tang History* made the change, we are told repeatedly, because the Japanese preferred the name "Riben," to what they felt was a rather demeaning appellation, "Wo," which could be interpreted literally as "slaves." Because the collapse of the imperial Tang administration in the tenth century precluded official historiographical opposition to the new name for Japan, "Riben," the precedent of the *Old Tang History* became institutionalized in later histories. In light of chapter 5 below, an important point here is the stability of the overall scheme of historiography. The shift from Wo to Riben was a minor change; the larger category, "eastern outsiders," persisted as evidence of the stability of the Tang organization of knowledge of other peoples. Chen Zhigui has pointed out that the Japanese embassy to the Tang court in 670 insisted that the name of their country was not Wo but Riben, and in records of the embassy of 702 Japan is consistently referred to as Riben. See his "Riben qian Tang shizhe chutan" [A preliminary investigation of Japanese envoys to the Tang], in *Zhong-Ri guanxishi lunji: Di er ji*, 4f. The best survey of early Chinese accounts of Wo and Riben is Wang Xiangrong, "Zhongguo zhengshi zhong de Riben zhuan" [The "Japan Biographies" in Chinese official histories], in his *Zhong-Ri guanxishi wenxian lunkao*, 1–65; see also Wu Anlong and Xiong Dayun, *Chūgokujin no Nihon kenkyū shi* [A history of Chinese studies of Japan] (Tokyo: Rokkō shuppan, 1989), 21–63. Two good comparisons between the early history of Japan and Chinese accounts of Wo are Shen Ren'an, *Wakoku to higashi Ajia*; and Nishijima Sadao, *Yamataikoku to Wakoku: Kodai Nihon to Higashi Ajia* [Yamato and Wo: ancient Japan and East Asia] (Tokyo: Ishikawa kobunkan, 1994).

36   See Wei, *Zengdu hai guo tu zhi*, 345 [*Ming shi*], and 348 [*Qing imperial compendium*]; and Gu Yanwu, *Tianxia junguo libing shu, juan* 48: 45b, 47a.

37   On the thirty-six, see Wei, *Zengdu hai guo tu zhi*, 351 [*Xing chao lu*]; as well as Dai Mingshi, *Riben fengtu ji*, [unpaginated]. On the seventy-two, see Wei, *Zengdu hai guo tu zhi*, 348 [*Hai guo wenjian lu*], and 350 [*Dili bei kao*]. I might add that in addition to the numerical designation, "seventy-two" in Chinese also has the meaning of "a great many" or "the entire group of."

38   See Wei, *Zengdu hai guo tu zhi*, 348 [*Hai guo wenjian lu*], 350 [Morrison], and 351 [Huang Zongxi].

39   Ibid., 349 [Gützlaff]. In an exceptional case, the two are described as emperor (*tianhuang*) and "domainal king" (*guowang*). This appellation is remarkable, because it

disregards the standing impropriety in naming a Japanese "emperor"; the Chinese court had been incensed in the seventh century, when the Japanese ruler sent an infamous letter to the Sui emperor, claiming to be the "emperor of the rising sun" writing to the [Chinese] "emperor of the setting sun." See ibid., 348 [*Qing Imperial Compendium*]. Since the *Qing Imperial Compendium* is the only one that mentions the office of *Kampaku*, regent or "chief advisor" to the Japanese emperor, its authors likely had access to Japanese texts.

40 Ibid., 351 [Morrison; Huang].

41 See ibid., 348 [*Hai guo wenjian lu*], 349 [*Qing Imperial Compendium*], 350 [*Dili hei kao*; Morrison].

42 Wei, *Zengdu hai guo tu zhi*, 348 [*Qing Imperial Compendium*]; and Gu Yingtai, *Ming shi jishi benmo*, 39.

43 Wei, *Zengdu hai guo tu zhi*, 348 [*Hai guo wenjian lu*].

44 Ibid., 349 [*Qing Imperial Compendium*].

45 Ibid., 351 [*Waiguo shi lue*].

46 Ibid., 349 [Gützlaff].

47 Ibid., 349 [Gützlaff]. That Gützlaff uniformly emphasizes differences extends even to his descriptions of China. He reserves "China" (*Zhongguo*) for cultural material—written characters—and instead refers to Chinese people by two other appellations: the Han people (*Hanren*); and the Tang People (*Tangren*). Unlike contemporary Cantonese and Mandarin usages of *Hanren* and *Tangren*, which generally mean "us," or "we Chinese," Gützlaff uses *Hanren* as a more racial characterization, to indicate physical qualities, and *Tangren* as a more cultural characterization, referring to behavior. (I have been told that nowadays *Hanren* is more prevalent in Hong Kong and China, *Tangren* more prevalent in Chinese-American communities.) Gützlaff's usage here is unique among these descriptions of Japan.

48 Ibid., 348 [*Hai guo wenjian lu*].

49 Gu Yanwu, *Tianxia junguo libing shu*, *juan* 48: 59–60.

50 Wei, *Zengdu hai guo tu zhi*, 354.

51 See Zhang Yunqiao and Zhang Lifan, "Wan Ming yi dui Riben yanjiu gaishu" [An outline of late Ming studies of Japan], in *Zhong-Ri guanxishi lunji: Di er ji*, 12–21; and Wu and Xiong, *Chūgokujin no Nihon kenkyū shi*, 65–92.

52 Xue Jun's *Riben kao lue* is reprinted in the *Congshu jicheng: Chu bian* [Complete collections: first series], *ce* 3,278 [vol. 131] (Shanghai: Shangwu yinyingben, 1935).

53 See Yong Rong et al. *Siku quanshu zongmu tiyao* [Annotated catalogue of the complete books of the Four Treasuries], vol. 16, *Shi bu*, *Dili lei cunmu* 7 [original chapters *juan* 78, i.e., *Shi bu* 34] ([Shanghai]: Shangwu yinshuguan, n.d.), 9–11. Unfortunately, the editors offer no examples of errors nor do they give any justification for their judgments, and I have not yet found any extant "draft reviews" that informed these judgments. On this matter of draft reviews, see R. Kent Guy, *The Emperor's Four Treasuries: Scholars and the State in the Late Ch'ien-lung Era* (Cambridge, Mass.: Harvard University, Council on East Asian Studies, 1987), 121–123.

54 The problematic authorship of this text is discussed by Wang Xiangrong, "Guanyu *Chou hai tu bian*" [On the *Illustrated Collection on Coastal Defense*], in his *Zhong-Ri guanxishi wenxian lunkao*, 159–217. Zheng Ruoceng (1505–1580) was apparently an advisor to Hu Zongxian (1511–1565). Because Hu financed the compilation and printing of the *Chou hai tu bian*, it was formally attributed to him in 1562; but when Hu's descendents reprinted the work ca. 1624, they erroneously designated Hu as the compiler and author.

55 Zuo Zongtang, *Zuo Wenxiang Gong zougao* [Collected memorials of Zuo Wenxiang], in *Zuo Wenxiang Gong quanji* [Complete works of Zuo Wenxiang] (Changsha: n.p., [1890]), 18:1–6.

56 Joseph Fletcher, "Sino-Russian Relations, 1800–1862" and "The Heyday of the Ch'ing Order in Mongolia, Sinkiang, and Tibet," in *The Cambridge History of China*, vol. 10, *Late Ch'ing, 1800–1911*, pt. 1, ed. John K. Fairbank (Cambridge: Cambridge University Press, 1978), 318–408.

57 Ibid., 375–382.

58 I return to this theme at the end of the book. Of particular value regarding the transition from traditional to Westernized diplomacy is Wang Ermin's "Wanqing waijiao sixiang de xingcheng" [The formation of diplomatic thought in the Late Qing], in *Zhongyang yanjiuyuan jindaishi yanjiusuo jikan* [Collected papers of the Modern History Institute of Academia Sinica], 1 (8/1969): 19–46.

59 *Chouban yiwu shimo: Tongzhi chao* [Complete records on managing foreign affairs, ser. 3, The Tongzhi Court], comp. Wen Qing (Peiping: Palace Museum, 1929–1930), 77:36b–37a.

60 The "International Office," or Zongli geguo shiwu yamen (abb. Zongli yamen), was created in 1861 under the direction of Yixin, the Prince Gong, in order to more directly handle affairs with the European nations. It became the Waiwu Bu (Department of Foreign Affairs) in 1901.

61 *Chouban yiwu shimo*, 77:34b–36a.

62 A fuller treatment from the viewpoint of diplomatic history is available in Key-hiuk Kim, *The Last Phase of the East Asian World Order: Korea, Japan, and the Chinese Empire, 1860–1882* (Berkeley: University of California Press, 1980), 136–153.

63 According to Joseph Fletcher, a tributary state was responsible for sending tribute to the Chinese court periodically, and the Chinese emperor theoretically confirmed the installation of the ruler of a tributary state; by contrast, a dependency was more integrated into the empire—Qing garrisons and officials watched over the people of a dependency, who paid Chinese taxes. Mongolia, Xinjiang, and Tibet were the most important of the Qing dependencies. See "Ch'ing Inner Asia c. 1800," in *The Cambridge History of China*, vol. 10, ed. Fairbank, 36–38.

64 *Chouban yiwu shimo*, 79:7b–8a.

65 This argument critical of Ming policy was made in the early Qing by the celebrated scholar Jiang Chenying (1628–1699); see his *Tongzhi haifang zonglun* [A comprehensive discussion for a united will to coastal defense], in his *Zhanyuan weidinggao* [Un-

finished manuscripts from the Clear Garden] ([ca. 1689]; reprinted in *Jiang Xiansheng quanji* [Complete works of Master Jiang], ed. Feng Baobian and Wang Dingxiang (n.p., 1930), 1:10b–30b.

66 *Chouban yiwu shimo*, 79:46a–48a. Li is referring to the second Opium War with Britain and France.

67 Ibid., 80:9b–11a.

68 Ibid., 80:10b.

69 The basic coverage of the official diplomacy is T. F. Tsiang, "Sino-Japanese Diplomatic Relations, 1870–1894," *Chinese Social and Political Science Review* 17 (1933): 1–106. See also Kim, *The Last Phase*, 187–203.

70 Tsiang, "Sino-Japanese Diplomatic Relations," 16–34. An interesting contextualization of the incident from the point of view of Japanese materials is provided in Marlene J. Mayo, "The Korean Crisis of 1873 and Early Meiji Foreign Policy," *JAS* 31, no. 4 (1972): 793–819.

71 See Prince Gong's memorials to the throne and letters to the Japanese embassy, in *Chouban yiwu shimo*, 93:25b–32a.

72 Jin Anqing, *Dong wo kao*, in *XFHZBP*, vol. 10 [unpaginated]. Cf. Wei Yuan, *Zengdu hai guo tu zhi*, 345–347.

73 The text of the decree is taken from the *Wei zhi* (The Wei treatise) in the *San guo zhi* (The treatise on the three kingdoms).

74 Chen Qiyuan, *Riben jinshi ji*, in *Xiaofanghuzhai yudi cong chao* [Collected reprints on geography from the "Little Square Hu" studio], comp. Wang Xiqi (Shanghai: Zhuyitang, [1877–1897]), *ce* 52: 265. I hereafter refer to this collection as *XFHZ*.

75 Jin Anqing, *Dong wo kao*, [unpaginated]; and Chen Qiyuan, *Riben jinshi ji*, 266.

76 Chen Qiyuan, *Riben jinshi ji*, 265a.

77 Jin Anqing, *Dong wo kao*, [unpaginated]. Note that Jin's argument reflects the ancient analysis of the *Mencius*, that virtue is necessarily opposed to profit.

78 Chen Qiyuan, *Riben jinshi ji*, 265a.

79 Ibid., 265a–265b.

80 Ibid., 265b.

81 See Li Hongnian's memorial in *Chouban yiwu shimo*, 93:41b–42a.

2 Civilization as Universal Practice

1 *Tong wen* is a problematic concept, which I explicate below. Wang Xiangrong concludes that Japan alone was singled out for this claim, because it does not seem to have been used in reference to Korea, Vietnam, or other Chinese tributaries. See his "Qianyan" [Preface], *Gudai de Zhongguo yu Riben*, 1.

2 For the background of Ōkōchi, I have relied on Saneto Keishū's introduction to *Ōkōchi bunsho* [The Ōkōchi documents] (Tokyo: Heibonsha, 1964), 3–14.

3 In addition to the originals at Waseda University, Tokyo University holds a set of photographs of the originals. There are also two partial transcriptions: Saneto Keishū

[ed. and trans.], *Ōkōchi bunsho*; and Zheng Ziyu and Sanetō Keishū, eds., *Huang Zunxian yu Riben youren bitan yigao* [Manuscripts of brushtalks between Huang Zunxian and his Japanese friends] (Taibei: Wenhai chubanshe, 1968). The latter work I hereafter refer to as *BTYG*.

4   See the prefaces by editors Zheng Ziyu and Sanetō Keishū in *BTYG*, as well as the reminiscence by Wang Xiangrong, "Bitan yigao," in his *Riben jiaoxi* [Japanese teachers] (Beijing: Sanlian shudian, 1988), 258–272.

5   For an excellent and concise tour of the nomenclature, see Jerry Norman, *Chinese* (Cambridge: Cambridge University Press, 1988), 135–138.

6   My evaluation of "official speech" is based on a Japanese textbook, contemporary with the brushtalks, for learning Chinese: Ōtsuki Fumihiko, *Shina bunten* [Chinese grammar] (Tokyo: n.p., [1877]).

7   See Yoshikawa Kōjirō, *Jinsai, Sorai, Norinaga: Three Classical Philologists of Mid-Tokugawa Japan* (Tokyo: Tōhō gakkai, 1983), 108–123; and Roy Andrew Miller, *The Japanese Language* (Chicago: University of Chicago Press, 1967), 112–135.

8   These issues have been rigorously and insightfully analysed by Naoki Sakai in *Voices of the Past: The Status of Language in Eighteenth-Century Japanese Discourse* (Ithaca: Cornell University Press, 1991), 211–239, 311–317.

9   See Chad Hanson, "Chinese Ideographs and Western Ideas," *JAS* 52, no. 2 (5/1993): 373–399.

10   John DeFrancis attempts to deny this point in *The Chinese Language: Fact and Fantasy* (Honolulu: University of Hawaii Press, 1984). While he recognizes that members of different cultures have been and continue to be able to read literary Chinese, he claims that their various pronunciation differences in reading—respective "mispronunciations"—alter the meanings of the characters. See pp. 154–156.

11   Brushtalking was a common occurence between Chinese and Japanese diplomats prior to the Sino-Japanese War in 1894. Wang Xiaoqiu has reproduced 1875 brushtalks between Li Hongzhang and Japan's ambassador to China, Mori Arinori, in *Jindai Zhong-Ri qishi lu* [Records of modern Chinese-Japanese revelations] (Beijing: Beijing chubanshe, 1987), 73–75. Japanese notes of diplomatic meetings between the members of the first Chinese embassy to Japan and their counterparts are reproduced in official documents of Japan's Foreign Office; see Gaimushō, ed., *Nihon gaikō monjo* (Tokyo: Gaimushō, 1949–), 13:377–379, 14:275–282, and passim.

12   Consider, for example, the discussion between Aoyama Nobutoshi and Shen Wenying concerning the differences between traditional Chinese and Japanese literary sensibilities, in *BTYG*, 30f.

13   A *ping* is roughly equal to six square feet; a *li* is roughly equal to one-third of an English mile.

14   *BTYG*, 107–109.

15   Compare brushtalks earlier in March and April 1878, in ibid., 15f, 22ff, 41f.

16   Yet about this same time, Huang wrote a number of poems exoticizing Japanese women; see his *Riben zashi shi* [Poems on divers Japanese affairs] (Hong Kong: Xunhuan baoguan, [1880]), 2:15–18. This text is referred to hereafter as *RBZSS*.

17 Cf. the awkward conversation over Japan's annexation of the Liuqiu Islands, from which Ōkōchi humorously extricates himself by declaring that he is "not Japanese" but a potential "enlightened being of Pūrvavideha," opting for the more universal affiliation of Buddhism. See *BTYG*, 251.

18 Huang Zunxian wrote a poem on this subject; see *RBZSS*, 1: 1b–2a. The story of Ugayafukiaezu-no-mikoto is found in chapter 45 of the *Kojiki*; see *Kojiki*, trans. Donald L. Philippi (Tokyo: University of Tokyo Press, 1965), 156–158.

19 The story, from the *Jiyi ji*, is translated by Stephen Owen in his *Great Age of Chinese Poetry: The High T'ang* (New Haven: Yale University Press, 1981), 91–93.

20 For the history of *keizai* in the Meiji period, see Kabashima Tadao et al., *Meiji/ Taishō shingo zokugo jiten* [Dictionary of new and colloquial expressions in the Meiji and Taishō periods] (Tokyo: Tokyodō, 1984), 110–111; and Suzuki Shūji, *Bunmei no kotoba*, 69–97.

21 V. N. Volosinov, *Marxism and the Philosophy of Language*, trans. Ladislav Matejka and I. R. Titunik (New York: Seminar Press, 1973), 17–24, 83–89.

22 In addition to "*tong wen*," a few writers use "*tong zhong*," "of a common seed" (i.e., race), or "*tong lei*," "of the same kind." These attributions of filiative connections between the Chinese and Japanese are rare, and occur in two specific contexts: (1) "*tong lei*" joins Chinese and Japanese in distinction to and in an alliance against the West; and (2) "*tong zhong*" refers to the legend of Xu Fu, the Chinese progenitor of Japan. (I discuss the legend in chapter 3.) For the one example of the former, see Huang Zunxian, *RBZSS*, 1:5b; for the latter, see ibid., 1:3a, and Hê Ruzhang, *Shi dong shulue* [A concise account of the eastern embassy] ([1878?]), reprinted in *Zaoqi Riben youji wuzhong* [Five early travel accounts of Japan], ed. Wang Xiaoqiu (Changsha: Renmin chubanshe, 1983), 67; hereafter *ZRYW*. In the 1880s and nineties, one runs across terms that, like (1) above, describe Chinese and Japanese as fellow Asians: "*tongzhou*" (shared continent), "*tongren*" (comrades), and so on. See, e.g., Yao Wendong, *Dong cha za zhu* [Miscellaneous writings from the eastern mission] (n.p., [1893]), 53f; and Sun Dian, ed., *Guiwei chongjiu yan jibian* [Collection from the feast held on Double Ninth Festival, 1883] (n.p., n.d.), passim.

Readers should not confuse my discussion of "*tong wen*" with the expression "*tong wen tong zhong*" ("of the same language and the same race"), which, to my knowledge, does not occur in the 1870s and 1880s. Noriko Kamachi mistakenly cites Huang Zunxian's unprecedented usage of "*tong lei tong wen*" ("same kind and same language") as "*tong wen tong zhong*" in her *Reform in China: Huang Tsun-hsien and the Japanese Model* (Cambridge, Mass.: Harvard University, Council on East Asian Studies, 1981), 55, q.v. 285n66. (Cf. Huang Zunxian, *RBZSS* 1: 5b.) Rather, "*tong wen tong zhong*" seems to have come into prominence at the turn of the century, with Zhang Zhidong's exhortations to Chinese students to pursue Western learning in Japan, and especially with Japanese imperialist justifications for encroaching on China. Wang Xiangrong states that "*tong wen tong zhong*" was most common as a slogan during the Japanese occupation of China between 1937 and 1945 and lingered into the 1950s; see his *Gudai de Zhongguo yu Riben*, [prefatory page] 1. In this respect, Sanetō Keishū's wartime discussion of "*tong wen tong zhong*" is an instructive example of imperialistic thought; see

Kindai Nisshi bunka ron [On modern Sino-Japanese culture] (Tokyo: Daitō Shuppansha, 1941), 153–160. Incidentally, Wang denies that *tong wen* can mean that Japanese share Chinese writing, but he overlooks both the fact of brushtalking and the high level of Japanese education in literary Chinese in the eighteenth and nineteenth centuries. See his essay "Zhongguo wenhua quan" [The Chinese cultural sphere] in *Gudai de Zhongguo yu Riben*, 1–25.

23 Some scholars interpret the deliberate linguistic symmetry of literary Chinese *textual* strategies (particularly during China's formative period) as an implicit demonstration of the proposition of *cosmic* symmetry. See John B. Henderson, *The Development and Decline of Chinese Cosmology* (New York: Columbia University Press, 1984), 44f., 125.

24 The Tongwen Guan, or "Office for/of Unified Language," was the Soong (960–1279) court's office in charge of receiving Korean ambassadors; during the Qing, the name was recirculated for the translation school established in 1862—this second Tongwen Guan was intended for the internal production of Chinese-language treaties and the training of embassy personnel. Both of these offices were especially concerned with reworking foreign languages into written documents presentable to the imperial court.

25 *Zhou Yi jinzhu jinyi* [The Zhou *Classic of Changes*, with contemporary annotations and translations], ann. and trans. Nan Huaijin and Xu Qinting (Taibei: Shangwu yinshuguan, 1974), 148f.

26 The argument could be extended to Korean language practices as well. See Ō, *A Korean Storyteller's Miscellany*, for several examples of Chinese language competence among fifteenth- and sixteenth-century Korean diplomats.

27 There may be readers who would prefer to translate "*tong wen*" as "shared culture." A number of scholars who write about the Confucian tradition do translate "*wen*" as "culture" and "cultural tradition"; e.g., Raymond Dawson, *Confucius* (Oxford: Oxford University Press, 1981), 19–21, 69; David L. Hall and Roger T. Ames, *Thinking through Confucius* (Albany: State University of New York Press, 1987), 44, 323. Indeed, one scholar who has specifically considered this mingling of Chinese and Japanese scholars refers to *tong wen* as "same culture": Noriko Kamachi, *Reform in China*, 55. By contrast, Kwang-Ching Liu has described this commonality as shared "civilization"; see his introduction to Kim, *The Last Phase*, vii–viii.

In considering an English translation, I have been persuaded by the linguistic backgrounds of "civilization" and "culture" provided by Raymond Williams in *Keywords: A Vocabulary of Culture and Society* (New York: Oxford University Press, 1976). Like "*wen*" and "*wenming*," "civilization" refers to a process and an achieved *condition of society* different from "barbarity" (pp. 48–50). By contrast, "culture" refers to specific processes of "tending" (agriculture, husbandry) and to the general process of human development (cultivation); under the influence of Romantics like Herder in the nineteenth century, "culture" became inextricably bound to the question of man's divergence from nature (pp. 76–82). Accordingly, I translate "*wen*" as Civilization because (1) by "*wenming*," the Chinese meant a process and achieved condition, and (2) this condition of *wenming* was considered to exist *within the natural world*.

28 Liu Xie, *Wenxin diaolong zhushi* [The annotated *Literary Mind and Carving Dragons*], ann. Zhou Zhenfu (Beijing: Renmin wenxue chubanshe, 1981), 420, 469.

29 See, for example, Huang Zunxian, *RBZSS*, 2:30b. *"Fangyan"* is also used to mean simply "regional vernacular" in general, as in Huang Zunxian, *Riben guozhi* [Japan treatise], 2d ed. (Shanghai: Tushu jicheng, [1898]; reprinted Taibei: Wenhai chubanshe, 1981), 33:15b; and in Wang Tao, *Fusang youji* [Travels in Fusang] (Tokyo: Kunten shuppan, [1880]), 1:18b.

30 See, for example, Luo Sen, *Riben riji* [Japan diary] ([1854]; reprinted in *ZRYW*), 39; Hê Ruzhang, *Shi dong shulue*, 45; and Wang Tao, in his preface to Huang Zunxian, *RBZSS*, 1:1b. Recall from chapter 1 the hostile Ming comments that claimed just the opposite—that the Dwarfs are a "warlike, unlettered people."

31 Stephen Owen, *Remembrances: The Experience of the Past in Classical Chinese Literature* (Cambridge, Mass.: Harvard University Press, 1986), 14.

32 Liu Xie, *Wenxin diaolong zhushi*, 469f. See also Zhu Ziqing, *Shi yan zhi bian* [A study of "Poetry verbalizes intention"] (Beijing: Guji chubanshe, 1956), [prefatory page] 1; 98f.

33 Liu Xie, *Wenxin diaolong zhushi*, 48ff. James Polachek points out that "aesthetic fellowships" became increasingly important during the late eighteenth and early nineteenth centuries in response to the Qianlong emperor's revival of verse composition on the civil service examination in the 1750s; *The Inner Opium War*, 25–28.

34 The best discussion of these issues is Zhu Ziqing's invaluable *Shi yan zhi bian*; in fact, Zhu points out that poetry was only distinguished as something different from *wen* (as "prose") during the Soong dynasty. See pp. 130, 158–160.

35 *BTYG*, 317.

36 Chinese versification relies strongly on the auditory effects of Chinese as a tonal language. Because monosyllabic characters are positioned according to modulations in pitch and contrasts between long and short syllables, tonal variation of "rising" and "level" tones is a striking complement to rhythm. See James J. Y. Liu, *The Art of Chinese Poetry* (Chicago: University of Chicago Press, 1962), 20–29.

37 Cao Xueqin, *Hong lou meng* (Taibei: Wenhua, 1979), 664.

38 Ibid., 681–687.

39 James Polachek discusses the poetry society as a model for Chinese literati behavior in *The Inner Opium War*, 47f. Sugishita Motoakira recounts an eighteenth-century precedent for poetry gatherings in Japan, in "Edo Kanshi ni okeru Nitchū kōryū no ichidanmen: Matsushita Umeoka to Shin no Wan Pon" [A phase of Japan-China interaction in Edo-period Chinese poetry: Matsushita Umeoka and China's Wang Peng], *Kokugo to kokubungaku* no. 838 (10/1993): 16–27.

40 Sanetō Keishū has meticulously catalogued these "great gatherings" (*da hui*) in *Meiji Nisshi bunka kōshō* [Sino-Japanese cultural interaction during Meiji] (Tokyo: Kofukan, 1943), 78–99.

41 We know from the Ōkōchi brushtalks that Ishikawa gave a manuscript copy of the volume to Hê Ruzhang for his inspection on July 15, 1878; it was printed six weeks later. See *BTYG*, 141, as well as Sanetō Keishū's account of the event in *Meiji Nisshi bunka kōshō*, 71–75.

42 Ishikawa Ei, comp., *Shibayama issho* (Tokyo: Bunshodō, [1878]), 1a.

43 Ibid., 1b–2a.

44 Ibid., 1a.

45 See especially the records of a poetry gathering held in 1883 in honor of Li Shu-chang, *Guiwei chongjiu yan jibian* [Collection from the feast held on Double Ninth Festival, 1883] (n.p., n.d.), ed. Sun Dian. This is a rare work; the only copy I have seen is in the Sanetō Keishū Archives in Tokyo.

46 Ishikawa, *Shibayama issho* [prefatory pages].

47 Ishikawa Ei, ed., *Nihon bunsho kihan* (Tokyo: Hogyokuto, [1879]), [preliminary pages].

48 I have learned a great deal about Chinese poetry in Meiji Japan from Kinoshita Hyō, *Meiji shika* [On Meiji poetry] (Tokyo: Bunchuto, 1943); Matsushita Tadashi, *Edo jidai no shifu shiron* [Theories and styles of poetry in the Edo period] (Tokyo: Meiji shoin, 1969); and *Meiji Kanshi bunshū* [A collection of Chinese poetry in the Meiji], ed. Okamoto Koseki (Tokyo: Chikuma, 1983).

49 *Dōjinsha hungaku zasshi* 41 (May 13, 1880): 8a–8b.

50 See Irokawa Daikichi, *Meiji no bunka* [Meiji culture] (Tokyo: Iwanami, 1970), 139–146.

51 *Meiji Kanshi bunshū*, 9. My translation is based on that by Donald Keene in "The Survival of Chinese Literary Traditions in the Meiji Era," in *Sino-Japanese Cultural Interchange: Aspects of Literature and Language Learning*, ed. Yue-him Tam (Hong Kong: Chinese University of Hong Kong, Institute of Chinese Studies, 1985), 80. A *koku* was the standard measurement for rice, in which samurai were paid, and corresponds roughly to five bushels.

52 See Maeda Ai, "Chinzan to Shuntō—Meiji shonen no kanshi tan" [Chinzan and Shuntō—Chinese Poetry societies in early Meiji], in his *Bakumatsu-Ishinki no bungaku* [Literature of the Bakumatsu and Meiji periods] (Tokyo: Hōsei Daigaku, 1972), 246–268.

II Prologue

1 In comparison to these "elite" or "ruling-class" interactions, see the account by Noriko Kamachi of strained relations between overseas Chinese merchant and working-class communities and the Japanese state: "The Chinese in Meiji Japan: Their Interactions with the Japanese before the Sino-Japanese War," in *The Chinese and the Japanese: Essays in Political and Cultural Interactions*, ed. Akira Iriye (Princeton: Princeton University Press, 1980), 58–73.

2 R. G. Collingwood, *The Idea of History* (New York: Oxford University Press, 1956), 269–282.

3 An indispensible aid to thinking about genres in literary Chinese is E. D. Edwards, "A Classified Guide to the Thirteen Classes of Chinese Prose," *Bulletin of the School of Oriental and African Studies* 12, nos. 3 and 4 (1948): 770–788.

4 During the Qing, the History Bureau (*Guoshiguan*) was a department within the

Hanlin Academy. Han Yu-shan describes the offices and historiographical functions of the two organizations in *Elements of Chinese Historiography* (Hollywood: W. M. Hawley, 1955), 209.

5 Although the genre of *ji* (as well as *youji*) can be traced to Tang writers of the eighth and ninth centuries, and particularly to the exemplary Liu Zongyuan (773–819), it was not until the Soong that *ji* became a significant genre. See James M. Hargett, "Yu-chi wen-hsüeh," in *The Indiana Companion to Traditional Chinese Literature,* ed. William H. Nienhauser Jr. (Bloomington: University of Indiana Press, 1986), 936–939; and his *On the Road in Twelfth-Century China: The Travel Diaries of Fan Chengda (1126–1193)* (Stuttgart: F. Steiner, 1989), 44–45.

6 See Bei Yunchen and Ye Youming, comps., *Lidai youji xuan* [Selections from travel diaries through the ages] (Changsha: Hunan renmin chubanshe, 1980), 4–6; and Hsu Hsia-k'o, *The Travel Diaries of Hsu Hsia-k'o,* trans. and ed. Li Chi (Hong Kong: Chinese University of Hong Kong, 1974), 13–28.

7 Based on references in the *Zhou li,* some scholars trace the local treatise to the Zhou period; unfortunately, no such early examples are extant. See Fu Zhenlun, *Zhongguo fangzhi xue tonglun* [A comprehensive study of the Chinese geographic treatise] (Shanghai: Shangwu yinshuguan, 1935), 1–2; and Tang Zupei, *Xin fangzhi xue* [A new study of the geographic treatise] (Taibei: Huaguo chubanshe, 1955), 1–3.

8 For a grounding of the treatise in historiography, see Li Taifen, *Fangzhi xue* [A study of the geographic treatise] (Shanghai: Shangwu yinshuguan, 1935), 1–17.

9 Two intermediate but short-lived genres bridging the *zhi* and the *fangzhi* were the *tujing* or "illustrated monograph" and the *tuzhi* or "illustrated treatise," both of which were compiled during the Sui and Tang (581–906) periods. See Chen Cheng-siang [Chen Zhengxiang], *Zhongguo fangzhi di dilixue jiazhi/Geographical Evaluation of the Chinese Fang-chih* (Hong Kong: Chinese University of Hong Kong, 1965), 7–11.

10 The best discussions of the development of the genre of local treatise are Wang Yong, *Zhongguo dilixue shi* [A history of Chinese geography] (Changsha: Shangwu yinshuguan, 1938), 127–216; and the proceedings of the International Conference on Chinese Local Gazetteers, "Fangzhi xue guoji yanjiu taohui lunwenjihao," *Hanxue yanjiu* 3, no. 2 (December 1985).

11 For a historical perspective on bibliography, see Tsien Tsuen-hsuin, "A History of Bibliographic Classification in China," *Library Quarterly* 22, no. 4 (10/1952): 307–324.

12 My description is indebted to the work of R. Kent Guy, *The Emperor's Four Treasuries: Scholars and the State in the Late Ch'ien-Lung Era* (Cambridge, Mass.: Harvard University, Council on East Asian Studies, 1987), especially 121–156. See also Frederick W. Mote, "Reflections on the First Complete Printing of the *Ssu-k'u Ch'üan-shu,*" *Gest Library Journal* 1, no. 2 (Spring 1987): 26–50.

13 For a concise and helpful analysis of the "school" phenomenon, see Benjamin Elman, "Ch'ing Dynasty 'Schools' of Scholarship," *Ch'ing-shih wen-t'i* 4, no. 6 (12/1979): 1–45. On Han vs. Soong learning see Benjamin Elman's *From Philosophy to Philology: Intellectual and Social Aspects of Change in Late Imperial China* (Cambridge, Mass.: Harvard University, Council on East Asian Studies, 1984), 57–60; and *Classi-*

cism, Politics, and Kinship: The Ch'ang-chou School of New Text Confucianism in Late Imperial China (Berkeley: University of California Press, 1990). The latter is an especially informative discussion of the interconnectedness of scholarly traditions in the eighteenth and nineteenth centuries.

14 Zhang Xuecheng, "Ji yu Dai Dongyuan lun xiu zhi" [A discussion with Dai Dongyuan on the compilation of treatises], in *Zhangshi yishu* [Posthumous works of Master Zhang] (Wuxing: Jiayetang, 1922), 14: 37a–39b. See also David S. Nivison, *The Life and Thought of Chang Hsüeh-ch'eng (1738–1801)* (Stanford: Stanford University Press, 1966), 45–49.

15 Another valuable perspective on the shifting ground of nineteenth-century "traditions" is provided in Theodore Huters, "From Writing to Literature: The Development of Late Qing Theories of Prose," *HJAS* 47, no. 1 (1987): 51–96.

3 Journeys to the East

1 The best discussion is Pauline Yu, *The Reading of Imagery in the Chinese Poetic Tradition* (Princeton: Princeton University Press, 1987). See also Stephen Owen, *Traditional Chinese Poetry and Poetics: Omen of the World* (Madison: University of Wisconsin Press, 1985), 44ff.; and Wai-kam Ho, "The Literary Concepts of 'Picture-Like' (*Ju-hua*) and 'Picture-Idea' (*Hua-i*) in the Relationship between Poetry and Painting," in *Words and Images: Chinese Poetry, Calligraphy, and Painting*, ed. Alfreda Murck and Wen C. Fong (New York: Metropolitan Museum of Art; Princeton: Princeton University Press, 1991), 359–404.

2 See Li Gui, *Dong you riji* [Diary of a journey to the East], pt. 4 of *Huanyou diqiu xinlu* [A new record of a trip around the world] ([1879]; reprinted Changsha: Hunan renmin chubanshe, 1980), 125; Wang Zhichun, *Dong you riji* [Diary of an eastern journey], in his *Tan ying lu* [Records from overseas] (n.p.: Shangyang wenyi zhai, [1880]), *juan* 1: 5a (hereafter referred to as *TYL*) and Hê Ruzhang, *Shi dong shulue*, reprinted in *ZRYW*, 49.

3 There are two extensive reviews of the material: the more credulous, Gustaaf Schlegel's "Problèmes géographiques: Les Peuples étrangers chez les historiens chinois: Fou-Sang Kouo," *T'oung Pao* 3 (1892): 101–168; and the more skeptical, E. Bretschneider's "Fu-Sang, or Who Discovered America?" *The Chinese Recorder* (October 1870): 114–120. This latter article was part of a bizarre dispute among nineteenth century sinologists, fueled by Hui Shen's account, over whether or not Buddhist monks had discovered America in the fifth century. Connoisseurs of the curious may consult Charles G. Leland, *Fusang, or the Discovery of America* (New York: Bouton, 1875).

4 Li Bo, "Shang yun yue," in *Li Bo ji jiaozhu* [The annotated collected works of Li Bo] (Shanghai: Guji chubanshe, 1980), 258–264.

5 Li Bo, "Ku Zhao Qing xing" [Lamenting Zhao Qing's departure], in ibid., 1503f; and Wang Wei, "Song mishu Zhao Jian hui Ribenguo" [For Secretary Zhao on his

return to Japan] in *Wang Ruocheng ji jianzhu* [Annotated selections from the works of Wang Ruocheng] (Beijing: Zhonghua shuju, 1961), 219–225. Abe is known in Chinese sources as both Zhao Qing and Chao Heng.

6　See Wang Xiangrong, "'Abei Zhongmalu' han jibei/zhenbei" [Abe Nakamaro and the mythical and real details], in *Cong Xu Fu dao Huang Zunxian* [From Xu Fu to Huang Zunxian], ed. Yang Zhengguang (Beijing: Shishi chubanshe, 1985), 79–99.

7　The earliest references to Japanese usages of "Fusang" that I have seen are a tenth-century collection of Chinese poetry by Japanese poets, *Fusōshū* [Fusang collection], and a twelfth-century Buddhist history of Japan, *Fusō ryakki* [Essential records of Fusang].

8　*Shan hai jing jiaozhu* [The annotated *Classic of Mountains and Oceans*], ann. Yuan Ke (Shanghai: Shanghai guji chubanshe, 1980), 260f. Huang Zunxian directly quotes the passage in *RBZSS*, 1:3b. I discuss this poem (number 6) below in chapter 6.

9　Hê Ruzhang, *Shi dong shulue*, 49.

10　Wang Zhichun, *Dong you riji, TYL, juan* 1: 5a.

11　I have not found a locus classicus for such a description, although the reduplicative *tongtong*—for which I so inadequately resort to "in the ending twilight"—can be traced to a pair of poems by the Tang contemporaries Li Shangyin and Bo Juyi.

12　See especially "Dong jun" ("The Lord of the East") among the "Nine Songs," as translated by and annotated by David Hawkes: *The Songs of the South: An Ancient Chinese Anthology of Poems by Qu Yuan and Other Poets*, rev. ed. (Harmondsworth: Penguin, 1985), 112–113, 121.

13　Wang Tao, *Fusang youji* [Travels in Fusang] (Tokyo: Kunten shuppan, [1880]), 3:11b. Hereafter referred to as *FSYJ*. For another example of Fusang and fantastic travel, see Huang Zunxian, *RBZSS*, 1:10a.

14　James Hargett makes a similar point regarding Fan Chengda's reference to a poem by Han Yu relating great distance to fantastic travel on the *luan* bird ("simurgh"). See *On the Road*, 102.

15　Huang Zunxian, *RBZSS*, 1:1a.

16　A collection of Ming poems commemorating the return departures of Japanese diplomats and monks has been assembled in the Qing encyclopedia *Gujin tushu jicheng* [Collections of the ancient and contemporary writings] ([ca. 1726]; reprinted n.p., Wenxing shudian, n.d.), *ce* 209, i.e., *Fangyu huibian* [Materials on the territories)]; *juan* 40: 397f.

17　Owen, *Remembrances*, 24.

18　*Shi ji* (Beijing: Zhonghua shuju, 1959), *juan* 6: 247–248, 258, 263; and *juan* 118: 3086; additionally, see the *Han shu* (Beijing: Zhonghua shuju, 1962) *juan* 25, pt. 2: 1260; and *juan* 45: 2172–2173.

19　*Hou Han shu* (Beijing: Zhonghua shuju, 1965), *juan* 85: 2822.

20　Wang Tao, "Introduction" to Huang Zunxian, *RBZSS*, 1:1a.

21　Wang Zhichun, *Dong you riji, TYL*, [preliminary page 8b] and *juan* 1: 5a.

22　Compare Wang Zhichun, *TYL, juan* 1: 4b, 7a; *juan* 2: 13; Hê Ruzhang, *Shi dong shulue*, 55, and *Shi dong za yong*, 73; Huang Qingdeng, *Dong you riji* [Diary of a journey to the East], in *ZRYW*, 230.

23 Hê Ruzhang, *Shi dong za yong* [Assorted verse from the Eastern Embassy], reprinted in *ZRYW,* 73.

24 Hê Ruzhang, *Shi dong shulue,* 55.

25 Huang Zunxian, *RBZSS,* 1:2b.

26 Ibid., 3a. See my comments on *tong zhong* (same seed/same race) in chapter 2, note 22.

27 For a compelling meditation on mankind's motives in constructing "mythic space"—from clarifying defective knowledge to familiarizing a worldview as "place"— see Yifu Tuan, "Mythical Space and Place," in his *Space and Place: The Perspective of Experience* (Minneapolis: University of Minnesota Press, 1977), 85–100.

28 See Mircea Eliade, *The Myth of the Eternal Return; or, Cosmos and History* (Princeton: Princeton University Press, 1965), xiv, 3–9.

29 Claude Lévi-Strauss, *The Savage Mind* (Chicago: University of Chicago Press, 1966), 17–22.

30 See, by contrast, the recent set of essays on religious pilgrimage, *Pilgrims and Sacred Sites in China,* ed. Susan Naquin and Chün-fang Yü (Berkeley: University of California Press, 1992). Susan Naquin discusses pilgrimage as popular ritual in "The Peking Pilgrimage to Miao-feng Shan: Religious Organizations and Sacred Site," esp. 358–366; and Pei-yi Wu discusses the problematic relationship between accounts of pilgrimages and travelogues in "An Ambivalent Pilgrim to T'ai Shan in the Seventeenth Century," 65–88.

31 A connection between place and literary remembrance was early on established in the *yong shi* ("celebrating history") tradition in Han poetry. See Hans H. Frankel, *The Flowering Plum and the Palace Lady: Interpretations of Chinese Poetry* (New Haven: Yale University Press, 1976), 104–127. The development of the travel record or *ji,* however, was a substantial modification of this early connection.

32 As a general phenomenon, see the valuable contextualization by Nancy D. Munn, "The Cultural Anthropology of Time: A Critical Essay," *Annual Review of Anthropology* 21 (1992): 93–123, esp. 112–116.

33 Owen, *Remembrances,* 26.

34 Accordingly, the community defined in a ritual remembrance is connected to the state structure by virtue of education—the basis of the political power of the ruling class, composed of a legal class of officials and an economic class of "gentry" landowners with access to education.

25 Marshall Sahlins, *Historical Metaphors and Mythical Realities: Structure in the Early History of the Sandwich Islands Kingdom* (Ann Arbor: University of Michigan Press, 1981).

36 Li Shuchang, *Zhuozunyuan cong gao* [Collected drafts from the Zhuozun Garden] ([1893]; reprinted Taibei: Wenhai chubanshe, n.d.), 6:35–36.

37 Even today, Xu Fu continues to exert a hold on certain Chinese who concern themselves with the whereabouts of his remains. See Hu Ying, "Xu Fu ji you yi kaozheng" [Another piece of evidential research on Xu Fu's tomb], in *Zhongguo yu Riben* [China and Japan] 21 (September 1971): 54; and Wang Xiangrong, "Xu Fu daole

Riben ma?" [Did Xu Fu reach Japan?], in *Gudai de Zhongguo yu Riben*, 64–106. Most recently, a group of Chinese archaeologists claim to have identified Xu Fu's native village along the Chinese coast in Jiangsu Province. See Luo Qixiang, "Xu Fu cun de faxian han Xu Fu dongdu" [The discovery of Xu Fu's village and Xu Fu's eastern crossing], in *Cong Xu Fu dao Huang Zunxian*, ed. Yang Zhengguang (Beijing: Shishi chubanshe, 1985), 24–51. By far the most spectacular obsession with Xu Fu has been that of Wei Tingsheng, whose work has resulted in three expansively circumstantial monographs, the aim of which has been to identify the first Japanese emperor Jimmu with Xu Fu: *Riben Shenwu kaiguo xinkao* [A new examination of the Japanese Jimmu's founding of the nation] (Hong Kong: Commercial Press, 1950); *Xu Fu yu Riben* [Xu Fu and Japan] (Hong Kong: Commercial Press, 1953); and a recapitulation and rebuttal of critics in English, *The Birth of Japan* (Taibei: China Academy, 1975).

38 Richard E. Strassberg mentions the related practice of engraving texts in stone (on rock walls or commemorative stele) as a part of the "tradition" of literary excursion, in *Inscribed Landscapes: Travel Writing from Imperial China* (Berkeley: University of California Press, 1994), 5f.

39 Yifu Tuan makes a valuable conceptual distinction between "space" and "place": *space,* the defining quality of which is a sense of freedom of movement, requires some structuring in order to become *place,* defined as a type of object and "familiar space." See *Space and Place*, 46.

40 The *Youli tujing yuji* (1889) is a complete diary of Fu's official travels between October 1887 and November 1889, which I discuss in chapter 5. The sections of Fu's diary (*juan* 3, 4, and 14) pertaining to his travels in Japan are separately titled *Youli Riben tujing yuji*; Wang Xiaoqiu titles them *Youli Riben yuji* in his reprint edition. See *ZRYW,* 109–218.

41 Wang Tao, *FSYJ,* 3:10a.

42 See Charles L. Batten Jr., *Pleasurable Instruction: Form and Convention in Eighteenth-Century Travel Literature* (San Francisco: University of California Press, 1978), 39–44 passim; and Percy G. Adams, *Travel Literature and the Evolution of the Novel* (Lexington: University of Kentucky Press, 1983), 40–50 passim.

43 *Dong you riji* [A diary of an eastern journey], in *XFHZ, zhi* 10: 302–304; and *Dong you jisheng* [Copious notes from an eastern journey], in *XFHZ, zhi* 10: 305.

44 James Hargett, by contrast, discusses Fan Chengda's travel records as "autobiographical," although he also states that "subjective" or "personal" aspects of travel literature were rare in the Soong period. See *On the Road,* 56, 106.

45 Wang Tao, *FSYJ,* 1:2a.

46 Owen, *Remembrances,* 17.

47 See Marshall Sahlins, *Islands of History* (Chicago: University of Chicago Press, 1985), 108f.

48 Compare Hê Ruzhang, *Shi dong za yong,* 85; Wang Zhichun, *Dong you riji, TYL, juan* 1: 17a ff.; and Wang Tao, *FSYJ,* 1:24b–25.

49 Compare Huang Zunxian, *RBZSS,* 1:8b, 10a; Wang Tao, *FSYJ,* 2:31b–32a; Wang Zhichun, *Dong you riji, TYL, juan* 2: 7.

50 Compare Wang Zhichun, *Dong you riji, TYL, juan* 1: 9; and Hê Ruzhang, *Dong you shulue*, 54.

51 Wang Tao, *FSYJ*, 3:15–22; Li Shuchang, *Zhuozunyuan cong gao*, 6: 32–33.

52 Both of these officials are tragic figures of the variety Japanese allude to in terms of *hōgan biiki*, "sympathy for the lieutenant"—that is, underdogs who died nobly in the service of a lost cause. See Ivan Morris, *The Nobility of Failure* (New York: Holt, Reinhart, and Winston, 1975).

53 See Murata Masashi, *Nanbokuchō ron* [On the northern and southern dynasties] (Tokyo: Shibundō, 1959), 209–211.

54 *Riben suo zhi* [Sundry records of Japan], in *XFHZ, zhi* 10: 306.

55 Wang Zhichun, *Dong yang suo ji* [Random notes on the East], *TYL, juan* 3: 7.

56 Hê Ruzhang, *Shi dong shulue*, 51.

57 Wang Tao, *FSYJ*, 2:10b–13a. Cf. 2:7a.

58 Some scholars describe this poetic (sub)genre of *yong wu* in contrast to the understanding of imagery represented in the theory that poetry "expresses intention" (discussed in chapter 4). This theory was based on the idea that inner intent, through writing, encodes the outward forms of things; images thus serve as the vehicle for a recovery of the author's presence before the object of his description. See, for example, Pauline Yu, *The Reading of Imagery in the Chinese Poetic Tradition*, 119ff., 168ff.

59 See Dore J. Levy, *Chinese Narrative Poetry: The Late Han through T'ang Dynasties* (Durham: Duke University Press, 1988), 34–53. In addition, Kang-i Sun Chang discusses the centrality of *yongwu* poetry to poetry gatherings during the Six Dynasties period, in *Six Dynasties Poetry* (Princeton: Princeton University Press, 1986), 122–125.

60 See Edward H. Schafer, *The Golden Peaches of Samarkand: A Study of T'ang Exotics* (Berkeley: University of California Press, 1963), 1–39.

61 See Ouyang Xiu, "Riben dao ge," *Ouyang Wenzhong Gong wenji* [Collected writings of Master Ouyang Wenzhong] (n.p., n.d.), *juan* 54 [*Waiji juan* 4]: 7; Liang Peilan, "Riben dao ge," *Qing shi duo* [Chimes of Qing poetry], ed. Zhang Yingchang (Beijing: Zhonghua shuju, 1960), 1:399; and Wang Tao, *FSYJ*, 2:26.

62 *Riben suo zhi*, in *XFHZ, zhi* 10: 306.

63 Luo Sen, *Riben riji* [Japan diary], in *ZRYW*, 34.

64 Compare the anonymous *Dong you jisheng*, in *XFHZ, zhi* 10: 305f; Li Gui, *Dong you riji*, 123; and Wang Zhichun, *Dong yang suo ji*, in *TYL, juan* 3: 15a.

65 The phrase is borrowed from Guo Songtao's account of his journey to Europe, the *Shi xi jicheng* [A full account of the embassy to the West], reprinted in *XFHZ, ce* 56: 147b.

66 Wang Zhichun, *Dong you riji, TYL, juan* 1: 18–20, and *juan* 2: 3–6.

67 Hê Ruzhang, *Shi dong za yong*, 78.

68 Li Gui, *Dong you riji*, 122.

69 Compare Hê Ruzhang, *Shi dong za yong*, 72; Wang Tao, *FSYJ*, 1:2b–4b, 2:10a, 12a; and Wang Zhichun, *Dong you riji, TYL, juan* 1: 13a ff., *juan* 2: 9–10.

70 Hayden White, *The Content of the Form: Narrative Discourse and Historical Representation* (Baltimore: Johns Hopkins University Press, 1987), 16.

71 Zeng Yongling, *Guo Songtao dazhuan* [The major biography of Guo Songtao] (Shenyang: Liaoning renmin chubanshe, 1989), 298–321. See also J. D. Frodsham, "Introduction," to *The First Chinese Embassy to the West: The Journals of Kuo Sung-t'ao, Liu Hsi-hung, and Chang Te-yi*, trans. and ann. J. D. Frodsham (Oxford: Clarendon Press, 1974), xxviii–liv.

72 Hê Ruzhang, *Shi dong shulue*, 60.

4 The Historiographical Use of Poetry

1 See Zhu Ziqing, *Shi yan zhi bian*, 1–42; and Pauline Yu, *The Reading of Imagery in the Chinese Poetic Tradition*, 67–84. For a suggestive discussion of the transition from oral to textual, see Steven Van Zoeren, *Poetry and Personality: Reading, Exegesis, and Hermeneutics in Traditional China* (Stanford: Stanford University Press, 1991), 17–51.

2 Pauline Yu, The *Reading of Imagery*, 69.

3 See Guy, *The Emperor's Four Treasuries*, 42–44; and Elman, *From Philosophy to Philology*, 212–221.

4 See Elman, *From Philosophy to Philology*, 179–185; and also the instructive comments of Wu Hongyi, *Qingdai shixue chutan* [Preliminary investigations of Qing poetic theory], rev. ed. (Taibei: Xuesheng shuju, 1985), 27–33. Zhu Ziqing describes other such usages of poetry, as early as the Chunqiu period, in *Shi yan zhi bian*, 60–62, 105–107.

5 In addition to Zhu Ziqing's preface to *Shi yan zhi bian*, an invaluable discussion of the broad issues is Barbara Herrnstein Smith, *Poetic Closure: A Study of How Poems End* (Chicago: University of Chicago Press, 1968), 1–37.

6 Two printings followed in 1880, by Wang Tao's newspaper company in Hong Kong, the Xunhuan baoguan, and by the Hōbun shobō in Tokyo. See Huang's preface to the reprint of 1885: Huang Zunxian, *Riben zashi shi*, reprinted in *Xizheng congshu* [Collected writings on Western administration], ed. "Qiuziqiangzhai Zhuren" ["Master of the Studio for Seeking Self-strengthening"] (n.p., [1897]), 25:1a. Three additional printings followed shortly thereafter, by the Zhonghua yinwuju (likely Shanghai) and bookstores in both Tokyo and Kyoto; the work was reprinted again in 1885 in Wuzhou (Guangxi). See Huang's afterword to the second edition, *Riben zashi shi*, 2d ed. (Taibei: Yiwen yinshuguan, 1974), 106. Wu Tianren has identified a total of thirteen printings (and a possible fourteenth) of the first edition; see his *Huang Gongdu xiansheng zhuan'gao* [A draft biography of Master Huang Gongdu] (Hong Kong: Zhongwen Daxue chuban, 1972), 305–307.

7 Because the Chinese practice of publishing differs from that in the United States, a word on terminology is in order. Each Chinese printing (*banben/kanban*) is technically an edition; however, I will refer to the various Chinese printings/editions of the 154-poem version as "the first edition." "Second edition" thus refers to Huang's later, 200-poem version.

8 In making this judgment, I have found the 1936 essay by Zhou Zuoren especially helpful: "Lun Huang Gongdu de *Riben zashi shi*" [On the *Poems on Divers Japanese*

Affairs by Huang Gongdu], in *Renjinglu congkao* [On the Renjing Hut Collections], ed. Zheng Ziyu (Singapore: Shangwu yinshuguan, 1959), 19–25.

9 Wang Tao, *FSYJ*, 1:21b.

10 Huang Zunxian, *Rěnjinglu shicao jianzhu* [The annotated draft poems from the Renjing Hut], ann. Qian Zhonglian (Hong Kong: Zhonghua shuju, 1963), 82–85. Hereafter *RJLSC*.

11 Huang Zunxian, *RBZSS*, 2:4. This is poem 122 in the second edition.

12 Wang Zhichun, *Dong you riji*, *TYL*, *juan* 1: 17a–b.

13 Arthur Waley, *Yuan Mei: Eighteenth-Century Chinese Poet* (New York: Macmillan, 1957), 166–168.

14 These are summarized in Huang Zunxian, *RBZSS*, 2:30; and Kang Youwei, "Xu" [Preface], in Huang Zunxian, *Riben zashi shi* [2d ed.], 1. (This text is reprinted in *Kang Youwei shi wen xuan* [Selected poetry and prose of Kang Youwei] (Guangdong: Renmin chubanshe, 1983), 369–377.)

15 My representations of general trends during the Qing are based upon Suzuki Torao, *Shina shiron shi* [A history of Chinese poetic theory] (Tokyo: Kobundō, 1927); Guo Shaoyu, *Zhongguo wenxue piping shi* [A history of Chinese literary criticism] (Shanghai: Shangwu yinshuguan, 1947); Aoki Masaru, *Shindai bungaku hyōron shi* [A history of Qing literary criticism] (Tokyo: Iwanami, 1950); and Liu Ruoyu [James J. Y. Liu], "Qingdai shishuo lunyao" [An outline of Qing poetic theory], in *Xianggang Daxue wushizhounian jinian lunwen ji* [Collected essays commemorating the fiftieth anniversary of Hong Kong University] (Hong Kong: Xianggang Daxue zhongwenxi, 1964), 1:321–342. On the matter of individual poetry circles as "schools"--with specific reference to Zha Shenxing and Li E—see Aoki, pp. 118–136. And on the relation of many concepts mentioned here to the practice of "poetry talk," see Wai-leung Wong, "Chinese Impressionistic Criticism: A Study of the Poetry-Talk (Shih-Hua Tz'u-Hua) Tradition" (Ph.D. diss., Ohio State University, 1976).

16 For a concise survey of Ming trends in poetics, see Yoshikawa Kōjirō, *Gen Min shi gaisetsu* (Tokyo: Iwanami, 1963), trans. John Timothy Wixted as *Five Hundred Years of Chinese Poetry, 1150–1650: The Chin, Yuan, and Ming Dynasties* (Princeton: Princeton University Press, 1989). On the Qing reaction to Ming poetics, see Aoki Masaru, *Shindai bungaku hyōron shi*, 1–39; Wu Hongyi, *Qingdai shixue chutan*, 105–146; and especially Richard John Lynn, "Tradition and the Individual: Ming and Ch'ing Views of Yuan Poetry," *Journal of Oriental Studies* 15, no. 1 (1977): 1–19; and "Orthodoxy and Enlightenment: Wang Shih-chen's Theory of Poetry and Its Antecedents," in *The Unfolding of Neo-Confucianism*, ed. Wm. Theodore de Bary (New York: Columbia University Press, 1975), 217–269. On the high Tang, see Owen, *The Great Age of Chinese Poetry*.

17 Li E, "Lüshan yeshi ji xu" [A preface to the collection from the Green Fir Hut], reprinted in Wu Hongyi and Ye Qingbing, eds., *Qingdai wenxue piping ziliao huibian* [Edited materials on Qing literary criticism] (Taibei: Chengwen chubanshe, 1979), 420 (hereafter *QWPZH*).

18 On the background of "scholarly poetry," see Richard John Lynn, "Orthodoxy and

Enlightenment," 231ff.; and "The Talent Learning Polarity in Chinese Poetics: Yan Yu and the Later Tradition," *Chinese Literature: Essays, Articles, Reviews* 5 (1983): 157–184. On the same, with specific reference to Weng Fanggang, see Guo Shaoyu, *Zhongguo wenxue piping shi*, 625–626; Li Fengmou, *Weng Fanggang ji qi shilun* [Weng Fanggang and his poetic theory] (Taibei: Chia Hsiu Foundation, 1978), 44–46; and Min Ze, *Zhongguo wenxue lilun piping shi* [A history of Chinese literary theory and criticism] (Beijing: Renmin chubanshe, 1981), 913ff.

19 Yuan Mei, from *Zhongyatang shiji* [Collected poems from Zhongya Hall], quoted in Wu Hongyi, *Qingdai shixue chutan*, 29.

20 Huang Zunxian, *RBZSS*, 1:1a.

21 Ibid., 1:2a.

22 Kurata Sadayoshi inexplicably refers Huang's "eccentric individualism" to the Ming poet of the Gong'an School, Yuan Hongdao. See *Shinmatsu-Minsho wo chūshin toshita Chūgoku kindai shi no kenkyū* [Studies of poetry in early modern China, with late Qing/early Republic as a focus] (Tokyo: Taishukan, 1969), 265.

23 Huang Zunxian, "Yu Langshan lun shi" [Discussing poetry with Langshan], *Lingnan xuebao* 2, no. 2 (July 1931): 184–185. Wu Tianren identifies Huang's addressee as Zhou Langshan in *Huang Gongdu Xiansheng zhuan'gao*, 381. Yang Tianshi dates this letter to 1876, prior to the writing of the *Poems on Divers Japanese Affairs*, but J. D. Schmidt believes Huang wrote it prior to 1874. Compare Yang Tianshi, *Huang Zunxian* (Shanghai: Renmin chubanshe, 1979), 132; and J. D. Schmidt, *Within the Human Realm: The Poetry of Huang Zunxian, 1848–1905* (Cambridge: Cambridge University Press, 1994), 318n7. Huang expresses similar ideas in his early poem, "Za gan" [Divers feelings], in *RJLSC*, 14–18.

24 *Fugu*, or "reviving antiquity," was a dominant motive among Ming poets, who were roundly criticized by many theorists of poetics during the Qing. Among Huang's contemporaries, followers of the Tongcheng School of Anhui would have advocated such an imitation of ancient style. See David Pollard, *A Chinese Look at Literature: The Literary Values of Chou Tso-jen in Relation to the Tradition* (Berkeley: University of California Press, 1973), 140–157. Cf. You Tong, "Wu Xusheng shi xu" [A preface to the poetry of Wu Xusheng], in *QWPZH*, 139; and Li E, "Lanyuan shichao xu" [A preface to copied poems from the Garden of Indolence], in *QWPZH*, 418–419.

25 According to Zhu Ziqing, a conflation of intention and emotion began with the later Han interpretation of "poetry verbalizes intention," and was formalized with Lu Ji's *Wen fu* (ca. 300) and Liu Xie's *Wenxin diaolong* (ca. 500). See *Shi yan zhi bian*, 33–42. Steven Van Zoeren offers an interesting account of this conflation in Confucius's *Analects*, in *Poetry and Personality*, 52–79.

26 See Stephen Owen, "Transparencies," *HJAS* 39, no. 2 (1979): 231–251, revised as chapter 2 of *Traditional Chinese Poetry and Poetics: Omen of the World* (Madison: University of Wisconsin Press, 1985), 54–77. Cf. Van Zoeren, *Poetry and Personality*, 104–108.

27 See Tu Wei-ming, "Profound Learning, Personal Knowledge, and Poetic Vision,"

in *The Vitality of the Lyric Voice: Shih Poetry from the Late Han to the T'ang*, ed. Shuen-fu Lin and Stephen Owen (Princeton: Princeton University Press, 1986), 3–31.

28 Huang Zunxian, "Zi xu" [Author's preface], *RJLSC*, 1. This interpretation of Huang is developed by Wu Jianqing in "Huang Zunxian de shige lilun han *Renjinglu shicao*" [Huang Zunxian's poetic theory and the *Draft Poems from the Renjing Hut*], *Hua'nan shiyuan xuebao—zhexue shehui kexue ban* [Journal of the Huanan Teachers' Academy—philosophy and social science edition] 26 (1980, no. 3): 85–95.

29 The fact of a body of conventional images would caution us against interpreting the *shi* in terms of a pure phenomenology. See Yu, *Reading Imagery*, 198; and Owen's caveat on "artificial construction" in *Traditional Chinese Poetry*, 40–44.

30 You Tong, "Wu Xusheng shi xu," in *QWPZH*, 139; and "Gong Zongbo shi xu" [A preface to the poetry of Gong Zongbo], in *QWPZH*, 143. See also Guo Shaoyu, *Zhongguo wenxue piping shi*, 604.

31 Zha Shenxing, "Guo Jielao yu zhi lun shi" [Encountering M. Jin Zhang and discussing poetry wtih him], in *QWPZH*, 366. See also Aoki Masaru, *Shindai bungaku hyōron shi*, 127.

32 Although he did not directly advocate the reconciliation of Han and Soong learning, Huang Zunxian was critical of both schools in an early poetic statement, and still maintained a sympathetic interest in both during his career. See "Gan huai" [Feelings aroused], in *RJLSC*, 1–12.

33 This simplistic discussion does not of course do justice to the complexities and subtleties of the differences. While there is a wealth of literature on the subject, the curious reader might start with Ying-shih Yu, "Some Preliminary Observations on the Rise of Ch'ing Confucian Intellectualism," *Tsing-Hua Journal of Chinese Studies* n.s. 11, nos. 1–2 (12/1975): 105–146; and Benjamin Elman, "Criticism as Philosophy: Conceptual Change in Ch'ing Dynasty Evidential Research," *Tsing-Hua Journal of Chinese Studies* n.s. 17 (1985): 165–98. See also Henderson, *The Development and Decline of Chinese Cosmology*, 104ff., 157ff.

34 Andrew H. Plaks, "Towards a Critical Theory of Chinese Narrative," in *Chinese Narrative: Critical and Theoretical Essays*, ed. Andrew H. Plaks (Princeton: Princeton University Press, 1977), 315. See also John B. Henderson, *Scripture, Canon, and Commentary: A Comparison of Confucian and Western Exegesis* (Princeton: Princeton University Press, 1991), 14.

35 Zhang Xuecheng, "*Shu* jiao" [The teaching of the *Classic of Documents*], in *Wenshi tongyi* 1:7–17; see also David S. Nivison, *The Life and Thought of Chang Hsüeh-ch'eng*, 222–229.

36 Zhang Xuecheng, "*Shi* jiao" [The teaching of the *Classic of Poetry*], in *Wenshi tongyi* 1:17–25; see also Nivison, *The Life and Thought*, 120–125. Wai-leung Wong discusses this issue in the context of Zhang's reflections on "poetry talk," in "Chinese Impressionistic Criticism," 7–8.

37 Guo Shaoyu, *Zhongguo wenxue piping shi*, 473–478, 481–485. Theodore Huters places Zhang in a more general process of emphasizing *wen* (writing) over evidential research in the late eighteenth century; "From Writing to Literature," 62–73.

38 Owen, *Traditional Chinese Poetry*, 192.

39 See Chow Tse-tsung, "The Early History of the Chinese Word *Shih* (Poetry)," in *Wen-lin: Studies in the Chinese Humanities*, ed. Chow Tse-tsung (Madison: University of Wisconsin Press, 1968), 151–209. Cf. Zhu Ziqing, *Shi yan zhi bian*, 1–2, 21.

40 See Irving Y. Lo and William Schultz, eds., *Waiting for the Unicorn: Poems and Lyrics of China's Last Dynasty, 1644–1911* (Bloomington: Indiana University Press, 1986), 18–19.

41 Zha Shenxing, "Guo Jielao yu zhi lun shi," in *QWPZH*, 366.

42 Alison Harley Black, *Man and Nature in the Philosophical Thought of Wang Fu-chih* (Seattle: University of Washington Press, 1989), 262–277; and Funatsu Tomohiko, *Chūgoku shiwa no kenkyū* [Studies of Chinese poetry talk] (Tokyo: Yakumo shobō, 1977), 134–139.

43 Li Fengmou, *Weng Fanggang*, 14–17, 52ff. Li describes Weng's interest in developing a theory of *li* as a response to Dai Zhen's famous critique of Soong interpretations of the *Mencius*. Weng was distressed that Dai, in rejecting material force and elevating principle, had ignored the issue of "human nature" (*xing*)—the manifestation of principle in man. Although Weng seems to have salvaged *xing*, it became but one in a set of elements (including feeling, event, and *wen*) encompassed by principle. Like Dai, Weng had little to say about material force. Hu Shi defends Dai Zhen's interpretations of *li* from Weng Fanggang's "inability to understand" in *Dai Dongyuan de zhexue* [Dai Zhen's philosophy] (Shanghai: Shangwu yinshuguan, 1927), 94–98; but Weng was in fact part of a larger reaction against Dai and Han learning generally in the early nineteenth century: see Benjamin Elman, "Criticism as Philosophy," 187ff.; and James Polachek, *The Inner Opium War*, 87–90.

44 Weng Fanggang, *Shizhou shihua* [Poetry talks from Shizhou], ed. Chen Erdong (Beijing: Renmin chubanshe, 1981), 123f.

45 Weng Fanggang, "Yueshan shiji xu" [A preface to the collected poems of Yueshan (Pan Liangyuan)], in *QWPZH*, 526.

46 Weng Fanggang, "Zhi yen ji xu" [A preface to the "Intentions Bespoken" collection], in *QWPZH*, 529.

47 Weng Fanggang, "Shenyun lun" [On Wang Shizhen's theory of "inspired tone"], in *QWPZH*, 536. Cf. Lo and Schultz, *Waiting for the Unicorn*, 20; and Li Fengmou, *Weng Fanggang*, 69.

48 Weng Fanggang, "Han shi yali li xungao lizi shuo" [A discussion of the character *Li* as beautifying and ordering in Han poetry], in *QWPZH*, 542. Scholars are divided over the status of this analysis in Weng's theory; Li Fengmou ignores it, while Guo Shaoyu makes it central. Cf. Guo, *Zhongguo wenxue piping shi*, 637.

49 Wu Hongyi, *Qingdai shixue chutan*, 243. Cf. Guo Shaoyu, *Zhongguo wenxue piping shi*, 637; and Li Fengmou, *Weng Fanggang*, 54, 57.

50 See Nivison, *The Life and Thought*, 225–226.

51 Kang Youwei, "Xu," in Huang Zunxian, *Riben zashi shi* [2d ed.], 1.

52 Ibid., 2.

53 Huang Zunxian, *RBZSS*, 1:2a.

54 W. B. Yeats, "He Mourns for the Change that Has Come upon Him and His Beloved, and Longs for the End of the World," in The *Variorum Edition of the Poems of W. B. Yeats* (New York: Macmillan, 1957), 153, 806f.

55 Ibid., 800.

56 You Tong, "Meicun ci xu" [A preface to Plum Village Lyrics], in *QWPZH*, 144; and "Cangwu ci xu" [A preface to Green Plane Tree Lyrics], in *QWPZH*, 145. See also Aoki Masaru, *Shindai bungaku hyōron shi*, 255–291; and David R. McCraw, *Chinese Lyricists of the Seventeenth Century* (Honolulu: University of Hawaii Press, 1990), 1–9. Chia-ying Yeh Chao recounts the Changzhou poet Zhang Huiyan's (1761–1802) inter-pretation of the lyric in terms of the "poetry verbalizes intention" tradition; see Chao, "The Ch'ang-chou School of *Tz'u* Criticism," in *Chinese Approaches to Literature from Confucius to Liang Ch'i-ch'ao*, ed. Adele Rickett (Princeton: Princeton University Press, 1978), 151–188.

57 See Li E, "Qunya ci ji xu" [A preface to the collected lyrics of a group of dandies], in *QWPZH*, 423.

58 Kang-i Sun Chang, *The Evolution of Chinese Tz'u Poetry: From Late T'ang to Northern Sung* (Princeton: Princeton University Press, 1980), 26–30. See also You Tong, "Mingci xuansheng xu" [A preface to a choice selection of famous lyrics], in *QWPZH*, 146f.

59 The best discussion of the *yuefu* form to date is Allen, *In the Voice of Others*, 37–68, 223–232.

60 Owen, *The Great Age of Chinese Poetry*, 94. Cf. Kang-i Sun Chang, *Evolution of Chinese Tz'u Poetry*, 18–19.

61 See the informative 1914 essay by Lou Zikuang and Ruan Changrui, "Zhuzhi ci de yanjiu" [Studies on the "bamboo stalk lyric"], in *Zhongshan Daxue minsu congshu* [Collected works on folklore from Zhongshan University] (1926; reprinted Taibei: Chinese Association for Folklore, 1969), 3:19–33. See also François Cheng, *Chinese Poetic Writing* (Bloomington: Indiana University Press, 1982), 120.

62 Wang Zhichun, *Dong you riji, TYL, juan* 2: 10.

63 Huang Zunxian, *RBZSS*, 2: 17. This is substantially revised as poem 107 in the second edition.

64 Shen Jiache et al., *Nan Song zashi shi* [Divers poems of the Southern Soong] (n.p., n.d.), *juan* [i]: 6a.

65 It is interesting, by comparison, that the genuine "lyric" too was used for descrip-tions of travel during the Qing. See David McCraw, *Chinese Lyricists*, 35ff, 102ff.

66 On the general topic of written vernacular forms, see the informative essay by Victor Mair, "Buddhism and the Rise of the Written Vernacular in East Asia: The Making of National Languages," *JAS* 53, no. 3 (8/1994): 707–751.

67 Hans H. Frankel, "*Yüeh-fu* Poetry," in *Studies in Chinese Literary Genres*, ed. Cyril Birch (San Francisco: University of California Press, 1974), 69–107.

68 I here rely on the terminology of Yuen Ren Chao, *A Grammar of Spoken Chinese* (Berkeley: University of California Press, 1968).

69 Huang Zunxian, *RBZSS*, 1:24b. Poem 66 in the second edition.

70 Ibid., 2:2a. Poem 85 in the second edition.

71 Ibid., 1:6b. Poem 13 in the second edition.

72 See Sheldon Hsiao-peng Lu, *From Historicity to Fictionality: The Chinese Poetics of Narrative* (Stanford: Stanford University Press, 1994), 1–11, 39–46. Andrew Plaks discusses *wen* in this opposition as "narrative" in "Towards a Critical Theory," 309–352.

73 I am drawing on Stephen Owen's "Voice," in *Traditional Chinese Poetry*, 108–142. See also his more recent "Meaning the Words: The Genuine as a Value in the Tradition of the Song Lyric," in *Voices of the Song Lyric in China*, ed. Pauline Yu (Berkeley: University of California Press, 1993), 30–69.

74 Bo Juyi, "Reading Zhang Ji's *Old Ballads*," in *Bo Xiangshan ji* [Collected works of Bo Xiangshan] (Changsha: Shangwu yinshuguan, 1934), 1:1–2.

75 See Lo and Schultz, eds., *Waiting for the Unicorn*, 17.

76 For Wang Shizhen, see Lynn, "Orthodoxy and Enlightenment"; for Wang Fuzhi, see Black, *Man and Nature*, 242–290.

77 See Owen, *Traditional Chinese Poetry*, 114–116; and James J. Y. Liu, *Chinese Theories of Literature* (Chicago: University of Chicago Press, 1975), 83–85. Funatsu Tomohiko refers Ye's position to an early Qing movement that linked voice and inspiration to a Confucian reading of the *Classic of Poetry* as molding character; see *Chūgoku shiwa no kenkyū*, 175–193.

78 Guo Shaoyu, *Zhongguo wenxue piping shi*, 630.

79 See Yoshikawa Kōjirō, *An Introduction to Sung Poetry*, trans. Burton Watson (Cambridge, Mass.: Harvard University Press, 1967), 38–42.

80 Yu-kung Kao and Tsu-lin Mei, "Syntax, Diction, and Imagery in T'ang Poetry," *HJAS* 31 (1971): 49–136.

81 You Tong, *Waiguo zhuzhi ci* [Bamboo stalk lyrics on the foreign domains], reprinted in *Zhaodai congshu* [Collected works reflecting the ages] (n.p.: Shikai tang, [1876]), (*Jia ji* [first series], *ce* 3, *juan* 3: 2.

82 Ibid., *juan* 3: 2b.

83 Shen Jiache et al., *Nan Song zashi shi, juan* 1: 4b.

84 Huang Zunxian, "Za gan" [Divers feelings], *RJLSC*, 14. A caveat is in order for some readers: Since Hu Shi first celebrated this line as one of the earliest calls for vernacular poetry, Huang Zunxian has been claimed by partisans of the vernacular movement, who did not advance their cause significantly until 1917, a decade after Huang's death. See Hu Shi, *Wushinian lai Zhongguo zhi wenxue* [Chinese literature of the last fifty years] (n.p.: Xinminguo shu, 1929), 42. Here I do *not* mean to suggest any equivalence between late Qing (including Huang's) poetic voice and vernacular language. In the first place, it would be difficult to identify a Qing vernacular. Reported speech in popular novels and plays—even the brushtalks—is stylized, assumes a knowledge of literary Chinese prose, and is not the same as actual speech; and as I indicated above, the stylistic peculiarities of Huang's *Poems* are as attributable to literary prose as to vernacular speech. Scholars who have taken seriously Huang Zunxian as a harbinger of vernacular poetry agree on only two aspects of his work: his use of new translation-word terminology and subject matter, and his adoption of this direct and prose-like

syntax. See Ch'en Shou-yi, *Chinese Literature: A Historical Introduction* (New York: Ronald Press, 1961), 626–628; Julia C. Lin, *Modern Chinese Poetry: An Introduction* (Seattle: University of Washington Press, 1972), 18–27; and especially J. D. Schmidt, *Within the Human Realm,* 62–68. In the second place, Hu Shi's vernacular movement, aside from advocating the use of vernacular speech, stressed with perhaps more vehemence the overthrowing of traditional poetic forms for the sake of "free verse" after the example of European poetry. According to Ono Jitsunosuke, Huang's formal and linguistic innovations are typical of only a *minor* portion of his poetic corpus. For the most part, he composed rather conventional five- and seven-syllable regulated verse and seven-syllable quatrains; the *Poems on Divers Japanese Affairs,* as I have said, are the latter. See Ono Jitsunosuke, "Keitaimen kara mita Kō Junken no shi" [Examining Huang Zunxian's poetry from the standpoint of form], *Chūgoku koten kenkyū* 12 (December 1964): 55–69.

85 Huang Zunxian, *Riben zashi shi* [2d ed.], 106. For Li Zhaolo, see *ECCP,* 448; his dictionary was published posthumously in 1871 at the direction of Li Hongzhang, so it would have been quite fresh to Huang. For Young J. Allen ("Lin Lezhi"), see *ECCP,* 851; Allen was a translator at the Jiangnan Arsenal and directed the translation of supplements to the third edition of Wei Yuan's geography.

86 Scholars are divided over the dominance of evidential research in the nineteenth century. Compare Elman, *Classicism, Politics, and Kinship,* 117–144, 246–249; Susan Mann Jones and Philip A. Kuhn, "Dynastic Decline and the Roots of Rebellion," in *Cambridge History of China,* vol. 10, *Late Ch'ing: 1800–1911,* pt. 1, ed. John K. Fairbank (Cambridge: Cambridge University Press, 1978), 144–154; and Theodore Huters, "From Writing to Literature," 63–65. In this context, I must reemphasize the uniqueness of Huang's *Poems* and his idiosyncratic approach to scholarship therein. If evidential research was on the decline in the nineteenth century, Huang and his admirers are exceptions to that general trend. My argument is thus an explication of Huang's eccentricity, and I note Huters's pertinent observation regarding Ruan Yuan's 1820s theory of prose—"[I]t represents the grafting of *kaoju* historicism onto the field of belles-lettres" (p. 87). Huang's *Poems* can be read in this light.

87 Huang commends evidential research in a pair of prefaces written during his stay in Japan; see "Renjinglu zawen chao" [Reprints of prose from the Renjing Hut], ed. Qian Zhonglian, in *Wenxian* 7 (1981): 66, 72. He also describes his work as evidential research in his 1887 preface to his *Japan Treatise;* see *Riben guozhi* (Shanghai: Tushu jicheng, [1898]; reprinted Taibei: Wenhai chubanshe, 1981), 5–6.

88 Huang Zunxian, *RBZSS,* 1:2a.

89 See W. G. Beasley and E. G. Pulleyblank, eds., *Historians of China and Japan* (Oxford: Oxford University Press, 1961), chaps. 9–11, passim.

90 Benjamin Elman, *From Philosophy to Philology.*

91 See Guy, *The Emperor's Four Treasuries,* 6–7; and Immanuel C. Y. Hsü, "Introduction" to his translation of Liang Qichao, *Intellectual Trends in the Ch'ing Period* (Cambridge, Mass.: Harvard University Press, 1959), 6–7.

92 See Yong Rong et al., *Siku quanshu zongmu tiyao* [Annotated catalogue of the

Complete Books of the Four Treasuries] ([Shanghai]: Shangwu yinshuguan, n.d.), [*juan* 142, i.e., *Zi bu* 52] vol. 27: *Zi bu, Xiaoshuo jia lei* 3:68–69.

93 Ibid., [*juan 78*, i.e., *Shi bu 7*] vol. 16: *Shi bu, Dili lei cunmu* 7:9–11.

94 Guy, *The Emperor's Four Treasuries,* 122–123, 129–154.

95 Of the two extant collections of draft reviews, that by Shao Jinhan (1743–1796) includes no works of geography; the other by Yao Nai (1732–1815) does. See Yao Nai, *Xibaoxuan shulu* [Book reviews by Yao Nai], ed. Mao Yusheng, in *Xibaoxuan yishu sanzhong* [Three posthumous works by Yao Nai], ed. Xu Zongliang (n.p., [1879]), *ce* 3.

96 Yong Rong et al., *Siku quanshu zongmu tiyao,* [*juan* 71, i.e., *Shi bu* 27] vol. 15, *Shi bu, Dili lei* 4:15.

97 Huang Zunxian, "Gan huai," *RJLSC,* 1.

98 See Bei and Ye, comps., *Lidai youji xuan,* 4–5.

99 See Irene Bloom, "On the 'Abstraction' of Ming Thought: Some Concrete Evidence from the Philosophy of Lo Ch'in-shun," in Wm. Theodore de Bary and Irene Bloom, eds., *Principle and Practicality: Essays in Neo-Confucianism and Practical Learning* (New York: Columbia University Press, 1979), 104–107. Hou Wailu makes an explicit connection between Gu Yanwu and *shixue* in *Zhongguo zaoqi qimeng sixiang shi* [A history of the philosophy of the early enlightenment in China] (Beijing: Renmin chubanshe, 1958), 231–232.

100 See Bei and Ye, comps., *Lidai youji xuan,* 5–6; and Hsu Hsia-k'o, *The Travel Diaries of Hsu Hsia-k'o,* 13–28.

101 Huang Zunxian, "Xunhui riji xu" [A preface to [Ikuta Mizutake's] diary of an official investigation and return], reprinted in "Renjinglu zawen chao," *Wenxian* 7 (1981): 66.

102 Wang Zhichun, *TYL, juan* 3: 1a.

103 See Stephen Owen, *Traditional Chinese Poetry,* 128–131.

104 Wang Zhichun, *TYL, juan* 3: 8a.

105 Wang Tao, *FSYJ,* 2:21a.

106 See the proceedings of the International Conference on Chinese Local Gazetteers, and in particular, the papers by Weng Tongwen, "Cong shehui-wenhuashi guandian lun fangzhi de fasheng fazhan" [On the appearance and development of local histories from the point of view of social and cultural history], and Chen Jiexian, "Lun Qingdai Taiwan diqu fangzhi de yili" [On the formal structure of local treatises on Taiwan during the Qing], *Hanxue yanjiu* 3, no. 2, pt. 1 (December 1985): 39–58, 157–231.

107 Some scholars trace this sensibility to Sima Guang (1019–1086) in the Soong; see E. G. Pulleyblank, "Chinese Historical Criticism: Liu Chih-chi and Ssu-ma Kuang," in Beasley and Pulleyblank, eds., *Historians of China and Japan,* 157–159.

108 See Willard Peterson, "The Life of Ku Yen-wu (1613–1682)," *HJAS* 28 (1968): 114–156; and 29 (1969): 201–247. See also Qian Mu, *Zhongguo jin sanbainian xueshu shi* [A history of learning in China during the past three hundred years] (Shanghai: Shangwu Shuju, 1939), 121–157; and Yamanoi Yū, "Ko Enbu no gakumonkan" [Gu Yanwu's view of scholarship], *Chūō Daigaku bungakubu kiyō* 35 (1964): 67–93.

109 Quan Zuwang, "Tinglin Xiansheng shendao biao" [Commemorating the mar-

vellous way of Master Tinglin], in his *Jiqiting ji* [Collections of the Jiqi Pavilion], 12: 1b, reprinted in *Ming Qing shiliao huibian* [Collected historical materials from the Ming and Qing] (Taibei: Wenhai chubanshe, n.d.), ser. 5, vol. 3 [vol. 41]: 543.

110 Poems 75 and 76 in the second edition, respectively.

111 Poems 2 and 55 in the second edition, respectively.

112 To be sure, the note was not new to evidential research scholarship—notelike jottings had been a popular form in the Ming period, and the genre of "poetry talk" (*shi hua*) too cultivated the note—but is did help to define the scholarly position of evidential research in that it was an alternative to the "commentary" and "recorded conversations" practiced by Soong learning scholars. See Daniel K. Gardner's "Modes of Thinking and Modes of Discourse in the Sung: Some Thoughts on the *Yü-lu* ('Recorded Conversations') Texts," *JAS* 50, no. 3 (8/1991): 574–603.

113 See Liang Qichao, *Qingdai xueshu gailun* [An outline of Qing learning], reprinted in *Liang Qichao lun Qingxueshi erzhong* [Two texts by Liang Qichao on the history of Qing learning] (Shanghai: Fudan Daxue chubanshe, 1985), 51–52, 159–162; and Qian Mu, *Zhongguo jin sanbainian xueshu shi*, 141–143. See also Elman, *From Philosophy to Philology*, 174–175.

114 In addition to the "notation book" (*zhaji cezi*), evidential research scholars produced a number of other new genres, among them the *buzheng* or "additions and corrections" and the *bianzheng* or "evaluation and correction"; see Henderson, *Scripture, Canon, and Commentary*, 221.

115 Huang Zunxian, *RBZSS*, 1:3b–4a. This is poem 8 in the second edition.

116 The example of cunning strategems in the poem—"fox cage and cattle coffin"—is in part, I believe, an allusion to an incident in the *History of the Han* biography of Chen Sheng As King of Chu, Sheng needed desperately to raise troops in his fight against Qin; he started a fire in a temple at night and imitated the cry of a fox calling, "Rise up, Great Chu, for King Chen Sheng"—whereupon the local militia were so terrified that they went forward in the morning to join Chen Sheng's ranks. See *Han shu*, 31:1786. Commentators read "cage" (*gou*) as a homonymic substitute for "set"—to set a fire. The other element here, "cattle coffin" (*niu jiu*), is still unclear.

117 Hê Ruzhang, *Shi dong zayong*, 69.

118 Huang Zunxian, *RBZSS*, 2:30a.

119 You Tong, *Waiguo zhuzhi ci*, 3:2. (The factual curiosities here have been discussed in chapter 1.)

120 See Zhu Yizun, "Ba *Wu qi jing*" [A Note on the *Mirror of Azuma*], in his *Pushuting ji* [Collections from the Pushu Pavilion] (Shanghai: Shangwu yinying, 1929), 44:12b–13a. See the comments by Feng Zuozhe and Wang Xiaoqiu, "*Azuma kagami* and *Wuqi jing bu*: Historical Evidence of Sino-Japanese Cultural Interaction," *Sino-Japanese Studies Newsletter* 1, no. 2 (March 1989): 28–40.

121 See the several forewords to the work by Zha Shenxing, Zhang Zaogong, and (presumably) Shen Jiache; these are included in the preliminary, unnumbered volume: Shen Jiache et al., *Nan Song zashi shi*.

122 Ibid., *juan* 1: 5a.

123 See Charles S. Gardner, *Chinese Traditional Historiography* (Cambridge, Mass.: Harvard University Press, 1938), 20–21.

124 *XFHZ, ce* 52: 283–301.

125 Rai San'yō also wrote a number of historical poems, which Huang undoubtedly saw, but which, I believe, did not significantly inform his own *Poems.*

126 *BTYG,* 153–55, 255–56. Cf. Wu Tianren, *Huang Gongdu,* 314ff.

127 Shigeno Yasutsugu (1827–1910), considered the best of the Meiji *kanbun* writers, served as vice director of the Bureau of Historical Compilation in the 1870s, a position from which he was removed by government "imperialist" officials for his revisions of the Japanese imperial lineage. Aoyama Nobutoshi (1820–1906), son of the famous historian Aoyama Nobuyuki (1776–1843), carried on the "independent" traditions of Rai San'yō. Miyajima Seiichiro (1838–1911), an ally of Ōkubo Toshimichi, also worked with the Bureau of Historical Compilation. Oka Senjin (1833–1914) was a private historian who wrote one of the first histories of the Meiji Restoration and a number of books on China. Huang writes of these Japanese friends in *RJLSC, juan* 3; see also Zheng Hailin, *Huang Zunxian yu jindai Zhongguo* [Huang Zunxian and modern China] (Beijing: Sanlian shudian, 1988), 102–107.

128 Huang Zunxian, *RBZSS,* 2:30b. This is poem 200 in the second edition.

129 Ibid., 2: 8a–11a. This is poem 145 in the second edition. The "Note" included in the poem is Huang's own. For a more extensive history of the chair in China, see C. P. Fitzgerald, *Barbarian Beds: The Origin of the Chair in China* (South Brunswick: A. S. Barnes, 1966). By contrast, Fitzgerald identifies the *hu chuang* or "barbarian bed" as a folding chair used out-of-doors, when it would have been awkward to sit on the ground.

130 Owen Lattimore claims that "Hu" was a generic term, including a number of existing tribes. See his *Inner Asian Frontiers of China* (Boston: Beacon Press, 1962), 450–454.

131 Yan Ruoju, quoted in Elman, *From Philosophy to Philology,* 30–31.

132 Dai Zhen, quoted in Liang Qichao, *Qingdai xueshu gailun,* 30. I have relied on the translations of Guy in *The Emperor's Four Treasuries,* 45, and Immanuel Hsu, in his translation of Liang Qichao, *Intellectual Trends in the Ch'ing Period,* 56.

133 Huang Zunxian, *RBZSS,* 1:1a. This remains poem 1 in the second edition.

134 Ibid., 1:1b–2a.

135 Ibid., 1:3a. This remains poem 5 in the second edition. Tokugawa (Mito) Mitsu-kuni (1628–1700) supervised the compilation of the *Dai Nihon shi* in its initial stages.

136 This theory is based on Emile Benveniste's distinction between *histoire* and *discours. Histoire,* or historical narration, is "the mode of utterance that excludes every 'autobiographical' linguistic form." The historian does not typically use the formal apparatus of discourse, which resides primarily in the relationship of the persons "I" and "you"; rather, a strict historical narrative typically employs only the forms of the third person. Discourse, by contrast, assumes "a speaker and a hearer, and in the speaker, the intention of influencing the other in some way." In other words, historical narration represents the "enounced," the narrated event from the past, while discourse represents the "enunciation," the interchange between speaking subjects in an "unceas-

ing present." See *Problems in General Linguistics* (Coral Gables: University of Miami Press, 1971), 206–209. Benveniste's ideas have been fruitfully reconsidered by Roman Jakobson, "Shifters, Verbal Categories, and the Russian Verb," in *Selected Writings* (Paris: Mouton, 1971), 2:130 147; and Anthony Easthope, *Poetry as Discourse* (London: Methuen, 1983), 40–47.

5 The Utility of Objectification in the Geographic Treatise

1 Li Hongzhang, *Li Wenzhong Gong quanji: Zougao* [Complete works of Li Wen-zhong: Memorials] (Nanjing: n.p., 1908), 24:26b.

2 Contemporaries mention two additional texts that were never completed or are no longer extant: (1) Yao Wendong (see below) was preparing a *Japan Treatise (Riben guozhi)* or *Draft Treatise on Japan (Riben zhigao)*, and although ten volumes were ready by 1884, only the table of contents was ever printed; see his *Dong cha za zhu* [Mis-cellaneous writings from the Eastern Mission] (n.p., [1893]), 47–50. Three of his Japanese friends wrote colophons for the work, which are reprinted in his *Haiwai tongren ji* [A collection from overseas fellows], ed. Kawada Kōshō (n.p., n.d.), 1: 1–3. (2) Xu Zhiyuan, a colleague of Chen Jialin (see below), claims to have been writing a *General Treatise on Japan (Riben tongzhi)* ca. 1885, which Chen allegedly used for his own work, but no one has verified this. See Satō Saburō, "Meiji ishin igo Nisshin sensō izen ni okeru Shinajin no Nihon kenkyū" [Chinese research on Japan between the Meiji Restoration and the Sino-Japanese War], *Rekishigaku kenkyū* 10, no. 11 [no. 83] (11/1940): 77. Moreover, as I mentioned in chapter 4, Wang Zhichun wrote a *Random Notes on the East* included in his *Tan ying lu* (*TYL*); although he begins this text within the format of a geographic treatise, he soon abandons such a formal structure and turns to miscellaneous notes. Accordingly, I do not treat his text in this chapter.

3 Yao's background is poorly known; his diplomatic travels (as a *gongsheng* of the sec-ond degree) are briefly mentioned in Wu Sheng et al., *Shanghai xian xuzhi* [A continu-ation of the Shanghai District treatise] (Shanghai, 1918; reprinted Taibei: Chengwen, 1970), 17:1. I have relied on Samuel Chu for the date of Yao's birth, but I do not know his source for this information nor have I been able to verify it; see "China's Attitudes toward Japan at the Time of the Sino-Japanese War," in *The Chinese and the Japanese,* ed. Akira Iriye, 86. Yao's various writings while in Japan are reviewed by Sanetō Keishū in *Meiji Nisshi bunka kōshō,* 113–149.

4 Nakane wrote his geography in 1872 while serving in the advisory office of the Japanese army; it was initially a textbook for army schools, but was widely used and reprinted in many editions during the first two decades of the Meiji period. Inciden-tally, Nakane's personal name, Shuku, is sometimes read "Kiyoshi."

5 In fact, Yao began his stay in Japan by translating a Japanese geography of the Liuqiu Islands, published in 1883 or 1884 in Chinese as *Liuqiu dili zhi* [A geographical treatise of the Liuqiu Islands] (n.p.: Dongying lishu, n.d.); see Sanetō, *Meiji Nisshi bunka kōshō,* 122–124.

6 Yao Wendong, *Riben dili bingyao* (Beijing: Tongwen guan, [1884]), *Liyan*: 5a (hereafter *RBDLBY*). To my knowledge, the Japanese geography of China to which Yao refers has not been identified; see Satō Saburō, *Kindai Nitchū kōshōshi no kenkyū* [Studies on modern Chinese-Japanese interaction] (Tokyo: Yoshikawa kōbunkan, 1983), 11.

7 Chen's biography is virtually unknown; he is listed as a recipient of the *gongsheng* degree and selected as a *bagong*, or "senior licentiate," for 1885, in Cheng Yaolie et al., *Liuhe xian xuzhi gao* [A draft continuation of the Liuhe District treatise] (n.p., 1920), 13:39b.

8 The fullest description of the background of this mission is Carol Tyson Reynolds, "East Meets East: Chinese Views of Early Meiji Japan" (Ph.D. diss., Columbia University, 1986), 176–189.

9 For summaries of the extant biographical material on both Gu and Fu, see ibid., 189–190, 215–221. Fu kept an extensive diary of his entire trip, which he published as *Youli tujing yuji* [Additional records from the illustrated monograph based on an official tour] (Tokyo: n.p., [1889]); the sections recounting his travels in Japan are reprinted in *ZRYW*, 109–218.

10 Little is known about the first edition of Gu's text, since the only extant copy is a two-volume reprint of 1897. See Satō Saburō, *Kindai Nitchū kōshōshi no kenkyū*, 18. It is likely that Gu's *Examination* was printed in Japan, since his colleague Fu Yunlong had his geography printed there in 1889.

11 Fu's choice of form is archaic; the *tujing* or "illustrated monograph" was a precursor of the local treatise and a dominant geographic genre during the Sui and Tang periods (ca. 600–900). See Chen Cheng-siang [Chen Zhengxiang], *Zhongguo fangzhi di dilixue jiazhi: Geographical Evaluation of the Chinese Fang-chih* (Hong Kong: Chinese University of Hong Kong, 1965), 6–11.

12 See Carol Tyson Reynolds, "East Meets East," 218–219. A few sections of Fu's monograph were reprinted in the 1890s in Wang Xiqi, comp., *Xiaofanghuzhai yudi cong chao* (*XFHZ*).

13 See the record of the poetry gathering to mark Ye Songshi's first return to China in 1876: Ye Songshi, *Fusang lichang ji* [A collection of parting songs from Fusang] (n.p., [1891]); and see Ye Songshi's "Preface" to *Ce ao za zhi* (Shanghai: n.p., [1889]) *Xu*: 5. (Hereafter *CAZZ*.)

14 Yuan recounted his world travel in *Tan ying lu* [Records from overseas] (Shanghai: Tongwen shuju, [1885]).

15 The printing of the 1890 edition, begun by the Canton Fuwenzhai, was not actually completed until 1895; the three editions of 1898 were printed by the Zhejiang shuju, the Shanghai tushu jicheng, and a Huiwen shuju. Zheng Hailin most fully surveys the various editions, mentioning as well a revised Fuwenzhai edition of 1897: *Huang Zunxian yu jindai Zhongguo*, 166–168. But see also Kamachi, *Reform in China*, 53, 168f; Satō, *Kindai Nitchū kōshōshi no kenkyū*, 14–17; and Wang Xiaoqiu, "Huang Zunxian *Riben guozhi* chutan" [A preliminary examination of Huang Zunxian's *Japan Treatise*],

in *Zhong-Ri wenhua jiaoliu shi lunwenji* [A collection of essays on the history of Sino-Japanese cultural interaction], ed. Beijingshi Zhong-Ri wenhua jiaoliushi yanjiuhui (Beijing: Renmin chubanshe, 1982), 234. There are in addition two worthwhile essays on the background of Huang's *Japan Treatise*: Cheng Guangyu, "Huang Zunxian yu Riren zhi qingyi ji qi *Riben guozhi*" [Huang Zunxian's Japanese friends and his *Japan Treatise*], in *Bainian lai Zhong-Ri guanxi lunwenji* (Essays on the past hundred years of Chinese-Japanese relations], ed. Shen Qinting (Taibei: n.p., 1969), 515–537; and Wang Xiaoqiu, *Jindai Zhong-Ri qishi lu*, 165–191.

16   E. Balazs, "L'Histoire comme guide de la pratique bureaucratique," in *Historians of China and Japan*, ed. W. G. Beasley and E. G. Pulleyblank (London: Oxford University Press, 1961), 84–87. See also the useful comments by B. J. Mansvelt Beck, *The Treatises of Later Han: Their Author, Sources, Contents, and Place in Chinese Historiography* (Leiden: E. J. Brill, 1990), 36–37, 52–55, 269–273.

17   See the instructive comments of P. van der Loon, "The Ancient Chinese Chronicles and the Growth of Historical Ideals," and A. F. P. Hulsewé, "Notes on the Historiography of the Han Period," in *Historians of China and Japan*, ed. Beasley and Pulleyblank, pp. 24–30 and 31–43 respectively.

18   On the background of the *fangzhi*, see Chen Cheng-siang, *Zhongguo fangzhi di dilixue jiazhi*, 4–12; Fu Zhenlun, *Zhongguo fangzhi xue tonglun* [A comprehensive study of the Chinese geographic treatise] (Shanghai: Shangwu yinshuguan, 1935), 23–29; Wang Yong, *Zhongguo dilixue shi* [A history of Chinese geography] (Changsha: Shangwu yinshuguan, 1938), 127–216; Weng Tongwen, "Cong shehui-wenhuashi guandian lun fangzhi de fasheng fazhan"; and Chen Jiexian, "Lun Qingdai Taiwan diqu fangzhi de yili."

19   Liang Qichao, "Fangzhi xue" [On local treatises], *Dongfang zazhi* [Eastern journal] 21, no. 18 (1924), 92; Fu Zhenlun, *Zhongguo fangzhi xue tonglun*, 24f; and Chen Cheng-siang, *Zhongguo fangzhi*, 12. Chen makes an analogous point about local treatises produced during the fifteenth century for the general gazetteer of the Ming dynasty; see also D. D. Leslie in *Essays on the Sources for Chinese History*, ed. Donald D. Leslie et al. (Columbia: University of South Carolina Press, 1973), 71.

20   See Chang Chung-li, *The Chinese Gentry: Studies on Their Role in Nineteenth-Century Chinese Society* (Seattle: University of Washington Press, 1955), 66.

21   Based on a similarity of content alone, Zheng Hailin compares Huang Zunxian's *Japan Treatise* to Zheng Qiao's (1104–1162) work of ca. 1149, the *Tong zhi* [Comprehensive treatises]. See Zheng Hailin, *Huang Zunxian yu jindai Zhongguo*, 158–166, 177. Although there is a convention of referring to a series of *tongzhi* or "institutional histories" based on Zheng Qiao's example, these were few by comparison to the local treatises, and in any case, as *zhi*, the contents of the *tongzhi* were similar to those of the *fangzhi*. See Han Yu-shan, *Elements of Chinese Historiography* (Hollywood: W. M. Hawley, 1955), 61, 154f.; and Endymion Wilkinson, *The History of Imperial China: A Research Guide* (Cambridge, Mass.: Harvard University, Council on East Asian Studies, 1973), 126–128.

22 Ye Qingyi and Yuan Zuzhi, *CAZZ*, 1:3b–4a. "Huo," pronounced "wa" in Japanese, allegedly represents the pronunciation of the ancient Japanese name for their land and ruling family, Yamato.

23 Huang Zunxian, *Riben guozhi*, 2d ed. (Shanghai: Tushu jicheng, [1898]; reprinted Taibei: Wenhai chubanshe, 1981), *Xu*: 2a. (Hereafter *RBGZ*.) Cf. Charles O. Hucker's descriptions in *A Dictionary of Official Titles in Imperial China* (Stanford: Stanford University Press, 1985), 236, 561.

24 Liang Qichao credits Zhang Xuecheng with promoting the analogy between the compilation of local treatises and the work of the "outer historian." See Liang's "Fangzhi xue," 95; and Zhang Xuecheng, *Wenshi tongyi* [General principles of writing and history] (Shanghai: Shangwu yinshuguan, 1933), 3:15–17.

25 Incidentally, Huang's disguise puts the reader into a similar position of duplicity, in that one surreptitiously sees documents intended for imperial eyes.

26 Zhu Chongsheng suggests that a progressive refinement of information took place in the local treatise during the Ming and Qing dynasties; see "Luanzhou zhi zhi zuanxiu jingguo ji qi shifa bijiao" [The compilation process of Luanzhou treatises and a comparison of their historical methods], *Hanxue yanjiu* 3, no. 2 (12/1985): 121–138.

27 Cf. Wilkinson, *The History of Imperial China*, 114–115; Han Yu-shan, *Elements of Chinese Historiography*, 33; and Charles Gardner, *Traditional Chinese Historiography*, 102. For a comparison of the contents of the *fangzhi* to official histories and other treatises, see Li Taifen, *Fangzhi xue*, 9–15.

28 Cf. the earlier "ethnographic descriptions" included in Wei Yuan's geography discussed above in chapter 1.

29 See Wolfgang Bauer, "The Encyclopaedia in China," *Cahiers d'Histoire Mondiale* 9, no. 3 (1966): 665–691.

30 Guy Alitto has discussed the motive of "social control" in the local treatise in "Zhongguo fangzhi yu Xifangshi de bijiao" [A comparison of Chinese local treatises and Western local histories], *Hanxue yanjiu* 3, no. 2 (12/1985): 59–71.

31 See the instructive "Translator's Introduction" by Djang Chu, in Huang Liuhong, *A Complete Book Concerning Happiness and Benevolence: Fu-hui ch'üan-shu: A Manual for Local Magistrates in Seventeenth-Century China*, trans. and ed. Djang Chu (Tucson: University of Arizona Press, 1984), 1–49.

32 Ibid., 129–130. I have modified Djang's translation somewhat, following my own reading of Huang Liuhong, *Fuhui quanshu* [A complete manual on prosperity and benevolence] (n.p., [1876]), 3:12b–13a.

33 See Ch'ü T'ung-tsu, *Local Government in China under the Ch'ing* (Cambridge, Mass.: Harvard University Press, 1962), 161–167.

34 In his monograph of 1935, Li Taifen quite deliberately discusses the geographic treatise as offering evidence of "civilization" in China—not Chinese Civilization, but "civilization" in a relative and comparative sense in the history of mankind. See his *Fangzhi xue*, 79ff.

35 Zhang Xuecheng, "Ji yu Dai Dongyuan lun xiuzhi," in *Zhangshi yishu* 14:37a–39b.

Credit for the formulation, "basic unit of official cultural production," goes to my friend the anthropologist Lin Kai-shyh.

36 A. C. Graham, *Disputers of the Tao: Philosophical Argument in Ancient China* (La Salle: Open Court, 1989), 6f., 315–319. For the sake of clarification, I note a second term that has figured in discussions of utility in the Chinese past: *li*, or "advantageous gain," a position advocated by the ancient philosopher Mozi (ca. 490–403 B.C.) and commonly translated as "utilitarianism," because, in a manner presumably reminiscent of the early-nineteenth-century British utilitarians, Mozi claimed that the virtue of an action was best defined in terms of its "advantage" to the greatest number of people. This notion has no bearing on my discussion of the usefulness of geography, but cf. "profit" in chapter 1 above. For my purposes, the best discussion of Mozi's utilitarianism is Kung-chuan Hsiao, *A History of Chinese Political Thought*, vol. 1, *From the Beginnings to the Sixth Century A.D.*, trans. F. W. Mote (Princeton: Princeton University Press, 1979), 225–235, 463f.

37 See Zhang Xuecheng, "Ji yu Dai Dongyuan lun xiuzhi," in *Zhangshi yishu*, 14:37a–39b; "Shi shi" [An explanation of "History"], in *Wenshi tongyi*, 1:66–69; as well as "Fangzhi li san shu yi" [A proposal for a three-part form for local treatises], in *Wenshi tongyi*, 6:1–7.

38 Document prepared by the Zongli Yamen, dated Guangxu 13, Fourth Month [May 1887]. Reprinted in *Huangchao zhengdian leizuan* [A compendium of imperial laws and regulations], comp. Xi Yufu and Shen Shixu (Shanghai, 1903; reprinted Taibei: Wenhai, 1974–), 485:2. This is also reprinted, with slight variations, in *Huangchao zhanggu huibian* [A collection of imperial documents], comp. Zhang Shouyong et al. (1902; reprinted Taibei: Wenhai, 1964), *Waibian* 29:28b–29; and Xue Fucheng, *Chushi siguo riji* [A diary of ambassadorial service to four nations] (n.p., [1892]; reprinted Changsha: Hunan renmin chubanshe, 1981), 107–108.

39 Chow Jen-hwa, *China and Japan: The History of Chinese Diplomatic Missions in Japan, 1877–1911* (Singapore: Chopman Enterprises, 1975), 129–141, 218–222; and Carol Tyson Reynolds, "East Meets East," 268–283.

40 I am drawing upon Kenneth Burke, *A Grammar of Motives* (Berkeley: University of California Press, 1969), 275–320; and Jürgen Habermas, *Knowledge and Human Interests*, trans. Jeremy J. Shapiro (Boston: Beacon Press, 1971), 67–139.

41 Yao Wendong, *RBDLBY, Liyan*: 2.

42 Fu Yunlong, *Youli Riben tujing* (Tokyo: n.p., [1889]), 4:32–34; hereafter *YLRBTJ*.

43 Burke, *A Grammar of Motives*, 282. In the same way that C. S. Peirce insisted that science is not knowledge but methodology, can we think of Chinese historiography too as primarily methodology? See Habermas, *Knowledge and Human Interests*, 91.

44 My reader should not confuse this sense of abstract with the perhaps more common, derogatory sense of "abstract" as being "opposed to the concrete"—in other words, something that could be, but is not, exemplified in its concretions, making it not easily understood (abstruse) or not practical (theoretical). It is this sense of abstract— abstruse or theoretical—that Irene Bloom opposes to "concrete" in her "On the 'Abstraction' of Ming Thought," 69.

45 Some scholars of Neo-Confucianism have translated *shi* as "practical" in their discussions of *shixue* as "practical learning." See Irene Bloom, "On the 'Abstraction' of Ming Thought," and Chung-ying Cheng, "Practical Learning in Yen Yuan, Chu Hsi, and Wang Yang-ming," also in *Principle and Practicality*, 37–67. Insofar as advocates of *shixue* were reacting to the metaphysical emphasis of Zhu Xi's interpretation of Confucianism (what became Soong learning during the Qing period) and so advocated *shi*—as substantive or concrete—in opposition to what they saw as Zhu Xi's preoccupation with *xu*—the empty or overly idealistic—it may be reasonable to interpret *shi* as "practical." But as H. D. Harootunian has pointed out, some of these scholars claim further that practical learning constitutes a form of empiricism and so prepared the way for Western science in China and Japan. See his review in *Journal of Japanese Studies* 7, no. 1 (1981): 11–31. While Chinese scholars were certainly gathering and explaining details, they did not inquire into the explanation process itself, which allegedly gave rise to the scientific method of hypothesis and experimentation. Indeed, the problem at hand is the *application* of information; it does not follow that details gathered or explained are necessarily practical. Hence my interpretation stresses the emphasis on the concrete in *shixue* as "substantive learning"—the observation of concrete things when conducting investigations, and the actual doing of things rather than the reading of books. See the instructive case of Wang Fuzhi, in Allison Black, *Man and Nature*, 164–180.

46 Zhang Zhidong, "Ciwen" [Foreword], in Huang Zunxian, *Riben guozhi* (Canton: Fuwenzhai, [1890]), [1b–2a].

47 Ye Qingyi and Yuan Zuzhi, *CAZZ*, 4:13, 22b–23a; and Gu Houkun, *Riben xinzheng kao* [An examination of Japan's new administration], reprinted in *Xizheng congshu* [Collected writings on Western administration], ed. "Qiuziqiangzhai zhuren" [Master of the Studio for Seeking Self-strengthening], vols. 25–26 (n.p., [1897]), 2:2a, 5b–8a (hereafter *RBXZK*). This relationship between learning and administration is discussed in chapter 6.

48 Chen Jialin, *Dong cha wenjian lu* [A record of things seen and heard on the Eastern Mission] (n.p., [1887]; reprinted in *XFHZ*, *zhi* 10: 371–407), 12b–14a. (Hereafter *DCWJL*.) N.B. In citing the reprint edition, I use the pagination specific to *Dong cha wenjian lu*, rather than the pagination of *XFHZ*.

49 Fu Yunlong, *YLRBTJ*, 20, pts. 1 and 2. Incidentally, this term *wenxue* is today the translation for "literature," but it denoted the broader field of book learning in the nineteenth century.

50 Huang Zunxian, *RBGZ*, *juan* 32–33.

51 Gu Houkun, *RBXZK*, 2:9a, 15a; and Ye Qingyi and Yuan Zuzhi, *CAZZ*, 3:1–2, 4:5–7.

52 Yao Wendong, *RBDLBY*, 1:55b; and Chen Jialin, *DCWJL*, 26b. Chen does mention Shinto by name on p. 4b, in connection with "Temples and Shrines," noting that the government recently created an office to manage shrines.

53 Fu Yunlong, *YLRBTJ*, 20, pt. 1:3a.

54 Huang Zunxian, *RBGZ*, 37:23b–29a.

55 See Yao Wendong, *RBDLBY*, 1:74a–81b; and Ye Qingyi and Yuan Zuzhi, *CAZZ*, 3:22b.

56 Chen Jialin, *DCWJL*, 27b.

57 Gu Houkun, *RBXZK*, 1.18b–19a; and Huang Zunxian, *RBGZ*, 32:10b–11a.

58 Kinai is sometimes considered not a circuit, but an exception, in which case the number of circuits is eight.

59 In general, we might identify three approaches. For one, both Yao and Huang reproduce the traditional geography of circuits and provinces. They describe the circuits and their respective provinces in turn; where Yao appends a section on "successive change" at the end of each province, Huang waits to summarize the whole in an extensive chart at the end of his descriptions (*RBGZ*, 12:28b–35.). Second, Fu and Gu Houkun—much of whose information seems to have been provided by official Japanese publications—take the prefectural system as their point of reference. After noting in general the shift from Tokugawa domains to Meiji prefectures, Gu abstracts the whole in a table that locates each prefecture in terms of the circuits and former domains (*RBXZK*, 2:18–19.). Fu, by contrast, provides a series of statistics on each prefecture, but then describes successive changes in extensive detail, with timely haste to include the most recent creation of Ehime and Kagawa prefectures from the former Sanuki domain (*YLRBTJ*, 3:3b–7a, 22b–41a). A third approach is the pair of utterly presentist representations by Chen Jialin and Ye Qingyi, who simply list the current prefectures one by one (*DCWJL*, 4; *CAZZ*, 3:3b–8a.).

60 Yao Wendong, *RBDLBY*, 1:56b–58a; Chen Jialin, *DCWJL*, 11b–12a; Ye Qingyi and Yuan Zuzhi, *CAZZ*, 4:1–24.

61 Chen Jialin, *DCWJL*, 11b; Fu Yunlong, *YLRBTJ*, 17:2a; Huang Zunxian, *RBGZ*, 13:1.

62 Fu Yunlong, *YLRBTJ*, 17:1–2a.

63 Gu Houkun, *RBXZK*, 2:12b–17b.

64 Fu and Huang call this section "Foreign Relations" and "Neighborly Relations," respectively, while Ye and Yuan call theirs, more prosaically, "Domain's Name Originally Wo."

65 Fu, and Ye and Yuan, call this history, respectively, "Domainal Records" and "Genealogical Records," while Huang calls it "Domainal Heritage." A revised edition of the "basic annals" and the biographies of the *Dai Nihon shi*, in literary Chinese, was published by 1854; this was the source of much of this history for the Chinese geographers.

66 Chen Jialin, *DCWJL*, 12a.

67 Huang Zunxian, *RBGZ*, 13:6b, 14:22–23.

68 Systematic divisions of the military during the Qing were a function of administrative structure; the more-or-less Chinese Green Standing Army, to which "water forces" were attached, was a provincial army, while the more-or-less Manchu Banner system was an imperial force. This was irrelevant to the Japanese case. Unfortunately for China, when it did begin to create a navy in the 1860s, it did so at the provincial level, which proved most inefficient, if not disastrous.

69 Fu Yunlong, *YLRBTJ*, 16:10b–11a.

70 This realization was voiced early on by Huang Zunxian in his *Poems*; see *RBZSS*, 1:18b.

71 For a discussion of regional stereotypes in China and a range of useful references, see Richard J. Smith, *China's Cultural Heritage: The Ch'ing Dynasty, 1644–1912* (Boulder: Westview Press, 1983), 18–21.

72 Yao Wendong, *RBDLBY*, 1:54b–55a; Chen Jialin, *DCWJL*, 26b; Fu Yunlong, *YLRBTJ*, 10:1.

73 Nakane Shuku, *Heiyō Nihon chiri shōshi*, rev. ed. (Tokyo: n.p., [1875]), 1:19b–20.

74 Ye Qingyi and Yuan Zuzhi, *CAZZ*, 3:10b; Huang Zunxian, *RBGZ*, 10:3b, 6b.

75 Huang Zunxian, *RBGZ*, 34:1.

76 Prose of course includes narration and description; both are expository representations in the syntax of the literary Chinese language. The list, by comparison, is printed within the vertical columns of prose, but dispenses with syntactical connections between items and relies instead on contiguity and the indexical ability of language to generate a structure approximating the logic of deduction. The reader understands that the list is a logical series and that it is completed when the structure of the list is interrupted and a new subject is signaled. The third mode of presentation, the table, is an orderly sequence of information into rows and columns for convenient reference, and relies for its coherence not on linguistic syntax but on visual perception.

77 Lien-sheng Yang, "The Organization of Chinese Official Historiography: Principles and Methods of the Standard Histories from the T'ang through the Ming Dynasty," in Beasley and Pulleyblank, eds., *Historians of China and Japan*, 56.

78 Benjamin Elman, *From Philosophy to Philology*, 187–188; and "Geographical Research in the Ming-Ch'ing Period," *Monumenta Serica* 35 (1981–1983): 15–16.

79 Yao Wendong, *RBDLBY*, 1:1b–2a. Ye Qingyi and Yuan Zuzhi give the standard longitudinal measurements of 124 and 156 in *CAZZ*, 3:1b.

80 Chen Jialin, *DCWJL*, 1b.

81 Gu Houkun, *RBXZK*, 2:17b–18a; Fu Yunlong, *YLRBTJ*, 1:1–3a; Huang Zunxian, *RBGZ*, 12:36–37a.

82 Wolfgang Bauer, "The Encyclopaedia in China," 670.

83 Chen Jialin, *DCWJL*, 2b; Ye Qingyi and Yuan Zuzhi, *CAZZ*, 6:1b.

84 Yao Wendong, *RBDLBY*, 1:21b–22a.

85 Fu Yunlong, *YLRBTJ*, 6:8a, 11a.

86 Huang Zunxian, *RBGZ*, 10:2b, 6.

87 Gu Houkun, *RBXZK*, 2:28b.

88 Ibid., 2:9–12.

89 The practice of mapmaking—which began as part of the investiture ceremony of imperial princes, with maps serving as implements symbolic of rule—developed apart from official geography; only in the twelfth century, and especially with the interest in naval exploration in the fifteenth century, did cartography advance and assume a significant position in geographical descriptions. If Tang and Soong Chinese had maps of Japan, no evidence survives. Joseph Needham implies that Chinese more often

concentrated on mapping central Asia and typically stopped eastward at the Korean peninsula. In fact, the earliest extant map that gives geographic information of Japan is a Korean world map produced ca. 1402, which may have been based on fourteenth-century Chinese maps produced after contact with Persians and Arabs. See his "Geography and Cartography," 543–556; and Cordell D. K. Yee, "Chinese Maps in Political Culture," 71–95.

90 Needham, "Geography and Cartography," 556–561.

91 J. V. Mills, "Chinese Coastal Maps," *Imago Mundi* 11 (1954): 151–168.

92 J. V. Mills identifies the Hu Zongxian maps of 1624 with Zheng Ruoceng's work of 1562, but I have examined only the edition of 1624. See chapter 1, note 54.

93 Joseph Needham, "Geography and Cartography," 583–586; Wang Yong, *Zhongguo dilixue shi*, 96–126; and Cordell D. K. Yee, "Taking the World's Measure: Chinese Maps between Observation and Text," in *The History of Cartography*, ed. Harley and Woodward, 96–127.

94 The Japanese themselves were experimenting with European-style cartography during the Tokugawa, but access to maps of Japan was strictly controlled by the shogunate. See Masayoshi Sugimoto and David L. Swain, *Science and Culture in Traditional Japan* (Cambridge: MIT Press, 1978), 342–343, 357; and Takagi Kikusaburō, *Nihon ni okeru chizu sokuryō no hattatsu ni kansuru kenkyū* [Studies on the development of map surveying in Japan] (Tokyo: Kazema shobō, 1966), 23–55.

95 Wang Yong, *Zhongguo dilixue shi*, 74–85; and Yee, "Chinese Maps in Political Culture," 91f.

96 Zhang Xuecheng, "Jiashu liu" [Family letter no. 6], *Zhangshi yishu* 9:73a. Cf. descriptions of Zhang's own local treatises: Nivison, *The Life and Thought*, 209; and Liang Qichao, "Fangzhi xue," 95–98.

97 Yao Wendong, *RBDLBY, Liyan*, 5. For the background of these early Meiji Japanese maps, see Takagi Kikusaburō, *Nihon ni okeru chizu sokuryō*, 56–70.

98 Knight Biggerstaff, "The T'ung Wen Kuan," *Chinese Social and Political Science Review* 18 (1934): 307–340.

6 Negotiating Civilization and Westernization

1 Chen Jialin, *DCWJL*, 1.

2 As I describe below, key Confucian texts imagined proceeding from study to practice. "Study" (*xue*) was an internalization of principles of behavior, which were, in turn, "modeled" or "imitated" (*mofang*) outwardly as practice, so that study and modeling were mutually confirming processes. The concept of *mofang* grew metaphorically in ancient Chinese from the use of physical casts or molds and calligraphic patterns (*mo*) to the imitating of ritual behavior (*fang*).

3 See James Hevia's comments on the "other" as "undifferentiated," in "Guest Ritual," 246.

4 Whether that understanding is misguided, erroneous, or illusory will not concern

me here; I am interested in describing cases of analogical reasoning among Chinese scholars in the nineteenth century.

5 See for example David Burrell, *Analogy and Philosophical Language* (New Haven: Yale University Press, 1973), 20, 223–226, 264–267. I have additionally learned much from Wendy Olmsted's work in progress, "A Rhetoric of Analogy" (University of Chicago).

6 On analogy in the *Mozi*, see A. C. Graham, *Later Mohist Logic, Ethics, and Science* (Hong Kong: Chinese University Press; London: School of Oriental and African Studies, 1978), 258–259, 336–365; D. C. Lau, "Some Logical Problems in Ancient China," *Proceedings of the Aristotelian Society* 53 (1952–3): 189–204; and Hu Shih, *The Development of the Logical Method in Ancient China* (Shanghai: Oriental Book Company, 1928), 99–108.

7 Robert M. Hartwell has determined that "historical models" first appear as a category of historiography with the seventh-century *Sui History*; during the reign of the Soong emperor Huizong (r. 1100–1125), the practice of consulting history in order to respond to change became an official component of planning policy. See his "Historical Analogism, Public Policy, and Social Science in Eleventh- and Twelfth-Century China," *American Hitorical Review* 76, no. 3 (June 1971): 690–727.

8 See Derk Bodde and Clarence Morris, *Law in Imperial China: Exemplified by 190 Ch'ing Dynasty Cases (Translated from the Hsing-an hui-lan), with Historical, Social, and Juridical Commentaries* (Philadelphia: University of Pennsylvania Press, 1967), 175–179, 517–533; and Fu-mei Chang Chen, "On Analogy in Ch'ing Law," *HJAS* 30 (1970): 212–224.

9 For three valuable alternative perspectives on Chinese reactions to the West, see John B. Henderson, "Ch'ing Scholars' Views of Western Astronomy," *HJAS* 46, no. 1 (1986): 121–148; Joanna Waley-Cohen, "China and Western Technology in the Late Eighteenth Century," *American Historical Review* 98, no. 5 (12/1993): 1525–1544; and Erh-min Wang, "The 'Turn of Fortune' (*Yun-hui*): Inherited Concepts and China's Response to the West," in *Cosmology, Ontology, and Human Efficacy: Essays in Chinese Thought*, ed. Richard J. Smith and D. W. Y. Kwok (Honolulu: University of Hawaii Press, 1993), 205–215.

10 On the development of *fa* into its later and now more common usage as "law," see Hu Shi, *The Development of the Logical Method*, 170–184.

11 See Wing-tsit Chan, *A Source Book in Chinese Philosophy* (Princeton: Princeton University Press, 1963), 86.

12 The great nineteenth-century *Imperial Compendium on Statecraft* by Hê Changling and Wei Yuan (the *Huangchao jingshi wenbian* of 1826) reproduces in its order of contents this progress from learning to practice.

13 See Chen Dengyuan, "Xixue lai Hua shi guoren zhi wuduan taidu" [The arbitrary attitudes of Chinese upon the coming of Western learning to China], *Dongfang zazhi* [Eastern miscellany] 27, no. 8 (April 1930): 61–76; and Henderson, "Ch'ing Scholars' Views of Western Astronomy."

14 See, for example, Joseph Levenson's discussion of perhaps the most forceful of these

"anti-Westerners," Woren, in his *Confucian China and Its Modern Fate*, vol. 1, *The Problem of Intellectual Continuity* (Berkeley: University of California Press, 1958), 70–76.

15 A valuable discussion of these arguments is Quan Hansheng's 1935 essay, "Qingmo de 'Xixue yuan chu Zhongguo' shuo" [The late Qing theory "Western learning originated in China"], in *Zhongguo jindaishi luncong* [Collected essays on modern Chinese history], ed. Li Dingyi (Taibei: Zhengzhong shuju, 1956), ser. 1, 5:216–258. Quan cites Feng Guifen as the first to reinterpret "reviving ancient ways" in this manner, during the 1860s.

16 Zeng Jize, *Chushi Ying/Fa riji* [A diary of the first embassy to England and France], reprinted in *XFHZ, ce* 58 [*zhi* 11, pt. 4]: 385. For an account of the confused history of this text and its variations, see Zhong Shuhe's introduction to the reprint of Zeng's handwritten manuscript, *Chushi Ying/Fa/Eguo riji* [A diary of the first embassy to England, France, and Russia] (Changsha: Yueli shushe, 1985), 39–45.

17 Zheng Hailin discusses Huang's references to the *Mozi* in the *Japan Treatise* in his *Huang Zunxian yu jindai Zhongguo*, 317–320.

18 Huang Zunxian, *RBZSS*, 1:19a. (Poem 54 in the second edition.) *N.B.* The statements in quotation marks are Huang's quotations of the *Mozi*.

19 Huang reiterates this explanation in the *Japan Treatise*; see *RBGZ* 32:11.

20 Huang Zunxian, *RBZSS*, 1:20b.

21 See Quan Hansheng, "Qingmo de 'Xixue yuan chu Zhongguo' shuo," 225–227.

22 In light of what follows, we can explain the transaction as a modified formal analogy: Huang claims that "Mo Di's transformation of metal is to transformations as transformations is to chemistry" ($A : B :: B : C$), or in other words, Huang produces the simple analogy or simile, "Mo Di's transformation of metal is like chemistry" ($A : C$).

23 On Huang's references to the idea of "progress" or "evolution" (*jinhua*) in the *Japan Treatise*, see Zheng Hailin, *Huang Zunxian yu jindai Zhongguo*, 181–184.

24 For a concise discussion of analogy and its usages in language, see Eva Feder Kittay, *Metaphor: Its Cognitive Force and Linguistic Structure* (Oxford: Clarendon Press, 1987), 150–160.

25 Aristotle cautioned against analogical argument for precisely this reason. See ibid., 2–4.

26 Huang Zunxian, *RBZSS*, 1:20b–21a.

27 Ibid., 1:21. (Poem 55 in the second edition.)

28 On the discussion of the need for men of talent during this period, see Mary Clabaugh Wright, *The Last Stand of Chinese Conservatism: The T'ung-Chih Restoration, 1862–1874* (Stanford: Stanford University Press, 1957), 68–95.

29 Huang Zunxian, *RBZSS*, 1:18b.

30 In fact, Huang rewrote this poem for the second edition in order to emphasize the Chinese precedent for Western newspapers, the "capital gazette" (*jingbao*), which collected reprints of the most important imperial decrees and memorials to the emperor. See *Riben zashi shi*, 2d ed., 29. This is poem 53.

31 Fukuzawa Yukichi, *Gakumon no susume* [An encouragement of learning], in *Fukuzawa Yukichi zenshū* (Tokyo: Iwanami, 1959), 3:48–56.

32 See issue 2 of the *Meiji Six Society Journal,* devoted to criticisms of Fukuzawa: *Meiroku zasshi: Journal of the Japanese Enlightenment,* trans. William Reynolds Braisted (Cambridge, Mass.: Harvard University Press, 1976), 21–29.

33 See Tsuchida Mitsufumi, *Meiji Taishō no shingo-ryūkōgo* [New and popular vocabulary in the Meiji and Taishō periods] (Tokyo: Kakugawa, 1983), 26–28.

34 There is a problem in our understanding of *"kaika."* Most early Meiji translators (e.g., Nishi Amane and Nakamura Keiu) used *"kaika"* interchangeably with *"bunmei"* and *"bunmeikaika"* as a translation word for "civilization"; early dictionaries likewise offer it as an equivalent for "civilization." (See especially Nishimura Shigeki's "Explanation of 'Civilization'" in issue 36 of the *Meiroku zasshi,* 446–449; he uses *"bunmeikaika"* and makes no mention of enlightenment—nor does anyone else in the journal.) "Enlightenment," and its German equivalent *"Aufklärung,"* do not appear in dictionaries until the 1890s, and *"kaika"* is not given as an equivalent for either of these terms. Although Nishi Amane began to use the Chinese word *"qimeng"* (J: *keimō*) for "enlightening" (in the active sense of "elucidating") early in the 1870s, it does not appear to have caught on as the (still current) translation word for the European Enlightenment (as a historical event) until much later. I suspect that the differential translation of *"bunmei"* and *"kaika"* is a historiographical move among American historians of Japan, motivated either by a need to identify the split in the movement or by the attempt to identify the Meiji interest in civilization with the European Enlightenment. In either case, the question remains—who initiated our habit of equating *"kaika"* and "enlightenment" so as to translate *"bunmeikaika"* as "civilization and enlightenment"?

35 The best history of this sociolinguistic process is Asukai Masamichi, *Bunmeikaika* [Civilization] (Tokyo: Iwanami, 1985), especially 109–165.

36 See Nakamura Keiu, "Gi taiseijin jōsho" [A memorial on the imitation of Westerners], a *kanbun* essay of 1871 reprinted in *Meiji keimō shisō shū* [Selections from the thought of the Meiji Enlightenment], ed. Ōkubo Toshiaki (Tokyo: Chikuma, 1967), 281–283. Many of Huang's perceptions of the "Western teaching method" mentioned above seem to have been formed by this essay.

37 Huang's use of *"wenming"* was a reaction to yet another Japanese neologism used in the first two decades of Meiji (1870s–80s) to translate the European word "civilization"—*"bunka,"* or *"wenhua"* in Chinese. *"Bunka,"* which Japanese understood as an abbreviation of *"bunmeikaika,"* was used quite interchangeably with *"bunmei."* In the 1890s, *"bunka"* began to be used to translate the German *"Kultur,"* and by the 1920s, *"bunmei"* assumed a pejorative connotation, referring to what was felt to be the merely materialistic civilization of Meiji, quite lacking in spiritual value. See Suzuki Shūji, *Bunmei no Kotoba,* 53–56.

38 Huang Zunxian, *RBZSS,* 1:3 (poem 6 in the second edition as well). My ambiguous syntax in the last paragraph here is intended to indicate the ambiguities of the original; Huang has distorted what might have otherwise been a typical quotation of the text, and indeed locates the Valley of Sunrise (and so on) *in the text.*

39 Huang does mention U.S. naval commodore Perry's "Black Ships" and the subsequent treaties with Western nations as events that contributed to Japanese adoption of

Western ways, but he makes much more of the Restoration as the origin and impetus for Western ways in Japan. See poems 9 and 10 in *RBZSS*, 1:5–6.

40 An eloquent and succinct discussion of the issue is Frederick W. Mote, "The Arts and the 'Theorizing Mode' of the Civilization," in *Artists and Traditions: Uses of the Past in Chinese Culture*, ed. Christian F. Murck (Princeton: Princeton University Press, 1976): 3–8.

41 The best introductions to the varied background of *fugu* are Yu-shih Chen, *Images and Ideas in Chinese Classical Prose: Studies of Four Masters* (Stanford: Stanford University Press, 1988); Luo Genze, *Zhongguo wenxue pipingshi* [A history of Chinese literary criticism] (Shanghai: Gudian wenxue chubanshe, 1957–1961), 2:113–165, 3:3–32; and Yoshikawa Kôjirô, *Five Hundred Years of Chinese Poetry*, 137–176.

42 For Zhu Xi's position, see his "Lun wen" [On *wen*], in *Zhuzi yulei* [Discussions with Master Zhu, by category], ed. Wang Xingxian (Beijing: Zhonghua shuju, 1986), 3297–3343. I am grateful to Matthew Levey for directing me to this.

43 On the role of *fugu* in both Han learning and the "New Text Movement" during the Qing, see Benjamin Elman, *Classicism, Politics, and Kinship*, 8off., 221ff.

44 Huang Zunxian, *RBZSS*, 1:6a. Poem 12 in the second edition.

45 This term replaced a near synonym and homonym, "*isshin*" (C: *yixin*), or "singular/total renovation," in the early years of Meiji. See Tsuchida Mitsufumi, *Meiji Taishô no shingo-ryūkōgo*, 14–16.

46 Unfortunately, the momentum of the *zhongxing* did not long outlive King Xuan, and the first phase of the Zhou, the Western Zhou, came to an end in 771 B.C., when the capital was moved eastward.

47 See Asukai, *Bunmeikaika*, 7–12.

48 On the elevation of and controversy surrounding Kusunoki during the Tokugawa and Meiji periods, see H. Paul Varley, *Imperial Restoration in Medieval Japan* (New York: Columbia University Press, 1971), 136–183. Although the Kemmu Restoration, because of Kusunoki, very quickly became an allusion central to the Meiji discourse on devotion to the emperor, it was in the years prior to and just after the Meiji Restoration primarily an allusion for the "return to ancient ways."

49 Huang Zunxian, *RBZSS*, 1:15a. (Poem 36 in the second edition as well.)

50 Nominally, the reform restored "ancient" tax practices, but E. H. Norman argues that in actuality it equaled and even exceeded Tokugawa rates. See his *Origins of the Modern Japanese State: Selected Writings of E. H. Norman* (New York: Pantheon, 1975), 243–273.

51 Conceptual reality was of course far more complex than Huang describes. The longstanding "reverence for the sovereign" (*sonnō*), emphasized by the Mito school during the Tokugawa period, was often accompanied by references to both Jimmu's inaugural laws and Godaigo's Kemmu Restoration, in terms of both *fukko* ("return to ancient ways") and *chūkō* ("restoration"). In the twilight years of the Tokugawa shogunate, some scholars questioned the appropriateness of alluding to Godaigo's futile "restoration." At the same time, *ōseifukko* ("return to the ancient ways of sovereign rule") became a dominant slogan. This was an explicit reference to Jimmu, as were the

subsequent popular terms: "total renovation" (C: *yixin*; J: *isshin*), and then the term now used, "renovation" or "new interweaving" (C: *weixin*; J: *ishin*). See Asukai, *Bunmeikaika*, 2–12; and H. D. Harootunian, *Toward Restoration: The Growth of Political Consciousness in Tokugawa Japan* (Berkeley: University of California Press, 1970), 1–46.

52 Huang Zunxian, *RBZSS*, 1:12b. (Poem 31 in the second edition as well.) I might mention that Huang is reproducing here a version of history that differs from present accounts. It is not at all clear that Jimmu established a "feudal" (*fengjian*) system; and it is even less clear why Huang understands "Kuni no Mikotomochi" ("domainal emissaries") in the way that he does. The common interpretation is that these were personal envoys of the emperor sent as temporary governors to provinces experiencing some emergency situation. Nevertheless, Huang means to differentiate the degree of connection between the emperor and his provincial rulers. Ostensibly the feudal "domainal princes" were largely independent of the emperor's court; by (dubious) contrast, the "domainal governors" recognized their direct accountability to the court. Huang's working analogy is that Jimmu's feudalism corresponds to that of Zhou China, and that Kōtoku's prefectural system corresponds to that of imperial Tang China.

53 Ibid., 1:13a.

54 Ibid., 1:13b. (Poem 32 in the second edition as well.)

55 As is commonly known, Huang later came to advocate a British parliamentary system and other Western institutions for China; he apparently passed these aspirations on to reform leaders after 1890. See Zhang Pengyuan, "Huang Zunxian de zhengzhi sixiang ji qi dui Liang Qichao de yingxiang" [The political thought of Huang Zunxian and its influence on Liang Qichao], in *Zhongyang yanjiuyuan jindaishi yanjiusuo jikan* [Collected papers of the Modern History Institute of Academia Sinica] 1 (8/1969): 217–237; and Wang Dezhao, "Huang Zunxian suo jian zhi Riben" [The Japan seen by Huang Zunxian], in *Sino-Japanese Cultural Interchange*, vol. 3, *The Economic and Intellectual Aspects*, ed. Yuehim Tam (Hong Kong: Chinese University of Hong Kong, 1985), 113–125.

56 By contrast, Chinese travelers to Europe and the United States in the 1860s through 1880s were struck by the utter difference of the West. See the bibliography for works by Bin Chun, Li Gui, Liu Xihong, Zhang Deyi, and Zhigang.

57 See Yen-p'ing Hao and Erh-min Wang, "Changing Chinese Views of Western Relations, 1840–95," in *The Cambridge History of China*, vol. 11, *Late Ch'ing, 1800–1911*, pt. 2, ed. John K. Fairbank and Kwang-ching Liu (Cambridge: Cambridge University Press, 1980), 189.

58 Feng Guifen, "Zhong zhuandui yi" (On the importance of directness), in *Jiaobinlu kangyi* [Protests from Jiaobin Hut] (n.p., [1884]; reprinted Taibei: Wenhai chubanshe, n.d.), 2:66.

59 Hê Ruzhang, *Shi dong shulue*, 59. See also Wang Tao, "He liu guo yi zhi E" [Unite the Six States to control Russia], in *Taoyuan wenlu waibian* [Additional essays from Taoyuan] (Hong Kong: n.p., [1883]), 4:27b–29a; and compare Huang Zunxian's lament for the cession of Taiwan to Japan after the Sino-Japanese War in 1895, where Japan is compared to Qin, and Taiwan to Chu (Qin's largest and southernmost rival): "Taiwan

xing," *RJLSC*, 245–247. In the late 1890s, some scholars were still reproducing this analogy; see, for example, Hê Shuling, "Lun jin zhi shiju yu Zhan'guo dayi" [On the major differences between the current situation and that of the Warring States], and Chen Shi, "Erenguo shikuleiqiang Qin lun" [On the Russians' harshness and strength of Qin], both in Mai Zhonghua, comp., *Huangqing jingshi wen xinlun* [A new collection of imperial statecraft writings] (Taibei: n.p., 1965), 1:124–126, and 2:293–295.

60 The Burlingame Mission was named after Anson Burlingame (1820–1870), American minister to China from 1861 to 1867, who, upon his retirement, represented the emperor of China on a diplomatic mission to "all the courts of the world."

61 Zhigang, *Chushi taixi ji* [A record of the first embassy to the West] (Beijing: Longfusi; Shishutang, [1877]; reprinted Changsha: Hunan renmin chubanshe, 1981), 132–133. By contrast, Li Gui's experience of circling the globe convinced him of the unity of the world; see *Huanyou diqiu xinlu*, 1–2.

62 Guo Songtao, *Shi Xi jicheng* [A full account of the embassy to the West], in *XFHZ*, *ce* 56: 153–155.

63 Huang Zunxian, "Xu" [Preface], *RBGZ*, 5.

64 Huang Zunxian, *RBZSS*, 1: 21. (Poem 55 in the second edition.)

65 I have relied especially on the travel diaries of Zhang Deyi, the Manchu bannerman who accompanied several of the first Chinese missions to Europe, and whose accounts were the earliest and most popular of the day: *Hang hai shu qi* [A description of curiosities overseas] ([1870]; reprinted Changsha: Hunan renmin chubanshe, 1981); *Zai shu qi* [A second description of curiosities] ([1875?]; reprinted as *Ou Mei huan youji* [An account of travels through Europe and America] Changsha: Hunan renmin chubanshe, 1981); and *San shu qi* [A third description of curiosities] ([1873?]; reprinted as *Sui shi Faguo ji* [An account of the diplomatic mission to France] Changsha: Hunan renmin chubanshe, 1982). In addition to previously cited texts by Li Gui and Zhigang, I have also consulted Bin Chun, *Chengcha biji* [Notes from a voyage] (n.d.; reprinted Changsha: Hunan renmin chubanshe, 1981); and Liu Xihong, *Ying yao siji* [Personal notes from a passage to England] ([1895?]; reprinted Changsha: Hunan renmin chubanshe, 1981).

66 Although he does not use the term *gonghe*, Zhang Deyi offers what is arguably the earliest personal description of a republic; he says of the government of France in 1871 that the "people and sovereign control national policy." See *San shu qi*, 91.

67 Early Chinese travelers to Europe and the United States noted the U.S. Congress or the British Parliament as the *huitang* ("meeting hall") or *gongyiting* ("public debate chamber"). By 1880, the term *yizhengyuan* ("court of policy debate") was generally used; Huang's term may be read as an abbreviation of this latter term. For *huitang*, see Zhang Deyi, *Zai shu qi*, 69, 129; and Liu Xihong, *Ying yao siji*, 59. For *gongyiting*, see Bin Chun, *Chengcha biji*, 25. For *yizhengyuan*, see Liu Xihong, 59, 81, 105ff.; and Li Gui, *Huanyou diqiu xinlu*, 61, 64f.

68 See Huang Zunxian, *RBZSS*, 2:7. This is poem 93 in the first edition, poem 129 in the second edition.

69 The main body of work is that of Gao Mingkai and Liu Zhengtan at Beijing

University. See their *Xiandai hanyu wailaici yanjiu* [Studies of loanwords in contemporary Chinese] (Beijing: Wenzi gaige chubanshe, 1958); and the more recent Liu Zhengtan et al., eds., *Hanyu wailaici cidian: A Dictionary of Loan Words and Hybrid Words in Chinese* (Shanghai: Cishu chubanshe, 1984). Their work is built upon that of Sanetō Keishū, who has argued that these words were borrowed by Chinese students in Japan *after* the Sino-Japanese War; but clearly, the readers of Huang's *Poems* had been exposed to some of them twenty years earlier. See *Chūgokujin Nihon-ryūgaku shi* [A history of Chinese overseas students in Japan], enlarged ed. (Tokyo: Kuroshio shuppan, 1981), 243–408.

70 It goes without saying that the theory of linguistics informing current studies of loanwords is indeed grounded in a practice of translation; I stand with V. N. Volosinov in criticizing such theories of language for their habit of reducing living language activity to the fixed status of "dead language." See *Marxism and the Philosophy of Language*, 69–71.

71 By contrast, Chinese travelers to Europe and the United States arrived with the assumption that the West was different, and set about explaining behaviors, customs, institutions, etc., from the start. A standard procedure was to describe a thing by way of naming it. See, for example, Li Gui's discussion of the major institutions he visited in Washington, D.C., including the Congress and the Federal Post Office: *Huanyou diqiu xinlu*, 61–65. The diaries of Zhang Deyi, who traveled repeatedly to Europe between 1866 and 1906, are very instructive as to his development from descriptions of things to naming things.

72 Joseph R. Levenson broached these issues in his formative *Confucian China and Its Modern Fate*, where he considers the growing domination of Western ideas in the twentieth century; but I remain unsatisfied by his analysis, which opposes the alternatives of a mere "change in language" and an "enrichment of vocabulary." See his *Confucian China and Its Modern Fate*, vol. 1, *The Problem of Intellectual Continuity*, 158–163.

73 Huang Zunxian, *RBGZ*, 1:1a.

74 The Sanetō Keishū Archives contains a number of rare records of poetry gatherings, the compilation of which is attributed to Yao: *Haiwai tongren ji* [A collection from the overseas fellows], ed. Kawada Kōshō (n.p., n.d.), which, in addition to the title collection, includes *Gui sheng zeng yan* [Words offered upon returning to the home province] and *Mojiang xiu shi shi* [Poems celebrating the Shi Festival on the Sumida River].

75 See, for example, "Shang Li xingshi shu" [A letter to Ambassador Li], in Yao Wendong, *Dong cha za zhu* [Miscellaneous writings from the Eastern Mission] (n.p., [1893]), 2a–3b. This collection was apparently first printed in 1885 as *Du haiwai qishushi zazhu* [Random writings from an overseas rare book room] (n.p., [1885]).

76 Yao Wendong, "Liyan" [Prefatory remarks], *RBDLBY*, 1:5a.

77 Yao Wendong, "Yu Ai Puyuan shu" [A letter to Ai Puyuan], in *Dong cha za zhu*, 1.

78 Yao Wendong, *RBDLBY*, 1:3a, 57a.

79 Yao Wendong, *Dong cha za zhu*, 53a, but see also the "Ba" [Afterword], 1a.

80 Yao Wendong, "Yu Ge Ziyuan shu" [A letter to Ge Ziyuan], in *Dong cha za zhu*, 25.

81 Compare, for example, the various treatments of the new Western concept, national debt (*guozhai*). Huang Zunxian and Fu Yunlong, as usual, give extended explanations, in addition to a plethora of statistical tables. See *RBGZ*, 18:13–18; and *YLRBTJ*, 14:23–24. Cf. Chen Jialin, *DCWJL*, 28b; Gu Houkun, *RBXZK*, 1:19b–20a; and Ye Qingyi, *CAZZ*, 3:21–22.

82 Not until 1898 is Chinese knowledge of Japan turned into a program of practical intent. In that year Kang Youwei submitted to the Guangxu emperor his *Riben xinzheng kao* [An examination of the new Japanese administration] a detailed chronicle of the first twenty-four years of the Meiji administration (1868–1890), describing the activities of the Japanese leadership as they constructed a new order in Japan. Kang's important text is reprinted in *Kang Youwei wuxu zhenzouyi* [Kang Youwei's genuine memorials of 1898], ed. Huang Zhangjian (Taibei: Zhongyang yanjiuyuan, Lishi yuyan yanjiusuo, 1974), 95–434. For a succinct discussion of the background of Kang's text and its role in the 1898 reforms, see Wang Xiaoqiu, *Jindai Zhong-Ri qishi lu*, 192–210.

83 Gu Houkun, *RBXZK*, 1:2a.

84 Ibid., 2:7b.

85 See ibid., 2:5b–6b.

86 See Huang Zunxian, *RBGZ*, 32:8b–11a, 33:15b–17a.

87 Fu Yunlong, *YLRBTJ*, 20, pt. 2: 17.

88 See the appropriate charts (unpaginated) in the 1888 *Outlines of the Modern Education in Japan*, trans. and published by the Department of Education, Tokyo, Japan.

89 See Hugh Keenleyside and A. F. Thomas, *History of Japanese Education and Present Educational System* (Tokyo: Hokuseido Press, 1937): 52–53. Because university courses were taught mainly in English and German during the 1870s and 1880s middle school students who hoped to go to university were implicitly expected to work harder at those languages. See James R. Bartholomew, "Japanese Modernization and the Imperial Universities, 1876–1920," *JAS* 37, no. 2 (2/1970): 251–271; and Donald Roden, *Schooldays in Imperial Japan: A Study in the Culture of a Student Elite* (Berkeley: University of California Press, 1980), 32–50. It was not until the 1930s that pragmatic interest in Chinese language study revived, as bureaucratic posts in Manchukuo and China became available to Japanese who could speak and were literate in Mandarin Chinese.

90 Chen Jialin, *DCWJL*, 13b–14a.

91 On the background of this argument, see H. D. Harootunian, *Things Seen and Unseen: Discourse and Ideology in Tokugawa Nativism* (Chicago: University of Chicago Press, 1988), 56–64. Fu is apparently paraphrasing Kamo Mabuchi.

92 Fu Yunlong, *YLRBTJ*, 20, pt. 1: 14b–15a.

93 See ibid., 20, pt. 1: 12a–16a. Huang Zunxian treats these arguments with much less detail in *RBGZ*, 33:12b–14a.

94 Chen Jialin, *DCWJL*, 14a.

95 Fu Yunlong, *YLRBTJ*, 20, pt. 1: 7.

96 Ye Qingyi and Yuan Zuzhi, *CAZZ*, 8:6b, 15a.

97 Fu Yunlong, *YLRBTJ*, 26:1–6b.

Afterword

1 Walter Benjamin, "Eduard Fuchs, Collector and Historian," in *One-Way Street and Other Writings* (London: Verso, 1985), 352. I develop Benjamin's theory in greater detail in "Constructing Perry's 'Chinaman' in the Context of Adorno and Benjamin," *positions: east asia cultures critique* 3, no. 2 (Fall 1995): 329–366.

2 See the monumental work by Sanetō Keishū, *Chūgokujin Nihon-ryūgaku shi;* and Paula Harrell, *Sowing the Seeds of Change: Chinese Students, Japanese Teachers, 1895–1905* (Stanford: Stanford University Press, 1992).

3 On Chinese translations of Japanese textbooks, see Sanetō, *Chūgokujin Nihon-ryūgaku shi,* 284–314; and his *Chūgoku ryūgakusei shitan* [On the history of Chinese foreign students] (Tokyo: Daiichi shobō, 1981), 141–147.

4 European textbooks had been introduced in China in the 1860s through new institutions like the Tongwen Guan. For an example, James Legge's 1864 *A Circle of Knowledge,* see Douglas Howland, "At the Crossroads of Victorian Ideology and Japanese Westernization," *Semiotics 1990*: 213–223.

5 Although the text is now reprinted as *Riben xinzheng kao* [An examination of Japan's new administration], it was originally titled either *Riben Mingzhi bianzheng ji* [An examination of Japan's political changes under the Meiji emperor] or, as I have put it, *Riben bianzheng kao.* See *Kang Yu-wei: A Biography and a Symposium,* ed. Jung-pang Lo (Tucson: University of Arizona Press, 1967), 446; Peng Tse-chou, *Chūgoku no kindaika to Meiji ishin* [China's modernization and the Meiji Restoration] (Kyoto: Dōbōsha, 1976), 1–158; and Wang Xiaoqui, *Jindai Zhong-Ri qishi lu,* 192–210.

6 Wang Xianqian, "Xu" [Preface], *Riben yuanliu kao* ([Changsha]: Sixian shuju, [1902]), 1:1–2.

7 Dai Jitao, *Riben lun* (Shanghai: Minzhi shuju, 1928).

8 See Xue [Hsüeh] Fucheng, *The European Diary of Hsieh Fucheng: Envoy Extraordinary of Imperial China,* trans. Helen Hsieh Chien (New York: St. Martin's Press, 1993), 30f., 74f., 99–198 passim. According to Cordell Yee, maps played a role in Soong treaties with the Jurchen and Khitan rulers in the eleventh century, but for the most part, they were used during the Qing to assist local administrators in land taxation; see his "Chinese Maps in Political Culture," 83, 90f. Joseph E. Schwartzberg, in the same volume, indicates that the first border maps of the Burma area were made by the British in conjunction with the Treaty of Yandabo (1826) that concluded the first Anglo-Burmese War; see his "Southeast-Asian Geographical Maps," in *The History of Cartography,* vol. 2, bk. 2, 747.

9 In addition to Benedict Anderson's seminal *Imagined Communities: Reflections on the Origin and Spread of Nationalism* (London: Verso, 1983), see Wah-kwan Cheng, "Vox Populi: Language, Literature, and Ideology in Modern China" (Ph.D. diss., University of Chicago, 1989); and Thongchai Winichakul, *Siam Mapped: A History of the Geo-Body of a Nation* (Honolulu: University of Hawaii Press, 1994).

10 On spoken drama as *wenming,* see Colin Mackerras, "The Drama of the Qing

Dynasty," in *Chinese Theater: From Its Origins to the Present Day*, ed. Colin Mackerras (Honolulu: University of Hawaii Press, 1983), 92–117.

11 See Wang Xiangrong, "Zhongguo wenhua quan" [China's cultural sphere], in *Gudai de Zhongguo yu Riben*, 1–25.

12 See Kamachi, *Reform in China*, 118–124; and Satō Saburō, "Kōakai ni kansuru ichi kosatsu" [One investigation of the Kōakai], *Yamagata Daigaku kiyō: jimbun kagaku* [Yamagata University bulletin: Human sciences] 1, no. 4 (August 1951): 399–411.

13 See Marius B. Jansen, "Konoe Atsumarō," in *The Chinese and the Japanese*, ed. Akira Iriye, 107–123; and Douglas R. Reynolds, "Training Young China Hands: Tōa Dōbunkai and Its Precursors, 1886–1945," in *The Japanese Informal Empire in China, 1895–1937*, ed. Peter Duus et al. (Princeton: Princeton University Press, 1989), 210–271.

14 Stefan Tanaka, *Japan's Orient: Rendering Pasts into History* (Berkeley: University of California Press, 1993).

15 *Zhong-Ri wenhua yu jiaoliu: Di yi ji* [Chinese-Japanese culture and interaction: first series], ed. Yang Zhengguang et al. (Beijing: Zhongguo zhanwang chubanshe, 1984), [vii].

16 *Nan shi* [History of the southern dynasties], *juan* 10, *Chen benji* [Basic annals of Chen] (Beijing: Zhonghua shuju, 1975), 1:307.

Bibliography

Adams, Percy G. *Travel Literature and the Evolution of the Novel.* Lexington: University of Kentucky Press, 1983.

Alitto, Guy. "Zhongguo fangzhi yu Xifangshi de bijiao" [A comparison of Chinese local treatises and Western local histories]. *Hanxue yanjiu* 3, no. 2 (12/1985): 59–71.

Allen, Joseph R. *In the Voice of Others: Chinese Music Bureau Poetry.* Ann Arbor: University of Michigan, Center for Chinese Studies, 1992.

Anderson, Benedict. *Imagined Communities: Reflections on the Origin and Spread of Nationalism.* London: Verso, 1983.

Aoki Masaru. *Shindai bungaku hyōron shi* [A history of Qing literary criticism]. Tokyo: Iwanami, 1950.

Asukai Masamichi. *Bunmeikaika* [Civilization]. Tokyo: Iwanami, 1985.

Balazs, E. "L'Histoire comme guide de la pratique bureaucratique." In *Historians of China and Japan,* ed. W. G. Beasley and E. G. Pulleyblank, 78–94. London: Oxford University Press, 1961.

Banno, Masataka. *China and the West, 1858–1861: The Origins of the Tsungli Yamen.* Cambridge, Mass.: Harvard University Press, 1964.

Barnett, Suzanne Wilson. "Wei Yuan and Westerners: Notes on the Sources of the *Hai-Kuo T'u-Chih.*" *Ch'ing-shih Wen-t'i* 2, no. 4 (November 1970): 1–20.

Bartholomew, James R. "Japanese Modernization and the Imperial Universities, 1876–1920." *JAS* 37, no. 2 (2/1970): 251–271.

Batten, Charles L., Jr. *Pleasurable Instruction: Form and Convention in Eighteenth-Century Travel Literature.* San Francisco: University of California Press, 1978.

Bauer, Wolfgang. "The Encyclopaedia in China." *Cahiers d'histoire mondiale* 9, no. 3 (1966): 665–691.

Beasley, W. G., and E. G. Pulleyblank, eds. *Historians of China and Japan.* Oxford: Oxford University Press, 1961.

Bei Yunchen and Ye Youming, comps. *Lidai youji xuan* [Selections from travel diaries through the ages]. Changsha: Hunan renmin chubanshe, 1980.

Biggerstaff, Knight. "The T'ung Wen Kuan." *Chinese Social and Political Science Review* 18 (1934): 307–340.

Bin Chun. *Chengcha biji* [Notes from a voyage]. N.d. Reprinted Changsha: Hunan renmin chubanshe, 1981.

Black, Alison Harley. *Man and Nature in the Philosophical Thought of Wang Fu-chih.* Seattle: University of Washington Press, 1989.

Bloom, Irene. "On the 'Abstraction' of Ming Thought: Some Concrete Evidence from the Philosophy of Lo Ch'in-shun." In *Principle and Practicality: Essays in Neo-*

Confucianism and Practical Learning, ed. Wm. Theodore de Bary and Irene Bloom, 69–125. New York: Columbia University Press, 1979.

Bo Juyi. *Bo Xiangshan ji* [Collected works of Bo Xiangshan]. Changsha: Shangwu yinshuguan, 1934.

Bodde, Derk, and Clarence Morris. *Law in Imperial China: Exemplified by 190 Ch'ing Dynasty Cases (Translated from the Hsing-an hui-lan), with Historical, Social, and Juridical Commentaries.* Philadelphia: University of Pennsylvania Press, 1967.

Bourdieu, Pierre. *Outline of a Theory of Practice.* Trans. Richard Nice. Cambridge: Cambridge University Press, 1977.

Bretschneider, E. "Fu-Sang, or Who Discovered America?" *The Chinese Recorder* (October 1870): 114–120.

Burke, Kenneth. *A Grammar of Motives.* Berkeley: University of California Press, 1969.

Cao Xueqin. *Hong lou meng* [The dream of the red chamber]. Taibei: Wenhua, 1979.

Chan, Wing-tsit. *A Source Book in Chinese Philosophy.* Princeton: Princeton University Press, 1963.

Chang Chung-li. *The Chinese Gentry: Studies on Their Role in Nineteenth-Century Chinese Society.* Seattle: University of Washington Press, 1955.

Chang, Hao. *Chinese Intellectuals in Crisis: Search for Order and Meaning (1890–1911).* Berkeley: University of California Press, 1987.

Chang, Kang-i Sun. *The Evolution of Chinese Tz'u Poetry: From Late T'ang to Northern Sung.* Princeton: Princeton University Press, 1980.

———. *Six Dynasties Poetry.* Princeton: Princeton University Press, 1986.

Chao, Chia-ying Yeh. "The Ch'ang-chou School of *Tz'u* Criticism." In *Chinese Approaches to Literature from Confucius to Liang Ch'i-ch'ao*, ed. Adele Rickett, 151–188. Princeton: Princeton University Press, 1978.

Chao, Yuen Ren. *A Grammar of Spoken Chinese.* Berkeley: University of California Press, 1968.

Chen Baochen. "Zou" [Memorial on the Liuqiu Incident]. In *Qing Guangxuchao Zhong-Ri jiaoshe shiliao* [Historical materials on Sino-Japanese relations during the Qing Guangxu court], 2:10–12. Beiping: Palace Museum, 1932.

Chen Cheng-siang [Chen Zhengxiang]. *Zhongguo fangzhi di dilixue jiazhi: Geographical Evaluation of the Chinese Fang-chih.* Hong Kong: Chinese University of Hong Kong, 1965.

Chen Dengyuan. "Xixue lai Hua shi guoren zhi wuduan taidu" [The arbitrary attitudes of Chinese upon the coming of Western learning to China]. *Dongfang zazhi* [Eastern miscellany] 27, no. 8 (April 1930): 61–76.

Chen, Fu-mei Chang. "On Analogy in Ch'ing Law." *HJAS* 30 (1970): 212–224.

Chen Jialin. *Dong cha wenjian lu* [A record of things seen and heard on the Eastern Mission]. N.p., [1887]. Reprinted in *XFHZ, zhi* 10: 371–407.

Chen Jiexian. "Lun Qingdai Taiwan diqu fangzhi de yili" [On the formal structure of local treatises on Taiwan during the Qing]. *Hanxue yanjiu* [Chinese studies] 3, no. 2 (12/1985): 157–231.

Chen Lunjiong. *Hai guo wenjian lu* [Recorded news of the sea kingdoms]. [1730].

Reprinted in *Siku quanshu zhenben* [Rare edition of the *Complete Books of the Four Treasuries*], ed. Wang Yunwu, ser. 5, vol. 2. Taibei: Shangwu yinshuguan, n.d.

Chen Qiyuan. *Riben jin shi ji* [An account of the recent affair with Japan]. In *XFHZ, ce* 52: 265–267.

Chen, Yu-shih. *Images and Ideas in Chinese Classical Prose: Studies of Four Masters.* Stanford: Stanford University Press, 1988.

Ch'en Shou-yi. *Chinese Literature: A Historical Introduction.* New York: Ronald Press, 1961.

Cheng, Chung-ying. "Practical Learning in Yen Yuan, Chu Hsi, and Wang Yang-ming." In *Principle and Practicality: Essays on Neo-Confucianism and Practical Learning,* ed. Wm. Theodore de Bary and Irene Bloom, 37–67. New York: Columbia University Press, 1979.

Cheng, François *Chinese Poetic Writing.* Bloomington: Indiana University Press, 1982.

Cheng Guangyu. "Huang Zunxian yu Riren zhi qingyi ji qi *Riben guozhi*" [Huang Zunxian's Japanese friends and his *Japan Treatise*]. In *Bainian lai Zhong-Ri guanxi lunwenji* [Essays on the past hundred years of Chinese-Japanese relations], ed. Shen Qinting, 515–537. Taibei: n.p., 1969.

Cheng, Wah-kwan. "Vox Populi: Language, Literature, and Ideology in Modern China." Ph.D. diss, University of Chicago, 1989.

Cheng Yaolie et al. *Liuhe xian xuzhi gao* [A draft continuation of the Liuhe District treatise]. N.p., 1920.

Chouban yiwu shimo: Tongzhi chao [Complete records on managing foreign affairs, ser. 3, *The Tong Zhi Court*], comp. Wen Qing. Peiping: Palace Museum, 1929–1930.

Chow Jen-hwa. *China and Japan: The History of Chinese Diplomatic Missions in Japan 1877–1911.* Singapore: Chopman Enterprises, 1975.

Chow Tse-tsung. "The Early History of the Chinese Word *Shih* (Poetry)." In *Wen-lin: Studies in the Chinese Humanities,* ed. Chow Tse-tsung, 151–209. Madison: University of Wisconsin Press, 1968.

Chu, Samuel C. "China's Attitudes toward Japan at the Time of the Sino-Japanese War." In *The Chinese and the Japanese: Essays in Political and Cultural Interactions,* ed. Akira Iriye, 74–95. Princeton: Princeton University Press, 1980.

Ch'ü T'ung-tsu. *Local Government in China under the Ch'ing.* Cambridge, Mass.: Harvard University Press, 1962.

Cohen, Paul A. *Between Tradition and Modernity: Wang T'ao and Reform in Late Ch'ing China.* Cambridge, Mass.: Harvard University Council on East Asian Studies, 1974.

———. *China and Christianity.* Cambridge, Mass.: Harvard University Press, 1963.

Collingwood, R. G. *The Idea of History.* New York: Oxford University Press, 1956.

Croizier, Ralph C. *Koxinga and Chinese Nationalism: History, Myth, and the Hero.* Cambridge, Mass.: Harvard University Press, 1977.

Dai Jitao. *Riben lun* [An essay on Japan]. Shanghai: Minzhi shuju, 1928.

Dai Mingshi. *Riben fengtu ji* [Notes on Japanese manners]. In *XFHZBP,* vol. 10 [unpaginated].

Dawson, Raymond. *Confucius*. Oxford: Oxford University Press, 1981.

DeFrancis, John. *The Chinese Language: Fact and Fantasy*. Honolulu: University of Hawaii Press, 1984.

Dennerline, Jerry. *The Chia-ting Loyalists: Confucian Leadership and Social Change in Seventeenth-Century China*. New Haven: Yale University Press, 1981.

Department of Education. *Outlines of the Modern Education in Japan*. Trans. and publ. Department of Education, Tokyo, Japan, 1888.

Dong you jisheng [Copious notes from an eastern journey]. In *XFHZ, zhi* 10: 305.

Dong you riji [A diary of an eastern journey]. In *XFHZ, zhi* 10: 302–304.

Drake, Fred W. *China Charts the World: Hsu Chi-yü and His Geography of 1848*. Cambridge, Mass.: Harvard University, East Asian Research Center, 1975.

Easthope, Anthony. *Poetry as Discourse*. London: Methuen, 1983.

Edwards, E. D. "A Classified Guide to the Thirteen Classes of Chinese Prose." *Bulletin of the School of Oriental and African Studies* 12, nos. 3–4 (1948): 770–788.

Eliade, Mircea. *The Myth of the Eternal Return; or, Cosmos and History*. Princeton: Princeton University Press, 1965.

Elman, Benjamin. "Ch'ing Dynasty 'Schools' of Scholarship." *Ch'ing-shih wen-t'i* 4, no. 6 (12/1979): 1–45.

——. *Classicism, Politics, and Kinship: The Ch'ang-chou School of New Text Confucianism in Late Imperial China*. Berkeley: University of California Press, 1990.

——. "Criticism as Philosophy: Conceptual Change in Ch'ing Dynasty Evidential Research." *Tsing-Hua Journal of Chinese Studies* n.s. 17 (1985): 165–98.

——. *From Philosophy to Philology: Intellectual and Social Aspects of Change in Late Imperial China*. Cambridge, Mass.: Harvard University, Council on East Asian Studies, 1984.

——. "Geographical Research in the Ming-Ch'ing Period." *Monumenta Serica* 35 (1981–1983): 1–18.

Fairbank, John K., ed. *The Cambridge History of China*. Vol. 10, *Late Ch'ing, 1800–1911*, pt. 1. Cambridge: Cambridge University Press, 1978.

——, ed. *The Chinese World Order: Traditional China's Foreign Relations*. Cambridge, Mass.: Harvard University Press, 1968.

Fang Hao. "Qingdai jinyang Tianzhujiao suo shou Riben zhi yingxiang" [Japanese influence on Qing suppression of Catholicism]. In *Fang Hao wenlu* [Writings of Fang Hao], 47–65. Beiping: Shangzhi bianyiguan, 1948.

Feng Guifen. *Jiaobinlu kangyi* [Protests from Jiaobin Hut]. N.p., [1884]. Reprinted Taibei: Wenhai chubanshe, n.d.

Feng Zuozhe and Wang Xiaoqiu. "*Azuma kagami* and *Wuqi jing bu*: Historical Evidence of Sino-Japanese Cultural Interaction." *Sino-Japanese Studies Newsletter* 1, no. 2 (March 1989): 28–40.

Fletcher, Joseph. "Ch'ing Inner Asia c. 1800." In *The Cambridge History of China*, vol. 10, ed. John K. Fairbank, 34–106.

——. "The Heyday of the Ch'ing Order in Mongolia, Sinkiang, and Tibet." In *The Cambridge History of China*, vol. 10, ed. John K. Fairbank, 351–408.

——. "Sino-Russian Relations, 1800–62." In *The Cambridge History of China*, vol. 10, ed. John K. Fairbank, 318–350.

Frankel, Hans H. *The Flowering Plum and the Palace Lady: Interpretations of Chinese Poetry*. New Haven: Yale University Press, 1976.

——. "Yüeh-fu Poetry." In *Studies in Chinese Literary Genres*, ed. Cyril Birch, 69–107. San Francisco: University of California Press, 1974.

Frodsham, J. D., trans. and ann. *The First Chinese Embassy to the West: The Journals of Kuo Sung-t'ao, Liu Hsi-hung, and Chang Te-yi*. Oxford: Clarendon Press, 1974.

Fu Yunlong. *Youli Riben tujing* [An illustrated monograph on Japan, based on an official tour]. Tokyo: n.p., [1889].

——. *Youli tujing yuji* [Additional records from the illustrated monograph based on an official tour]. Tokyo: n.p., [1889].

Fu Zhenlun. *Zhongguo fangzhi xue tonglun* [A comprehensive study of the Chinese geographic treatise]. Shanghai: Shangwu yinshuguan, 1935.

Fukuzawa Yukichi. *Gakumon no susume* [An encouragement of learning]. In *Fukuzawa Yukichi zenshū*, 3:21–144. Tokyo: Iwanami, 1959.

Funatsu Tomohiko. *Chūgoku shiwa no kenkyū* [Studies of Chinese poetry talk]. Tokyo: Yakumo shobō, 1977.

Gaimushō, ed. *Nihon gaikō monjo* [Japanese foreign relations documents]. Tokyo: Gaimushō, 1949–.

Gao Mingkai and Liu Zhengtan. *Xiandai Hanyu wailaici yanjiu* [Studies of loanwords in contemporary Chinese]. Beijing: Wenzi gaige chubanshe, 1958.

Gardner, Charles S. *Chinese Traditional Historiography*. Cambridge, Mass.: Harvard University Press, 1938.

Gardner, Daniel K. "Modes of Thinking and Modes of Discourse in the Sung: Some Thoughts on the Yü-lu ('Recorded Conversations') Texts." *JAS* 50, no. 3 (8/1991): 574–603.

Graham, A. C. *Disputers of the Tao: Philosophical Argument in Ancient China*. La Salle: Open Court, 1989.

——. *Later Mohist Logic, Ethics, and Science*. Hong Kong: Chinese University Press; London: School of Oriental and African Studies, 1978.

Gu Houkun. *Riben xinzheng kao* [An examination of Japan's new administration]. N.p., [1889]. Reprinted in *Xizheng congshu* [Collected writings on Western administration], ed. Qiuziqiangzhai zhuren [Master of the Studio for Seeking Self-strengthening], vols. 25–26, n.p., [1897].

Gu Yanwu. *Tianxia junguo libing shu* [On the gains and ills of the administrative domains under Heaven]. Reprinted in *Sibu congkan: San bian*. Shanghai: Shanghai shangwu yinying, 1936.

Gu Yingtai. *Yanhai wo luan* [The Dwarf Rebellion along the coast]. In *Ming shi jishi benmo* [Highlights of Ming history, beginning to end], vol. 8, 40–61. Shanghai: Shangwu yinshuguan, 1933.

Guo Shaoyu. *Zhongguo wenxue piping shi* [A history of Chinese literary criticism]. Shanghai: Shangwu yinshuguan, 1947.

Bibliography 307

Guo Songtao. *Shi xi jicheng* [A full account of the embassy to the West]. Reprinted in *XFHZ, ce* 56: 146–159.

Guy, R. Kent. *The Emperor's Four Treasuries: Scholars and the State in the Late Ch'ien-Lung Era*. Cambridge, Mass.: Harvard University, Council on East Asian Studies, 1987.

Habermas, Jürgen. *Knowledge and Human Interests*. Trans. Jeremy J. Shapiro. Boston: Beacon Press, 1971.

Hall, David L., and Roger T. Ames. *Thinking through Confucius*. Albany: State University of New York Press, 1987.

Han Yu-shan. *Elements of Chinese Historiography*. Hollywood: W. M. Hawley, 1955.

Hanson, Chad. "Chinese Ideographs and Western Ideas." *JAS* 52, no. 2 (5/1993): 373–399.

Hao, Yen-p'ing, and Erh-min Wang. "Changing Chinese Views of Western Relations, 1840–95." In *The Cambridge History of China*, vol. 11, *Late Ch'ing, 1800–1911*, pt. 2, ed. John K. Fairbank and Kwang-ching Liu, 142–201. Cambridge: Cambridge University Press, 1980.

Hargett, James M. *On the Road in Twelfth-Century China: The Travel Diaries of Fan Chengda (1126–1193)*. Stuttgart: F. Steiner, 1989.

——. "Yu-chi wen-hsüeh." In *The Indiana Companion to Traditional Chinese Literature*, ed. William H. Nienhauser Jr., 936–939. Bloomington: University of Indiana Press, 1986.

Harootunian, H. D. Review of *Principle and Practicality: Essays in Neo-Confucianism and Practical Learning*, ed. Wm. Theodore de Bary and Irene Bloom. *Journal of Japanese Studies* 7, no. 1 (1981): 11–31.

——. *Things Seen and Unseen: Discourse and Ideology in Tokugawa Nativism*. Chicago: University of Chicago Press, 1988.

——. *Toward Restoration: The Growth of Political Consciousness in Tokugawa Japan*. Berkeley: University of California Press, 1970.

Harrell, Paula. *Sowing the Seeds of Change: Chinese Students, Japanese Teachers, 1895–1905*. Stanford: Stanford University Press, 1992.

Hartwell, Robert M. "Historical Analogism, Public Policy, and Social Science in Eleventh- and Twelfth-Century China." *American Historical Review* 76, no. 3 (June 1971): 690–727.

Hawkes, David, trans. and ann. *The Songs of the South; An Ancient Chinese Anthology of Poems by Qu Yuan and Other Poets*. Rev. ed. Harmondsworth: Penguin, 1985.

Hê Ruzhang. *Shi dong shulue* [A concise account of the Eastern Embassy]. Reprinted in *ZRYW*, 45–68.

——. *Shi dong za yong* [Assorted verse from the Eastern Embassy]. Reprinted in *ZRYW*, 69–86.

Henderson, John B. "Ch'ing Scholars' Views of Western Astronomy." *HJAS* 46, no. 1 (1986): 121–148.

——. *The Development and Decline of Chinese Cosmology*. New York: Columbia University Press, 1984.

———. *Scripture, Canon, and Commentary: A Comparison of Confucian and Western Exegesis*. Princeton: Princeton University Press, 1991.

Hevia, James L. *Cherishing Men from Afar: Qing Guest Ritual and the Macartney Embassy of 1793*. Durham: Duke University Press, 1995.

———. "Guest Ritual and Interdomainal Relations in the Late Qing." Ph.D. diss., University of Chicago, 1986.

Ho, Wai-kam. "The Literary Concepts of 'Picture-Like' (*Ju-hua*) and 'Picture-Idea' (*Hua-i*) in the Relationship between Poetry and Painting." In *Words and Images: Chinese Poetry, Calligraphy, and Painting*, ed. Alfreda Murck and Wen C. Fong, 359–404. New York: Metropolitan Museum of Art; Princeton: Princeton University Press, 1991.

Hou Wailu. *Zhongguo zaoqi qimeng sixiang shi* [A history of the philosophy of the early enlightenment in China]. Beijing: Renmin chubanshe, 1958.

Hsiao, Kung-chuan. *A History of Chinese Political Thought*. Vol. 1, *From the Beginnings to the Sixth Century A.D.* Trans. F. W. Mote. Princeton: Princeton University Press, 1979.

Hsu Hsia-k'o. *The Travel Diaries of Hsu Hsia-k'o*. Trans. and ed. Li Chi. Hong Kong: Chinese University of Hong Kong, 1974.

Hsü, Immanuel C. Y. *China's Entrance into the Family of Nations: The Diplomatic Phase, 1858–1880*. Cambridge, Mass.: Harvard University Press, 1960.

Hu Shi. *Dai Dongyuan de zhexue* [Dai Zhen's philosophy]. Shanghai: Shangwu yinshuguan, 1927.

———. *Wushinian lai Zhongguo zhi wenxue* [Chinese literature of the last fifty years]. N.p.: Xinminguo shu, 1929.

Hu Shih [Hu Shi]. *The Development of the Logical Method in Ancient China*. Shanghai: Oriental Book Company, 1928.

Hu Ying. "Xu Fu ji you yi kaozheng" [Another piece of evidential research on Xu Fu's tomb]. *Zhongguo yu Riben* [China and Japan] 21 (September 1971): 54.

Huang Liuhong. *Fuhui quanshu*. N.p., [1876]. Trans. and ed. Djang Chu as *A Complete Book Concerning Happiness and Benevolence: Fu-hui ch'üan-shu, A Manual for Local Magistrates in Seventeenth-Century China*. Tucson: University of Arizona Press, 1984.

Huang Qingdeng. *Dong you riji* [Diary of a journey to the East]. [1893]. Reprinted in *ZRYW*, 219–276.

Huang Zunxian. *Renjinglu shicao jianzhu* [The draft poems from the Renjing Hut]. Ann. Qian Zhonglian. Hong Kong: Zhonghua shuju, 1963.

———. "Renjinglu zawen chao" [Reprints of prose from the Renjing Hut]. Ed. Qian Zhonglian. *Wenxian* [Literature] 7 (1981): 62–78; 8 (1981): 77–96.

———. *Riben guozhi* [Japan treatise]. 2d ed. Shanghai: Tushu jicheng, [1898]. Reprinted Taibei: Wenhai chubanshe, 1981.

———. *Riben zashi shi* [Poems on divers Japanese affairs]. Hong Kong: Xunhuan baoguan, [1880]; 2d ed., Taibei: Yiwen yinshuguan, 1974.

———. "Yu Langshan lun shi" [Discussing poetry with Langshan]. *Lingnan xuebao* [Lingnan research reports] 2, no. 2 (July 1931): 184–185.

Hucker, Charles O. *A Dictionary of Official Titles in Imperial China.* Stanford: Stanford University Press, 1985.

Hummel, Arthur, ed. *Eminent Chinese of the Ch'ing Period (1644–1912).* Taibei: Ch'eng Wen Publishing, 1970.

Huters, Theodore. "From Writing to Literature: The Development of Late Qing Theories of Prose." *HJAS* 47, no. 1 (1987): 51–96.

Iriye, Akira, ed. *The Chinese and the Japanese: Essays in Political and Cultural Interactions.* Princeton: Princeton University Press, 1980.

Irokawa Daikichi. *Meiji no bunka* [Meiji culture]. Tokyo: Iwanami, 1970.

Ishikawa Ei, ed. *Nihon bunsho kihan* [Models for Japanese composition]. Tokyo: Hogyokutō, [1879].

———, comp. *Shibayama issho* [A laugh on Shiba Hill]. Tokyo: Bunshodō, [1878].

Jansen, Marius B. *China in the Tokugawa World.* Cambridge, Mass.: Harvard University Press, 1992.

———. "Konoe Atsumarō." In *The Chinese and the Japanese: Essays in Political and Cultural Interactions,* ed. Akira Iriye, 107–123. Princeton: Princeton University Press, 1980.

Jiang Chenying. *Tongzhi haifang zonglun* [A comprehensive discussion for a united will to coastal defense]. In *Zhanyuan weidinggao* [Unfinished manuscripts from the Clear Garden], *juan* 1, 10b–30b [ca. 1689]. Reprinted in *Jiang Xiansheng quanji* [Complete works of Master Jiang], ed. Feng Baobian and Wang Dingxiang, n.p., 1930.

Jin Anqing. *Dong wo kao* [An investigation of the eastern Dwarfs]. In *XFHZBP,* vol. 10 [unpaginated].

Jones, Susan Mann, and Philip A. Kuhn. "Dynastic Decline and the Roots of Rebellion." In *The Cambridge History of China,* ed. John K. Fairbank, vol. 10, 107–162.

Kabashima Tadao et al. *Meiji/Taishō shingo zokugo jiten* [Dictionary of new and colloquial expressions in the Meiji and Taishō periods.] Tokyo: Tokyodō, 1984.

Kamachi, Noriko. "The Chinese in Meiji Japan: Their Interactions with the Japanese before the Sino-Japanese War." In *The Chinese and the Japanese: Essays in Political and Cultural Interactions,* ed. Akira Iriye, 58–73. Princeton: Princeton University Press, 1980.

———. *Reform in China: Huang Tsun-hsien and the Japanese Model.* Cambridge, Mass.: Harvard University, Council on East Asian Studies, 1981.

Kang Youwei. *Kang Youwei shi wen xuan* [Selected poetry and essays of Kang Youwei]. Guangdong: Renmin chubanshe, 1983.

———. *Riben xinzheng kao* [An examination of the new Japanese administration]. In *Kang Youwei wuxu zhenzouyi* [Kang Youwei's genuine memorials of 1898], ed. Huang Zhangjian, 95–434. Taibei: Zhongyang yanjiuyuan, Lishi yuyan yanjiusuo, 1974.

Kao, Yu-kung, and Tsu-lin Mei. "Syntax, Diction, and Imagery in T'ang Poetry." *HJAS* 31 (1971): 49–136.

Keene, Donald. "The Survival of Chinese Literary Traditions in the Meiji Era." In *Sino-Japanese Cultural Interchange: Aspects of Literature and Language Learning,* ed.

Yue-him Tam, 75–90. Hong Kong: Chinese University, Institute of Chinese Studies, 1985.

Keenleyside, Hugh, and A. F. Thomas. *History of Japanese Education and Present Educational System*. Tokyo: Hokuseido Press, 1937.

Kim, Key-hiuk. *The Last Phase of the East Asian World Order: Korea, Japan, and the Chinese Empire, 1860–1882*. Berkeley: University of California Press, 1980.

Kinoshita Hyō. *Meiji shika* [On Meiji poetry]. Tokyo: Bunchutō, 1943.

Kittay, Eva Feder. *Metaphor: Its Cognitive Force and Linguistic Structure*. Oxford: Clarendon Press, 1987.

Kojiki. Trans. with intro. and notes by Donald L. Philippi. Tokyo: University of Tokyo Press, 1965.

Kurata Sadayoshi. *Shinmatsu-Minsho wo chūshin toshita Chūgoku kindai shi no kenkyū* [Studies of poetry in early modern China, with late Qing/early Republic as a focus]. Tokyo: Taishukan, 1969.

Lau, D. C. "Some Logical Problems in Ancient China." *Proceedings of the Aristotelian Society* 53 (1952–3): 189–204.

Leland, Charles G. *Fusang, or The Discovery of America*. New York: Bouton, 1875.

Leonard, Janet Kate. *Wei Yuan and China's Rediscovery of the Maritime World*. Cambridge: Harvard University, Council on East Asian Studies, 1984.

Leslie, Donald D., et al., eds. *Essays on the Sources for Chinese History*. Columbia: University of South Carolina Press, 1973.

Levenson, Joseph R. *Confucian China and Its Modern Fate*. Vol. 1, *The Problem of Intellectual Continuity*. Berkeley: University of California Press, 1958.

Lévi-Strauss, Claude. *The Savage Mind*. Chicago: University of Chicago Press, 1966.

Levy, Dore J. *Chinese Narrative Poetry: The Late Han through T'ang Dynasties*. Durham: Duke University Press, 1988.

Li Bo. *Li Bo ji jiaozhu* [The annotated collected works of Li Bo]. Shanghai: Guji chubanshe, 1980.

Li Fengmou. *Weng Fanggang ji qi shilun* [Weng Fanggang and his poetic theory]. Taibei: Chia Hsiu Foundation, 1978.

Li Gui. *Dong you riji* [Diary of a journey to the East]. In *Huanyou diqiu xinlu* [A new record of a trip around the world]. [1879]. Reprinted Changsha: Hunan renmin chubanshe, 1980.

Li Hongzhang. *Li Wenzhong Gong quanji: Zougao* [Complete works of Li Wenzhong: Memorials]. Nanjing: n.p., 1908.

Li Shuchang. *Zhuozunyuan conggao* [Collected drafts from the Zhuozun Garden]. [1893]. Reprinted Taibei: Wenhai chubanshe, n.d.

Li Taifen. *Fangzhi xue* [A study of the geographic treatise]. Shanghai: Shangwu yinshuguan, 1935.

Liang Peilan. "Riben dao ge" [Song of the Japanese sword]. In *Qing shi duo* [Chimes of Qing poetry], ed. Zhang Yingchang, 1:399. Beijing: Zhonghua shuju, 1960.

Liang Qichao. "Fangzhi xue" [On local treatises]. *Dongfang zazhi* [Eastern journal] 21, no. 18 (1924): 91–102.

——. *Intellectual Trends in the Ch'ing Period.* Trans. Immanuel C. Y. Hsü. Cambridge, Mass.: Harvard University Press, 1959.

——. *Qingdai xueshu gailun* [An outline of Qing learning]. Reprinted in *Liang Qichao lun Qingxueshi erzhong* [Two texts by Liang Qichao on the history of Qing learning]. Shanghai: Fudan Daxue chubanshe, 1985.

Lin, Julia C. *Modern Chinese Poetry: An Introduction.* Seattle: University of Washington Press, 1972.

Liu, James J. Y. *The Art of Chinese Poetry.* Chicago: University of Chicago Press, 1962.

——. *Chinese Theories of Literature.* Chicago: University of Chicago Press, 1975.

Liu Ruoyu [James J. Y. Liu]. "Qingdai shishuo lunyao" [An outline of Qing poetic theory]. In *Xianggang Daxue wushizhounian jinian lunwen ji* [Collected essays commemorating the fiftieth anniversary of Hong Kong University] 1:321–342. Hong Kong: Xianggang Daxue zhongwenxi, 1964.

Liu Xie. *Wenxin diaolong zhushi* [The *literary mind and carving dragons*]. Ann. Zhou Zhenfu. Beijing: Renmin wenxue chubanshe, 1981.

Liu Xihong. *Ying yao siji* [Personal notes from a passage to England]. [1895?]. Reprinted Changsha: Hunan renmin chubanshe, 1981.

Liu Zhengtan et al. *Hanyu wailaici cidian: A Dictionary of Loan Words and Hybrid Words in Chinese.* Shanghai: Cishu chubanshe, 1984.

Lo, Irving Y., and William Schultz, eds. *Waiting for the Unicorn: Poems and Lyrics of China's Last Dynasty, 1644–1911.* Bloomington: Indiana University Press, 1986.

Lo, Jung-pang, ed. *Kang Yu-wei: A Biography and a Symposium.* Tucson: University of Arizona Press, 1967.

Lou Zikuang and Ruan Changrui. "Zhuzhi ci de yanjiu" [Studies on the Bamboo Stalk Lyric]. In *Zhongshan Daxue minsu congshu* [Collected works on folklore from Zhongshan University], 3:19–33. Taibei: Chinese Association for Folklore, 1969.

Lu, Sheldon Hsiao-peng. *From Historicity to Fictionality: The Chinese Poetics of Narrative.* Stanford: Stanford University Press, 1994.

Luo Genze. *Zhongguo wenxue pipingshi* [A history of Chinese literary criticism]. Shanghai: Gudian wenxue chubanshe, 1957–1961.

Luo Qixiang. "Xu Fu cun de faxian han Xu Fu dongdu" [The discovery of Xu Fu's village and Xu Fu's eastern crossing]. In *Cong Xu Fu dao Huang Zunxian* [From Xu Fu to Huang Zunxian], ed. Yang Zhengguang, 24–51. Beijing: Shishi chubanshe, 1985.

Luo Sen. *Riben riji* [Japan diary]. [1854]. Reprinted in *ZRYW,* 27–44.

Lynn, Richard John. "Orthodoxy and Enlightenment: Wang Shih-chen's Theory of Poetry and Its Antecedents." In *The Unfolding of Neo-Confucianism,* ed. Wm. Theodore de Bary, 217–269. New York: Columbia University Press, 1975.

——. "The Talent Learning Polarity in Chinese Poetics: Yan Yu and the Later Tradition." *Chinese Literature: Essays, Articles, Reviews* 5 (1983): 157–184.

——. "Tradition and the Individual: Ming and Ch'ing Views of Yuan Poetry." *Journal of Oriental Studies* 15, no. 1 (1977): 1–19.

Maeda Ai. "Chinzan to Shuntō—Meiji shonen no kanshi tan" [Chinzan and Shuntō—

Chinese poetry societies in early Meiji]. In *Bakumatsu-Ishinki no bungaku* [Literature of the Bakumatsu and Meiji periods], 246–268. Tokyo: Hōsei Daigaku, 1972.

Mai Zhonghua, comp. *Huangying jingubi nuen rinlun* [A new collection of imperial statecraft writings]. Taibei: n.p., 1965.

Mair, Victor. "Buddhism and the Rise of the Written Vernacular in East Asia: The Making of National Languages." *JAS* 53, no. 3 (1994): 707–751.

Mackerras, Colin. "The Drama of the Qing Dynasty." In *Chinese Theater: From Its Origins to the Present Day*, ed. Colin Mackerras, 92–117. Honolulu: University of Hawaii Press, 1983.

Mansvelt Beck, B. J. *The Treatises of Later Han: Their Author, Sources, Contents, and Place in Chinese Historiography*. Leiden: E. J. Brill, 1990.

March, Andrew L. *The Idea of China: Myth and Theory in Geographic Thought*. New York: Praeger, 1974.

Matsushita Tadashi. *Edo jidai no shifu shiron* [Theories and styles of poetry in the Edo period]. Tokyo: Meiji shoin, 1969.

Mayo, Marlene J. "The Korean Crisis of 1873 and Early Meiji Foreign Policy." *JAS* 31, no. 4 (1972): 793–819.

McCraw, David R. *Chinese Lyricists of the Seventeenth Century*. Honolulu: University of Hawaii Press, 1990.

Meiroku Zasshi: Journal of the Japanese Enlightenment, trans. William Reynolds Braisted. Cambridge, Mass.: Harvard University Press, 1976.

Miller, Roy Andrew. *The Japanese Language*. Chicago: University of Chicago Press, 1967.

Mills, J. V. "Chinese Coastal Maps." *Imago Mundi* 11 (1954): 151–168.

Min Ze. *Zhongguo wenxue lilun piping shi* [A history of Chinese literary theory and criticism]. Beijing: Renmin chubanshe, 1981.

Morris, Ivan. *The Nobility of Failure*. New York: Holt, Reinhart, and Winston, 1975.

Mote, Frederick W. "The Arts and the 'Theorizing Mode' of the Civilization." In *Artists and Traditions: Uses of the Past in Chinese Culture*, ed. Christian F. Murck, 3–8. Princeton: Princeton University Press, 1976.

——. "Reflections on the First Complete Printing of the *Ssu-k'u Ch'üan-shu*." *Gest Library Journal* 1, no. 2 (Spring 1987): 26–50.

Munn, Nancy D. "The Cultural Anthropology of Time: A Critical Essay." *Annual Review of Anthropology* 21 (1992): 93–123.

Murata Masashi. *Nanbokuchō ron.* [On the northern and southern dynasties]. Tokyo: Shibundō, 1959.

Nakamura Keiu. "Gi taiseijin jōsho" [A memorial on the imitation of Westerners]. In *Meiji keimō shisō shū* [Selections from the Thought of the Meiji Enlightenment], ed. Ōkubo Toshiaki, 281–283. Tokyo: Chikuma, 1967.

——, ed. *Dōjinsha bungaku zasshi* [The literary journal of the Society for a Common Humanity]. 1880.

Nakane Shuku. *Heiyō Nihon chiri shōshi* [A short treatise on the military essentials of Japanese geography]. Rev. ed. Tokyo: n.p., [1875].

Naquin, Susan, and Chün-fang Yü, eds. *Pilgrims and Sacred Sites in China*. Berkeley: University of California Press, 1992.

Needham, Joseph. "Geography and Cartography." In *Science and Civilization in China*, vol. 3, *Mathematics and the Sciences of the Heavens and the Earth*. Cambridge: Cambridge University Press, 1959.

Nishijima Sadao. *Yamataikoku to Wakoku: Kodai Nihon to Higashi Ajia* [Yamato and Wo: Ancient Japan and East Asia]. Tokyo: Ishikawa kobunkan, 1994.

Nivison, David S. *The Life and Thought of Chang Hsüeh-ch'eng (1738–1801)*. Stanford: Stanford University Press, 1966.

Norman, E. H. *Origins of the Modern Japanese State: Selected Writings of E. H. Norman*. New York: Pantheon, 1975.

Norman, Jerry. *Chinese*. Cambridge: Cambridge University Press, 1988.

Ŏ Sukkwŏn. *A Korean Storyteller's Miscellany: The P'aegwan Chapki of Ŏ Sukkwŏn*, [trans.] Peter H. Lee. Princeton: Princeton University Press, 1989.

Okamoto Koseki, ed. *Meiji Kanshi bunshū* [A collection of Chinese poetry in the Meiji]. Tokyo: Chikuma, 1983.

Ono Jitsunosuke. "Keitaimen kara mita Kō Junken no shi" [Examining Huang Zunxian's poetry from the standpoint of form]. *Chūgoku koten kenkyū* 12 (December 1964): 55–69.

Ōtsuki Fumihiko. *Shina bunten* [Chinese grammar]. Tokyo: n.p., [1877].

Ouyang Xiu. "Riben dao ge" [Song of the Japanese sword]. In *Ouyang Wenzhong Gong wenji* [Collected writings of Master Ouyang Wenzhong], *juan* 54 [*waiji juan* 4]: 7. N.p., n.d.

Owen, Stephen. *The Great Age of Chinese Poetry: The High T'ang*. New Haven: Yale University Press, 1981.

——. "Meaning the Words: The Genuine as a Value in the Tradition of the Song Lyric." In *Voices of the Song Lyric in China*, ed. Pauline Yu, 30–69. Berkeley: University of California Press, 1993.

——. *Remembrances; The Experience of the Past in Classical Chinese Literature*. Cambridge, Mass.: Harvard University Press, 1986.

——. *Traditional Chinese Poetry and Poetics: Omen of the World*. Madison: University of Wisconsin Press, 1985.

Peng Tse-chou. *Chūgoku no kindaika to Meiji ishin* [China's modernization and the Meiji Restoration]. Kyoto: Dōbōsha, 1976.

Peterson, Willard. "The Life of Ku Yen-wu (1613–1682)." *HJAS* 28 (1968): 114–156; 29 (1969): 201–247.

Plaks, Andrew H. "Towards a Critical Theory of Chinese Narrative." In *Chinese Narrative: Critical and Theoretical Essays*, ed. Andrew H. Plaks, 309–352. Princeton: Princeton University Press, 1977.

Polachek, James M. *The Inner Opium War*. Cambridge, Mass.: Harvard University, Council on East Asian Studies, 1992.

Pollard, David. *A Chinese Look at Literature: The Literary Values of Chou Tso-jen in Relation to the Tradition*. Berkeley: University of California Press, 1973.

Proceedings of the International Conference on Chinese Local Gazetteers. Published as "Fangzhi xue guoji yanjiu taohui lunwenjihao." *Hanxue yanjiu* 3, no. 2 (December 1985).

Qian Mu. *Zhongguo jin sanbainian xueshu shi* [A history of learning in China during the past three hundred years]. Shanghai: Shangwu shuju, 1939.

Quan Hansheng. "Qingmo de 'Xixue yuan chu Zhongguo' shuo" [The late Qing theory "Western learning originated in China"]. In *Zhongguo jindaishi luncong* [Collected essays on modern Chinese history], ed. Li Dingyi, ser. 1, 5:216–258. Taibei: Zhengzhong shuju, 1956.

Quan Zuwang. "Tinglin Xiansheng shendao biao" [Commemorating the marvellous way of Master Tinglin]. In *Jiqiting ji* [Collections of the Jiqi Pavilion], *juan* 12. Reprinted in *Ming Qing shiliao huibian* [Collected historical materials from the Ming and Qing], ser. 5, vol. 3 [vol. 41], Taibei: Wenhai chubanshe, n.d.

Ren Hongzhang. "Cong *Zhupi yuzhi* kan Kang/Yong shiqi de Zhong-Ri jiaoshe." [Chinese-Japanese interactions during the Kang Xi and Yong Zheng reigns, as seen in *Imperial Comments in Vermilion*]. In *Zhong-Ri quanxishi lunji: Di er ji*, 38–53.

Reynolds, Carol Tyson. "East Meets East: Chinese Views of Early Meiji Japan." Ph.D. diss., Columbia University, 1986.

Reynolds, Douglas R. "Training Young China Hands: Tōa Dōbunkai and Its Precursors, 1886–1945." In *The Japanese Informal Empire in China, 1895–1937*, ed. Peter Duus et al., 210–271. Princeton: Princeton University Press, 1989.

Riben suo zhi [Sundry records of Japan]. In *XFHZ, zhi* 10: 306.

Roden, Donald. *Schooldays in Imperial Japan: A Study in the Culture of a Student Elite.* Berkeley: University of California Press, 1980.

Ross, Kristin. *The Emergence of Social Space: Rimbaud and the Paris Commune.* Minneapolis: University of Minnesota Press, 1988.

Sahlins, Marshall. *Historical Metaphors and Mythical Realities: Structure in the Early History of the Sandwich Islands Kingdom.* Ann Arbor: University of Michigan Press, 1981.

——. *Islands of History.* Chicago: University of Chicago Press, 1985.

Sakai, Naoki. *Voices of the Past: The Status of Language in Eighteenth-Century Japanese Discourse.* Ithaca: Cornell University Press, 1991.

Sanetō Keishū. *Chūgokujin Nihon-ryūgaku shi* [A history of Chinese overseas students in Japan]. Enlarged ed. Tokyo: Kuroshio shuppan, 1981.

——. *Chūgoku ryūgakusei shitan* [On the history of Chinese foreign students]. Tokyo: Daiichi shobō, 1981.

——. *Kindai Nisshi bunka ron* [On modern Sino-Japanese culture]. Tokyo: Daitō Shuppansha, 1941.

——. *Meiji Nisshi bunka kōshō* [Sino-Japanese cultural interaction during Meiji]. Tokyo: Kofukan, 1943.

——, ed. and trans. *Ōkōchi bunsho* [The Ōkōchi documents]. Tokyo: Heibonsha, 1964.

Satō Saburō. *Kindai Nitchū kōshōshi no kenkyū* [Studies on modern Chinese-Japanese interaction]. Tokyo: Yoshikawa kōbunkan, 1983.

——. "Kōakai ni kansuru ichi kosatsu" [One investigation of the Kōakai]. *Yamagata Daigaku kiyō: jimbun kagaku* [Yamagata university bulletin: Human sciences] 1, no. 4 (August 1951): 399–411.

——. "Meiji ishin igo Nisshin sensō izen ni okeru Shinajin no Nihon kenkyū" [Chinese research on Japan between the Meiji Restoration and the Sino-Japanese War]. *Rekishigaku kenkyū* 10, no. 11 [no. 83] (11/1940): 47–87.

Schafer, Edward H. *The Golden Peaches of Samarkand: A Study of T'ang Exotics.* Berkeley: University of California Press, 1963.

Schlegel, Gustaaf. "Problèmes géographiques: Les Peuples étrangers chez les historiens chinois: Fou-Sang Kouo." *T'oung Pao* 3 (1892): 101–168.

Schmidt, J. D. *Within the Human Realm: The Poetry of Huang Zunxian, 1848–1905.* Cambridge: Cambridge University Press, 1994.

Shan hai jing jiaozhu [The *Classic of Mountains and Oceans*], ann. Yuan Ke. Shanghai: Shanghai guji chubanshe, 1980.

Shen Jiache et al. *Nan Song zashi shi* [Divers poems of the Southern Soong]. N.p., n.d.

Shen Ren'an. *Wakoku to higashi Ajia* [The Wo Kingdom and east Asia]. Tokyo: Rokkō Shuppan, 1990.

Smith, Barbara Herrnstein. *Poetic Closure: A Study of How Poems End.* Chicago: University of Chicago Press, 1968.

Smith, Richard J. *China's Cultural Heritage: The Ch'ing Dynasty, 1644–1912.* Boulder: Westview Press, 1983.

Strassberg, Richard E. *Inscribed Landscapes: Travel Writing from Imperial China.* Berkeley: University of California Press, 1994.

Sugimoto, Masayoshi, and David J. Swain. *Science and Culture in Traditional Japan.* Cambridge: MIT Press, 1978.

Sugishita Motoakira. "Edo Kanshi ni okeru Nitchū kōryū no ichidanmen: Matsushita Umeoka to Shin no Wan Pon" [A phase of Japan-China interaction in Edo-period Chinese poetry: Matsushita Umeoka and China's Wang Peng]. *Kokugo to kokubungaku* no. 838 (10/1993): 16–27.

Sun Dian, ed. *Guiwei chongjiu yan jibian* [Collection from the feast held on Double Ninth Festival, 1883]. N.p., n.d.

Suzuki Shūji. *Bunmei no kotoba* [The vocabulary of enlightenment]. Hiroshima: Bunka hyōron, 1981.

Suzuki Torao. *Shina shiron shi* [A history of Chinese poetic theory]. Tokyo: Kobundō, 1927.

Takagi Kikusaburō. *Nihon ni okeru chizu sokuryō no hattatsu ni kansuru kenkyū* [Studies on the development of map surveying in Japan]. Tokyo: Kazema shobō, 1966.

Tanaka, Stefan. *Japan's Orient: Rendering Pasts into History.* Berkeley: University of California Press, 1993.

Tang Zupei. *Xin fangzhi xue* [A new study of the geographic treatise]. Taibei: Huaguo chubanshe, 1955.

Toby, Ronald P. *State and Diplomacy in Early Modern Japan: Asia in the Development of the Tokugawa Bakufu.* Princeton: Princeton University Press, 1984.

Tsiang, T. F. "Sino-Japanese Diplomatic Relations, 1870–1894." *Chinese Social and Political Science Review* 17 (1933): 1–106.

Tsien Tsuen-hsuin. "A History of Bibliographic Classification in China." *Library Quarterly* 22, no. 4 (10/1952): 307–324.

Tsuchida Mitsufumi. *Meiji Taishō no shingo-ryūkōgo* [New and popular vocabulary in the Meiji and Taishō periods]. Tokyo: Kakugawa, 1983.

Tu Wei-ming. "Profound Learning, Personal Knowledge, and Poetic Vision." In *The Vitality of the Lyric Voice: Shih Poetry from the Late Han to the T'ang*, ed. Shuen-fu Lin and Stephen Owen, 3–31. Princeton: Princeton University Press, 1986.

Tuan, Yifu. *Space and Place: The Perspective of Experience*. Minneapolis: University of Minnesota Press, 1977.

Van Zoeren, Steven. *Poetry and Personality: Reading, Exegesis, and Hermeneutics in Traditional China*. Stanford: Stanford University Press, 1991.

Varley, H. Paul. *Imperial Restoration in Medieval Japan*. New York: Columbia University Press, 1971.

Volosinov, V. N. *Marxism and the Philosophy of Language*. Trans. Ladislav Matejka and I. R. Titunik. New York: Seminar Press, 1973.

Waley, Arthur. *Yuan Mei: Eighteenth-Century Chinese Poet*. New York: Macmillan, 1957.

Waley-Cohen, Joanna. "China and Western Technology in the Late Eighteenth Century." *American Historical Review* 98, no. 5 (12/1993): 1525–1544.

Wang Dezhao. "Huang Zunxian suo jian zhi Riben" [The Japan seen by Huang Zunxian]. In *Sino-Japanese Cultural Interchange*, vol. 3, *The Economic and Intellectual Aspects*, ed. Yuehim Tam, 113–125. Hong Kong: Chinese University of Hong Kong, 1985.

Wang, Erh-min. "The 'Turn of Fortune' (*Yun-hui*): Inherited Concepts and China's Response to the West." In *Cosmology, Ontology, and Human Efficacy: Essays in Chinese Thought*, ed. Richard J. Smith and D. W. Y. Kwok, 205–215. Honolulu: University of Hawaii Press, 1993.

Wang Ermin [Wang, Erh-min]. "Wanqing waijiao sixiang de xingcheng" [The formation of diplomatic thought in the late Qing]. In *Zhongyang yanjiuyuan jindaishi yanjiusuo jikan* [Collected papers of the Modern History Institute of Academia Sinica] 1 (8/1969): 19–46.

Wang Peng. *Xiu hai bian* [An essay on ocean passages]. [1764?]. Reprinted in *XFHZ*, zhi 10: 269–273.

Wang Tao. *Fusang youji* [Travels in Fusang]. Tokyo: Kunten shuppan, [1880].

——. *Taoyuan wenlu waibian* [Additional essays from Taoyuan]. Hong Kong: n.p., [1883].

Wang Wei. "Song mishu Zhao Jian hui Ribenguo" [For Secretary Zhao on his return to Japan]. In *Wang Ruocheng ji jianzhu* [Annotated selections from the works of Wang Ruocheng]. Beijing: Zhonghua shuju, 1961.

Wang Xiangrong. "'Abei Zhongmalu' han jibei/zhenbei" [Abe Nakamaro and the mythical and real details]. In *Cong Xu Fu dao Huang Zunxian* [From Xu Fu to Huang Zunxian], ed. Yang Zhengguang, 79–99. Beijing: Shishi chubanshe, 1985.

———. *Gudai de Zhongguo yu Riben* [China and Japan in antiquity]. Beijing: Sanguan shudian, 1989.

———. *Riben jiaoxi* [Japanese teachers]. Beijing: Sanlian shudian, 1988.

———. *Zhong-Ri guanxishi wenxian lunkao* [Critical examinations of documents for the history of Chinese-Japanese relations]. Changsha: Yuelu shushe, 1985.

Wang Xianqian. *Riben yuanliu kao* [An examination of Japan's origin and development]. [Changsha]: Sixian shuju, [1902].

Wang Xiaoqin. "Huang Zunxian *Riben guozhi* chutan" [A preliminary examination of Huang Zunxian's *Japan Treatise*]. In *Zhong-Ri wenhua jiaoliu shi lunwenji* [A collection of essays on the history of Sino-Japanese cultural interaction], ed. Beijingshi Zhong-Ri wenhua jiaoliushi yanjiuhui, 222–256. Beijing: Renmin chubanshe, 1982.

———. *Jindai Zhong-Ri qishi lu* [Records of modern Chinese-Japanese revelations]. Beijing: Beijing chubanshe, 1987.

———, ed. *Zaoqi Riben youji wuzhong* [Five early travel accounts of Japan]. Changsha: Hunan renmin chubanshe, 1983.

Wang Xiqi, comp. *Xiaofanghuzhai yudi cong chao* [Collected reprints on geography from the "Little Square Hu" Studio]. Shanghai: Zhuyi tang, [1877–1897].

———, comp. *Xiaofanghuzhai yudi cong chao bupian* [Supplement to the collected reprints on geography from the "Little Square Hu" Studio]. Shanghai: [1877–1897?]; reprinted Taibei: Guangwen shuju, 1964.

Wang Yi-t'ung. *Official Relations between China and Japan, 1368–1549*. Cambridge, Mass.: Harvard University Press, 1953.

Wang Yong. *Zhongguo dilixue shi* [A history of Chinese geography]. Changsha: Shangwu yinshuguan, 1938.

Wang Zhichun. *Qingchao rouyuan ji* [Records of Qing dynastic grace to distant peoples]. N.p., [1876]. Reprinted Beijing: Zhonghua shuju, 1989.

———. *Tan ying lu* [Records from overseas]. N.p.: Shangyang wenyi zhai, [1880].

Wei Tingsheng. *The Birth of Japan*. Taibei: China Academy, 1975.

———. *Riben Shenwu kaiguo xinkao* [A new examination of the Japanese Jimmu's founding of the nation]. Hong Kong: Commercial Press, 1950.

———. *Xu Fu yu Riben* [Xu Fu and Japan]. Hong Kong: Commercial Press, 1953.

Wei Yuan. *Hai guo tu zhi* [Illustrated treatise on the sea kingdoms]. Shanghai: Shanghai shuju shiyin, [1895]. Reprinted as *Zengdu hai guo tu zhi* [The enlarged treatise on the sea kingdoms]. Taibei: Guiting chubanshe, 1979.

Weng Fanggang. *Shizhou shihua* [Poetry talks from Shizhou], ed. Chen Erdong. Beijing: Renmin chubanshe, 1981.

Weng Tongwen. "Cong shehui-wenhuashi guandian lun fangzhi de fasheng fazhan" [On the appearance and development of local histories from the point of view of social and cultural history]. *Hanxue yanjiu* [Chinese studies] 3, no. 2 (12/1985): 39–57.

White, Hayden. *The Content of the Form: Narrative Discourse and Historical Representation*. Baltimore: Johns Hopkins University Press, 1987.

Wilkinson, Endymion. *The History of Imperial China: A Research Guide*. Cambridge, Mass.: Harvard University, Council on East Asian Studies, 1973.

Williams, Raymond. *Keywords: A Vocabulary of Culture and Society*. New York: Oxford University Press, 1976.

Winichakul, Thongchai. *Siam Mapped: A History of the Geo-Body of a Nation*. Honolulu: University of Hawaii Press, 1994.

Wong, Wai-leung. "Chinese Impressionistic Criticism: A Study of the Poetry-Talk (Shih-Hua Tz'u-Hua) Tradition." Ph.D. diss., Ohio State University, 1976.

Wright, Mary Clabaugh. *The Last Stand of Chinese Conservatism: The T'ung-Chih Restoration, 1862–1874*. Stanford: Stanford University Press, 1957.

Wu Anlong and Xiong Dayun. *Chūgokujin no Nihon kenkyū shi* [A history of Chinese studies of Japan]. Tokyo: Rokkō shuppan, 1989.

Wu Hongyi. *Qingdai shixue chutan* [Preliminary investigations of Qing poetic theory]. Rev. ed. Taibei: Xuesheng shuju, 1985.

Wu Hongyi and Ye Qingbing, eds. *Qingdai wenxue piping ziliao huibian* [Edited materials on Qing literary criticism]. Taibei: Chengwen chubanshe, 1979.

Wu Jianqing. "Huang Zunxian de shige lilun han *Renjinglu shicao*" [Huang Zunxian's poetic theory and the *Draft Poems from the Renjing Hut*]. *Hua'nan shiyuan xuebao—zhexue shehui kexue ban*. [Journal of the Huanan Teachers' Academy—philosophy and social science edition] 26 (1980, no. 3): 85–95.

Wu Sheng et al. *Shanghai xian xuzhi* [A continuation of the Shanghai District treatise.] Shanghai, 1918. Reprinted Taibei: Chengwen, 1970.

Wu Tianren. *Huang Gongdu Xiansheng zhuan'gao* [A draft biography of Master Huang Gongdu]. Hong Kong: Zhongwen Daxue chuban, 1972.

Xi Yufu and Shen Shixu, comps. *Huangchao zhengdian leizuan* [A compendium of imperial laws and regulations]. Shanghai, 1903. Reprinted Taibei: Wenhai, 1974–.

Xu Gongsheng. "Fuzhou yu Neishuang guanxishi chu tan" [Preliminary investigations into the history of relations between Fuzhou and Naha]. In *Zhong-Ri guanxishi lunji: Di er ji*, 23–38.

Xu Jiyu. *Ying huan zhi lue* [A short treatise on the ocean circuits]. [1850]. Reprinted Taibei: Huawen shuju, n.d.

Xue Fucheng. *Chushi siguo riji* [A diary of ambassadorial service to four nations]. N.p., [1892]. Reprinted Changsha: Hunan renmin chubanshe, 1981.

——. *The European Diary of Hsieh Fucheng: Envoy Extraordinary of Imperial China*. Trans. Helen Hsieh Chien. New York: St. Martin's Press, 1993.

Xue Jun. *Riben kao lue* [Concise investigations of Japan]. [1523]; reprinted in the *Congshu jicheng: Chu bian* [Complete collections; First series], *ce* 3,278 [vol. 131]. Shanghai: Shangwu yinyingben, 1935.

Yamanoi Yū. "Ko Enbu no gakumonkan" [Gu Yanwu's view of scholarship]. *Chūō Daigaku bungakubu kiyō* 35 (1964): 67–93.

Yang, Lien-sheng. "The Organization of Chinese Official Historiography: Principles and Methods of the Standard Histories from the T'ang through the Ming Dynasty." In *Historians of China and Japan*, ed. W. G. Beasley and E. G. Pulleyblank, 44–59. London: Oxford University Press, 1961.

Yang Tianshi. *Huang Zunxian*. Shanghai: Renmin chubanshe, 1979.

Yao Nai. *Xibaoxuan shulu* [Book reviews by Yao Nai]. Ed. Mao Yusheng. In *Xibaoxuan yishu sanzhong* [Three posthumous works by Yao Nai], ed. Xu Zongliang, *ce* 3. N.p., [1879].

Yao Wendong. *Dong cha za zhu* [Miscellaneous writings from the Eastern Mission]. N.p., [1893].

——. *Haiwai tongren ji* [A collection from overseas fellows]. Ed. Kawada Kōshō. N.p., n.d.

——. *Riben dili bingyao* [The military essentials of Japanese geography]. Beijing: Zongli yamen, [1884].

Ye Qingyi and Yuan Zuzhi. *Ce ao za zhi* [Random pickings from a dragon ride]. Shanghai: n.p., [1889].

Ye Songshi. *Fusang lichang ji* [A collection of parting songs from Fusang]. N.p., [1891].

Yee, Cordell D. K. "Chinese Maps in Political Culture." In *The History of Cartography*, vol. 2, bk. 2, *Cartography in the Traditional East and Southeast Asian Societies*, ed. J. B. Harley and David Woodward, 71–95. Chicago: University of Chicago Press, 1994.

Yin Guangren and Zhang Rulin. *Aomen ji lue* [A short record of Macao]. Reprinted in *Zhongshan wenxian*, vol. 8. Taibei: Taiwan xuesheng shuju, 1965.

Yong Rong et al. *Siku quanshu zongmu tiyao* [Annotated catalogue of the *Complete Books of the Four Treasuries*]. [Shanghai]: Shangwu yinshuguan, n.d.

Yoshikawa Kōjirō. *Gen Min shi gaisetsu*. Tokyo: Iwanami, 1963. Trans. John Timothy Wixted as *Five Hundred Years of Chinese Poetry, 1150–1650: The Chin, Yuan, and Ming Dynasties*. Princeton: Princeton University Press, 1989.

——. *An Introduction to Sung Poetry*. Trans. Burton Watson. Cambridge, Mass.: Harvard University Press, 1967.

——. *Jinsai, Sorai, Norinaga: Three Classical Philologists of Mid-Tokugawa Japan*. Tokyo: Tōhō gakkai, 1983.

You Tong. *Waiguo zhuzhi ci* [Bamboo stalk lyrics on the foreign domains]. Reprinted in *Zhaodai congshu* [Collected works reflecting the ages], *Jia ji* [first series], *ce* 3, *juan* 3. N.p.: Shikai tang, [1876].

Yu, Pauline. *The Reading of Imagery in the Chinese Poetic Tradition*. Princeton: Princeton University Press, 1987.

Yu, Ying-shih. "Some Preliminary Observations on the Rise of Ch'ing Confucian Intellectualism." *Tsing-Hua Journal of Chinese Studies* n.s. 11, nos. 1–2 (12/1975): 105–146.

Yu Zhengxie. *Guisi lei gao* [Classified Manuscripts of the Year "Guisi"]. [1833]. Reprinted in *Anhui cong shu* [Collected works from Anhui Province], ser. 3, *ce* 7–18.

Yuan Zuzhi. *Tan ying lu* [Records from overseas]. Shanghai: Tongwen shuju, [1885].

Zeng Jize. *Chushi Ying/Fa/Eguo riji* [A diary of the first embassy to England, France, and Russia]. Changsha: Yueli shushe, 1985.

——. *Chushi Ying/Fa riji* [A diary of the first embassy to England and France]. Reprinted in *XFHZ*, *ce* 58 [*zhi* 11, pt. 4]: 385–405.

Zeng Yongling. *Guo Songtao dazhuan* [The major biography of Guo Songtao]. Shenyang: Liaoning renmin chubanshe, 1989.

Zhang Deyi. *Hang hai shu qi* [A description of curiosities overseas]. [1870]. Reprinted Changsha: Hunan renmin chubanshe, 1981.

——. *San shu qi* [A third description of curiosities]. [1873?]. Reprinted as *Sui shi Faguo ji* [An account of the diplomatic mission to France]. Changsha: Hunan renmin chubanshe, 1982.

——. *Zai shu qi* [A second description of curiosities]. [1875?]. Reprinted as *Ou Mei huan youji* [An account of travels through Europe and America]. Changsha: Hunan renmin chubanshe, 1981.

Zhang Pengyuan. "Huang Zunxian de zhengzhi sixiang ji qi dui Liang Qichao de yingxiang" [The political thought of Huang Zunxian and its influence on Liang Qichao]. In *Zhongyang yanjiuyuan jindaishi yanjiusuo jikan* [Collected papers of the Modern History Institute of Academia Sinica] 1 (8/1969): 217–237.

Zhang Shouyong et al., comps. *Huangchao zhanggu huibian* [A collection of imperial documents]. 1902. Reprinted Taibei: Wenhai, 1964.

Zhang Xuecheng. *Wenshi tongyi* [General principles of writing and history]. Shanghai: Shangwu yinshuguan, 1933.

——. *Zhangshi yishu* [Posthumous works of Master Zhang]. Wuxing: Jiayetang, 1922.

Zhang Yunqiao and Zhang Lifan. "Wan Ming yi dui Riben yanjiu gaishu" [An outline of Late Ming studies of Japan]. In *Zhong-Ri guanxishi lunji: Di er ji*, 12–21.

Zheng Hailin. *Huang Zunxian yu jindai Zhongguo* [Huang Zunxian and modern China]. Beijing: Sanlian shudian, 1988.

Zheng Ziyu and Sanetō Keishū, eds. *Huang Zunxian yu Riben youren bitan yigao* [Manuscripts of brushtalks between Huang Zunxian and his Japanese friends]. Taibei: Wenhai chubanshe, 1968.

Zhigang. *Chushi taixi ji* [A record of the first embassy to the West]. Beijing: Longfusi; Shishutang, [1877]. Reprinted Changsha: Hunan renmin chubanshe, 1981.

Zhong-Ri guanxishi lunji: Di er ji [Collected articles on the history of Chinese-Japanese relations, 2d ser.]. Ed. Dongbei diqu Zhong-Ri guanxishi yanjiuhui [Manchuria Research Group on the History of Chinese-Japanese Relations]. Jilin: Renmin chubanshe, 1984.

Zhong-Ri guanxishi ziliao huibian [Collected materials on the history of Chinese-Japanese relations]. Ed. Wang Xiangrong and Xia Yingyuan. Beijing: Zhonghua shuju, 1984.

Zhong-Ri wenhua yu jiaoliu: Di yi ji [Chinese-Japanese culture and interaction, 1st ser.]. Ed. Yang Zhengguang et al. Beijing: Zhongguo zhanwang chubanshe, 1984.

Zhou Yi jinzhu jinyi [The Zhou *Classic of Changes*, with contemporary annotations and translations]. Ann. and trans. Nan Huaijin and Xu Qinting. Taibei: Shangwu yinshuguan, 1974.

Zhou Zuoren. "Lun Huang Gongdu de *Riben zashi shi*" [On the *Poems on Divers Japanese Affairs* by Huang Gongdu]. In *Renjinglu congkao* [On the Renjing Hut collections], ed. Zheng Ziyu, 19–25. Singapore: Shangwu yinshuguan, 1959.

Zhu Chongsheng. "Luanzhou zhi zhi zuanxiu jingguo ji qi shifa bijiao" [The compilation process of Luanzhou treatises and a comparison of their historical methods]. *Hanxue yanjiu* 3, no. 2 (12/1985): 121–138.

Zhu Xi. *Zhuzi yulei* [Discussions with Master Zhu, by category], ed. Wang Xingxian. Beijing: Zhonghua shuju, 1986.

Zhu Yizun. "Ba *Wu qi jing*" [A note on the *Mirror of Azuma*]. In *Pushuting ji* [Collections from the Pushu Pavilion], *juan* 44: 12b–13a. Shanghai: Shangwu yining, 1929.

Zhu Ziqing. *Shi yan zhi bian* [A study of "poetry verbalizes intention"]. Beijing: Guji chubanshe, 1956.

Zito, Angela Rose. "Re-presenting Sacrifice: Cosmology and the Editing of Texts." *Ch'ing-shih wen-t'i* 5, no. 2 (12/1984): 47–78.

Zuo Zongtang. *Zuo Wenxiang Gong zougao* [Collected memorials of Zuo Wenxiang]. In *Zuo Wenxiang Gong quanji* [Complete works of Zuo Wenxiang]. Changsha: n.p., [1890].

Glossary

Aomen ji lue 澳門紀略

baishi 稗史

banben 板本

bian 編

biange 變革

bianye yao tou, you gou yao wei 辮爺搖頭猶狗搖尾

biji 筆記

bitan 筆談

bu zhi changshi shi he chong 不知常世是何蟲

bunmeikaika 文明開化

Ce ao za zhi 策鰲雜摭

chaogong zhi guo 朝貢之國

Chen Jialin 陳家麟

Chen Lunjiong 陳倫炯

Chen Qiyuan 陳其元

Chenglin 成林

Chou hai tu hian 籌海圖編

Chunxiang zhui bi 蓴鄉贅筆

ci 詞

Dai Jitao 戴季陶

Dai Zhen 戴震

de 的

dianqibao 電氣報

dianxin 電信

dili 地理

Dili bei kao 地理備考

Dili shuo lue 地理說略

Dong cha wenjian lu 東槎聞見錄

Dong Han 董含

dong ren   東人

Dong wo kao   東倭考

dong yi   東夷

dong ying   東瀛

dong you   東遊

donglaifa   東來法

dongyangche   東洋車

er   耳

er . . . nai . . .   而 . . . 乃 . . .

eryue chang kai xian'ai hua   二月常開仙艾花

fa   法

falü (J: *hōritsu*)   法律

Fan hai xiao lu   汎海小錄

fang   方

fangyan   方言

fangzhi   方志 (誌)

fenfen min   紛紛民

Feng Guifen   馮桂芬

fengtuji   風土記

fu (narrative poem)   賦

fu (prefecture)   府

Fu Yunlong   傅雲龍

fugu   復古

Fusang   扶桑

ge (form)   格

ge (song)   歌

ge wu   格物

geng   更

gonghe (J: *kyōwa*)   共和

Gu Houkun   顧厚焜

Gu Yanwu   顧炎武

guan hua   官話

Guisi lei gao   癸巳類稿

guo   猓

Guo Songtao　郭嵩燾

guo yu　國語

guowang　國王

Hai guo tu zhi　海國圖志

Hai guo wenjian lu　海國聞見錄

han　藩

hanwen (J: *kanbun*)　漢文

hanzi (J: *kanji*)　漢字

Hê Ruzhang　何如璋

Heiyō Nihon chiri shōshi　兵要日本地理小誌

hitsuwa　筆話

Hong Shiwei　洪士偉

houlai geng za xiexing shu　後來更雜蟹行書

hu chuang　胡床

Hu Zongxian　胡宗憲

Huang Liuhong　黃六鴻

Huang Qing tong kao　皇清通考

Huang Zongxi　黃宗羲

Huang Zunxian (Gongdu)　黃遵憲 (公度)

huaxue　化學

huo (J: wa / Yamato)　和

huolunche　火輪車

huolunchuan　火輪船

Ishikawa Ei (Hongzhai)　石川英 (鴻齋)

Iwagaki Matsunae　巌垣松苗

ji (note / record)　記

ji (stool)　几

jiaming (J: *kana*)　假名

jian ai　兼愛

jiangyu　疆域

jili　肌理

jin　近

Jin Anqing　金安清

jingli　經理

jingshijimin (J: *keiseisaimin*)   經世濟民

jishu   技術

jiyu   寄語

jueju   絕句

jun   君

junxian   郡縣

kanben   刊本

Kang Youwei   康有為

kaozheng   考證

ke yong   可用

ken   縣

koku   石

Kokushi ryaku   國史略

Kunyu tu shuo   坤輿圖說

lei   類

leishu   類書

li (1/3 mile)   里

li (principle, reason, order)   理

li (propriety)   禮

li (utility, benefit)   利

Li E   厲鶚

Li Hongzhang   李鴻章

Li Shuchang   黎庶昌

Li Wei   李衛

Li Xiaopu   李篠圃

Li Xingong   李信恭

Li Xu   李煦

Liao Xi'en (Quxian)   廖錫恩 (樞仙)

liezhuan   列傳

Lin Zexu   林則徐

Liu Xi   劉熙

lu   錄

Luo Sen   羅森

lüshi   律詩

Ma Jishi　瑪吉士

Mai Ersen　麥爾森

Mao Yuanyi　茅元儀

minfa (J: *minpō*)　民法

ming　名

minquan (J: *minken*)　民權

mofang xifa　模仿西法

Mori Shuntō　森春濤

Nakane Shuku　中根淑

nan yang　南洋

Nansong zashi shi　南宋雜事詩

Oka Senjin (Lumen)　岡千仞 (鹿門)

Ōkōchi Teruna (Guige)　大河内輝聲 (桂閣)

Ōnuma Chinzan　大沼枕山

ping　坪

putong hua　普通話

qi　氣

Quan Zuwang　全祖望

Rai San'yō　賴山陽

renliche　人力車

renqing　人情

Riben bianzheng kao　日本變政考

Riben dili bingyao　日本地理兵要

Riben fengtu ji　日本風土記

Riben guozhi　日本國志

Riben jinshi ji　日本近事記

Riben kao　日本考

Riben kao lue　日本考略

Riben lun　日本論

Riben tu zuan　日本圖纂

Riben xinzheng kao　日本新政考

Riben yuanliu kao　日本源流考

Riben za yong　日本雜詠

Riben zhuan　日本傳

Sha Qiyun　沙起雲

shei shuo furong jiang shang mao/hong yan yidai you weiji
　　誰說芙蓉江上貌／紅顏一代有危機

Shen Jiache　沈嘉轍

Shen Wenying (Meishi)　沈文熒 (梅史)

shendao (J: Shintō)　神道

shenjiao　神教

shi (event)　事

shi (poem)　詩

Shi ming　釋名

shi shi qiu shi　實事求是

shi yan zhi　詩言志

Shigeno Yasutsugu　重野安繹

shihui (J: *shikai*)　詩會

shixue　實學

shu　書

shuchu (J: *yushutsu*)　輸出

shuguo　屬國

shuru (J: *yu'nyū*)　輸入

Si zhou zhi　四洲志

Siku quanshu　四庫全書

Song shi ji shi　宋詩紀事

Tai e　太阿

Takezoe Shin'ichirō　竹添進一郎

ti　體

ti wu　體物

Tianxia junguo libing shu　天下郡國利病書

tiaofen　條分

tiaoli (proportionally ordered)　條例

tiaoli (reasonably ordered/"reasoned order")　條理

tiaolie　條列

tiedao　鐵道

tielu　鐵路

tong lei　同類

tong ren   同人

tong wen   同文

tong wen zhi bang   同文之邦

tong wen zhi guo   同文之國

tong zhong   同種

tong zhou   同洲

tongji (J: *tōkei*)   統計

wabun   和文

Waiguo shi lue   外國史略

Waiguo zhuzhi ci   外國竹枝詞

Waishi   外史

Wang Fanqing (Qinxian)   王藩清 (菜仙)

Wang Fuzhi   王夫之

Wang Shizhen   王士禎

Wang Tao   王韜

Wang Xianqian   王先謙

Wang Yun   王惲

Wang Zhiben (Qiyuan)   王治本 (黍園)

Wang Zhichun   王之春

Wanguo dili quantuji   萬國地理全圖集

Wei Yuan   魏源

weixin (J: *ishin*)   維新

wen yi zai dao   文以載道

Weng Fanggang   翁方綱

wenhua   文化

wenli   文理

wenming   文明

wenxue   文學

wenyan wen   文言文

wenzi   文字

Wo guo   倭國

Wokou   倭寇

Wonu guo   倭奴國

Wu bei zhi   武備志

wugong　武功

xi (detailed)　細

xi (practice)　習

Xi Hé you guo zai kongsang　義和有國在空桑

xian　縣

xianfa (J: *kenpō*)　憲法

xiang (detailed)　詳

xiang (image)　象

xiaoshuo　小説

Xiaoxingren　小行人

xiezhen (J: *shashin*)　寫真

Xing chao lu　行朝錄

xingfa (J: *keihō*)　刑法

xinpai (J: *shinpai*)　信牌

xinwen　新聞

Xu Chengzu　徐承祖

Xu Fu (Xu Shi)　徐福 (徐市)

Xu Jiyu　徐繼畬

Xu Xiake　徐霞客

xuan　眩

Xue Fucheng　薛福成

Xue Jun　薛俊

xue xixue　學西學

xueshu　學術

xuexiao　學校

yan　言

Yan Ruoju　閻若璩

Yanagihara Sakimitsu　柳原前光

yan'ge　沿革

Yanzi　晏子

Yao Wendong　姚文棟

ye　也

Ye Qingyi　葉慶頤

Ye Songshi　葉松石

Ye Xie　葉燮

yeshi　野史

yi (completion particle)　矣

yi (meaning, intention)　意

yi ge　一個

yi yi dai shui　一衣帶水

yibian　一變

yili　義理

yiming　異名

Yin Guangren　印光任

Ying Baoshi　應寶時

Ying Han　英翰

Ying huan zhi lue　瀛環志略

Yingzhou　瀛洲

yiyuan (J: *giin*)　議院

yizi　異字

yong　用

yong wu　詠物

You Tong　尤侗

you yong　有用

youji　遊記

Youli Riben tujing　遊歷日本圖經

Youli tujing yuji　游歷圖經餘紀

yu (locative particle)　於

yu (speech)　語

Yu Zhengxie　俞正燮

Yuan Zuzhi　袁祖志

yudi　輿地

yuefu　樂府

Zeng Guofan　曾國藩

Zeng Jize　曾紀澤

Zha Shenxing　查慎行

Zhang Deyi　張德彝

Zhang Rulin　張汝霖

Zhang Shusheng　張樹聲

Zhang Sigui　張斯桂

Zhang Xuecheng　章學誠

Zhang Zhidong　張之洞

Zhao Diancheng　趙殿成

Zhao Xin　趙信

Zhao Yu　趙昱

zhaoxiang　照相

zhen　真

zheng　正

Zheng Chenggong　鄭成功

Zheng Hê　鄭和

Zheng Ruoceng　鄭若曾

zhengquan (J: *shōken*)　證券

zhi (intention)　志

zhi (treatise)　志 (誌)

Zhigang　志剛

zhiguan　職官

zhong wen　中文

zhongxing (J: *chūkō*)　中興

zhou　州

zhu　註

Zhu Yizun　朱彝尊

Zhupi yuzhi　硃批諭旨

Zhuzhi ci　竹枝詞

zi (J: *azana*)　字

ziyou (J: *jiyū*)　自由

ziyouzizai　自由自在

zongli　綜理

zu zi kaozheng　足資考證

Zuo Zongtang　左宗棠

Index

International Office (Zongli yamen), 31, 106, 158, 159, 164, 173, 191, 259n60
international treaties, 28–31, 34, 39–40
Ishikawa Ei (Hongzhai), 58–60, 62–65, 148
Iwagaki Matsunae, 148

Japan: abandonment of Chinese Civilization, 236–41; administration according to Chinese historical accounts, 23–24; Chinese evaluations of Taiwan Incident, 35–41, 158–59; in Chinese historical record, 5–6, 18–28, 35–41, 143–44, 253–54n12, 257n35; contact with Ming emperors, 254n14; contact with Qing emperors, 17–18; as example for China to follow, 29, 299n82; facility with Chinese poetry, 66–67; having its own language, 237–40; imperial ideology during Meiji, 98; inclusion within Civilization, 5–8, 31–32, 34–35, 43, 56–57, 65–66; incorporation of Liuqiu Islands, 158–59; Kemmu Restoration in, 218; landmarks of interest to travelers, 97–99; latitude and longitude of, 186–87; "learning" analyzed, 178–79; Meiji administrative system analyzed, 180–82, 289n59; Meiji Constitution, 99; military system analyzed, 184; nativism (kokugaku), 161, 238–39; origins of imperial institutions in China, 88–89; overhaul of education system in, 209–210; pan-Asian associations in, 247–48; poetic images of, 81–86; regional characteristics of people, 184–85; resemblance to China, 23–25; as "Riben," 11, 82, 257n35; seclusion during Tokugawa period, 11–12; sending students to West, 235; Sino-Japanese Friendship Treaty (1871), 12, 15, 18, 29, 30, 31–35, 100; swords as emblematic of, 101–102; Westernization in, 2, 5,

28–29, 33, 103, 198, 207, 210, 211–14, 219–22, 227–33, 235. See also Dwarf; Wo kingdom
"Japan Biography" (in the Ming History), 17, 19, 21, 26, 36, 38, 72
ji (memoir/record), 74, 100, 139, 266n5
Jin Anqing, 36–38, 40
Jingū Kōgō, 36, 103, 143–44

kanbun, 45–47, 237. See also literary Chinese language
Kang Youwei, 127–28, 245, 300n5
kao (investigation), 26–28
Konoe Atsumarō, 248
Korea, 7, 14–15, 18, 21, 32, 36, 99, 102, 143–44, 232, 253n6
Kusunoki Masashige, 98, 218, 295n48

language: formal definitions of, 46–47; issue of borrowing, 231; Japanese theories of, 238–39. See also literary Chinese language; speech
Lévi-Strauss, Claude, 89
li: as order in poetry, 118, 125–26; as order in treatise, 177; as principle, 123, 184; as reason, 40
Liang Peilan, 101
Liang Qichao, 106, 157
Liao Xi'en (Quxian), 48–51
Li Bo, 83, 85, 86
Li E, 118, 119, 120, 129, 146. See also Seven Masters of Wulin
Lifan Yuan (Office of Frontier Affairs), 252n4
Li Gui, 82
Li Hongzhang, 29, 32–33, 35, 42, 158, 159, 164, 205
Lin Zexu, 19
Li Shuchang, 62, 91–92, 98, 100, 104, 160, 233, 243
literary Chinese language (wenyan wen), 6–7, 14, 28, 45–47, 85–86; as effacing differences in speech, 45–47

literary name (C: *zi* / J: *azana*), 52–53
Liuqiu Islands, 17, 32, 35, 102, 158, 159, 232, 233
Liu Xie, 43
Liu Yuxi, 129–30, 132
Li Wei, 17–18
Li Xiaopu, 95
Li Xingong, 26–27
Li Xu, 17
lordship (*jun*), 13–17
lu (record), 74, 106–107
Luo Sen, 102

Mai Ersen, 17
Ma Jishi, 19
Mao Yuanyi, 19, 188
maps and cartography, 161, 162, 188–94, 246, 290–91n89
Martin, W. A. P., 194
Meiji Restoration (Renovation), 6, 12, 28, 44, 66, 88, 216–23, 295–96n51
Miyajima Seiichirō, 149, 282n127
Mori Shuntō, 67
Morrison, Robert, 19, 20, 24, 25, 28
Mountains of the Immortals, 81, 87, 88
Mount Fuji, 97, 187
mythos, 89–91, 97

Nagasaki trade, 17–18
Nakamura Keiu, 66, 212–13
Nakane Shuku, 159, 185, 283n4
narrative: as description (*fu*), 100–101; in song, 112; in travelogue, 95–96, 104
Neo-Confucianism, 64, 161, 184. *See also* Soong learning
neologisms (for Westernization), 208, 215, 228–31, 294n37, 297n67, 297–98n69, 299n81
notes (*biji*), 21, 128, 143, 281n112; vs. annotations, 145–48

objectivity, as criterion for knowledge, 4, 75, 78. *See also* truth

official passes (*xinpai*), 17, 253–54n12
Ogyū Sorai, 46, 142
Oka Senjin (Lumen), 58, 149, 282n127
Ōkōchi Teruna (Guige), 44–45, 48–53, 58–60, 62, 65, 149
Ōnuma Chinzan, 66–67, 111
Opium Wars, 12, 30, 217
origin: as means of coopting Westernization, 203; myth of Xu Fu as origin for travel to Japan, 87; as object of study, 78, 153; as that which can be recovered, 37; as that which is repeated, 88
Ouyang Xiu, 101
Owen, Stephen, 56, 86, 91, 96, 130, 132

performative (or poetic) representation, 4, 74, 80, 90, 116, 176, 204, 223; as invitation to share subjectivity, 96–97; as subjective or undisciplined, 104–105
Perry Expedition to Japan, 12, 102, 294–95n39
place: as historiographical site, 90–91, 104; vs. space, 270n39
Poems on Divers Affairs of the Southern Soong, 118, 124, 127, 132, 135, 146–48, 155
poetry, 44, 57, 61; bamboo stalk lyric, 118, 129–32; *ci* (lyric), 118, 129; composition of, 7, 57–58, 60–62, 109, 122, 129; fictional persona in, 130; and form, 118, 121–22, 134; *ge* (song), 112; as historiography, 64–65, 90, 108–110, 112, 119–21, 126–27, 130, 155; intellectualization of, 119; *jueju* (quatrain), 59, 110, 121, 130; linking word and event, 124–25; *lüshi* (regulated verse), 111, 121; and method (*fa*), 118, 134; occasional poetry, 57–65, 108, 111–12; poetry gatherings (*shikai*), 62–65, 233–34, 247, 298n74; "poetry verbalizes intention" (*shi yan zhi*), 4, 96, 121–28, 175, 271n58; as a public practice, 133; recognition of associations in, 61, 63; as scholarly

poetry (*cont.*)

practice, 7, 54–55; as self-expression, 134; *shi* tradition, 121–22, 124–25, 132, 133–34, 154; Soong poetry, 118, 125, 135; as structure of feeling, 112; syntax in, 133, 134–35; Tang poetry, 60, 121, 135; usage of analogy (metaphor) in, 114; and *yan* (voice/wording), 122, 123–24, 129, 134–35, 154; and *yi* (intention/meaning), 122; *yong shi* (celebrating history), 269n31; *yong wu* (celebrating things), 100–102, 271n58; *yuefu*, 117, 129–32, 155. See also *Classic of Poetry*; image

Prince Gong (Yixin), 31, 35, 158, 259n60

proximity (*jin*), 12–15, 34–35, 39, 40–41, 252–53n5

Qing Emperors: treaties with Russia, 30; treaty with Kokand, 30; unofficial contacts with Japan, 17–18

Qing Imperial Compendium, 19, 25, 255n19

Qin Shi Huang, 54, 63, 87, 181

Quan Zuwang, 141

Rai San'yō, 142, 148, 154

representation, 2–5, 16, 71–79, 157–58, 165–67, 174, 244–46. *See also* expository representation; geography; performative representation; text

reviving ancient ways (*fugu*), 12, 118, 134, 216–17, 218, 274n24

Riben, 11, 257n35, as poetic image, 82. *See also* Japan

ritual, 15–16, 32, 57–58, 86; of remembrance, 86, 90–92, 96–97, 269n34

Ryūkyū Islands. *See* Liuqiu Islands

Sahlins, Marshall, 91

Said, Edward, 3

Saigō Takemori, 67, 99

sakura (cherry blossoms), 97, 103, 111–16

Sanetō Keishū, 44

Satsuma Rebellion, 67, 99

Schafer, Edward, 101

Schwab, Raymond, 3

Seven Masters of Wulin, 118, 119, 135, 146

Sha Qiyun, 146

Shen Jiache, 146, 147. *See also* Seven Masters of Wulin

Shen Wenying (Meishi), 48, 49, 51, 64, 65

Shigeno Yasutsugu, 80, 95–96, 106, 149, 282n127

Shinto, 113–14, 145; analyzed in treatises, 179

shixue (substantive/practical learning), 139, 173, 177, 288n45

shu (writings), 106

Sima Qian, 87, 164, 252n2

Sino-Japanese War (1894–1895), 2, 110, 160, 164, 174, 194, 241

Songs of the South, 85

Soong learning, 76–77, 122–23, 126

speech, 44–46, 55, 231, 238–39; *fangyan* (regional speech/dialect), 56; as *logos*, 56; as requiring translation, 239–40; used in poetry, 132–33

Spence, Jonathan, 170

statecraft, 76

Su Shi (Dongbo), 125, 140

Taiping rebellion, 12, 33, 217

Taiwan Incident (1874), 35–41, 233

Takezoe Shin'ichirō, 94

Tanaka, Stefan, 248

text: as form of representation, 4, 16, 72–79; grounded in language, 71–72; as harboring a utility, 174–75; and intertextual relations, 86, 104, 142, 152; as site of author-reader interchange, 96–97. See also *wen yi zai dao;* writing

ti wu (embodying objects), 100

tong lei (common kind), 262–63n22

Zha Shenxing, 118, 122, 125

Zheng Chenggong, 23

Zheng Hê, 188

Zheng Ruoceng, 27, 259n54

zhi (treatise), 74–75, 266n9; abstraction in, 177, 178–80; analytical depth in, 183–85; distribution of details in, 183; evaluated as *tiao* (orderly), 177; evidential research in, 181–82; forms of presenting information in, 185–88; historical depth in, 180–83; and imperial administration, 158, 164; maps in, 188–94; as objectification of place, 158; organization in, 177; as prototype of geographical representation, 164; re-

placed by Western textbooks, 244–45; six geographic treatises of 1880s, 158–64, 198, 223, 235–36, 283n2; strategies of objectification, 176–88; truthfulness of, 158; utility of, 158, 173–76, 287n36. See also *fangzhi*

Zhigang, 266

Zhou dynasty, 45, 108, 181, 295n46; as ground of nineteenth-century analogies, 200–201, 214–15, 217–18, 223–24, 229, 231, 296n52

Zhu Xi, 64, 76, 122, 138, 150, 216

Zhu Yizun, 146

Zito, Angela, 16

Zuo Zongtang, 29, 205

D. R. Howland is Assistant Professor of History at DePaul University. His ongoing research focuses on intellectual and cultural processes of Westernization in China and Japan. *Borders of Chinese Civilization* is his first book.

Howland, Douglas, 1955-
Borders of Chinese civilization : geography and history at Empire's end / by D. R. Howland.
p.   cm. — (Asia-Pacific)
Includes bibliographical references and index.
ISBN 0-8223-1775-3 (cloth). — ISBN 0-8223-1772-9 (ptk.)
1. Japan—Civilization—Chinese influences.   2. Japan—Relations—China.   3. China—Relations—Japan.   4. Chinese—Japan—Ethnic identity.   I. Title.   II. Series.
DS821.5.C5H68   1996
303.48′251052—dc20   95-49999   CIP